THE GRAND NATIONAL

THE HISTORY OF THE
AINTREE SPECTACULAR

THE GRAND NATIONAL

THE HISTORY OF THE AINTREE SPECTACULAR

STEWART PETERS

WITH PHOTOGRAPHS BY BERNARD PARKIN

TEMPUS

FRONT COVER – Just In Debt (red colours, blue stars) jumps a fence in the 2005 Grand National preceded by Forest Gunner (red cap).

BACK COVER – The field race away from Becher's Brook in the 1989 race.

FRONTISPIECE – Classified (17) leads St Alezan (hidden), Rupertino (24) and West Tip over Becher's in the 1986 race.

AUTHOR'S ACKNOWLEDGEMENTS

Bernard Parkin, Josh Gifford, Henrietta Knight, Dickon White, Emma Owen, Lisa Rayman, Clare Hooper, John Randall, Laura Hitchcock, Holly Bennion, Rob Sharman, Emma Jackson and James Howarth.

First published 2005

Tempus Publishing Ltd
The Mill, Brimscombe Port
Stroud, Gloucestershire GL5 2QG
www.tempus-publishing.com

© Stewart Peters, 2005

British Library Cataloguing in Publication Data.
A catalogue record for this book is available from the British Library.

ISBN 0 7524 3547 7

Typesetting, design and origination by Tempus Publishing.
Printed in Great Britain

STEWART PETERS

Stewart Peters is a freelance sports writer and leading author of horse racing history. His previous works include popular books about the Cheltenham Festival and Epsom Derby. It is with a deep, lifelong passion for racing, in particular the intensity and bravery attached to steeplechasing, that his work is driven, seeking to document and rekindle the achievements of man and beast.

The Grand National is unique, and more than just a race. It is something very special, not only for the unrivalled adrenalin it provides or the monumental efforts of the competitors, but also for what it means traditionally as an historical, sporting centrepiece of our nation.

To remember and chronicle horses like Teal, Nicolaus Silver, Red Rum, Aldaniti and Corbiere is inspiring and, for me, provides the basis for wanting to embrace and enthuse about our great race more fervently each time it comes around.

Stewart Peters.

BERNARD PARKIN

This book's chief photographer, Bernard Parkin, was for many years racing photographer to HM Queen Elizabeth the Queen Mother and currently serves HM The Queen in the same capacity. A racing photographer for over fifty years, it was an early ambition to capture racehorses flying over Becher's Brook with emphasis on the grace and splendour of the steeplechasers in action. This he has achieved time and time again, never using remote control or a motor-winder and always working with a standard 50mm lens. He has an extreme dislike of distorted photographs of horses and of exaggerated and unnatural perspectives.

Racing is about excitement. Race photography is all about recording the moment. Before you can take a decent action photo of the latter, the excitement factor has to be conquered.

To remain ice cool as the field approaches Becher's with the mighty thunder of 160 hooves getting ever closer is very difficult. It is the most exhilarating feeling I have experienced.

Bernard Parkin.

Amberleigh House on his way to winning the National in 2004.

FOREWORD

The Grand National has always held a very special place in my heart, and was a race that I always dreamed of winning. I first rode in the National in 1962 on an outsider called Siracusa and, as a jockey, I had many memorable moments at Aintree. I experienced the thrill of completing for the first time on Vulcano in 1966 and was going well for a very long way on Bassnet in 1969.

Perhaps my greatest chance of winning came on a very good horse called Honey End, trained by Captain Ryan Price. Honey End was favourite the year the 100/1 shot Foinavon won, and we were just starting to make our move when chaos erupted at the twenty-third fence. The riderless Popham Down caused a huge pile-up, stopping every horse bar Foinavon. I put Honey End to the fence a number of times, and we eventually set off in pursuit of the runaway leader. Honey End ran his heart out and made up tremendous ground and, on the run for home, we, together with Brian Fletcher on Red Alligator and Terry Biddlecombe on Greek Scholar, had Foinavon in our sights. But sadly it was just too big a gap to bridge, and eventually we finished second. Anything can happen in the National, and obviously it did that day, but I am convinced Honey End would have gone mightily close with a clear run.

As a trainer, I think it is safe to say it was a fairytale result when Aldaniti won in 1981. I trained the horse, who had suffered terrible leg problems, and the first accomplishment was that he even got to Aintree at all, so badly had he broken down previously. But Aldaniti was given total care in his recovery and had been a high-class horse before his injuries. Of course, as has been well documented, Bob Champion had come through a frightening ordeal, successfully battling cancer, and when the two of them won the race, I think it touched the nation, particularly knowing the struggles Bob had encountered. That was a truly special day, one that will never be forgotten.

After Aldaniti, I had plenty more good horses run in the race, of which You're Welcome, Topsham Bay and Brave Highlander all deserve a mention. Brave Highlander was certainly a real Aintree horse, very consistent over the fences and

Josh Gifford.

such a safe and clever jumper. There were a few times with him when it looked as though winning the race again was very possible. Since I retired, my son Nick has had his first National runners as a trainer in Skycab and Joly Bey, and seeing them run for him similarly filled me with pride.

The Grand National has given me some wonderful memories, many of which are featured in this book, together with all the significant moments in the history of the great race. Stewart Peters has captured the spirit of the National, reliving the events of each year in what is a thoroughly satisfying record of the race's history.

Josh Gifford.

Josh Gifford rode 642 winners as a jockey between 1959 and 1970 and was National Hunt Champion Jockey four times. He took over as a trainer from Captain Ryan Price in 1970 and trained 1,587 winners between then and his retirement in 2003. He trained Aldaniti to win the Grand National in 1981 in one of the most emotional victories of all time.

INTRODUCTION

From the time the very first Grand National – then known as the Grand Liverpool Steeplechase – was run back in 1839, this magnificent and unique sporting occasion has delivered enthralling stories and races of gripping excitement with every single edition. With its status currently as strong as it has ever been, the Grand National proudly positions itself as the most popular, nation-binding race of the year, and is justifiably considered one of the most important and prestigious events in the entire sporting calendar.

It is to Liverpool hotel owner William Lynn that the origins of the Grand National can be traced. Having leased an area of country land at Aintree (close to the major city of Liverpool) from Lord Sefton, a racing enthusiast, the forward-thinking Lynn set about organising Flat races over the countryside. Seeing an opportunity for progression and expansion, Lynn proceeded with plans for a grandstand at Aintree, and it was Lord Molyneux that laid the original foundation stone for the building. Molyneux later had a race over the Grand National fences named after him.

After Lynn staged the first Flat fixture on 7 July 1829, his brainchild went from strength to strength, despite a rival course at nearby Maghull. Lynn gradually introduced Hurdles races to Aintree, with October 1835 proving a landmark fixture dedicated to that particular sphere of racing. The fixture proved a total success, with the now infamous Captain Martin Becher riding the brilliant horse Vivian to a pair of victories.

At the same time at a course in St Albans, the most important steeplechase of the time – the Great St Albans Steeplechase – was already up and running and developing as a spectacle in a way that added a different dimension to racing than purely Flat and Hurdle contests. Having experimented with chases at Maghull in conjunction with the owner of that course, John Formby, Lynn was inspired, and began promoting and preparing the first 'Grand Liverpool Steeplechase' to be run at Aintree on 26 February 1839. It is unclear as to why Lynn then resigned from the Aintree Management Committee just weeks before the first edition of the great race, but the groundwork laid for the glorious future that lay in wait was undoubtedly down to him, and while names like Sefton, Topham, Molyneux and Becher have had races run over the most famous fences in the world named after them, Lynn sadly never received that honour.

So the first running of what would become known as the Grand National took place in 1839. Aintree today resembles the original course, in terms of the left-handed circuit and the positioning of many of the fences. The biggest difference between now and then was the state of the ground and the make-up of the obstacles. In 1839, the race – thought to be around four miles in length after two circuits had been completed – was run over total country or farmland, including stretches of ploughed land that became treacherous in wet conditions. Most of the fences were smallish banks topped with rails or bundles of gorse and there were two flights of hurdles to finish the race. The difficult fences of the original course included a brutal 4ft 8in stone wall and a pair of devilish brooks. The first of the brooks had an exaggerated 'drop' landing (a feature of many of the Grand National fences today) and, in that first running, Captain Becher was flung from his horse Conrad and took shelter in the deepest part of the brook before emerging unscathed. From then on, that fence was known as Becher's Brook. The second brook, though not as severe as Becher's, received its name a year later. The Irish jockey Mr Alan Power had wagered a considerable amount of money that he would be first to the stone wall fence, which was at the halfway point in the race. Charging off in the lead, Power looked certain to win his bet when his horse, Valentine, came to a standstill before the second brook – seemingly ready to refuse – before apparently changing his mind and leaping over the fence in a most peculiar style, enabling Power to reach the stone wall first: hence the christening of Valentines Brook.

Finishing touches are put to the awesome Chair fence prior to the 1997 meeting.

Polyfemus (25), Bigsun (19) and Lastofthebrownies jump the modified Becher's Brook in 1990.

The notoriously evil and much-disliked stone wall was replaced in 1844 with a water jump and, following a tragic accident in 1862 at the fence before the water, a gaping open ditch (designed to slow down the runners before they faced the long jump over the water a fence later) was placed in front, and this fence became known as The Chair because of its positioning next to the seat manned by the distance judge.

By 1885, the whole of the Grand National course had been turfed. Over time, the fences were gradually made bigger and bigger, with the bases of the fences comprising of thick branches and stacked to their respective heights with the tightly-packed green spruce that is in evidence today, making the fences the most distinctive of any racecourse the world over. The fences got so big in the 1950s that a frequent number of accidents led to alterations in 1960 to the size of some of the fences, as well as the stiff, upright obstacles being given a slope on the take-off side so to benefit the horses as they judged their jumps. Nowadays, the fence-building at Aintree starts a month prior to the National, with spruce collected predominantly from the Lake District.

Sadly, further accidents to horses did take place and, after one particularly unfortunate race in 1989, the fences were modified for good – offering a safer if less spectacular Aintree challenge. Even so, with fences such as the still-spine-tingling Becher's Brook, the formidable Chair (where the ground on the landing side is higher than the take-off side, unlike most of the 'drop' fences on the course), Valentines and the ninety-degree Canal Turn, horses competing in the Grand National must be brave and able to jump, as the race still offers the supreme test in steeplechasing. A suspect jumper in standard chases would still have a torrid time if asked to compete over the National fences, notwithstanding the modifications.

As it has from the early part of its existence, the Grand National trip is a four-and-a-half-mile marathon, with thirty fences jumped over two circuits of the course – The Chair and water being jumped only once – with the long, stamina-sapping run to the finish from the last fence rounding the famous 'elbow', where runners carve to the right (to avoid the by then bordered-off Chair).

The most famous family associated with Aintree were the Topham family, who owned areas of land around Aintree and had been involved with the management of the course from the early years of the National. Indeed, it was Edward William Topham who was asked to handicap the race for the first time in 1843 and, in that year, the race's name changed from The Grand Liverpool Steeplechase to The Liverpool and National Handicap Steeplechase.

In 1949, the then-Lord Sefton sold the course to the Topham family, and it was the charismatic, forward-thinking Mrs Mirabel Topham who was appointed to manage

Young Hustler (1), Sure Metal (centre) and Three Brownies land over The Chair in 1996.

it. Mrs Topham instantly added a new chase to the Grand National meeting to be run over one circuit of the National course, called the Topham Trophy. It was a fine idea, as it gave horses that were perhaps not blessed with the stamina for the full National distance a chance of glory over the famous fences, while also serving as a test of Aintree ability for horses that aspired to future Grand National participation. As well as the new race, Mrs Topham also established a new track within the Grand National course, naming it the Mildmay Course after the late jockey Lord Anthony Mildmay, one of the finest amateurs of his generation and a man who came close to National glory in 1936 aboard his father's horse Davy Jones. Mrs Topham also showed her willingness to listen to the concerns of others, sanctioning the modification of the fences in 1960 when there was rampant outcry that the Grand National was becoming too severe and brutal a test.

In the mid-1960s, with Aintree Racecourse suffering some lean and worrying times, it was announced that the course was being sold to property developers, sparking fears each time the National came round that it would be the last. It was not until 1973 that the course was sold to developer Bill Davies and, although thankfully he vowed to keep the National going, attendances were slipping and the general outlook appeared bleak for the future. The great race looked doomed until bookmakers Ladbrokes agreed to manage the National from 1976 to 1978

and, with their intuition, the race enjoyed an upturn in fortune, one of the reasons being the elimination of Flat racing from the Grand National meeting.

Even with the help of Ladbrokes (help that eventually lasted seven committed years), Mr Davies remained ready to sell Aintree at any time, condemning the Grand National to extinction, although there were some porous suggestions that the race could be transferred to a different course (in name only obviously). However, in 1983, Davies sold Aintree to the Jockey Club and a year later Canadian whisky firm Seagram moved in to categorically solidify the race's future. Inspired by a newspaper article about the Grand National written by Lord Oaksey (who as a jockey had finished runner-up in the 1963 race aboard Carrickbeg), Seagram chairman Major Ivan Straker – whose horse The Tsarevich finished second in the 1987 National – stepped up to at last secure the future of the world's greatest race.

Ever since the first Seagram-sponsored race in 1984, the Grand National steadily rose to security, then prosperity and now, in the twenty-first century, has gloriously risen to magnificent new heights and can safely bask in its history with an assured future, with its popularity growing worldwide by the year. Seagram subsidiary company Martell took up the mantle with magnificent effect in 1992 and, after thirteen superb years of sponsorship, handed over the reigns to John Smiths for the 2005 renewal.

Speed undoes the leaders at the first fence in 2005. Frenchman's Creek (22) and Lord Atterbury (33) are about to depart the race, while the grey Strong Resolve, Spot The Difference (29) and Glenelly Gale (black, red cap) make mistakes but survive.

Aintree legend Red Rum with jockey Tommy Stack.

Every year the Grand National somehow provides stories that enchant and capture countless hearts like no other race can. From the very first victory of Lottery in 1839, names such as The Lamb, Manifesto, Reynoldstown, Red Rum and Aldaniti have enshrined themselves a place in racing folklore, helping to provide a rich and romantic history. Since its very conception, the Grand National has featured spectacular races with combative contestants, breathtaking finishes, crushing falls, jubilation, desolation, heartache and hope, all played out on the natural oasis of Aintree Racecourse, set beneath a simple backdrop comprising of housing and industry. It is hoped that the races that lie in wait in the future bring a blend of as many fascinating qualities that make up the unrivalled history of the greatest and most famous race of them all, the Grand National.

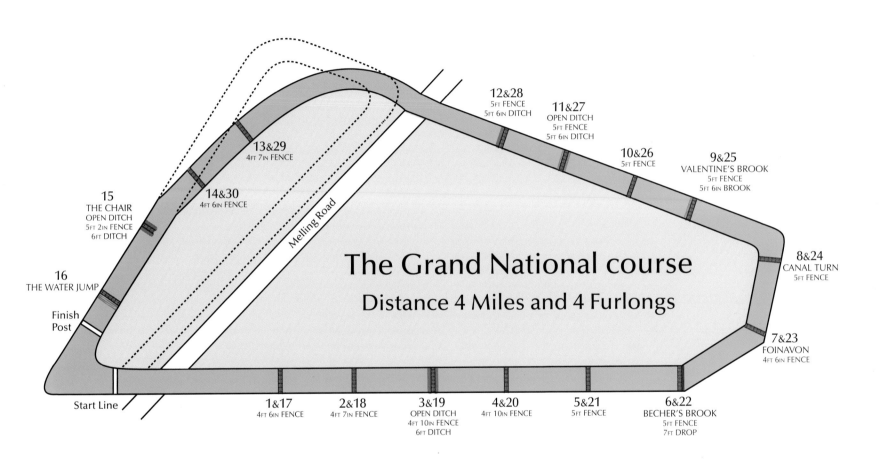

12&28
5FT FENCE
5FT 6IN DITCH

11&27
OPEN DITCH
5FT FENCE
5FT 6IN DITCH

10&26
5FT FENCE

9&25
VALENTINE'S BROOK
5FT FENCE
5FT 6IN BROOK

13&29
4FT 7IN FENCE

14&30
4FT 6IN FENCE

15
THE CHAIR
OPEN DITCH
5FT 2IN FENCE
6FT DITCH

8&24
CANAL TURN
5FT FENCE

Melling Road

The Grand National course

Distance 4 Miles and 4 Furlongs

16
THE WATER JUMP

Finish
Post

7&23
FOINAVON
4FT 6IN FENCE

Start Line

1&17
4FT 6IN FENCE

2&18
4FT 7IN FENCE

3&19
OPEN DITCH
4FT 10IN FENCE
6FT DITCH

4&20
4FT 10IN FENCE

5&21
5FT FENCE

6&22
BECHER'S BROOK
5FT FENCE
7FT DROP

THE GRAND NATIONAL HANDICAP
STEEPLECHASE ROLL OF HONOUR

YEAR	WINNER	JOCKEY	ODDS
1839	Lottery	Jem Mason	5/1 Fav.
1840	Jerry	Mr B. Bretherton	12/1
1841	Charity	Mr A. Powell	14/1
1842	Gay Lad	Tom Olliver	7/1
1843	Vanguard	Tom Olliver	12/1
1844	Discount	Mr H. Crickmere	5/1 Jt Fav.
1845	Cure-All	Mr W.J. Loft	N/A
1846	Pioneer	W. Taylor	N/A
1847	Matthew	D. Wynne	10/1
1848	Chandler	Capt. J.L. Little	12/1
1849	Peter Simple	T. Cunningham	20/1
1850	Abd-El-Kader	C. Green	N/A
1851	Abd-El-Kader	T. Abbot	7/1
1852	Miss Mowbray	Mr A. Goodman	N/A
1853	Peter Simple	Tom Olliver	9/1
1854	Bourton	J. Tasker	4/1 Fav.
1855	Wanderer	J. Hanlon	25/1
1856	Freetrader	G. Stevens	25/1
1857	Emigrant	C. Boyce	10/1
1858	Little Charley	W. Archer	100/6
1859	Half Caste	C. Green	7/1
1860	Anatis	Mr T. Pickernell	7/2 Fav.
1861	Jealousy	J. Kendall	5/1
1862	Huntsman	H. Lamplugh	3/1 Fav.
1863	Emblem	G. Stevens	4/1
1864	Emblematic	G. Stevens	10/1
1865	Alcibiade	Capt. H. Coventry	100/7
1866	Salamander	Mr A. Goodman	40/1
1867	Cortolvin	J. Page	16/1
1868	The Lamb	Mr G. Ede	9/1
1869	The Colonel	G. Stevens	100/7
1870	The Colonel	G. Stevens	7/2 Fav.
1871	The Lamb	Mr T. Pickernell	11/2
1872	Casse Tete	J. Page	20/1
1873	Disturbance	Mr J.M. Richardson	20/1
1874	Reugny	Mr J.M. Richardson	5/1 Fav.
1875	Pathfinder	Mr T. Pickernell	100/6
1876	Regal	J. Cannon	25/1
1877	Austerlitz	Mr F.G. Hobson	15/1
1878	Shifnal	J. Jones	7/1
1879	The Liberator	Mr G. Moore	5/1

YEAR	WINNER	JOCKEY	ODDS
1880	Empress	Mr T. Beasley	8/1
1881	Woodbrook	Mr T. Beasley	11/2 Jt Fav.
1882	Seaman	Lord Manners	10/1
1883	Zoedone	Count C. Kinsky	100/7
1884	Voluptuary	Mr E.P. Wilson	10/1
1885	Roquefort	Mr E.P. Wilson	100/30 Fav.
1886	Old Joe	T. Skelton	25/1
1887	Gamecock	W. Daniels	20/1
1888	Playfair	G. Mawson	40/1
1889	Frigate	Mr T. Beasley	8/1
1890	Ilex	A. Nightingall	4/1 Fav.
1891	Come Away	Mr H. Beasley	4/1 Fav.
1892	Father O'Flynn	Capt. E.R. Owen	20/1
1893	Cloister	W. Dollery	9/2 Fav.
1894	Why Not	A. Nightingall	5/1 Jt Fav.
1895	Wild Man From Borneo	Mr Joseph Widger	10/1
1896	The Soarer	Mr D.G.M. Campbell	40/1
1897	Manifesto	T. Kavanagh	6/1 Fav.
1898	Drogheda	J. Gourley	25/1
1899	Manifesto	G. Williamson	5/1
1900	Ambush II	A. Anthony	4/1
1901	Grudon	A. Nightingall	9/1
1902	Shannon Lass	D. Read	20/1
1903	Drumcree	P. Woodland	13/2 Fav.
1904	Moifaa	A. Birch	25/1
1905	Kirkland	F. Mason	6/1
1906	Ascetic's Silver	Mr A. Hastings	20/1
1907	Eremon	A. Newey	8/1
1908	Rubio	H.B. Bletsoe	66/1
1909	Lutteur III	G. Parfrement	100/9 Jt Fav.
1910	Jenkinstown	R. Chadwick	100/8
1911	Glenside	Mr J.R. Anthony	20/1
1912	Jerry M	E. Piggott	4/1 Jt Fav.
1913	Covertcoat	P. Woodland	100/9
1914	Sunloch	W.J. Smith	100/6
1915	Ally Sloper	Mr J.R. Anthony	100/8
1919	Poethlyn	E. Piggott	11/4 Fav.
1920	Troytown	Mr J.R. Anthony	6/1
1921	Shaun Spadah	F.B. Rees	100/9
1922	Music Hall	L.B. Rees	100/9
1923	Sergeant Murphy	Capt. G.H. Bennet	100/6
1924	Master Robert	R. Trudgill	25/1
1925	Double Chance	Major J.P. Wilson	100/9
1926	Jack Horner	W. Watkinson	25/1
1927	Sprig	T.E. Leader	8/1 Fav.
1928	Tipperary Tim	Mr W.P. Dutton	100/1

YEAR	WINNER	JOCKEY	ODDS
1929	Gregalach	R. Everett	100/1
1930	Shaun Goilin	T.B. Cullinan	100/8
1931	Grakle	R. Lyall	100/6
1932	Forbra	J. Hamey	50/1
1933	Kellsboro' Jack	D. Williams	25/1
1934	Golden Miller	G. Wilson	8/1
1935	Reynoldstown	Mr F. Furlong	22/1
1936	Reynoldstown	Mr F. Walwyn	10/1
1937	Royal Mail	E. Williams	100/6
1938	Battleship	B. Hobbs	40/1
1939	Workman	T. Hyde	100/8
1940	Bogskar	M.A. Jones	25/1
1946	Lovely Cottage	Capt. R. Petre	25/1
1947	Caughoo	E. Dempsey	100/1
1948	Sheila's Cottage	A.P. Thompson	50/1
1949	Russian Hero	L. McMorrow	66/1
1950	Freebooter	J. Power	10/1 Jt Fav.
1951	Nickel Coin	J.A. Bullock	40/1
1952	Teal	A.P. Thompson	100/7
1953	Early Mist	B. Marshall	20/1
1954	Royal Tan	B. Marshall	8/1
1955	Quare Times	P. Taaffe	100/9
1956	ESB	D.V. Dick	100/7
1957	Sundew	F.T. Winter	20/1
1958	Mr What	A. Freeman	18/1
1959	Oxo	M. Scudamore	8/1
1960	Merryman II	G. Scott	13/2 Fav.
1961	Nicolaus Silver	H.R. Beasley	28/1
1962	Kilmore	F.T. Winter	28/1
1963	Ayala	P. Buckley	66/1
1964	Team Spirit	G.W. Robinson	18/1
1965	Jay Trump	Mr T.C. Smith	100/6
1966	Anglo	T. Norman	50/1
1967	Foinavon	J. Buckingham	100/1
1968	Red Alligator	B. Fletcher	100/7
1969	Highland Wedding	E.P. Harty	100/9
1970	Gay Trip	P. Taaffe	15/1
1971	Specify	J. Cook	28/1
1972	Well To Do	G. Thorner	14/1
1973	Red Rum	B. Fletcher	9/1 Jt Fav.
1974	Red Rum	B. Fletcher	11/1
1975	L'Escargot	T. Carberry	13/2
1976	Rag Trade	J. Burke	14/1
1977	Red Rum	T. Stack	9/1
1978	Lucius	B.R. Davies	14/1
1979	Rubstic	M. Barnes	25/1
1980	Ben Nevis	Mr C. Fenwick	40/1
1981	Aldaniti	R. Champion	10/1
1982	Grittar	Mr C. Saunders	7/1
1983	Corbiere	B.De Haan	13/1
1984	Hallo Dandy	N. Doughty	13/1
1985	Last Suspect	H. Davies	50/1
1986	West Tip	R. Dunwoody	15/2
1987	Maori Venture	S.C. Knight	28/1
1988	Rhyme 'N' Reason	B. Powell	10/1
1989	Little Polveir	J. Frost	28/1
1990	Mr Frisk	Mr M. Armytage	16/1
1991	Seagram	N. Hawke	12/1
1992	Party Politics	C. Llewellyn	14/1
1993	RACE VOID	N/A	N/A
1994	Miinnehoma	R. Dunwoody	16/1
1995	Royal Athlete	J. Titley	40/1
1996	Rough Quest	M.A. Fitzgerald	7/1 Fav.
1997	Lord Gyllene	A. Dobbin	14/1
1998	Earth Summit	C. Llewellyn	7/1 Fav.
1999	Bobbyjo	P. Carberry	10/1
2000	Papillon	R. Walsh	10/1
2001	Red Marauder	Richard Guest	33/1
2002	Bindaree	J. Culloty	20/1
2003	Monty's Pass	B.J. Geraghty	16/1
2004	Amberleigh House	G. Lee	16/1
2005	Hedgehunter	R. Walsh	7/1 Fav.

Notes

From 1839 to 1842, the race was known as The Grand Liverpool Steeplechase.

From 1843 to 1846, the race was known as The Liverpool and National Handicap Steeplechase.

There was no race at Aintree in 1916, 1917 or 1918 because of the First World War, although replacement races took place at Gatwick in those years.

There was no race between 1941 and 1945 because of the Second World War.

1839-1940

Huge crowds watch the drama unfold at the fearsome Becher's Brook in 1928.

With Aintree and the first ever running of the Grand Liverpool Steeplechase the talk of the entire racing community, come 26 February 1839, the crowds flocked to the course to witness the inaugural event. What the very first race had in common with every subsequent edition was drama, a slice of the unexpected, a certain degree of criticism, a thoroughly thrilled and entertained audience and a most grand and deserving winner.

Setting off over ploughed land that would make the journey particularly taxing were seventeen brave horses, including a trio of Irish runners owned by Tom Ferguson, one of these being the extremely well-fancied Rust, an English mare called The Nun and a tall, brown horse named Lottery, ridden by one of the leading horseman of the era: 'Dandy' Jem Mason. The thrills and spills of the big race were soon in evidence, with Captain Becher thrown over the fence at the first brook, hiding in its deepest part as the remaining horses soared over him, before collecting his horse Conrad and continuing the race. Becher's Brook was born.

Meanwhile the Irish challenger Rust was running a race of immense promise under his amateur rider William McDonough, until ill luck intervened. As another Irish raider, Daxon (ridden by Ferguson himself), was delighting the crowd with a trailblazing effort at the head of affairs, Rust had taken on a part of the course – quite legally – that was a narrow lane. Here, a mob of money-hungry crooks whose design on glory lay with another in the race, trapped the talented animal by surrounding him and giving the horse nowhere to run, ending his chance. An even worse fate befell poor Dictator who collapsed at the second brook – eventually known as Valentines – following a fall and died instantly, becoming the first fatality in the race's history.

The horse that was relishing the unique occasion was Lottery and, having thrilled the spectators in front of the stands by leaping the treacherous stone wall with admirable power and grace, he proceeded to dominate the remainder of the race. Daxon had fallen by the wayside, as had over half the field and, clearing the final two flights, which were ordinary hurdles, with some extraordinarily extravagant leaps, Lottery drew gasps from the crowd and announced himself as the first star of steeplechasing.

Lottery was a fine winner, although the dark side of the race surfaced in the very first edition, with complaints over the severity of a number of the obstacles (the two brooks and the stone wall being the chief objects of anger) and the obvious alarm caused by the death of Dictator. These were feelings that now, as then, will always be associated with the Grand National and have surfaced continually down the years – at times so fiercely that changes were made.

Thankfully however, the skulduggery that ruined the event for Rust was a side of racing confined to the first few years of the race, although a number of the early Nationals had shadows of evil and wrong-doing cast over them. Lottery's winning time of almost fifteen minutes – though hideously slow by modern comparisons – did not detract from the fact he was the sport's first superstar. In winning the race over very heavy, ploughed ground, his career ascended into a whirlwind of excellence, winning regularly throughout his racing days. Indeed, he was often penalised for being 'too good', such as in subsequent editions of the big race in 1841 and 1842 where – although a race run at level weights before the first handicapped National in 1843 – Lottery was required to carry an 18lb penalty on both occasions. Owned by Mr John Elmore (who also owned the winner of the

1842 race, Gay Lad), Lottery proved a fine flag-bearer for the new race, running in the first five editions and finishing seventh on his last attempt in 1843.

Inspired by the mighty Lottery, the race grew in stature and popularity with fields regularly consisting of between twenty and thirty runners. Matthew became the first of twenty-two (to date) Irish-trained winners when triumphing in 1847 when the race was officially called The Grand National for the first time, while Peter Simple in 1853 became the oldest winner on record at fifteen. Peter Simple had also won in 1849, making him the second horse to win twice, the first being the small bay Abd-El-Kader in 1850 and 1851. Another National first occurred in 1862 when Huntsman became the first of only two French-trained winners of the race. That same year saw the tragic death of jockey James Wynne, who was killed at the fence that would become known as The Chair.

There were twenty-one in the line-up the year that the tiny grey horse The Lamb first ran in the Grand National in 1868. The Lamb can lay claim to being – most likely – the smallest Grand National competitor of all time at fifteen hands high, if that, though his diminutive stature did not detract from the fact he was a beautiful-looking animal. The Lamb's sire, Zouave, was bred by Mr Courtenay, owner of the 1847 winner Matthew, and was named after the son of a farmer, who owned The Lamb's dam. The farmer's son himself, like the young foal, was a delicate, fragile figure who sadly died very early in his life. Delicate in appearance The Lamb may have been but, on the racecourse, he jumped with authority and was well-fancied for the 1868 National as a six-year-old behind the favourite Chimney Sweep (tragically killed on the run to the first fence having struck a large rock, fracturing a pastern). The Lamb prevailed in the mud to become the first grey to win the Grand National, and one of only two that have succeeded to date. The fine horseman George Ede was the man that guided The Lamb to victory. The fact that The Lamb became an Aintree legend was most heart-warming; he had overcome his frail structure to triumph in 1868, but after being laid low for the best part of two years soon after because of a wasting disease, it seemed impossible that he would return to Aintree to win again. But win again he did, this time in the 1871 National, a result that caused the delighted crowd to literally raise the roof. Some of the spectators cut pieces off The Lamb's tail for souvenirs as he was led back victorious. Sadly, George Ede had been killed in the 1870 Grand Sefton Chase – also run over the Grand National course – and the winning jockey in 1871 was Tommy Pickernell, or 'Mr Thomas' as he was known.

Soon after The Lamb's second Grand National, racing lost one of its finest jockeys and arguably the greatest Grand National jockey of them all. George Stevens won a record five Grand Nationals, the first aboard Freetrader in 1856. Hailing from Cheltenham, Stevens rode the good-looking, near-black horse The Colonel to victories in both 1869 and 1870, and finished sixth in the 1871 National on the same horse. A mere three months after that race, Stevens met his end far away from the hazards of Aintree when hacking on Cleeve Hill in Cheltenham. His mount whipped round suddenly, flinging Stevens from the saddle; the great jockey fractured his head after cracking it against a rock, resulting in his most untimely death.

Stevens was, without doubt, the finest Grand National jockey of the nineteenth century, but the greatest horse in the same period was surely the exceptionally handsome Manifesto. Taking part in the National for the first time in 1895, Manifesto finished fourth as a seven-year-old. He won the race in 1897, destroying a field that included former winners Wild Man From Borneo and The Soarer. Such was his dominance at that particular time he would almost certainly have won a year later if injury had not caused his absence, but he returned to Aintree to win the National in 1899 under the maximum burden of 12st 7lbs – one of only four horses to ever do that in the race, the others being the brilliant, bold-jumping stayer Cloister in 1893, Jerry M in 1912 and Poethlyn (who was also the shortest-priced winner ever at 11/4) in 1919. Although the maximum burden was later altered to 12 stone, Manifesto's feat is all the more remarkable considering that, in modern times, no horse between Rhyme 'N' Reason's win in 1988 and Hedgehunter's in 2005 carried 11 stone or more to victory. Manifesto then ran in four of the next five Nationals, eight altogether (the last at the unfathomable age of sixteen), and cemented himself as an everlasting Aintree god by finishing third on three of those four runs.

Royal runners have been infrequent in the history of the Grand National, and the most famous of these select band of competitors is more famous for losing the race than winning but, in 1900, the royal colours of HRH The Prince of Wales – later King Edward VII – were carried to victory by the six-year-old Ambush II. It was a resounding start to the century for Aintree and the Grand National, and a most successful one for the future King, whose Diamond Jubilee won the Epsom Derby later that season. Although Ambush II would run in a further pair of Grand Nationals, he never won again, and his success in 1900 remains the only occasion a member of the Royal Family has won the race.

There was a sense of irony that there could have been a second winner for King Edward VII in the form of Moifaa, yet His Majesty only became owner of the horse (described as being the 'ugliest' winner of any Grand National and having the 'head of a camel') after Moifaa had won the big race in 1904. The interesting thing about Moifaa – a giant brown horse – was that he was bred in New Zealand and spent at least the first six years of his life there, where he took the country's chasing scene by storm. Sent to England two years before the 1904 National, the gelding was said to have been shipwrecked off the coast of Ireland and had been found on a beach by fishermen. Under the guidance of the little-known Surrey-based trainer Mr Hickey, the towering beast jumped the Aintree course in fine style to defeat the following year's victor, Kirkland, by eight lengths. Moifaa was purchased on behalf of King Edward VII to run in the 1905 National, but unfortunately came down at Becher's. Moifaa's 1904 victory was a groundbreaking success for competitors born and raised overseas, and helped to spread the worldwide acclaim of the Grand National. He was the first

Miss Dorothy Paget leads in Golden Miller and jockey Gerry Wilson after the 1934 race. The great horse remains the last to win both the Gold Cup and National in the same year.

winner that had truly hailed from a distant land, though he would not be the last as, in time, the United States and New Zealand again would enjoy National glory, while an Australian descendant came mighty close to one of the most scintillating victories ever.

Another massive horse, Troytown, won in 1920, providing a third win in the race for the finest amateur of the era, Jack Anthony, while another interesting winner in the 1920s was Sergeant Murphy, the first American-owned winner and only the second thirteen-year-old horse to triumph in the National (Why Not had previously triumphed in 1894) to this day.

In 1928, with the course long established to the form of today (with the exceptions of the fence modifications), the National proved emphatically that it was a race where 'anything could happen', a phrase that no other race can justifiably claim to use. As the prize money increased in the early 1920s, so the size of the fields began to creep up in number. The forty-two that went to post in 1928 was then a record, and included the fine young chaser Easter Hero, the imminent winner of the 1929 and 1930 Cheltenham Gold Cups. Easter Hero was, a year later, to prove himself a horse worthy of winning the National; finishing second carrying 12st 7lbs he was generally seen as unlucky not to have won. But in 1928 he was very much the villain of the piece. Taking the field along at a terrific pace, Easter Hero misjudged the ditch in front of the Canal Turn and landed awkwardly on top of the fence, struggling desperately to get back on to the ground on the take-off side. Those behind him either refused or unseated their jockeys, while a number of loose horses stopped other contestants dead in their tracks. Only a few were able to continue the race and, by the second Becher's, only five were left in the contest. At the last fence, the American challenger Billy Barton fell, leaving 100/1 shot Tipperary Tim free to win by a distance. Billy Barton was remounted to finish second, but no other horse completed.

Encouraged by the shock result and general unpredictable nature of the Grand National, an all-time record of sixty-six starters lined-up for the 1929 race. The ditch in front of the Canal Turn – a fence that comes at a critical moment when the runners have to swing left-handed at a ninety-degree angle, meaning most cut across the inside of the fence – was filled in to the state it is today, so to avoid the mayhem that occurred in 1928 happening again. Easter Hero was favourite and unluckily spread a plate on the second circuit, but still managed to hold the lead until after the second last, when he was overtaken by 100/1 outsider Gregalach, receiving 14lbs from Easter Hero. A shock winner he may have been, but Gregalach became an Aintree regular, running in the next five Nationals and finishing a close second to former stablemate Grakle in 1931.

It was 1933 that saw the first appearance in the Grand National of the sensational, five-time Cheltenham Gold Cup winner Golden Miller. Essentially a park horse, 'The Miller' was never wholeheartedly in love with the National fences, and he either fell, unseated or refused in the race in 1933, 1935, 1936 and 1937. But in 1934, facing a field that included the Mr Frank Furlong-ridden prospect Really True, a two-time Cheltenham Gold Cup runner-up in the high-class Thomond II and former National winners Gregalach and Forbra (1932), Golden Miller's class came through. Ridden by Gerry Wilson (who was on board for two of the horse's Gold Cup triumphs), Golden Miller won by five lengths and became the only horse to ever win the Gold Cup and Grand National in the same season. In his first Grand National attempt in 1933, Golden Miller had been ridden by Ted Leader, who had won the 1927 National on the favourite Sprig and whose father Tom had trained Gregalach to win in 1929, while Golden Miller was also the horse that brought famous owner Miss Dorothy Paget into the limelight. Miss Paget would have many more decent National horses in years to come.

It proved to be a family affair in 1935 with Reynoldstown winning the National for owner/trainer Major Noel Furlong, ridden by his son Frank – an outstanding amateur. The near-black Reynoldstown won again a year later, but only after Lord Mildmay's son Anthony had his reigns broken aboard the outsider Davy Jones when landing in the lead at the second last, causing the horse to run out. When Reynoldstown won in 1936 (the same year the magnificent race favourite Avenger – the mount of future four-time National-winning trainer Fred Rimell – was killed after breaking his neck from a fall at the seventeenth), he was partnered by another amateur, Fulke Walwyn, a man who would become one of the finest trainers to ever grace the sport, and who would enjoy Grand National success in that area with Team Spirit in 1964. Reynoldstown – who nowadays has an important novice chase named after him – was the first winner of successive Nationals since The Colonel in 1869 and 1870, showing that if the demands of winning one Grand National are hard enough, then to achieve more than that is truly something special, a fact brought gloriously to life by the legendary Red Rum in the 1970s.

The tiny, American-owned stallion Battleship was the first Grand National winner bred in the United States when he won in 1938 (although the 1908 winner Rubio had been bred in California but dispatched to England as a yearling) and, in doing so, highlighted Bruce Hobbs – riding for his trainer/father Reg – as the youngest ever winning rider of the race at seventeen. With the exception of The Lamb, Battleship was the smallest horse to triumph in the National, denying the seven-year-old Royal Danieli as he did so.

The 1938 third Workman became the first Irish-trained winner since Troytown when he won for trainer Jack Ruttle of County Dublin in the 1939 National. Workman beat Macmoffat by three lengths, with the runner-up again filling second place in 1940. With five Aintree Grand Nationals missed because of the Second World War, Macmoffat incredibly returned to Aintree to run in the 1946 and 1947 editions – the latter when aged fifteen.

War was already in progress by the time of the 1940 Grand National, and many in the crowd were dressed in military uniform. A good number of the jockeys were on leave, including Flight Sergeant Mervyn Jones, who won the race on Bogskar, and his brother Hywel, who fell from National Night. Sadly, Mervyn was one of many who lost their lives serving the Allies in the Second World War, as was Frank Furlong. There had been no Aintree Nationals in the years 1916, 1917 and 1918 because of the First World War (although three substitute races did take place at Gatwick, but bore no resemblance to the big race at Aintree apart from the race distance), and now there would be no more until 1946. Aintree Racecourse was used as a truck depot during the war years, housing 16,000 troops. All the while, the course was carefully watched over by the Topham family.

1946

LOVELY COTTAGE

The Grand National returned to Aintree in 1946 having been sadly missed during the torrid war years. Under the caring and thorough guidance of Mrs Topham and the Topham family, the racecourse was prepared for the eagerly awaited renewal of the great race, with more than 300,000 people cramming into the course to watch the National. Due to the special demand to see the race, Aintree acted by putting up extra crash barriers around the course to protect the vast number of viewers from the action.

There could not have been a better boost for the National's reappearance than the presence in the field of the finest chaser of the era. Owned by Mr James Rank and trained in Ireland by Tom Dreaper, the powerful bay Prince Regent had taken all before him in Ireland, where racing had been nowhere near as badly affected by the Second World War as England. Indeed, one-third of the 1946 National field were Irish-trained. A clever, bold jumper, Prince Regent had proved most versatile, adapting to many different styles of course and conditions, winning the Irish Grand National in 1942 in a quagmire and had, just three weeks before Aintree, won the Gold Cup at Cheltenham. Despite being considered a near certainty for the National on the day, Prince Regent had a hefty 12st 5lbs to carry and his stamina reserves were taken on trust. However, his class was expected to tell in what was generally opined to be a poor year because of war ramifications. In the saddle, Workman's jockey in 1939 Tim Hyde was expected to steer Prince Regent home in first place to become the first favourite to win the Grand National since Sprig in 1927.

As well as the 1945 Cheltenham Gold Cup winner Red Rower, the first two from the 1940 National, Bogskar and Macmoffat, reappeared, while the nimble Dunshaughlin was considered the best of Miss Dorothy Paget's three challengers. France too sent over a pair of talented raiders in Symbole and Kami and among the remainder thought most capable of upsetting Prince Regent were Limestone Edward, Knight's Crest, Suzerain II and Lovely Cottage.

Mrs Mirabel Topham.

Owned by Mr Clifford Nicholson, the Northern-trained Limestone Edward had long been considered a leading candidate for the National, being a safe conveyance and a smart jumper. Although his race weight of 10st 2lbs was handy, Limestone Edward's chance had been somewhat tarnished by a recent injury setback, and although connections attempted to dispel any lingering fears, plenty doubted whether the horse had recovered in time for such a race.

Trained by Noel Murless at Hambleton near Thirsk, Knight's Crest joined Limestone Edward as a leading hope of the North. Formerly trained in Ireland (where, with a huge weight advantage, he had beaten Prince Regent in the 1944 Irish Grand National), Knight's Crest had been given a relatively light campaign by his trainer and just two weeks before the National, he had won at Wetherby to show his wellbeing.

A win for Suzerain II would have been rich compensation for trainer Bill Payne, who had been the seventeen-year-old jockey aboard Great Span in the 1928 Grand National. Great Span had looked certain to win the race only for his saddle to slip at the second-last fence. Suzerain II was considered to hold a live outside chance, having won well at Fontwell Park the week before, with his confident owner, Mr Ben Davis, claiming Prince Regent to be the only horse he feared.

A nine-year-old bay gelding, Lovely Cottage – a former hunter-chaser – was another previously trained in Ireland. Now trained in Hampshire by Tommy Rayson, the horse was ridden at Aintree by Captain Robert Charles Petre, an officer in the Scots Guards who had returned from service in Italy earlier in the year. Without the class of Prince Regent, Lovely Cottage had bountiful stamina, having won over four miles at Punchestown earlier in his career.

With firm ground looking likely the day before the race, overnight rain softened the going to good and, with tremendous excitement, the first Grand National for six years began, with Prince Regent the market leader at 3/1.

It was Mr J. Cousins on his own horse Gyppo that led the charge to the first fence, where another Miss Paget-owned horse, Astrometer, became the first casualty. Lord Roseberry's horse Jock smashed through the third fence leaving behind a gaping hole, and Dunshaughlin came down when going through the same hole rather than jumping a more solid section of the obstacle.

Prince Regent, while not overly convincing jumping the National fences for the first time, had survived without serious alarm on the first circuit but, with fellow Gold Cup winner Red Rower out of the race by the time the water had been reached, the favourite began to display his class, as he confidently hunted the Irish-trained front-runner Lough Conn and Miss Paget's third representative, Housewarmer. In behind these came Limestone Edward, Tulyra, Bricett, Silver

Fame, Lovely Cottage and Suzerain II, and in that order they marched onwards to the second circuit.

The big ditch second time round also looked like it had recently returned from a wartime battle, so exaggerated was the canyon-like hole that Jock had created on the first lap, and numerous horses paid the penalty for going straight through the space, including Lough Conn and the trailing Knight's Crest, while further ahead Becher's brought about the downfall of the French horses Kami and Symbole. Kami was well in touch and travelling smoothly when he departed, but sadly Symbole met his end, killed when breaking his neck in his fall.

Prince Regent and Limestone Edward began to draw clear of the remainder, having jumped the Canal Turn and Valentines, although the number of loose horses around them was a cause for concern. Then Limestone Edward put pay to his chance by clouting the twenty-sixth so hard he lost nearly twenty lengths.

The crowd were already showing their appreciation for the great Prince Regent as he jumped the last fence in the country and made his way back towards the stands. But the race was far from over, and the loose horses surrounding the favourite were forcing Hyde to drive Prince Regent forward, wasting valuable

Lovely Cottage wins from Jack Finlay and Prince Regent.

energy through excess speed in order to avoid interference. In behind, Lovely Cottage was running on stoutly, with Suzerain II and Jack Finlay – a 100/1 outsider – also improving.

Lovely Cottage was still many lengths behind Prince Regent two out (where trainer Payne suffered more bad luck as Suzerain II came down when full of running), but the extra energy asserted by the favourite had proved critical, and he was clearly tiring badly.

Enjoying the thorough examination of stamina, Lovely Cottage had cut the gap to two lengths as Prince Regent jumped the last. On the run-in, he was finishing twice as fast, and he soon swallowed up Prince Regent and galloped all the way to the line to win by four lengths, with Jack Finlay also passing the gallant favourite in the closing stages. Housewarmer filled fourth place ahead of the veteran Schubert and Limestone Edward.

The crowd had been won over by the courageous run of Prince Regent, but although in receipt of almost 2 stone, Lovely Cottage confirmed himself to be the best stayer in the field, landing a huge victory for Captain Petre (the leading amateur of the 1937/38 season), Rayson and the owner of Lovely Cottage, Mr John Morant, who before the Second World War trained a number of point-to-pointers in the New Forest.

Aintree was relaunched back into the limelight with another marvellous chapter to add its already famed history, and Lovely Cottage proudly became the first post-war winner of the Grand National.

1946 GRAND NATIONAL RESULT

FATE	HORSE	AGE/WEIGHT	JOCKEY	ODDS
1st	LOVELY COTTAGE	9.10.8	CAPT. R. PETRE	25/1
2nd	JACK FINLAY	7.10.2	W. KIDNEY	100/1
3rd	PRINCE REGENT	11.12.5	T. HYDE	3/1
4th	HOUSEWARMER	9.10.2	A. BRABAZON	100/1
5th	Schubert	12.11.0	C. Beechener	100/7
6th	Limestone Edward	12.10.2	D. Doyle	13/2
Fell	Symbole	aged.11.11	W. Redmond	33/1
Fell	Largo	7.10.13	J. Cooke	66/1
Fell	Heirdom	14.10.10	P. Cahalin	66/1
Fell	Bogskar	13.10.9	R. Matthews	66/1
Fell	Kami	9.10.9	H. Bonneau	33/1
Fell	Macmoffat	14.10.8	I. Alder	50/1
Fell	Astrometer	8.10.3	M. Gordon	50/1
Fell	Knight's Crest	9.10.3	P. Murphy	22/1
Fell	Suzerain II	8.10.3	G. Archibald	33/1
Fell	Vain Knight	13.10.2	R. Curran	100/1
Fell	Silver Fame	7.10.0	D. Ruttle	40/1
Fell	Historical Revue	8.10.0	S. Ryan	66/1
Fell	Tulyra	10.10.0	Mr D.A. Jackson	100/1
Fell	Dunshaughlin	8.10.0	R.J. O'Ryan	100/8
Fell	Double Flush	10.10.0	E. Newman	100/1
Fell	Yung-Yat	10.10.0	T. Cullen jnr	100/1
Fell	Lough Conn	10.10.0	D. McCann	33/1
Fell	Jock	8.10.2	F. Gurney	50/1
Fell	Musical Lad	9.10.0	M. Browne	100/1
Fell	Bricett	9.10.2	J. Brogan	28/1
Fell	Gyppo	12.10.0	Mr J. Cousins	40/1
Fell	Alacrity	13.10.0	G. Bowden	100/1
Fell	Closure	9.10.0	Mr H. Applin	100/1
Fell	Elsich	10.10.0	W. Balfe	100/1
Pulled-Up	Red Rower	12.11.7	G. Kelly	22/1
Pulled-Up	E.P.	11.10.2	M. Molony	50/1
Brought Down	Newark Hill	12.10.1	P. Lay	50/1
Refused	King Gesson	10.10.0	R. Burford	100/1

Weight is in stone & pounds
5 April 1946
Going – Good
Winner – £8,805
Time – 9mins 38 1/5secs
34 Ran
Favourite – Prince Regent

Top Weight – Prince Regent
Winner trained by Tommy Rayson at
Headbourne Worthy, Hampshire
Winner owned by Mr J. Morant
Lovely Cottage, bay gelding by
Cottage – The Nun III.

1947

CAUGHOO

When Prince Regent's stamina had evaporated in the closing stages of the 1946 Grand National, it was not because of the conditions underfoot. The ground that day had been perfectly good but, twelve months on, the country was still in the midst of enduring a miserable period of weather, with many of the winter fixtures lost because of dreadful conditions. The schedules and preparations of many horses had been severely hampered and, with so much racing lost in the preceding months, a huge field of fifty-seven lined up for the 1947 Grand National, with overnight rain leaving the ground very heavy, increasing the chance of fallers and – to Prince Regent's detriment the year before – loose horses.

In spite of the unsuitable going, there were those that considered the now twelve-year-old Prince Regent to have seen his best days, and the fact that the horse had 12st 7lbs to carry (only four horses had ever carried that weight to win a National) was a further negative aspect to consider. An 8/1 favourite, seventeen hands high and the class horse Prince Regent may have been, but many believed it would be one of the other eight Irish-trained horses in the field that would prove best, among them Revelry and Lough Conn. Revelry was a son of the 1932 Epsom Derby winner April The Fifth, and was regarded as having fine stamina and a strong liking for soft going. Lough Conn was one of a number of horses – including Bricett, Silver Fame and Kami – running in 1947 that had competed admirably in the 1946 National without completing. A bold-jumping front-runner, Lough Conn was a winner of the four-mile Conyngham Cup at Punchestown, a race previously won by the 1946 Grand National winner Lovely Cottage (absent on this occasion through injury).

One Irish runner thought to have no chance, however, was Caughoo. One of an astonishing twenty-six in the race listed at 100/1, Caughoo was a little eight-year-old brown gelding trained by Herbert McDowell and ridden by Aintree debutant Eddie Dempsey. Caughoo had won a pair of Ulster Grand Nationals

at Downpatrick, but the horse's recent form was so poor that his odds seemed a very fair reflection of his chance.

While some of the interesting contenders included the very tall grey six-year-old Soda II and the well-handicapped seven-year-old Luan Casta (a winner of the Stanley Chase over a shorter distance on the National course), a pair of leading home-trained runners were Silver Fame and Bricett. Silver Fame had been in tremendous form during the season, winning four of his five races, and Lord Bicester's horse was clearly on the rise. One cause for concern was Silver Fame's fall in the Grand Sefton Chase over the National fences earlier in the season, but in his favour was the booking to ride him of the previous year's winning jockey, Captain Petre. Bricett had long been regarded in the North as a serious Grand National horse and, despite a scare in his preparation when suffering an over-reach, the horse started third favourite on the day behind only Prince Regent and Revelry, at generous odds of 22/1. Many of Bricett's supporters had remembered the 1946 National when the horse had appeared to be travelling as well as eventual winner Lovely Cottage before departing the race on the second circuit. Bricett was regarded as a sound jumper and resolute galloper, and his finest performance of the season had arrived when winning the Stayers' Chase at Cheltenham's December meeting, showing he would relish the full distance of the Grand National.

As the runners assembled at the start, a haunting mist hovered eerily over the racecourse, causing near impossible visibility from the stands once the horses were out in the country. Nevertheless, the usual cocktail of excitement and tension was very much in effect as the enormous field tore away on what was sure to be a most gruelling Grand National. Among the first to show were Lough Conn, Domino, Refugio, Gormanstown, Prince Regent, Silver Fame, Rearmament, First Of The Dandies and Schubert, but groans soon rippled around the spectators when it was learned the much-fancied Revelry had come down at the first, bringing down the outsider EP.

Michael's Pearl and Bullington both struck the upright fence with such force that they crashed down on the landing side of the third, while a mistake by Prince Regent at the same fence saw him lose a good deal of ground as well as his position among the leaders.

As the runners approached Becher's for the first time the mist had really set in, and from the stands, it was almost a mystery as to what was happening. Many of the crowd may have wanted to close their eyes anyway, as Becher's ended the hopes of another leading fancy, Luan Casta, as well as Black Jennifer. Jockey Sheehan was to remount the latter, only for the partnership to come unstuck again at the tenth. Sheehan remounted for a second time, but when Black Jennifer fell again at the second Becher's, he wisely called it a day.

The field was beginning to get strung out as Lough Conn led on. The number of loose horses were increasing too, although one sad accident occurred at Valentines when Linthill made a mistake and injured a leg so badly that he had

Caughoo passes the post a shock winner.

to be destroyed. Sheila's Cottage was another to suffer ill luck of a different kind. Jumping very well under jockey Arthur Thompson, the Neville Crump-trained mare was crossed by a loose horse at the twelfth, causing her to fall.

As the field emerged from the gloom coming back towards the stands, the Irish raider Lough Conn was churning along in front from Musical Lad, Kilnaglory, Klaxton, Bricett and Tulyra, followed by Caughoo, Jack Finlay, Domino, Border Command and the favourite Prince Regent.

The race lost First Of The Dandies at the thirteenth and almost lost Prince Regent at The Chair when another loose horse jumped across him, hampering the top weight and causing him to surrender vital ground.

Lough Conn was jumping each fence like a buck, clearly thriving on the Aintree experience, and by the time the second Canal Turn was reached, the race really began to take shape. Bricett was travelling well at this stage but he was bumped so badly by a rival that he fell, unluckily put out of the race by being so rudely hampered.

At the second Valentines, the field was well strung out, with Lough Conn still in front. However, the unconsidered Caughoo was full of running behind him and making up ground rapidly, while Prince Regent had bravely moved up to challenge the leading group, which included the grey horses Kilnaglory and Refugio, the American hope.

More casualties took place behind the leading group as they raced down the back of the course, with Soda II falling at the twenty-sixth and the unlucky Silver Fame put out of the race when Tulyra ran across him two fences later. Silver Fame had been slowly moving into contention and was clearly a horse of quality. He ran in further Nationals but never found much luck. However, his day arrived at Cheltenham in 1951 when, as a twelve-year-old, he won the Gold Cup.

Lough Conn, despite his bold run, had also suffered interference from loose horses on the second circuit but, as he approached the second last, it was clear that the rank outsider Caughoo was going the best. According to jockey Eddie Dempsey, Caughoo almost came down on his head at the opening three fences, but had soon got a grasp of the drop effect and, having never fallen in his life, began to relish the unique challenge. Looking behind for potential dangers, Dempsey sent Caughoo past the gallant Lough Conn, and the outsider came home an easy winner, finishing totally unflustered with twenty lengths to spare over Lough Conn. Kami followed up his promising run in 1946 by staying on to take third, ahead of the much-loved Prince Regent, who under the circumstances had perhaps run an even finer race than the year before when he almost won.

With the Grand National having been moved from its traditional Friday slot to Saturday for economic reasons at the suggestion of the government, the vast crowd were predominantly stunned by the performance of Caughoo and the ease with which the outsider strolled home. There was a myth attached to the 1947 renewal that, because of the dense mist hovering over the course, Dempsey had been able to wait with Caughoo beside the Canal Turn and rejoined the race when the leaders returned on the second circuit. However, photographic evidence shows Caughoo jumping the water jump just behind the leaders, emphatically dispelling this theory! Caughoo's success was a family one. Trained by Herbert McDowell, the horse was owned by his brother John, a Dublin jeweller, and cost a mere 50 guineas before being named after the Irish estate of the owner's father.

1947 GRAND NATIONAL RESULT

FATE	HORSE	AGE/WEIGHT	JOCKEY	ODDS
1st	CAUGHOO	8.10.0	E. DEMPSEY	100/1
2nd	LOUGH CONN	11.10.1	D. McCANN	33/1
3rd	KAMI	10.10.13	MR J. HISLOP	33/1
4th	PRINCE REGENT	12.12.7	T. HYDE	8/1
5th	Some Chicken	10.10.2	R. Turnell	40/1
6th	Housewarmer	10.10.6	R.J. O'Ryan	25/1
7th	Refugio	9.11.0	F. Adams	100/1
8th	Kilnaglory	12.11.1	B. Marshall	40/1
9th	Clyduffe	12.10.0	M. Hogan	50/1
10th	Ocultor	12.11.0	B. Marshall	100/1
11th	Toyette	10.10.6	Major R. Waugh Harris	100/1
12th	Halcyon Hours	7.11.2	M. Gordon	50/1
13th	Brick Bat	8.10.0	E. Newman	66/1
14th	Schubert	13.10.11	C. Beechener	66/1
15th	Leap Man	10.11.0	T.F. Rimell	50/1
16th	Brighter Sandy	9.10.7	Capt. J. Eustace-Smith	66/1
17th	Rearmament	10.11.1	G. Kelly	33/1
18th	Rowland Boy	8.10.3	Mr R. Black	66/1
19th	Handy Lad	12.10.0	Capt. W. Williams	100/1
Fell	Bricett	10.11.1	M.C. Prendergast	22/1
Fell	Revelry	7.10.12	D. Moore	100/6
Fell	Silver Fame	8.10.12	R. Petre	33/1
Fell	Jack Finlay	8.10.8	W. Kidney	33/1
Fell	Luan Casca	7.10.7	A. Brabazon	22/1
Fell	Bullington	11.10.6	J. Bissill	66/1
Fell	EP	12.10.5	M. Molony	100/1
Fell	Klaxton	7.10.5	J. Maguire	66/1
Fell	Musical Lad	10.10.4	M.J. Prendergast	33/1
Fell	Bogskar	14.10.4	R. Burford	100/1
Fell	First Of The Dandies	10.10.3	J. Moloney	66/1
Fell	Macmoffat	15.10.4	I. Alder	100/1
Fell	Sheila's Cottage	8.10.1	A.P. Thompson	40/1
Fell	Michael's Pearl	8.10.0	E. Reavey	100/1
Fell	Bomber Command	8.10.0	A. Jarvis	100/1
Fell	Parthenon	8.10.0	P. Murray	40/1
Fell	Soda II	6.10.2	F. Gurney	50/1
Fell	Prattler	12.10.0	P. Conlon	50/1
Fell	Black Jennifer	7.10.0	J. Sheehan	50/1
Fell	Double Sam	12.10.0	H. Haley	100/1
Fell	Gyppo	13.10.0	Mr J. Cousins	100/1
Fell	Good Date	9.10.0	J. Dowdeswell	100/1
Fell	Border Bob	9.10.0	J. Neely	100/1
Fell	Tribune	13.10.0	K. Gilsenan	100/1
Fell	Oh Joe	7.10.0	E. Vinall	100/1
Fell	Shanakill	9.10.0	W. Denson	100/1
Pulled-Up	Day Dreams	8.10.0	M. Browne	100/1
Pulled-Up	Linthill	11.10.0	P. Taylor	100/1
Pulled-Up	Wicklow Wolf	7.10.0	M.J. Hogan	100/1
Pulled-Up	Yung-Yat	11.10.1	J. Brogan	100/1
Pulled-Up	Gormanstown	7.10.9	T. Molony	40/1
Pulled-Up	Domino	7.10.0	D. Morgan	28/1
Pulled-Up	Martin M	7.10.0	Major Skrine	66/1
Pulled-Up	Jubilee Flight	12.10.0	E. Hannigan	100/1
Brought Down	Grecian Victory	10.10.0	P. Lay	100/1
Refused	Tulyra	11.10.0	Mr D.A. Jackson	100/1
Refused	Granitza	8.10.0	N. Dixon	100/1
Carried Out	Patrickswell	9.10.0	P. Cahalin	100/1

29 March 1947
Going – Heavy
Winner – £10,007
Time – 10mins 3⅘secs
57 Ran
Favourite – Prince Regent
Top Weight – Prince Regent
Winner trained by Herbert McDowell at Malahide, County Dublin, Ireland
Winner owned by Mr J.J. McDowell
Caughoo, brown gelding by Within The Law – Silverdale.

1948

SHEILA'S COTTAGE

Although the forty-three runners for the 1948 Grand National was down in number (by fourteen) from the year before, the competitive nature of the race was intensely high, with many confirmed Aintree performers in the field. Indeed, eighteen of the runners had competed in the 1947 renewal and, once more, Lovely Cottage was back after a year's absence.

Having run well in the two most recent Grand Nationals, the nine-year-old chestnut Silver Fame seemed to be at his peak as he attempted to make it third time lucky in the race. Silver Fame had proved in both 1946 and 1947 that he could handle the National fences, and had been desperately unlucky to be put out of the 1947 race late on when well placed. Trained by George Beeby and owned by Lord Bicester (who also ran the big, talented but somewhat clumsy seven-year-old Roimond and the outsider Parthenon), Silver Fame had been in magnificent form during the season, winning all five of his races and, despite having to carry 8lbs more than in 1947, was one of the few contenders whose form warranted a place among the market leaders. Sensing a horse at the top of his game, punters made Silver Fame – a half-brother to the 1940 hero Bogskar – the 9/1 favourite.

Many Aintree veterans took their chance once more, including the now-thirteen-year-old Prince Regent, Housewarmer (fourth and sixth in the previous two Nationals), the 1947 runner-up Lough Conn and the two most recent winners Caughoo and Lovely Cottage. Yet through the likes of Loyal Antrim, Happy Home, Cromwell, War Risk and Cloncarrig there were, however, enough newcomers with ability to give the 1948 Grand National a mouth-watering array of possibilities.

Enjoying plenty of support on the day was Ireland's leading hunter-chaser Loyal Antrim. The horse was a brave, exuberant jumper, fully expected to adapt to the unique National fences, and a recent win at Naas confirmed his wellbeing. Happy Home was one of four horses in the race trained by Fulke Walwyn (the improving 1947 finisher Rowland Boy and the ex-Irish-trained pair

Housewarmer and Revelry the other three) and the Glen Kelly-ridden horse was one of the class acts in the race, twice having been placed in the Cheltenham Gold Cup. Anthony Mildmay – so unlucky aboard Davy Jones in the 1936 race – had since succeeded his father as Lord Mildmay and now owned a healthy number of horses that he had in training with his close friend Peter Cazalet. Among those horses was Mildmay's mount in the Grand National, Cromwell, a highly promising seven-year-old that had beaten more fancied National contenders Roimond and Rowland Boy recently at Lingfield. One of the horses in the field with winning experience over the National fences was the grey War Risk. Trained by Battleship's 1938 winning jockey Bruce Hobbs, War Risk had won a Grand Sefton Chase, while the giant eight-year-old Cloncarrig had been purchased by owner Sir Allan Gordon-Smith as a replacement for the ill-fated 1947 third Kami. Talented and well handicapped, Cloncarrig was a horse on the rise, yet some questioned if his jumping was sufficient for the National, with his doubters pointing to a recent fall at Cheltenham.

As the field lined-up at the start watched by a record attendance of over 500,000, there were many horses – including Bricett, the massive grey Soda II, First Of The Dandies and the temperamental mare Sheila's Cottage – hopeful of making a greater impact on the race than twelve months previously. Sheila's Cottage – though not as well-fancied as in 1947 – had proved her stamina at Haydock Park on more than one occasion and, at 50/1, was generally unconsidered by the public: surprising considering she had jumped beautifully before unluckily being put out of the race in 1947.

Musical Lad, who had given a bold showing in 1947, lashed out with a reckless kick just before the starter released them, almost striking Cromwell, but the field were soon dispatched and quickly headed by Lough Conn, setting off like a train in front as he had done the year before.

Tracked by Zahia, First Of The Dandies, Happy Home, Sheila's Cottage, Cloncarrig, Weevil and Schubert, the leader rose at the first, where Serpentine and Bricett were the first to depart. Some Chicken fell at the second while at the big ditch, Cromwell's stablemate Ultra Bene came down and Platypus hit the fence so hard it was a miracle he survived – but he did, and the mistake served as a warning to the horse, who proceeded to jump immaculately the rest of the way.

Becher's, as it so often does, brought misfortune. Travelling nicely within himself and looking set for another bold run, Silver Fame took off at the fence only for Gormanstown to jump across him. Unluckily crashing into the outsider, Silver Fame fell, once more receiving no luck at all in the Grand National.

Silver Fame's stablemate Roimond departed at the Canal Turn, and soon the leader Lough Conn began to struggle. It transpired the horse had broken a blood vessel and was pulled-up. Cloncarrig had jumped impressively, silencing his critics in the early stages, and at Valentines he took command from Zahia, First Of The Dandies and Sheila's Cottage, with Rowland Boy and the old campaigner Schubert close on their heels.

Three lengths to the good and fencing with power and precision, Cloncarrig was warming to his task and really attacking the National fences when he blundered the fourteenth and was down on his knees. Although Cloncarrig did not fall, his jockey Mr J. Hislop had no hope of staying in the saddle. He had failed to get round but Cloncarrig had shown that, with more experience, he had the potential to develop into a serious Grand National contender in future years.

Half the field remained in the race as they crossed the water, with First Of The Dandies the new leader from Zahia, Happy Home, Sheila's Cottage, Le Daim, Rowland Boy and Cromwell, while cutting a forlorn figure and tailed-off at the rear was Lovely Cottage, a light of former years.

Confidently ridden by Jimmy Brogan, First Of The Dandies marched the leading bunch down towards Becher's again – Housewarmer falling at the nineteenth – and by the time they reached the Canal Turn, there were six in contention; the leader followed by Sheila's Cottage, Happy Home, Rowland Boy, Zahia and Cromwell.

Cromwell appeared to be travelling mightily when ill luck again struck Lord Mildmay. The jockey cruelly aggravated an old injury that affected his neck and head. Jarring the suspect area jumping the Canal Turn, Lord Mildmay was virtually unable to lift his head to view the fences in the closing stages of the race, and later said he did not even see the final two obstacles, adding testament to the effort of Cromwell for guiding his pilot home safely.

First Of The Dandies was still in front as they approached two out, but the 100/1 shot Zahia – ridden by Eddie Reavey – now loomed up to challenge him, apparently ready to cause another huge Grand National shock. Having jumped the penultimate fence, another savage twist occurred in a style typical of Grand National stories. Veering off to the left, Reavey appeared to be taking the wrong course and, when he realised his error, he was so wide of the last fence he had no chance of jumping it and was forced to run out.

Brogan could not believe his luck, and First Of The Dandies surged on with the race at his mercy. All his rivals had been seen off, with the important exception of the Arthur Thompson-ridden Sheila's Cottage. Despite a mistake at the second Becher's, the mare had stayed well in touch, and now her already proven stamina came into play. Drawing level with the long-time leader 100 yards from the finish, her bravery and finishing power saw her overthrow First Of The Dandies and relegate that horse to a hard-fought, one-length defeat. Six lengths back in third, amid thoughts of 'what might have been' came Lord Mildmay on Cromwell, with Happy Home fourth ahead of the fast-finishing Platypus.

A rangy, rugged mare with strength and courage, Sheila's Cottage (by the same sire, Cottage, that produced Lovely Cottage and the 1948 Welsh Grand National winner Bora's Cottage) was, by her trainer Neville Crump's own admission, a moody, angry individual but became the horse that really set the trainer's career alight. Crump had originally held a commission in the Fourth Hussars but began

Sheila's Cottage and jockey Arthur Thompson are led in.

training two years prior to the outbreak of the Second World War, while Dublin-born jockey Arthur Thompson had served five years in the Royal Northumberland Fusiliers, including a harrowing three as a prisoner of war, having been captured at Tobruck.

For Crump, Thompson and winning owner John Procter of Lincolnshire, it had been a thrilling Grand National – won by their horse in gritty but admirable fashion. Sheila's Cottage had become the first mare to win the National since Shannon Lass in 1902, and her reward was retirement and a place at stud.

1948 GRAND NATIONAL RESULT

FATE	HORSE	AGE/WEIGHT	JOCKEY	ODDS
1st	SHEILA'S COTTAGE	9.10.7	A.P. THOMPSON	50/1
2nd	FIRST OF THE DANDIES	11.10.4	J. BROGAN	25/1
3rd	CROMWELL	7.10.11	LORD MILDMAY	33/1
4th	HAPPY HOME	9.11.10	G. KELLY	33/1
5th	Platypus	7.10.6	A. Jack	66/1
6th	Rowland Boy	9.11.8	B. Marshall	100/9
7th	Parthenon	9.10.0	P. Murray	100/1
8th	Maltese Wanderer	9.10.0	K. Gilsenan	100/1
9th	Offaly Prince	9.10.5	Mr A. Parker	100/1
10th	Klaxton	8.11.8	R. Smyth	40/1
11th	War Risk	9.11.1	R. Turnell	33/1
12th	Revelry	8.11.6	D. Moore	33/1
13th	Schubert	14.10.2	L. McMorrow	66/1
14th	Lovely Cottage	11.11.4	C. Hook (remounted)	66/1
Fell	Roimond	7.11.7	R. Black	22/1
Fell	Caddie II	10.11.7	J. Maguire	50/1
Fell	Silver Fame	9.11.6	M. Molony	9/1
Fell	Bricett	11.11.3	T. Molony	100/1
Fell	Rearmament	11.11.2	D. Ruttle	66/1
Fell	Cloncarrig	8.10.13	Mr J. Hislop	22/1
Fell	Clonaboy	10.10.10	E. Hannigan	66/1
Fell	Gormanstown	8.10.9	M. Hogan	66/1
Fell	Housewarmer	11.10.6	H. Nicholson	25/1
Fell	Sir John	7.10.3	Major C. Blacker	100/1
Fell	Tudor Close	11.10.3	T. Maher	100/1
Fell	Loyal Antrim	11.10.3	E. Newman	22/1
Fell	Ulster Monarch	9.10.1	Capt. J. Eustace-Smith	100/1
Fell	Musical Lad	11.10.1	M. Browne	100/1
Fell	Ultra Bene	9.10.1	A. Grantham	100/1
Fell	Le Daim	9.10.1	S. Pinch	100/1
Fell	Soda II	7.10.0	H. Bonneau	40/1
Fell	Highland Lad	9.10.0	E. Kennedy	50/1

FATE	HORSE	AGE/WEIGHT	JOCKEY	ODDS
Fell	Some Chicken	11.10.0	W. Redmond	50/1
Fell	Serpentine	10.10.0	C. Mitchell	100/1
Fell	Bora's Cottage	10.10.0	E. Vinall	100/1
Pulled-Up	Caughoo	9.11.1	E. Dempsey	28/1
Pulled-Up	Lough Conn	12.10.5	J. Fitzgerald	22/1
Pulled-Up	Skouras	8.10.0	A. Power	100/1
Brought Down	Weevil	9.10.11	V. Mooney	33/1
Unseated Rider	Tommy Traddles	7.10.0	C. Harrison	100/1
Refused	Halcyon Hours	8.11.5	M.C. Prendergast	50/1
Carried Out	Prince Regent	13.12.2	T. Hyde	25/1
Took Wrong Course	Zahia	8.10.2	E. Reavey	100/1

20 March 1948
Going – Good
Winner – £9,103
Time – 9mins 25²/₅secs
43 Ran
Favourite – Silver Fame
Top Weight – Prince Regent
Winner trained by Neville Crump at Middleham, Yorkshire
Winner owned by Mr J. Procter
Sheila's Cottage, bay mare by Cottage – Sheila.

1949

RUSSIAN HERO

With the first three Grand Nationals since the Second World War returning winners priced 25/1, 100/1 and 50/1, it was with some trepidation and very careful planning that punters selected their fancies for the 1949 renewal. It was the year that Mrs Mirabel Topham and her family officially owned the course for the first time, having purchased Aintree from Lord Sefton, and with the National meeting extended to four days for the first time, the days preceding the great race had seen three fine races run over the National fences: the new Topham Chase, the Champion Chase and the Foxhunter Chase – the 1949 renewal of the lattermost being the final time that particular race was run over the full National course and distance.

In what was considered something of a sub-standard Grand National, many horses that had contested the most recent Nationals were again present, including Happy Home, Bricett, Loyal Antrim and Caughoo, while the 1948 third, Cromwell, was the elected market leader. Having endured torturous luck in the race the year before, Lord Mildmay was again back to ride Cromwell, a horse that was blossoming into the prime of his career aged eight, and had enjoyed a fruitful season. Never outside the first three places from six runs, Cromwell had won twice, the most recent of which coming at the expense of the safe-jumping Happy Home at Windsor. With no Sheila's Cottage or Lough Conn in the field in 1949, many remembered how well Cromwell had jumped in the 1948 race before cruel fate had intervened, and with that in mind, Cromwell started the race as 6/1 favourite, with Happy Home next best at 10/1.

As well as the outsider Barn Dance, Major J. Powell saddled the two most fancied newcomers in Cavaliero and Royal Mount. Cavaliero was an eight-year-old, rich in talent but somewhat unreliable and inconsistent, and was partnered by Jimmy Brogan – second the year before on First Of The Dandies. Two years older than Cavaliero was Royal Mount, a horse considered a touch small for the big Aintree fences. His stamina too remained in question, having failed to last home in the Welsh Grand National earlier in the season. Royal Mount had,

otherwise, enjoyed a decent season, being one of the few horses to finish ahead of Cromwell when impressively beating the National favourite at Kempton Park in February.

The massive chestnut Ulster Monarch and the powerful Cloncarrig were similar in that they had both failed to complete the 1948 National, had both since won over the big fences and were both now high in the handicap. Ulster Monarch, trained in Berwickshire by Stuart Wight, had won over the National fences in the Valentine Chase in November over a shorter distance than the big race, really impressing with his fencing, while Cloncarrig – despite his lingering tendency to clout the odd fence, like in the 1948 National – had also displayed fine stamina when winning over four miles at Cheltenham during the season.

In another open Grand National, the chance of an outsider, such as Acthon Major or Russian Hero, winning remained a possibility. Trained in the North by Walter Easterby, Acthon Major had never attempted such an extreme distance as the National before, but had won over three-and-a-half miles at Haydock Park in November, giving the impression that the further he went, the better he was. Acthon Major had a sprinkling of supporters but, having apparently lost his form, Russian Hero was friendless. A nine-year-old bay gelding trained by former jockey George Owen in Cheshire, Russian Hero was considered more of a two-and-a-half-mile horse, winning over that distance at Leicester in January. Soon after, however, a pair of falls and a poor run at Cheltenham shattered his confidence, seemingly leaving him with only a remote chance at Aintree.

On what was sure to be lightning-quick ground, the forty-three runners were sent on their way, with Roimond, Acthon Major, Cloncarrig, Cavaliero, San Michele, Astra and Wot No Sun in the front rank as they approached the first fence. Parthenon, normally a reliable jumper, crashed out instantly, as did Stone Cottage, while Caughoo's saddle slipped at the fourth and the horse ran out.

Roimond, giving late booking and National debutant Dick Francis a fine ride, led the field on over Becher's and, a fence later, Cloncarrig became the race's first major casualty, falling at the smallest fence on the course.

Roimond, Acthon Major, Astra and Wot No Sun (representing the winning trainer of 1948, Neville Crump) led over Valentines Brook, where the drop caught out Cavaliero, while Acthon Major was another to fall by the wayside as they made their way back towards the stands.

A large number of the survivors had bunched up as the field prepared to pass the stands, with Leap Man the only faller at The Chair and, receiving a tremendous cheer from the vast number of onlookers upon taking the water, Roimond ventured on from the always well-placed Russian Hero (under Irish jockey Leo McMorrow). Then came Wot No Sun, Astra, Ulster Monarch, San Michele, Royal Mount, Monaveen and the favourite Cromwell.

It was Monaveen that shot through rapidly to dispute the lead early on the second circuit, but then the horse sent the spruce flying when coming down at the nineteenth, and from there the falls came like an onrushing avalanche.

Russian Hero and jockey Leo McMorrow are led in victorious.

The high number of casualties meant the survivors were given the added headache of loose horses to contend with and, although the leading pair of Russian Hero and Royal Mount were largely untroubled as they cleared Valentines and beyond, Cromwell – moving up to challenge the leaders – did suffer some slight interference, though it is hard to imagine it affected the outcome.

Royal Mount had pulled into a five-length lead at the twenty-eighth fence and was looking the likely winner. In behind, Roimond was hampered by a loose horse, forcing him to jump at an angle and resulting in a collision with Astra that put that horse on the floor, while the improving Gallery also went when moving up to challenge.

All these incidents had left just three horses with a chance of winning, as the impressive Royal Mount turned for home ahead of Russian Hero and Roimond. But Royal Mount hit the second last with a shuddering thump, and Russian Hero, who came to take the race full of running, swiftly overtook Pat Doyle's partner.

The big green fences had ignited Russian Hero and, jumping the last, the jockey in the black-and-white-quartered colours of owner Fernie Williamson raced away to victory by eight lengths from Roimond. The tired Royal Mount had simply ran out of stamina and his mistake two out had only accelerated the inevitable, for Russian Hero had been travelling ominously well behind him. Cromwell came home safely in fourth, while among the eleven finishers were Bricett who, despite falling in his fourth consecutive Grand National, had been remounted by Tim Molony to finish ninth.

The race had sadly witnessed the fatality of Bora's Cottage through a fall on the second circuit, but the winning time of Russian Hero had been bettered by only Golden Miller, Reynoldstown and Bogskar in the past thirty years.

Another surprise winner he had been, yet Russian Hero had taken to Aintree most magnificently and was a thoroughly deserving winner. The horse was an ex-hunter with the Cheshire Hounds and the win gave trainer Owen his most glorious success since giving up riding three years previously.

Perhaps the happiest man at Aintree that day was owner Williamson. As well as proudly owning the Grand National winner, Williamson had also turned down an offer of 4,500 guineas for Russian Hero two weeks prior to the National and could now also collect on a bet he had placed earlier in the season, when he had backed his horse to win the race at ante-post odds of 300/1.

Outsider Bruno II fell at the fence before Becher's and, at the Brook second time, the tiring Wot No Sun was a casualty, together with 33/1 shot Royal Cottage.

Roimond had been giving Francis a marvellous first National ride, and their lead lasted until the second Canal Turn, where the horse was out-jumped by the improving pair of Russian Hero and Royal Mount, who then took it up. Ulster Monarch was creeping into contention when he came down at the Canal Turn, bringing down Southborough and Brighter Sandy as he did so. It was the second consecutive Grand National that the big chestnut Ulster Monarch had failed to complete – another statistic he now shared with Cloncarrig.

1949 GRAND NATIONAL RESULT

FATE	HORSE	AGE/WEIGHT	JOCKEY	ODDS
1st	RUSSIAN HERO	9.10.8	L. McMORROW	66/1
2nd	ROIMOND	8.11.12	R. FRANCIS	22/1
3rd	ROYAL MOUNT	10.10.12	P.J. DOYLE	18/1
4th	CROMWELL	8.11.3	LORD MILDMAY	6/1
5th	Flaming Steel	8.10.9	Mr J. Spencer	33/1
6th	Happy Home	10.11.10	B. Marshall	10/1
7th	Tonderman	12.10.4	Mr J. Bloom	66/1
8th	Lucky Purchase	11.10.2	A. Jack	50/1
9th	Bricett	12.10.9	T. Molony (remounted)	20/1
10th	Clyduffe	14.10.0	J. Power	66/1
11th	Perfect Night	11.10.0	Mr D. Ancil	66/1
Fell	Cloncarrig	9.11.7	K. Gilsenan	18/1
Fell	Ulster Monarch	10.11.2	R. Curran	28/1
Fell	Cavaliero	8.11.1	J. Brogan	100/8
Fell	Acthon Major	9.10.11	R.J. O'Ryan	50/1
Fell	Caddie II	11.10.10	J. Maguire	66/1
Fell	Leap Man	12.10.10	E. Vinall	66/1
Fell	Bruno II	9.10.9	M. Pringle	66/1
Fell	San Michele	9.10.5	Mr J. Boddy	66/1
Fell	Astra	8.10.4	A.P. Thompson	50/1
Fell	Magnetic Fin	10.10.4	L. Vick	50/1
Fell	Loyal Antrim	12.10.4	Mr A. Scannell	50/1
Fell	Bora's Cottage	11.10.3	E. Kennedy	50/1
Fell	Monaveen	8.10.3	A. Grantham	50/1
Fell	Wot No Sun	7.10.3	G. Kelly	40/1
Fell	Replica	11.10.3	E. Reavey	66/1

FATE	HORSE	AGE/WEIGHT	JOCKEY	ODDS
Fell	Arranbeg	12.10.2	R. McCarthy	66/1
Fell	Martin M	9.10.1	Major W.H. Skrine	66/1
Fell	Southborough	11.10.1	P. Murray	66/1
Fell	Stone Cottage	8.10.1	M. Hogan	66/1
Fell	Celtic Cross	11.10.0	J. Parkin	66/1
Fell	Morning Star II	10.10.0	G. Bowden	66/1
Fell	Ship's Bell	9.10.0	M. O'Dwyer	66/1
Fell	Offaly Prince	10.10.4	Mr A. Parker	66/1
Fell	Barn Dance	10.10.0	E. Newman	50/1
Fell	Parthenon	10.10.5	R. Bates	66/1
Fell	Sagacity	11.10.0	A. Power	66/1
Brought Down	Brighter Sandy	11.11.2	R. Turnell	40/1
Brought Down	Gallery	11.10.8	G. Slack	40/1
Brought Down	Ardnacassa	11.10.5	R. Connors	66/1
Brought Down	Sen Toi	14.10.5	T. Cusack	66/1
Refused	Royal Cottage	9.10.12	R. Black	33/1
Ran Out	Caughoo	10.11.0	D. McCann	66/1

26 March 1949

Going – Slightly Firm

Winner – £9,528

Time – 9mins 24⅕secs

43 Ran

Favourite – Cromwell

Top Weight – Roimond

Winner trained by George Owen at Malpas, Cheshire

Winner owned by Mr W.F. Williamson

Russian Hero, bay gelding by Peter The Great – Logique.

1950

FREEBOOTER

For the first time since 1908, there was a Royal runner in the Grand National. HRH Prince of Wales had been the last Royal to win the race when his Ambush II triumphed in 1900, and it was another of his horses (although he had become King Edward VII by then), Flaxman, that had been the last to grace the National, finishing fourth in 1908. However, through the inspiration of Lord Mildmay, Her Majesty Queen Elizabeth entered into National Hunt ownership, and in the Peter Cazalet-trained Monaveen, Her Majesty now owned a horse that would make her the first British queen since Queen Anne to be associated with racing.

Monaveen was a little nine-year-old bay gelding that was to officially run in the colours of HRH Princess Elizabeth, who was listed as joint-owner with her mother. Monaveen had been specially selected by Mildmay and Cazalet as a horse capable of winning the Grand National, having run so boldly until falling at the nineteenth fence in 1949. There was a huge deal of interest surrounding the Royal runner, and his chance was decent, given that he had won four of five races during the season, beating a host of Grand National rivals during those successes. However, his sole defeat had arrived over the National fences in the Grand Sefton Chase, and there was a suspicion that the Royal horse may lack sufficient stamina in the big one itself. Proudly taking the mount on the special occasion was Tony Grantham, who had also ridden the horse in the 1949 race.

With an enormous field of forty-nine ensuring a plethora of possible outcomes, punters chose to side with horses with experience over the daunting fences. Indeed, of the first fourteen in the betting, no fewer than nine had run in the National before (including the most recent winner Russian Hero), while a tenth, Freebooter, had twice won over the National fences in the Champion Chase at the 1949 Grand National meeting and the Grand Sefton Chase earlier in the current campaign.

Those two Aintree performances highlighted Freebooter as a potential Grand National winner, and he quite rightly commanded a position as joint-favourite, despite a heavy burden of 11st 11lbs, with the 1949 second Roimond. A grand,

powerful individual, Freebooter seemed the ideal sort for the National, really impressing on his previous visits to Aintree. Now as a nine-year-old, he was in his prime, and his form during the season – including an undemanding victory in Doncaster's Great Yorkshire Chase – suggested he was the horse to beat at Aintree. Trained in Yorkshire by Robert Renton, Freebooter was partnered by Jimmy Power, who had finished tenth on his National debut in 1949 aboard the veteran chaser Clyduffe.

Both joint-top weight and joint-favourite, Roimond was again well-fancied, as were National regulars Cloncarrig (who had added muscle to his already rugged frame since 1949), Lord Mildmay's mount Cromwell and the beanpole Soda II (a cat-like jumper and a winner over four miles during the season), while among the interesting newcomers were Shagreen and Angel Hill. Shagreen was the big hope of Ireland and was trained by Tom Dreaper and owned by Mr James Rank of Prince Regent fame. Shagreen had solid Irish form behind him, although he had a hefty 11st 8lbs to contend with. Conversely, the 10st 3lbs allotted to the strong-staying mare Angel Hill made her one of the most appealing outsiders in the field.

It promised to be a most interesting Grand National, with so many horses holding sound claims, including bold performers from the 1949 race Royal Mount, Rowland Boy, Acthon Major, Wot No Sun and Gallery, while also in the line-up was the French raider Garde Toi – third in the recent Cheltenham Gold Cup – and Cadamstown, winner of the first ever Topham Trophy over the National fences. It was with a huge sense of excitement (exaggerated by the presence of the Royal runner) that the race began.

With forty-nine horses thundering towards the first fence, each trying to secure an ideal position, it was inevitable that the usual breakneck pace would result in casualties. Beginning a trend that would continue as the century wore on, the previous year's winner Russian Hero bowed out at the first. Also among the six to go at the opener were the giant Tommy Traddles and Comeragh, who had never fallen before in his life.

The main feature of the first circuit was the extremely high number of fallers, with runners crashing out everywhere. Monaveen delighted the crowd by blazing a trail down to Becher's in front, followed by Wot No Sun, Roimond, Barney VI, Gallery and Acthon Major, but the National's most unforgiving fence put pay to the chances of a quartet, including Gallery and Cavaliero. For the first time, Freebooter showed among the leaders, with an enormous leap at Becher's taking him level with Monaveen.

Travelling with the leaders, but not jumping with the same gusto that had so delighted Dick Francis the year before, the big chestnut Roimond caused a shock when capsizing at the seventh, while the next two fences took their toll, claiming, among others, Cadamstown at the Canal Turn and Castledermot – the quietly fancied mount of Tim Molony – at Valentines. Tragedy ensued at the ditch at the eleventh, as the 1949 third Royal Mount crashed out, falling right across Cromwell who was forced back into the ditch, hampering Saintfield

The magnificent Freebooter clears the final fence.

who refused. Sadly, Royal Mount had broken a leg and became a heartbreaking National fatality.

With over half of the huge field out of the contest by the time the survivours raced in front of the stands, Monaveen's chance of victory had clearly increased, yet just when he seemed ready to seriously challenge for glory, the horse blundered the fourteenth so badly that Grantham was thrown forward in the saddle alarmingly.

If Monaveen's blunder had been bad, Freebooter's at The Chair was even worse. Clouting the fence with his chest, Power too was sent rocketing up the horse's neck, but the jockey skilfully recovered, while it was testament to the raw power and intelligence of Freebooter that the horse was able to maintain his feet while losing little ground in the process.

With Monaveen and Freebooter making errors, Cloncarrig had gradually moved into a leading position and was jumping better than in his previous National attempts, proudly leading the pack out for the second circuit, followed by Wot No Sun, Acthon Major and Monaveen, while next came a bunch of

hopefuls including Shagreen, Rowland Boy, Column, Inchmore, Freebooter, Angel Hill and Confucius.

The remainder were getting badly strung out and, running down to the second Becher's, the race was taking shape, with the big grey Soda II another to depart. At Becher's, Angel Hill had arrived on the scene to threaten Cloncarrig for supremacy, while Monaveen now began to struggle, and the only other horses in contention were Wot No Sun, Shagreen, Acthon Major and the gradually improving Freebooter.

But when the Irish horse Shagreen (running a mightily impressive race under Glen Kelly) came down at the twenty-third, followed by a spectacular dive by Angel Hill at the Canal Turn, the race developed into a duel between Cloncarrig and Freebooter; two fine, strapping chasers, neither of whom displayed any sign of distress or weakness.

The two were virtually inseparable as they came to the second last having drawn well clear of the rest, but then the mistakes that had haunted Cloncarrig's previous National raids surfaced once more. As Power kicked Freebooter on,

Bob Turnell realised he had to respond on Cloncarrig. Charging fast at the fence, Cloncarrig got in too close, hitting the top of the obstacle and crashing down in a heap. Both horses appeared full of running at the time, but Freebooter had remained ice cool under pressure and was then left free to come home at his leisure, winning by fifteen lengths. Wot No Sun and Acthon Major had proved they were true Aintree horses by following Freebooter home, having both shown well throughout, while Rowland Boy took fourth place and Monaveen returned home safely in fifth, his stamina proving insufficient for the Grand National.

Freebooter was hailed as the best horse to win the race since Golden Miller, and it was a hard claim to argue. He had carried a colossal weight, jumped superbly (apart from his scare at The Chair), had steered clear of the loose horse hazards and kept his composure to see off the imposing danger of Cloncarrig. Freebooter was a real powerhouse – resilient, tough and with a touch of class. He maintained his 100 per cent record over the National fences while providing the greatest moments in the respective careers of Renton and Power. Freebooter later confirmed his status as one of the finest performers over the big National fences when winning a second Grand Sefton Chase as well as a Becher Chase.

1950 GRAND NATIONAL RESULT

FATE	HORSE	AGE/WEIGHT	JOCKEY	ODDS
1st	FREEBOOTER	9.11.11	J. POWER	10/1
2nd	WOT NO SUN	8.11.8	A.P. THOMPSON	100/7
3rd	ACTHON MAJOR	10.11.2	R.J. O'RYAN	33/1
4th	ROWLAND BOY	11.11.7	R. BLACK	40/1
5th	Monaveen	9.10.13	A. Grantham	100/7
6th	Ship's Bell	10.10.0	M. O'Dwyer	66/1
7th	Inchmore	13.10.0	R. Curran	100/1
Fell	Garde Toi	9.12.1	Marquis de Portago	100/1
Fell	Roimond	9.12.1	R. Francis	10/1
Fell	Klaxton	10.11.13	J. Maguire	40/1
Fell	Cloncarrig	10.11.9	R. Turnell	25/1
Fell	Shagreen	9.11.8	G. Kelly	20/1
Fell	Cavaliero	9.11.6	J.A. Bullock	66/1
Fell	Russian Hero	10.11.4	L. McMorrow	22/1
Fell	Cromwell	9.11.4	Lord Mildmay	18/1
Fell	Stockman	8.11.1	D. Thomas	100/1
Fell	Royal Mount	11.11.0	Mr A. Corbett	40/1
Fell	Mermaid IV	11.11.0	Mr T.B. Palmer	100/1
Fell	Battling Pedulas	11.10.11	D. Marzani	50/1
Fell	Castledermot	8.10.9	T. Molony	20/1
Fell	Gallery	12.10.8	G. Slack	28/1

FATE	HORSE	AGE/WEIGHT	JOCKEY	ODDS
Fell	Cadamstown	10.10.8	E. Dempsey	66/1
Fell	Ardnacassa	12.10.5	Mr T. Brookshaw	100/1
Fell	Soda II	9.10.5	K. Mullins	33/1
Fell	Knockirr	10.10.4	T. Cusack	66/1
Fell	Angel Hill	10.10.3	T. Shone	33/1
Fell	Cottage Welcome	11.10.3	C. Hook	100/1
Fell	Inverlochy	11.10.3	P.J. Doyle	50/1
Fell	Barney VI	12.10.2	T.P. Burns	100/1
Fell	Possible	10.10.1	P. Conlon	50/1
Fell	Tommy Traddles	9.10.1	F. O'Connor	66/1
Fell	San Michele	10.10.0	J. Boddy	100/1
Fell	Highland Cottage	10.10.0	M. Hogan	66/1
Fell	Limestone Cottage	10.10.0	J. Dowdeswell	100/1
Fell	Pastime	9.10.0	C. Sleator	66/1
Fell	Southborough	12.10.0	E. Reavey	100/1
Fell	Ivan's Choice	9.10.0	P.J. O'Brien	100/1
Fell	Ole Man River	8.10.0	G. Bonas	100/1
Fell	Comeragh	9.11.0	P.J. Kelly	50/1
Fell	Zarter	10.10.0	Mr J. Straker	66/1
Pulled-Up	Confucius	9.10.0	C. O'Connor	40/1
Pulled-Up	Happy River	7.10.12	D. McCann	40/1
Pulled-Up	Binghamstown	11.10.7	Mr L. Furman	100/1
Pulled-Up	Safety Loch	9.10.0	Mr D. Punshon	100/1
Brought Down	Column	10.10.2	A. Mullins	100/1
Brought Down	Dynovi	9.10.0	A. Jack	100/1
Unseated Rider	Skouras	10.10.2	M. Browne	100/1
Refused	Fighting Line	11.10.8	Mr E. Greenway	50/1
Refused	Saintfield	13.10.0	Mr M. Gosling	100/1

25 March 1950
Going – Good
Winner – £9,314
Time – 9mins 24⅕secs
49 Ran
Joint Favourites – Roimond and Freebooter
Top Weights – Garde Toi and Roimond
Winner trained by Robert Renton at Ripon, Yorkshire
Winner owned by Mrs L. Brotherton
Freebooter, bay gelding by Steel Point – Proud Fury.

1951

NICKEL COIN

Having contested such a captivating duel the previous year, Freebooter and Cloncarrig were back at Aintree for the 1951 Grand National. Although a specialist over the National fences, the handicapper had made winning races extremely tough for Freebooter, and if he was to record successive wins in the race, the horse would have to overcome the maximum burden of 12st 7lbs, a feat last managed by Poethlyn in 1919. Like Freebooter, Cloncarrig would have proved a most popular winner. The big horse had run a fine race the year before, but he too was now in the handicapper's tight grasp, the eleven-year-old having to carry 12 stone on this occasion. Since the 1950 race, Cloncarrig had undergone an operation to help his wind, and the horse entered the race with jockey Bob Turnell bubbling with confidence over the horse's chance at Aintree.

Splitting Freebooter and Cloncarrig at the top of the handicap was another horse that had impressed many the year before, Shagreen. The horse had proven that National showing to be no fluke when winning the Grand Sefton Chase earlier in the season (beating Freebooter in the process), yet Glen Kelly's mount now had a huge weight of 12st 2lbs to shoulder. Even so, Shagreen's previous visits to Aintree had left a most-favourable impression, so much so that he shared second place in the betting market at 10/1 with both Freebooter and Cloncarrig.

Lord Bicester's Roimond and the out-of-form Russian Hero were also back in 1951, but it was to a newcomer that punters looked for inspiration. Having registered some fine performances since the announcement of the Grand National weights, Mr Jock Whitney's Arctic Gold had leapt to favourite for the race and was clearly the best handicapped chaser in the field. Mr Whitney had come very close to winning the National when his Easter Hero had been second in 1929, and the owner had also seen his Sir Lindsay finish third in 1930 and Thomond II finish third in both 1934 and 1935. The front-running, bold-jumping chestnut Arctic Gold had put together a hat-trick of wins during the season and had beaten Freebooter at Doncaster in February. Improving all the time and

partnered by Tim Molony, the obvious worry for Arctic Gold was inexperience, as no horse of his age – six – had won the National since Ally Sloper in 1915.

With chances ranging from considerable to moderate, some of the most interesting newcomers to the race included Finnure, Royal Tan, Dog Watch and Nickel Coin. Finnure, like Roimond owned by Lord Bicester and trained by George Beeby, was a giant chestnut and the selected mount of Dick Francis. Finnure had drawn attention as a possible National winner the year before when winning the Champion Chase over the big fences. Apart from Shagreen and the outsider Derrinstown, Royal Tan was the only runner from Ireland, the seven-year-old chestnut representing the yard of Vincent O'Brien (the yard that would have a huge impact on the race in upcoming years), while the ten-year-old brown stayer Dog Watch hailed from the same George Owen yard as Russian Hero. A strong jumper and tough stayer, the nine-year-old bay mare Nickel Coin carried a mere 10st 1lb in the race. With a Classic-winning sire in Pay Up, Nickel Coin was not without class, and her form (she had run no fewer than twelve times during the season) was consistent, winning the Manifesto Chase at Lingfield en route to Aintree. Trained by Jack O'Donaghue and ridden by one time prisoner of war John Bullock, Nickel Coin looked to join Shannon Lass and Sheila's Cottage as Grand National-winning mares in the twentieth century, and was allowed to start at 40/1.

One person sadly missing from Aintree on this occasion was the much-loved Lord Anthony Mildmay. Tragically, he had lost his life through drowning after the 1950 Grand National, and the loss was felt throughout racing. Fittingly, Mrs Topham would name the new course the Mildmay course (consisting of regular hurdles and park fences and built in the centre of the Grand National course, with National fences thirteen, fourteen, fifteen and sixteen, as well as twenty-nine and thirty on the second circuit situated on the new 'racecourse proper') when it was ready for the 1953 meeting.

It was to be the most bizarre National since Tipperary Tim's victory in 1928 and, although the heavy ground had contributed largely to the mayhem of that race together with the Easter Hero debacle at the Canal Turn, on this occasion, it was unfortunately human error that caused much of the commotion.

The start can only be described as a shambles, as many of the horses were still circling round when starter Mr Leslie Firth inexplicably let the field go. Cloncarrig was one that was caught out for he had his back turned, and Freebooter was struck in the jaw by the tape as it rose, causing him to lose ground.

Amid the mayhem, the normal frantic dash to the first was replaced by a kamikaze charge as many runners tried to compensate for the lost ground, and a fierce rush to the first fence ensued that bordered on panic. Hitting the first at breakneck speed, the situation caused the departure of twelve runners – a National record – and those left bitter by the incident were the connections of fallers Stockman, Parsonshill, Column, Confucius, Cadamstown, Texas Dan, Irish Lizard, Revealed, Stalbridge Rock and the well-fancied Finnure, while

Nickel Coin (left) and Gay Heather jump
the seventeenth fence together.

promising amateur Michael Scudamore was brought down on East A' Calling and Fred Rimell's Welsh Grand National runner-up Land Fort – partnered by Bryan Marshall – was last over when he clipped the top and come down. Cloncarrig and Freebooter were down the field at the first, while the chestnut Royal Tan was also well to the rear.

With exactly one-third of the field eliminated after one fence, there was no let up in the pace, and the veteran Gallery was next to go, his fall followed by groans from the crowd as Freebooter was consequently brought down, while at the fifth, Shagreen paid the price for an uncharacteristically awful jump. Staying out of trouble up front was Arctic Gold and, jumping boldly, he led on from Armoured Knight, Nickel Coin, Glen Fire, Roimond and the grey horse Caesar's Wife.

Becher's claimed only Morning Cover, but the chaos continued at the seventh with four exiting, while the Canal Turn again proved dramatic as the leader Arctic Gold put in a careless leap and fell, bringing down Armoured Knight. In behind, Glen Fire – a first National ride for Fred Winter – landed on his head

and Cloncarrig and Prince Brownie also came to grief. Roimond never left the ground at Valentines, Partpoint fell and Caesar's Wife came down in the lead a fence later, causing Queen Of The Dandies to fall.

The stunned crowd looked on in amazement as a mere seven horses headed for The Chair, preceded by a herd of loose horses in a race where survival would have been a mighty achievement. It was Russian Hero that had taken control, Aintree again bringing the former winner to life, and he approached The Chair with a strong command on proceedings, tracked by Gay Heather, Dog Watch, Nickel Coin, Broomfield, Royal Tan and Derrinstown.

At this stage, Russian Hero would have been favourite, given his 1949 triumph, but the loose horses – including the grey Caesar's Wife – were causing mayhem by running in all directions. Clearly distracted, Russian Hero then slowed going into the fence, hit it hard and deposited McMorrow to the turf. In behind, his stablemate Dog Watch was interfered with by the loose runners and barely took off, landing on top of The Chair and sending Tim Brookshaw flying as the horse fell back into the ditch. This left Gay Heather with a clear lead over Nickel Coin and the other three, and the five survivors made their way out for the second circuit before a disbelieving audience.

With half the race still to run, it was the mare Nickel Coin that pushed into the lead, closely followed by Gay Heather, and the pair proceeded to jump beautifully down to Becher's. Taking the Brook with a super leap, the white-socked Nickel Coin touched down narrowly in front, but Gay Heather paid the price for getting in too close and came down, with Derrinstown crashing into the stricken horse from behind, resulting in a tangled mess, although both horses were soon remounted.

Broomfield did not last much longer and, by the second Canal Turn, Nickel Coin and the Irish horse Royal Tan had the race to themselves. Racing together out in the country, Nickel Coin hugged the inside with a 12lb concession from Royal Tan giving her the advantage.

As they raced back towards the stands, roars went up as Royal Tan rallied, but the mare appeared to have his number when the Irish horse hit the last very hard and almost fell. Royal Tan recovered well, but his chance of winning had been buried by that mistake, and Nickel Coin strode home a six-length winner. Having been two fences behind when Nickel Coin crossed the line, the game Derrinstown received a warm cheer by taking third – and last.

It had been an extraordinary race, with the runner-up – only a seven-year-old – receiving much credit in defeat having also finished second in the Irish National twelve days before. But it was Nickel Coin that had jumped better than any on the day, providing the first major win for Reigate-based Irishman O'Donaghue and providing the thrill of a lifetime for owner Mr Jeffrey Royle, a Surrey farmer who had ridden Nickel Coin twice during the season. Nickel Coin was the first horse he owned.

Once again, the Grand National had proved it was a race like no other, where anything is possible and the unexpected should be expected.

1951 GRAND NATIONAL RESULT

FATE	HORSE	AGE/WEIGHT	JOCKEY	ODDS
1st	NICKEL COIN	9.10.1	J.A. BULLOCK	40/1
2nd	ROYAL TAN	7.10.13	MR A.S. O'BRIEN	22/1
3rd	DERRINSTOWN	11.10.0	A. POWER (remounted)	66/1
Fell	Shagreen	10.12.2	G. Kelly	10/1
Fell	Cloncarrig	11.12.0	R. Turnell	10/1
Fell	Roimond	10.12.0	A. Jarvis	100/7
Fell	Finnure	10.12.0	R. Francis	22/1
Fell	Land Fort	7.11.3	B. Marshall	20/1
Fell	Russian Hero	11.11.1	L. McMorrow	40/1
Fell	Arctic Gold	6.10.13	T. Molony	8/1
Fell	Rowland Boy	12.10.12	D.V. Dick	50/1
Fell	Prince Brownie	9.10.9	A. Grantham	33/1
Fell	Stalbridge Rock	8.10.5	Mr R. McCreery	66/1
Fell	Cadamstown	11.10.4	J. Dowdeswell	50/1
Fell	Gallery	13.10.4	A. Mullins	50/1
Fell	Dog Watch	10.10.2	T. Brookshaw	33/1
Fell	Partpoint	9.10.5	A.P. Thompson	33/1
Fell	Broomfield	10.10.4	R. Emery	33/1
Fell	Glen Fire	8.10.1	F.T. Winter	33/1
Fell	Confucius	10.10.0	M. O'Dwyer	100/1
Fell	Queen Of The Dandies	10.10.0	R. Carter	100/1
Fell	Column	11.10.1	Mr A. Corbett	100/1
Fell	Gay Heather	10.10.0	R. Curran	66/1
Fell	Morning Cover	10.10.0	G. Slack	40/1
Fell	Revealed	11.10.0	Mr W. Beynon-Brown	100/1
Fell	Caesar's Wife	9.10.8	Mr G.B. Rogers	100/1
Fell	Binghamstown	12.10.0	Mr L. Furman	100/1
Fell	Parsonshill	12.10.2	Mr J. Seely	100/1
Brought Down	Freebooter	10.12.7	J. Power	10/1
Brought Down	Sergeant Kelly	10.10.12	R. De'Ath	40/1
Brought Down	Armoured Knight	7.10.8	T. Cusack	66/1
Brought Down	East A' Calling	10.10.2	Mr M.J. Scudamore	50/1
Brought Down	Stockman	9.10.2	G. Vergette	100/1
Brought Down	Irish Lizard	8.10.1	P. Taaffe	50/1
Brought Down	Texas Dan	9.10.1	P. Fitzgerald	66/1
Refused	Tasman	11.10.0	C. Hook	100/1

7 April 1951
Going – Soft
Winner – £8,815
Time – 9mins 48⅘secs
36 Ran
Favourite – Arctic Gold

Top Weight – Freebooter
Winner trained by Jack O'Donaghue at
  Reigate, Surrey
Winner owned by Mr J. Royle
Nickel Coin, bay mare by Pay Up
  – Viscum.

1952

TEAL

When trainer Neville Crump and jockey Arthur Thompson won the Grand National in 1948, they did so with a horse in Sheila's Cottage that was largely unconsidered pre-race by connections and punters. However, when Thompson stated that – bar interference – he was confident that Teal would win the 1952 Grand National, it certainly caught the attention of many. A bay ten-year-old with stamina and finishing speed, Teal was a strong, relentless galloper, well-weighted for his first tilt at the National and in fine form leading up to the event. Despite a worrying tendency to spank the odd park fence, Thompson was adamant that the horse's jumping would stand up to the rigours of Aintree. Teal had shown his wellbeing prior to the National, with a three-mile-three-furlong success at Birmingham (one of three he enjoyed during the season) enough to see the horse start 100/7 second favourite.

Another huge field (forty-seven) was again headed by Freebooter in both the handicap and the betting market. Partnered on this occasion by Bryan Marshall, Freebooter had rolled up four consecutive victories to begin the season as he returned stunningly to the form of his Grand National-winning campaign of two seasons before. A narrow defeat by the 1951 Gold Cup winner and former National favourite Silver Fame at Sandown, followed by a rare fall in the Cheltenham Gold Cup behind Mont Tremblant (Nagara, a French challenger for the National was fourth) did little to deter public belief that Freebooter, again shouldering the maximum 12st 7lbs, could recapture his National crown.

Despite the 1951 winner Nickel Coin not taking part, it was a most competitive Grand National field in 1952, with experienced-if-ageing Aintree old hands Wot No Sun, Russian Hero, Roimond and Cloncarrig joined by the newcomers such as Skyreholme, the Welsh Grand National winner, and Cardinal Error, an eight-year-old Haydock Park winner. However, three of the strongest challengers looked to be Miss Dorothy Paget's grand chaser Legal Joy and the Irish pair of Royal Tan and Early Mist – future stablemates.

Having run so well in 1951, Royal Tan had 7lbs more to carry on this occasion, but brought with him the supreme confidence of Irish supporters, convinced the horse could go one place better, with the chestnut certainly holding solid claims, winning a recent chase at Cheltenham. Another chestnut, the promising young Early Mist – trained by Tom Dreaper and ridden by Pat Taaffe – was to find himself the most fancied of the Irish runners following a campaign of rich potential. Sandwiched between Teal at 100/7 and Early Mist at 18/1 was the extremely well-handicapped Legal Joy. From the yard of Fulke Walwyn, Legal Joy was more commonly raced over far shorter distances than the National, but had illustrated both speed and stamina when winning three times in high-class company during the season. Legal Joy had the same sire – Within The Law – as the 1947 winner Caughoo, and had in the saddle the blossoming talent of Michael Scudamore, now a professional.

A dispute between the Tophams and the BBC over the radio broadcast rights to the race had led to the vanquishing for one year of the live expert coverage that listeners had come to expect from the unrivalled BBC. As a compromise, Mrs Topham arranged for her own team of assembled commentators to provide live coverage of the race. This, however, proved both farcical and distinctly amateurish, the commentary being littered with hesitation, mistakes and general comedy, hardly good advertising for the greatest race in the world.

Grand National day was damp, cold and misty. As the big field milled round at the start with the previous year's debacle still fresh in everyone's mind, the tension and anticipation reached mountainous levels.

With many determined not to be caught out by another poor start, a band of runners broke the tape, causing a ten-minute delay as a replacement was sent for, and in this interim period, Marshall dismounted Freebooter to relieve some of the horse's hefty burden.

Away second time to a thunderous roar, it was the Spanish amateur the Duque de Alburquerque that led on his own horse, the Peter Cazalet-trained Brown Jack III, yet despite being advised by officials to steady the pace of the first fence approach, the initial gallop was frenetic, as Freebooter, Wot No Sun, Roimond, Skyreholme, Teal and Legal Joy joined the front rank. Not surprisingly, another high casualty number resulted, with ten horses coming to grief and, although most of the fancied runners survived, Early Mist and Cardinal Error bit the dust, as did (for a second time in the National) Russian Hero. Another five fell by the wayside at the big ditch, including the grey Caesar's Wife and the promising youngster Whispering Steel, who sent his jockey somersaulting over the fence, and with Brown Jack III, Cloncarrig and Nagara all departing before Becher's, the field had once more been decimated in the race's early stages.

At Becher's, Freebooter held the lead from Printer's Pie, Another Delight, Starlit Bay and Wot No Sun, and here Wolfschmidt and Skouras came down, the latter sadly having to be destroyed having suffered a very bad injury. One could sense the anti-Grand National campaigners preparing their attack on the race, as a

Above: Captain Neville Crump meets the Duke and Duchess of York at Aintree in 1989.

Right: Teal (left) jumps the last fence with Legal Joy.

second consecutive National was blitzed with fallers and misfortune, and more dropped out at the next fence as fancied outsiders Skyreholme and Pearly Prince fell, with Another Delight crumbling at Valentines.

At the head of affairs, Teal and Freebooter were clearly enjoying themselves and began a duel that would last until the second Canal Turn. Both horses were jumping with tremendous power, exhibiting passion in their task, and as they headed back towards the stands, they led from Legal Joy, Wot No Sun, Roimond, Border Luck and Menzies, and in that order they took The Chair and water and, even though half the field were already out of the race, the massive number of starters had – this time – ensured that there were still plenty of competitors (twenty) by the start of the second circuit.

As the field began to get strung out, Freebooter and Teal continued to dominate, although there were a number of unlucky incidents in behind. The veteran Roimond clipped the seventeenth and fell, bringing down Menzies in the process when the pair were both travelling well, while the seven-year-old Border Luck was cruising into a threatening position when falling at the fence before Becher's.

In a glorious example of National Hunt racing at its finest, Freebooter and Teal went stride for stride into Becher's, the most fearsome obstacle in the land, and flew the fence as if presented with wings, thrilling the spectators in the vicinity (who were still somewhat downhearted by the sight of the stricken Skouras). On the landing side, Teal pecked slightly, his nose scraping the ground, yet he lost little momentum, and then received some luck when Freebooter hit the top of the Canal Turn two fences later and tumbled to the ground.

Freebooter's exit left Teal clear in front and seemingly on the way to victory, but in behind, Scudamore was bringing Legal Joy through to challenge, with the Irish horse Royal Tan also beginning to make significant progress. With half-a-mile to run, Legal Joy joined Teal in the lead and the two enjoyed a memorable battle as they left the back stretch behind them and rounded the turn for home.

With nothing between them they took the last fence together while, in behind, Royal Tan again made a last-fence blunder – but whereas he had survived in 1951 to take second place, this time he fell, hitting the ground when apparently still full of running.

But it was the front-running Teal that had most left to give and, shaking off the worthy challenge of the larger-framed Legal Joy, the horse ran on to win by five lengths to give the North their fourth National win in five years, and Crump and Thompson their second. Placed for the second time, although a long way behind the first two, was Wot No Sun (also trained by Crump) with the 100/1 shot Uncle Barney able to steal a place following Royal Tan's last-fence fall.

It had been a spectacular display of front-running from Teal, who had jumped with style and courage. Teal was bred in Ireland and purchased by Mr Harry Lane for £2,000 after winning a race at Kelso the previous May. Remarkably, that Kelso win was Teal's first in a proper steeplechase, although he had previously gained experience in a number of point-to-points. Having had just five runs under the guidance of the great Yorkshire trainer Crump, it was huge testament to both trainer and horse that the inexperienced Teal should win a race as daunting and demanding as the Grand National.

For Thompson, Teal's win highlighted him as perhaps the finest rider of the era over the National fences, and those that had listened to the Irishman's bold prediction that Teal would win the National were now considerably richer.

1952 GRAND NATIONAL RESULT

FATE	HORSE	AGE/WEIGHT	JOCKEY	ODDS
1st	TEAL	10.10.12	A.P. THOMPSON	100/7
2nd	LEGAL JOY	9.10.4	M. SCUDAMORE	100/6
3rd	WOT NO SUN	10.11.7	D.V. DICK	33/1
4th	UNCLE BARNEY	9.10.4	J. BODDY	100/1
5th	Overshadow	12.10.5	E. Newman	22/1
6th	Printers Pie	8.10.0	G. Slack	100/1
7th	Hierba	7.10.0	A. Mullins	66/1
8th	Column	12.10.0	P. Pickford	100/1
9th	Parsonshill	13.10.1	Mr J. Seely	100/1
10th	Sergeant Kelly	11.10.9	R. Cross (remounted)	100/1
Fell	Freebooter	11.12.7	B. Marshall	10/1
Fell	Roimond	11.11.13	T. Molony	33/1
Fell	Cloncarrig	12.11.13	Mr W. Dugdale	50/1
Fell	Nagara	10.11.7	P. Hieronimus	100/1
Fell	Royal Tan	8.11.6	Mr A.S. O'Brien	22/1
Fell	Skyreholme	9.11.3	R. Francis	40/1
Fell	Skouras	12.10.13	Mr R. Keith	66/1
Fell	Dominick's Bar	8.10.13	A. Prendergast	66/1
Fell	Tantivy	11.11.1	Mr M. Westwick	50/1
Fell	Russian Hero	12.10.11	L. McMorrow	50/1

FATE	HORSE	AGE/WEIGHT	JOCKEY	ODDS
Fell	Whispering Steel	7.10.11	R. Morrow	40/1
Fell	Early Mist	7.10.11	P. Taaffe	18/1
Fell	Another Delight	9.10.10	G. Kelly	25/1
Fell	Possible	12.11.0	Mr E. Weymouth	100/1
Fell	Hal's Venture	7.10.8	J. Foster	45/1
Fell	Pearly Prince	9.10.5	D. Leslie	25/1
Fell	Starlit Bay	8.10.3	Mr C. Straker	50/1
Fell	Inter Alia	9.10.3	C. Sleator	66/1
Fell	Wolfschmidt	12.10.3	F. O'Connor	100/1
Fell	Bronze Arrow	10.10.2	Mr J. Straker	100/1
Fell	St Kathleen II	9.10.2	P.J. Doyle	50/1
Fell	Rocket VI	8.10.1	V. Speck	100/1
Fell	Traveller's Pride	9.10.1	L. Stephens	100/1
Fell	Golden Surprise	7.10.3	Mr T. Clarke	100/1
Fell	Brown Jack III	9.10.10	Duque de Alburquerque	40/1
Pulled-Up	Icy Calm	9.11.0	Marquis de Portago	33/1
Pulled-Up	Tavoy	9.10.0	D. McCann	100/1
Pulled-Up	Derrinstown	12.10.0	A. Power	100/1
Brought Down	Cardinal Error	8.11.8	J. Power	33/1
Brought Down	Menzies	10.10.4	M. O'Dwyer	33/1
Brought Down	Irish Lizard	9.10.3	R.J. Hamey	33/1
Unseated Rider	Border Luck	7.10.12	T. Shone	20/1
Unseated Rider	Caesar's Wife	10.10.6	Mr G. Rogers	50/1
Refused	Kelek	8.10.13	C. Hook	40/1
Refused	Royal Stuart	9.10.3	T. Brookshaw	50/1
Refused	Court Painter	12.10.0	F. Carroll	100/1
Refused	Cream Of The Border	7.10.0	A. Kelly	50/1

5 April 1952

Going – Good

Winner – £9,268

Time – 9mins 21½secs

47 Ran

Favourite – Freebooter

Top Weight – Freebooter

Winner trained by Neville Crump at Middleham, Yorkshire

Winner owned by Mr H. Lane

Teal, bay gelding by Bimco – Miltown Queen.

1953

EARLY MIST

The field of thirty-one for the 1953 Grand National was the smallest since the Second World War and, disappointingly, the quality also seemed inferior to previous years. With the exception of the 1952 Cheltenham Gold Cup winner Mont Tremblant and a handful of others, the field was bereft of class, and adding a sense of sadness to the occasion was the recent death in the Gold Cup of the excellent 1952 National winner Teal. Injuring himself at the water jump at Cheltenham, Teal had ruptured a bowel and, although valiant attempts were made to save him, the horse later suffered a relapse and was lost.

Teal had long been the ante-post favourite for the Grand National, so as an alternative, punters latched onto a horse that had enjoyed success in other races over the National fences, albeit at shorter distances. From the Robert Renton stable that had produced Freebooter to win in 1950, the consistent eleven-year-old brown gelding Little Yid had won the Molyneux Chase at the November meeting and had also been second in the Topham Trophy at the 1952 Grand National meeting. A fine jumper, Little Yid had posted the best Grand National trial of the season when coming third behind the subsequent Gold Cup winner Knock Hard and the ill-fated Teal in the Great Yorkshire Chase at Doncaster. That form, coupled with the presence in the saddle of Freebooter's jockey Jimmy Power, saw Little Yid start as the 7/1 favourite.

Unquestionably the class horse of the field, Mont Tremblant had won the Gold Cup as a six-year-old and was owned by Miss Dorothy Paget. Trained by Fulke Walwyn, Mont Tremblant had finished fourth in the most recent Gold Cup, and the chestnut had run well at both Sandown and Kempton before that. Trying the Aintree fences for the first time, Mont Tremblant was a fearless, accurate jumper, and it was only his huge weight burden of 12st 5lbs – a stone more than any other 1953 National runner – that kept Dave Dick's mount from starting shorter than his price of 18/1.

With the Sid Mercer-trained Glen Fire surprisingly high in the betting market – despite having twice failed to get round over the big fences, including when

falling in the 1951 National – other horses that came into the 1953 race with high aspirations included Whispering Steel, Cardinal Error, Lucky Dome and Early Mist. A true stayer who had fallen early in the 1952 race, Whispering Steel had leapt into contention on this occasion by winning over three-and-a-half miles at Sandown in January, beating the 1952 runner-up Legal Joy in the process. Cardinal Error was another of the casualties from the previous year's race expected to fair better in 1953, and was a popular selection to win for Stuart Wight's yard. Having seen Royal Tan go close in two previous Nationals (Royal Tan was absent through injury in 1953), Vincent O'Brien had a pair of serious contenders in Lucky Dome and Early Mist. The diminutive, lightly weighted brown seven-year-old Lucky Dome was highly rated in Ireland, having won a big chase at Leopardstown since the announcement of the Aintree weights, yet it was Early Mist that seemed to have the better credentials for the National, despite a first fence fall in 1952. Normally an excellent jumper, the chestnut was held in the highest regard at O'Brien's yard, and both trainer and jockey Bryan Marshall were quietly confident the horse would atone for the previous year's mishap.

There were no former National winners in the line-up on this occasion, but among those in the field were Irish Lizard, winner of the Topham Trophy over the National fences forty-eight hours earlier, and the grand old campaigner Cloncarrig, now thirteen and competing in his sixth Grand National – yet incredibly still to complete the race despite challenging seriously for glory on a number of occasions.

The attendance on the day was down on previous years, yet once the tape rose and the field shot away, the adrenalin flowed through the veins of all present, as it does so vigorously on Grand National day.

Off to a fine start on good ground, it was Michael Scudamore aboard Ordnance that led the charge to the first fence, joined in the front line by Tim Molony aboard Quite Naturally, then came Little Yid, Knuckleduster (a winner of the 1950 Stanley Chase over the National fences), Mont Tremblant and Wait And See. Not rising sufficiently at the fence, Quite Naturally was the first to go, coming down in a heap, while outsider Grand Truce was another faller.

The signs were worrying for little Lucky Dome; he was dwarfed by his fellow contestants in the paddock and parade, and it was obvious from an early stage that the Grand National fences were unsuitable for a horse his size. Struggling mightily with the spruce mountains, Lucky Dome had become detached by Becher's, and was wisely pulled-up by Pat Doyle.

Land Fort, Wait And See and Steel Lock were all eliminated on the run to Becher's, with the fifth fence – normally one of the most incident-starved on the course – was the scene of a particularly sad episode, when the popular Cardinal Error died instantly from a fall that broke his neck.

Ordnance had delighted Michael Scudamore by fencing with relish, and the horse had carved open a handy advantage by Becher's, with Little Yid, Glen Fire, Knuckleduster, Armoured Knight, Mont Tremblant and Hierba the closest

Early Mist jumps the final fence.

to him, but a catalogue of grief lay in wait at the Canal Turn, where the riderless Head Crest (a Becher's victim) cannoned into the improving Whispering Steel, bringing the horse to his knees and unshipping jockey Morrow in the process. Independently, the fence claimed both Hierba and Parasol II, the latter also a tragic fatality in what was developing into a most brutal National.

Glen Fire's increasing disdain towards Aintree was again evident at the eleventh when, attempting to refuse, he was sent hurtling into the open ditch by the following Larry Finn, who also ended up in there, while the domino effect also hampered Irish Lizard, who landed on top of the fence and had to wade out of the obstacle before continuing his journey.

With all the market leaders bar Little Yid, Mont Tremblant and Early Mist out of the race, the outsiders saw their prospects grow, and Ordnance was a full ten lengths in front as they turned into the home stretch for the first time, running onto the brand new Mildmay Course as they did so. Maintaining his lead over The Chair and water, Ordnance was followed by Little Yid, Mont Tremblant, Armoured Knight and Early Mist, and next came a hungry pack including the awkward-jumping Senlac Hill (the mount of Dick Francis), Witty, Overshadow, Pearly Prince, Cloncarrig, Irish Lizard and, slightly adrift of these, Uncle Barney and Knuckleduster.

The principal move on the second circuit was conducted by Marshall on Early Mist, who sent his horse forward with intent and, by the twentieth, he was right up with Ordnance. Having held sole possession of the lead for so long, Ordnance seemed distracted by the presence of another horse and made his one and only error, coming down in unfortunate style, while Armoured Knight was another still going well when falling a fence later.

All this left the three most-fancied survivors – Early Mist, Mont Tremblant and Little Yid – with a distant advantage over the chasing pack, and jumping Becher's in that order, they began their long way home.

Little Yid, having previously only run over shorter distances on the National track, was the first to break, tiring badly from the second Canal Turn and, having lost ground on the other two, cried enough when refusing the twenty-seventh. With Little Yid out of it, the veteran Cloncarrig had plugged through into third place and, just as it seemed he was finally going to complete the Grand National, he committed one of his trademark race errors, smacking the twenty-eighth and coming down.

Mont Tremblant had run a fine race and his class and jumping had seen off all but Early Mist, but conceding 17lbs to a tremendously gifted rival in his own right, the former Gold Cup winner had to settle for second best and, over the closing fences, Early Mist drew clear having jumped beautifully throughout. Despite a brief rally from the top weight, Early Mist asserted himself having jumped the last and galloped on grandly to become the totally convincing winner of the 1953 Grand National by twenty lengths. Having fallen at the first in two previous Nationals, Irish Lizard – who had not had a clear passage on this occasion either – took a gallant third having won the Topham two days before, with Overshadow and Senlac Hill the only others to complete. Naturally, the low number of finishers and the deaths of two more horses led to suggestions the course was too severe, yet these were suggestions that would not provoke any alterations for some years yet.

Early Mist had proved a brilliant winner of the race, joining Freebooter and Teal as the best post-war winners and continuing the dominant spell enjoyed by County Tipperary-based O'Brien. Still a young trainer, O'Brien had now saddled winners of four Gold Cups, three Champion Hurdles, an Irish Grand National and now the Grand National. Even without his perceived 'first choice' Royal Tan, O'Brien had produced Early Mist at his absolute peak, with the horse totally unaffected by his first-fence fall in 1952. The O'Brien era was in full flow and, at Aintree, that dominance was set to continue for a number of years.

In the aftermath of Early Mist's victory, there was a sense of sorrow felt for the horse's previous owner, Mr James Rank. Having harboured a lifelong dream to win the race, Mr Rank had died after the 1952 National, and Early Mist was sold for 5,300 guineas to Mr Joe Griffin, a businessman from Dublin.

1953 GRAND NATIONAL RESULT

FATE	HORSE	AGE/WEIGHT	JOCKEY	ODDS
1st	EARLY MIST	8.11.2	B. MARSHALL	20/1
2nd	MONT TREMBLANT	7.12.5	D.V. DICK	18/1
3rd	IRISH LIZARD	10.10.6	R. TURNELL	33/1
4th	OVERSHADOW	13.10.4	P. TAAFFE	33/1
5th	Senlac Hill	8.10.10	R. Francis	66/1
Fell	Cardinal Error	9.11.5	R. Curran	100/7
Fell	Cloncarrig	13.11.5	Mr R. McCreery	66/1
Fell	Land Fort	9.10.13	Mr H. Oliver jnr	50/1
Fell	Quite Naturally	9.10.8	T. Molony	18/1
Fell	Parasol II	8.10.4	Mr A. Oughton	25/1
Fell	Ordnance	7.10.3	M. Scudamore	25/1
Fell	Armoured Knight	9.10.1	T. Mabbutt	66/1
Fell	Pearly Prince	10.10.0	R.E. Jenkins	66/1
Fell	Baire	7.10.0	J. Foster	40/1
Fell	Head Crest	7.10.0	S. Barnes	40/1
Fell	Uncle Barney	10.10.4	J. Boddy	40/1
Fell	Grand Truce	9.10.0	D. Leslie	66/1
Fell	Hierba	8.10.0	A. Mullins	50/1
Fell	Happy Days	13.10.0	A. Benson	66/1
Pulled-Up	Knuckleduster	9.11.0	Mr P.B. Browne	25/1
Pulled-Up	Lucky Dome	7.10.0	P.J. Doyle	10/1
Pulled-Up	Desire	12.10.0	T. Cullen	66/1
Brought Down	Whispering Steel	8.10.13	R. Morrow	9/1
Brought Down	Larry Finn	9.10.11	A.P. Thompson	40/1
Brought Down	Wait And See	8.10.5	A. Freeman	50/1
Brought Down	Cream Of The Border	8.10.0	B. Wilkinson	66/1
Unseated Rider	Witty	8.10.5	G. Slack	22/1
Refused	Glen Fire	10.10.8	M. Lynn	10/1
Refused	Little Yid	11.10.1	J. Power	7/1
Refused	Steel Lock	9.10.0	Mr E. Maggs	66/1
Refused	Punchestown Star	9.10.0	S. McComb	66/1

28 March 1953

Going – Good

Winner – £9,330

Time – 9mins 22⅘ secs

31 Ran

Favourite – Little Yid

Top Weight – Mont Tremblant

Winner trained by Vincent O'Brien at Cashel, County Tipperary, Ireland

Winner owned by Mr J.H. Griffin

Early Mist, chestnut gelding by Brumeux – Sudden Dawn.

1954

ROYAL TAN

Although his 1953 Grand National hero Early Mist was unable to participate twelve months on, Vincent O'Brien had a more than capable replacement in the ten-year-old Royal Tan. Having already run two fine races in the National, Royal Tan was made top weight for the 1954 race and arrived at Aintree having most recently finished second in a three-mile chase at Cheltenham. Owner Joe Griffin had seen his Early Mist step in for an absent Royal Tan the year before, and now he hoped that lightning would strike twice with the horses reversing roles. In addition to having the same owner and trainer as Early Mist, Royal Tan also had the same jockey, with Bryan Marshall on board.

If the 1953 race had been slightly sub-standard in terms of quality, then the 1954 race was perhaps an even poorer renewal. Royal Tan was top weight but had 12lbs less to carry than Mont Tremblant in 1953 and a stone less than Freebooter in 1952, indicating the inferior quality of the 1954 contest. Only Royal Tan and former runner-up Legal Joy (now woefully out of form) were asked to carry more than 11 stone. The fact that Irish Lizard – twice a first-fence faller in the National – was favourite, also suggested a weak renewal. Trained by Frenchie Nicholson, Irish Lizard was a solid stayer, had finished third in 1953, had won a Topham Trophy and had the excellent Michael Scudamore on his back, yet he was hardly a mouth-watering favourite, considering the likes of Prince Regent, Silver Fame and Freebooter, who had topped the markets in the post-war years. Still, Irish Lizard had a strong liking for Aintree, having also finished runner-up in the season's Grand Sefton Chase, and while not having the class of many in the race (even in a poor year), he was a dour stayer that was certain to give his best.

Two newcomers were seen as potential Kings of Aintree in 1954, both hailing from Ireland. Like Royal Tan, Churchtown – a strong, bay nine-year-old – was trained by O'Brien and had good form in staying chases, making him a more than useful 'second-string' for the yard. Also trained in Ireland, the giant Coneyburrow caught the eye of many, not least in the pre-race build-up where – the size of a mammoth – he dwarfed his rivals as he strolled around the paddock, radiating

power and strength. An eight-year-old bay, Coneyburrow had been one of the top novices the year before, winning the Broadway Chase at the Cheltenham Festival, and had then leapt into Grand National consideration by winning the Grand Sefton Chase earlier in the current season. With Pat Taaffe on board, the one concern over Coneyburrow's chance was stamina, or potential lack of it.

Trained in Yorkshire by Robert Renton and owned by Mrs E. Truelove (who had owned the 1953 favourite Little Yid), Tudor Line was one of the most interesting candidates in 1954 for the sheer confidence placed on the horse by his trainer. An Aintree virgin aged nine, Tudor Line had indeed been in fine form during the season, yet his wins had all come between two and two-and-a-half miles, and he had never even attempted three. Even so, Renton was ultra-confident his horse would stay the trip, stating it would take a fine horse to lower Tudor Line's colours.

Breaking away evenly on good ground, the first fence brought about the downfall of Gentle Moya, Alberoni, Swinton Hero and Whispering Steel, while Minimax fell at the second – where Tim Molony received a ghastly looking fall from Dominick's Bar. The outsider Baire fell right into the yawning open ditch at the third, while a fence later, Paris New York's fall was sadly fatal.

Out in front, Coneyburrow was devouring the fences with rare brilliance, with Legal Joy, Sanperion, Ordnance, Punchestown Star and Royal Stuart chasing him, and although Becher's claimed no victims either time, there was further disaster

Vincent O'Brien: a master trainer of both National Hunt and Flat horses.

Royal Tan jumps the final fence ahead
of Tudor Line.

waiting back on the racecourse. Well-positioned under Dave Dick, Legal Joy came down hard at the thirteenth, and it was with great sadness and sorrow that he was later destroyed having injured himself beyond repair.

Jumping The Chair like a stag, Coneyburrow continued to dictate proceedings but, at the water, the leader stood right off the fence, landing awkwardly and sending splashes everywhere. The horse was all but down, yet Taaffe skilfully recovered his mount and they were able to continue, albeit twelve lengths further back than before.

Beginning the second circuit, it was now Royal Stuart, Punchestown Star and Sanperion that led the charge, tracked by the ever-improving Churchtown – who had taken marvellously to the fences – and Ordnance, while just off the pace were the well-fancied trio of Royal Tan, Irish Lizard and Tudor Line, with Coneyburrow responding well to Taaffe's urges and storming through to again take a prominent position.

With Ordnance a faller at the fence after Becher's when still in touch, the race took its shape for the decisive final third. Churchtown had forged into the lead at the twentieth and he remained in control at Valentines, jumping with confidence and class but being hunted up by the ever-improving Tudor Line, still on the bridal and going incredibly easily for a horse untested at the trip. Next came Sanperion, Royal Tan and Irish Lizard, with a gap back to the only other horse in contention, Coneyburrow.

Churchtown blundered badly three out, as the chestnut pair of Tudor Line and Royal Tan flashed past him mercilessly together with Sanperion. The same fence saw another tragic twist as Coneyburrow made an error causing him to fall. The giant horse had damaged himself severely, and it was a bitterly sad moment when he too was put down. It had not been a rough-and-tumble National, but the accidents were hard to take and left a rotten taste to accompany what was becoming an enthralling race.

Churchtown had recovered admirably from his mistake and, coming back onto the racecourse, had passed the tiring Sanperion and set his sights on the two chestnuts, of which Tudor Line was still travelling imperiously for George Slack while Marshall was hard at work on Royal Tan.

Two out and Churchtown made another error that ended his hopes, leaving Tudor Line alone in front, with Royal Tan the one to chase him. Hard driven, Royal Tan was the one with proven stamina and, as he began to cut down the leader, a good jump at the last appeared to give him the advantage. It seemed that Royal Tan – so close in previous Nationals – would finally achieve victory in the great race as he took a three-length lead at the elbow. But fighting back ferociously under Stack, Tudor Line came with one final flourish that sent the crowd into a frenzy. However, Marshall showed why he was one of the finest jockeys of his era, keeping Royal Tan near the inside rail and holding the demon-esque finishing speed of Tudor Line. At the line, Royal Tan had prevailed by a neck in a thrilling finish. Plugging on ten lengths behind was the favourite Irish Lizard with Churchtown fourth, having thrown away a winning chance with late jumping errors. Nine horses had completed but, of course, the race ended with a dark cloud hovering over it as three horses had died from falls, while a fourth, Dominick's Bar, had dropped dead in the early stages, leading to the most intense criticism of the race yet.

On reflection, it was a majestic performance from Royal Tan, as the horse was conceding a stone to Tudor Line and had jumped far better than in his previous National runs. Royal Tan's win marked the first time in sixty-nine years a jockey had won successive Nationals, while the last owner to win with different horses was Sir Charles Assheton-Smith in 1912 and 1913, courtesy of Jerry M and Covertcoat. Royal Tan had originally been owned by Mrs M. Keogh, for whom O'Brien had trained the great hurdler Hatton's Grace. Mr Griffin had purchased the horse midway through the 1951/52 season, and now Royal Tan had given him a most memorable second Grand National success.

1954 GRAND NATIONAL RESULT

FATE	HORSE	AGE/WEIGHT	JOCKEY	ODDS
1st	ROYAL TAN	10.11.7	B. MARSHALL	8/1
2nd	TUDOR LINE	9.10.7	G. SLACK	10/1
3rd	IRISH LIZARD	11.10.5	M. SCUDAMORE	15/2
4th	CHURCHTOWN	9.10.3	T. TAAFFE	10/1
5th	Sanperion	9.10.2	D. Leslie	20/1
6th	Martinique	8.10.1	Mr E. Greenway	66/1
7th	Uncle Barney	11.10.0	L. McMorrow	50/1
8th	Southern Coup	12.10.10	A.P. Thompson	40/1
9th	Ontray	6.10.8	Mr R. Brewis	66/1
Fell	Legal Joy	11.11.3	D.V. Dick	33/1
Fell	Whispering Steel	9.10.12	R. Morrow	40/1
Fell	Alberoni	11.10.12	Mr E. Cousins	66/1
Fell	Coneyburrow	8.10.11	P. Taaffe	8/1
Fell	Dominick's Bar	10.10.7	T. Molony	33/1
Fell	Swinton Hero	10.10.6	Mr C. Harty	66/1
Fell	Prince Of Arragon	13.10.2	J. Gorey	66/1
Fell	Gay Monarch II	8.10.4	T. Brookshaw	50/1
Fell	Ordnance	8.10.1	J. Dowdeswell	18/1
Fell	Baire	8.10.0	J. Foster	66/1
Fell	Hierba	9.10.0	R.J. Hamey	66/1
Fell	Border Luck	9.10.0	T. Shone	66/1
Fell	Paris New York	7.10.0	M. Roberts	66/1
Fell	Statesman	8.10.0	E. Newman	50/1
Fell	Gentle Moya	8.10.0	Mr J. Straker	100/6
Pulled-Up	Icy Calm	11.10.5	R. Francis	40/1
Unseated Rider	Triple Torch	8.10.0	D. Ancil	66/1
Refused	Royal Stuart	11.10.0	J. Power	66/1
Refused	Minimax	10.10.0	Capt. M. MacEwan	66/1
Refused	Punchestown Star	10.10.0	S. McComb	66/1

27 March 1954
Going – Good
Winner – £8,571
Time – 9mins 32⅘ secs
29 Ran
Favourite – Irish Lizard
Top Weight – Royal Tan
Winner trained by Vincent O'Brien at Cashel, County Tipperary, Ireland
Winner owned by Mr J.H. Griffin
Royal Tan, chestnut gelding by Tartan – Princess Of Birds.

1955

QUARE TIMES

With Grand National attendances experiencing a recent steady decline, the last thing Aintree needed was a spell of utterly foul weather come the 1955 meeting. Unfortunately the heavens opened in staggering fashion and, when heavy rain fell on the course the night before the big race, the Grand National track more closely resembled an ocean than the venue for the world's greatest steeplechase. A steady downpour continued on the day of the race and, with puddles of water cluttering the turf, an 11 a.m. inspection was called, leading to fears the race may be abandoned. Following the inspection, the course and fences were deemed to be safe, with the exception of the water jump, which was omitted for the first time since it replaced the stone wall in the previous century. One thing was for certain, the ground was extremely heavy and the race was going to become a thorough examination of stamina.

Ireland held an incredibly strong hand in 1955, with no fewer than eight of their horses featuring among the first thirteen in the betting, including the two most recent National winners, Early Mist and Royal Tan. Because of faltering business, Mr Griffin had sold his two Aintree heroes before the 1955 race: Early Mist to Mr John Dunlop and Royal Tan to Prince Aly Khan, although the pair remained in training with Vincent O'Brien.

Among the Irish raid was the race favourite Copp, a bay eleven-year-old trained by Paddy Sleator. Well weighted with just 10st 8lbs, Copp was formerly a superb hunter-chaser and, having recently been switched to regular handicaps, had displayed tremendous spirit and enthusiasm in his new sphere, winning three races in a row, including an eye-catching performance over three-and-a-half miles at Leopardstown, with conditions on that occasion almost identical to those at Aintree in 1955.

Mr Linnett and Carey's Cottage gave Ireland two of the most promising youngsters in the field. A fast improving seven-year-old, Mr Linnett had won his last two chases, although both were over much shorter distances than the National, while Carey's Cottage was a most consistent performer, trained by Tom Taaffe and ridden by his son Tosse.

As well as Early Mist, Royal Tan and Fred Winter's mount Oriental Way, O'Brien also saddled the highly regarded nine-year-old Quare Times. A quick, economical jumper with very good flat speed, Quare Times had won a four-mile chase at Cheltenham the year before and had on board yet another Taaffe, this time the truly brilliant horseman Pat, hoping for better luck on Quare Times than on poor Coneyburrow the year before.

With such a powerful Irish invasion, the English runners were somewhat swamped in the betting market but, as well as the 1954 runner-up Tudor Line and the representative of HM Queen Elizabeth The Queen Mother, M'as Tu Vu, the home challenge was stocked with a number of worthy contenders, most notably Mariner's Log and Gigolo. The long-time dream of winning the Grand National had so far eluded Lord Bicester, despite having been represented in the past by the likes of Silver Fame, Roimond and Finnure, but there was a feeling that his Mariner's Log could be the horse to end the waiting. A class horse trained by George Beeby and ridden by Dick Francis, Mariner's Log had been second in the 1954 Cheltenham Gold Cup and shouldered 11st 12lbs in the National, while the ten-year-old Gigolo was a lightly raced National newcomer, hailing from the yard of Stuart Wight.

Although Carey's Cottage was slightly slow getting away, the field broke nicely, and the pounding by thirty runners over the saturated turf created a cyclone of spray and flying mud as they ploughed their way to the first. Groans of despair rippled round the rain-sodden crowd as the well-backed Mariner's Log came down at the opener (Lord Bicester's dream over for another year), with Blue Envoy also a faller.

There were surprisingly few casualties on the way down to Becher's, with the heavy ground forcing a slower pace than normal, and it was the tall chestnut Sundew – another Irish horse – that settled into a front-running rhythm, taking the field along from Moogie, ESB, M'as Tu Vu and Quare Times.

Becher's claimed Roman Fire, Moogie and ESB but, as Sundew hacked on in front, there were still a large number of horses in contention crossing The Chair, with the pace sensibly set as jockeys tried to coax their mounts home without exhaustion.

Jumping the big fences in the style of a genuine Grand National horse, Sundew marched on up front under Pat Doyle, with Carey's Cottage and Quare Times hunted up next by the Taaffe brothers, both travelling imperiously. Positioning themselves in behind were M'as Tu Vu, Gentle Moya, Wild Wisdom, Tudor Line, Ontray and Gigolo, while the two previous winners (who were also the highest in the handicap), Early Mist and Royal Tan, were struggling in the mud under their heavy burdens.

From the second Becher's, the race divided the contenders from the strugglers as many horses rapidly began to fade, unable to cope with the energy-draining ground,

Quare Times and jockey Pat Taaffe are clear winners in 1955.

and it was Quare Times and Carey's Cottage that asserted themselves, jumping past the tiring Sundew at the Canal Turn, and took Valentines together with Tudor Line chasing them further back. M'as Tu Vu, carrying the Royal colours, had been prominent at the second Becher's, but he too began to tire badly and later fell.

The leading trio had shot well clear and the race was between them as they came back onto the racecourse. Quare Times was going best of all on the inside while Tudor Line lost some ground at the last two fences by jumping out to his right. Although all three remained in contention as they came over the final fence, it was Quare Times that raced on the strongest and, driven out in commanding style by Pat Taaffe, the horse ripped through the mud and ran out a very convincing twelve-length winner. Tudor Line had again excelled himself around Aintree, yet was a horse that was far better on good ground, while four lengths back in third came Carey's Cottage, having run a bold first Grand National. Of the thirteen that finished (a high number considering conditions but nevertheless strung out emphatically), Gigolo stayed on best to take fourth while Early Mist and Royal Tan came home in their own time in ninth and twelfth respectively, but the favourite Copp had been among the fallers. No serious injury had been suffered by any horse or rider, a huge relief following the tragedies of 1954, and was a bright spot for a Grand National that was again attended poorly.

Quare Times had relished the extreme conditions and proved an excellent winner, giving O'Brien the honour of training three consecutive National winners. The 1955 race witnessed no fewer than five past, present or future winners. 1955 was the last time O'Brien would win the great race; before long, the brilliant trainer would set his mind to mastering Flat racing, where he would take his success to fantastic new heights, including training the winner of the most prestigious Classic – the Epsom Derby – a record six times.

1955 GRAND NATIONAL RESULT

FATE	HORSE	AGE/WEIGHT	JOCKEY	ODDS
1st	QUARE TIMES	9.11.0	P. TAAFFE	100/9
2nd	TUDOR LINE	10.11.3	G. SLACK	10/1
3rd	CAREY'S COTTAGE	8.10.11	T. TAAFFE	20/1
4th	GIGOLO	10.11.3	R. CURRAN	100/6
5th	Ontray	7.10.8	Mr R. Brewis	66/1
6th	Gentle Moya	9.10.0	Mr J. Straker	50/1
7th	Clearing	8.10.2	R.J. Hamey	50/1
8th	Wild Wisdom	10.10.0	Lt Col W. Holman	66/1
9th	Early Mist	10.12.3	B. Marshall	9/1
10th	Red Rube	8.10.3	A. Oughton	66/1
11th	Irish Lizard	12.10.9	M. Scudamore	100/8
12th	Royal Tan	11.12.4	D.V. Dick	28/1
13th	Uncle Barney	12.10.0	L. McMorrow	50/1
Fell	Mariner's Log	8.11.12	R. Francis	100/8
Fell	Sundew	9.11.3	P.J. Doyle	28/1
Fell	ESB	9.11.1	T. Cusack	66/1
Fell	Oriental Way	7.10.12	F.T. Winter	33/1
Fell	Copp	11.10.8	T. Molony	7/1
Fell	M'as Tu Vu	9.10.7	A. Freeman	22/1
Fell	No Response	9.10.2	D. Ancil	45/1
Fell	Dark Stranger	10.10.5	Mr J. Bosley	40/1
Fell	Blue Envoy	10.10.1	Mr E. Greenway	66/1
Fell	Another Rake	10.10.1	D. Leslie	45/1
Fell	Moogie	12.10.0	J. Neely	66/1
Fell	Munster King II	8.10.0	V. Speck	66/1
Fell	Sun Clasp	7.10.0	J. Power	66/1
Pulled-Up	Mr Linnett	7.11.5	Mr J.R. Cox	20/1
Pulled-Up	Little Yid	13.10.10	R. Emery	50/1
Brought Down	Roman Fire	12.10.0	J. Dowdeswell	66/1
Knocked Over	Steel Lock	11.10.0	J.A. Bullock	66/1

26 March 1955

Going – Heavy

Winner – £8,934

Time – 10mins 19⅕ secs

30 Ran

Favourite – Copp

Top Weight – Royal Tan

Winner trained by Vincent O'Brien at Cashel, County Tipperary, Ireland

Winner owned by Mrs W.H.E. Welman

Quare Times, bay gelding by Artist's Son – Lavenco.

1956

ESB

One hundred and nine Grand Nationals had passed prior to the 1956 renewal, each one bringing with them a blend of excitement, romance, disaster and, of course, drama. Easter Hero wiping out virtually the entire field in one fell swoop in 1928, Golden Miller achieving the Gold Cup/Grand National double in 1934, and the 'mad' start of the 1951 race were some of the most dramatic moments thus far. Even to this day, however, the most famous image the Grand National has ever produced arrived in the 1956 running – an episode filled with such purpose for the connections and such mystery in its occurrence that it is a tale frequently told but never fully understood.

Although the twenty-nine-runner field was again on the small side, the crowd number had swelled with the exciting news that The Queen Mother was to have two runners, hoping to realise her ambition of winning the great race. As well as M'as Tu Vu, who had run well for a long way in 1955, Her Majesty was represented by the high-class bay ten-year-old Devon Loch. Both horses were trained by Peter Cazalet, but it was the engaging bay Devon Loch that most captured the public's hearts and imagination, fuelling dreams of a long-awaited Royal winner. A beautiful-looking horse with a distinctive white mark on his forehead, Devon Loch was a gazelle-like jumper expected to adapt to Aintree with a minimum of fuss. Although he had a hefty weight of 11st 4lbs, Devon Loch had won the three-and-a-half-mile Mildmay Memorial Chase at Sandown in preparation for the National, had the full confidence of his stable, and also had former Champion Jockey Dick Francis on board.

Quare Times was missing this time through injury, but former winners Early Mist and Royal Tan returned, although the latter was now trained by jockey Bryan Marshall and had been in distinctly average form throughout the season. Sadly, enthusiastic owner Lord Bicester had passed away after the 1954 race, yet his colours were carried one last time out of respect by Mariner's Log, a first-fence faller twelve months before, while Sundew, Carey's Cottage, Ontray and Gentle Moya all figured prominently in the betting, having made favourable impressions in the 1955 race.

ESB, High Guard and Key Royal were other notable and serious challengers to the Queen Mother's horses. Trained by Fred Rimell (whose father Tom had trained Forbra to win in 1932) and ridden by Dave Dick, ESB (so named because of the starting initials of his dam, English Summer, and sire Bidar) was one of the class horses in the field having been runner-up in a Cheltenham Gold Cup as a six-year-old. Now ten, the dark-bay gelding came into the race in encouraging form, having won his last two races. The bold-jumping grey High Guard hailed from the powerful Neville Crump yard and was a sure stayer with Aintree form, having finished second in the Becher Chase earlier in the season, while Key Royal was an improving bay eight-year-old and a winner of three recent chases. Although by a sire in Royal Charger that was a recognised sprinter, and despite the fact that most of his success had come over far shorter trips than the National, there was a long-standing theory that classy two-and-a-half mile horses were ideal for the race on good ground, and Key Royal fell into that category. It was a theory often contested but not totally unfounded.

Despite a whole cluster of worthy contenders, it was a horse in rapidly ascending form that started favourite for the 1956 race in the shape of the eight-year-old Must. A fine jumper and proven stayer, Must had shown his liking for a marathon trip by winning over four miles at Cheltenham in December, following that up with an admirable performance behind Devon Loch in the Mildmay Memorial at Sandown to earn a 7/1 starting price for the National.

Beneath a pleasant March sky with anticipation hanging in the air, the crowd settled to watch the race, not one person possibly aware of the incredible outcome that lay in store for an unforgettable National. The shocks and sensations began at the very first fence when a rippling groan spread through the

Dick Francis later became a top-selling author.

Eagle Lodge (25) leads (from left to right) Devon Loch, Gentle Moya, ESB and Ontray.

stands on realisation that Must had fallen, as had Early Mist, the normally grand jumper High Guard and Reverend Prince, but although No Response went at the third and Mariner's Log crashed a fence later, there were very few casualties on the first circuit, with the majority of the field – including the two Royal runners – jumping in splendid fashion.

It was Armorial III, ridden by Jack Dowdeswell, that had surged into an early lead, with another noted front-runner – the giant Sundew – also in the front rank jumping Becher's and beyond, followed next by Much Obliged, M'as Tu Vu, Ontray, Polonius and Eagle Lodge. Only Athenian, who fell at the twelfth, was lost from the contest as they came back onto the racecourse, with Armorial III still leading and Devon Loch warming to his task as he progressed through the field, flying each obstacle like a bird.

There was a sense of 'the calm before the storm' as twenty-two of the twenty-nine starters set out for the second circuit, but M'as Tu Vu was soon to depart, sending jockey Arthur Freeman to the ground at the eighteenth, although they were some ten lengths behind the leaders at the time. There were a number of falls and refusals towards the rear as the gallant Armorial III led on, rising at the second Becher's in fine style, but Sundew hit the famous fence with such force he gave himself no chance of staying on his feet on the landing side. Next over the daunting obstacle and still very much in the hunt were Eagle Lodge, ESB, Ontray and Devon Loch, with a break back to Gentle Moya, Key Royal, Merry Windsor, Carey's Cottage, Much Obliged and Royal Tan; the winner was sure to come from these eleven.

With Armorial III turning on the speed jumping Valentines, the field was stretched out by some margin, and chasing the leader with most impression were

Eagle Lodge, Devon Loch, ESB and Much Obliged, but the race was about to take a dramatic twist at the twenty-sixth fence. Having never been headed in the race and a few lengths to the good, Armorial III clipped the fence with his back legs and crashed to the ground, while on the wide outside and moving forward at the time, Much Obliged also came down, narrowly avoiding wiping out Devon Loch as he did so, while ESB and jockey Dave Dick performed wonders to swerve the fallen Armorial III just in front of them. Much Obliged had looked menacing, and his fall frustrated his jockey Michael Scudamore as he searched for his first National victory, but now Devon Loch had been left in front on the outside together with Eagle Lodge on the inner, while ESB and Ontray (whose owner Captain Scott Briggs had owned Macmoffat, runner-up in 1939 and 1940) came next as the excitement grew with the Royal horse hitting the front.

Heading back to the racecourse, the crowd rose to their feet as Francis pushed the willing Devon Loch two lengths clear of Eagle Lodge, and the prospect of an historic result loomed large. With real power apparently left in the Royal horse, Eagle Lodge dropped away, and it was ESB that emerged as the last remaining threat to Devon Loch over the final two fences.

Devon Loch had jumped the course in wonderful fashion and had plenty more to give, taking the last with precision and, once on the flat, asserted his superiority as ESB could give no more. Rounding the elbow, Devon Loch drew further and further clear of ESB, the Royal horse strongly driven by an inspired Francis and as he did so, a crescendo of noise poured down onto the course and boomed out loud and joyous with the most deafening yet spectacular volume.

Then in one horrible, awful action, Devon Loch was down. The applause that had been so rapturous seconds earlier stopped in an instant, a ghastly silence spreading itself around Aintree as spectators struggled to believe what they had seen. Approaching the outside of the water jump just fifty yards from the line (with the rail in between himself and the fence), Devon Loch had taken off as if jumping an imaginary fence before collapsing on his belly, skidding agonisingly for ten yards with Francis clinging desperately to his neck. Unable to regain his composure, Devon Loch stood like a statue, rooted to the spot as Francis watched helplessly as ESB cantered past him for a most fortunate National win. With Devon Loch all at sea, Francis – dejected and despondent – dismounted the horse, who was eventually led away. Gentle Moya, Royal Tan and Eagle Lodge filled out the minor places, but of course the only horse that mattered was the one that did not win, such was the popularity of The Queen Mother and the public desire for her horse to win.

After the race, a veterinary examination showed nothing to be wrong with Devon Loch, thus beginning the inquest into the mystery of why the horse collapsed. So many suggestions were put forward; the 'phantom' water jump theory, a patch of soft, false ground that unbalanced the horse, excess glucose in his diet causing cramp, a weak hind leg, a heart attack, a black tongue (sighted by Dick at the last fence) indicating a lack of oxygen – yet the widely accepted answer, one that Francis himself concedes to, was that the tremendous tornado of noise filtering down from the stands had caught Devon Loch's attention and frightened the horse into his reaction. Certainly no horse had ever been cheered home with such volume as Devon Loch.

Whatever the correct theory, it is a mystery that will sadly never be solved with any true satisfaction. The sense of disappointment for The Queen Mother was unanimous, yet in the true sporting manner that made her the most loved and cherished owner of her lifetime, she only had concerns for the welfare of Devon Loch, Francis and Cazalet, as well as a most sporting message of congratulations for the winners, masking her own disappointment with commendable grace. Indeed, Rimell and Dick were almost apologetic on meeting Her Majesty after the race, as they too shared in the sympathy for the owner and horse.

It was a shame for ESB too, for although most fortunate to win, the horse never received much credit for his National triumph, even though his finishing time was merely a second outside of Golden Miller's race record from 1934. This showed just how powerfully the Royal horse had been racing before his mishap, for he surely would have obliterated that time. ESB, owned by the elderly Mrs Lionel Carver, was a horse at his best at distances of around three miles, and it was his class and jumping that got him as close as he did to Devon Loch at the finish.

Francis never rode in the Grand National again, eventually becoming a world-renowned author of thrillers. Devon Loch also never attempted the National again, yet the impact he had on it will never be forgotten, for he had played his part in shaping the history of the great race.

1956 GRAND NATIONAL RESULT

FATE	HORSE	AGE/WEIGHT	JOCKEY	ODDS
1st	ESB	10.11.3	D.V. DICK	100/7
2nd	GENTLE MOYA	10.10.2	G. MILBURN	22/1
3rd	ROYAL TAN	12.12.1	T. TAAFFE	28/1
4th	EAGLE LODGE	7.10.1	A. OUGHTON	66/1
5th	Key Royal	8.10.8	T. Molony	28/1
6th	Martinique	10.10.0	S. Mellor	40/1
7th	Carey's Cottage	9.10.13	R. Turnell	10/1
8th	Clearing	9.10.1	J.A. Bullock	66/1
9th	Wild Wisdom	11.10.1	Mr L. Bridge	66/1
Fell	Early Mist	11.12.2	B. Marshall	25/1
Fell	Mariner's Log	9.11.11	R. Emery	22/1
Fell	Sundew	10.11.4	F.T. Winter	8/1
Fell	High Guard	9.11.1	A.P. Thompson	22/1
Fell	Much Obliged	8.11.0	M. Scudamore	50/1
Fell	Dunboy II	12.11.0	Mr R. Brewis	66/1
Fell	Armorial III	7.10.10	J. Dowdeswell	20/1
Fell	Merry Windsor	8.10.10	L. McMorrow	28/1
Fell	Must	8.10.10	R. Morrow	7/1
Fell	M'as Tu Vu	10.10.6	A. Freeman	40/1
Fell	Reverend Prince	10.10.5	Mr C. Pocock	40/1
Fell	Witty	11.10.4	P.A. Farrell	66/1
Fell	Domata	10.10.4	D. Ancil	66/1
Fell	Athenian	7.10.3	R.J. Hamey	66/1
Fell	No Response	10.10.1	C. Finnegan	50/1
Fell	Ontray	8.10.0	R. Curran	100/6
Refused	Polonius	10.10.3	E.F. Kelly	66/1
Refused	Border Luck	11.10.0	M. O'Dwyer	66/1
Refused	Pippykin	8.10.0	J. Power	100/7
Slipped-Up	Devon Loch	10.11.4	R. Francis	100/7

24 March 1956
Going – Good
Winner – £8,695
Time – 9mins 21²/₅secs
29 Ran
Favourite – Must
Top Weight – Early Mist
Winner trained by Fred Rimell at Kinnersley, Worcestershire
Winner owned by Mrs L. Carver
ESB, bay or brown gelding by Bidar – English Summer.

Jockey Dick Francis is left dejected after Devon Loch slipped up fifty yards from the winning post with the race at his mercy.

1957

SUNDEW

For the first time since 1947 the race, as it had been originally, was run on the Friday in an attempt to improve the dwindling attendances that had become a feature of the Grand National in the 1950s. However, it was only a temporary switch, and was neither successful in its aim nor worthwhile financially for Aintree.

ESB returned to Aintree with 10lbs more to carry than in 1956, but had run poorly in the recent Cheltenham Gold Cup, and stronger arguments were reserved for others on this occasion. One of these was the nine-year-old Goosander from Neville Crump's yard. Subject of a huge gamble, the horse's odds had plummeted to 5/1 and, good horse though he was, it seemed an alarmingly short price based predominantly on a pair of wins at Haydock Park during the season, the latter of which was the Grand National Trial. Goosander had been one of the favourites for the 1956 race before falling victim of injury at the eleventh hour and, although a sound stayer, his best form had been found in the mud, whereas the Aintree going in 1957 was good.

Among those that had failed to get round in 1956 were Much Obliged and Sundew. Much Obliged was a strongly made horse and a real stayer. An impressive Sandown winner earlier in the season, many recalled just how sweetly Much Obliged was running before coming down five out in 1956, and accordingly he was backed down to 10/1 second favourite. Sundew had given a bold, front-running performance in the 1956 National before suffering a very heavy fall at the second Becher's. Some questioned whether the horse had the necessary stamina or jumping ability to even complete the course, yet the big chestnut remained a talented animal, and retained some support courtesy of his partnership with a Champion Jockey, the great Fred Winter.

At the top of the handicap were the Peter Cazalet-trained Becher Chase runner-up Rose Park, a superb jumper of park fences and third in the recent Gold Cup, and the declining talent of 1954 Gold Cup winner Four Ten, a giant bay with a striking white blaze on his face, trained by Alec Kilpatrick. Interesting newcomers included Wyndburgh, Tiberetta, Hart Royal, Glorious Twelfth and Tutto. The stocky brown

gelding Wyndburgh and the mare Tiberetta were both real sloggers, proven over extreme distances, while Hart Royal was a former hunter, trained by Ian Lomax near Marlborough, and came into the race in splendid form with three wins from four races during the season, enhancing the chestnut's reputation as a beautiful, natural jumper. Another magnificent jumper was the hotly tipped grey Glorious Twelfth from the yard of Robert Renton, with the horse finishing second over the National fences in the Grand Sefton Chase in the autumn, while the Leopardstown Chase winner Tutto was the chief hope of a relatively weak Irish challenge that included the veteran Royal Tan, running in his sixth and final Grand National.

It was a misty afternoon with light drizzle filling the Aintree air, but once the thirty-five runners were sent on their way, the sheer thrill of the spectacle was enough to warm the hearts of all present. Armorial III, Sundew and Hart Royal were the first to meet the opening obstacle but, on the inside, the last named came down in a rare fall, together with the French-bred horse Rendezvous III and Virginius, who dumped National debutant Mr Alan Lillingston rudely to the turf.

There were many fallers on the first circuit, including the trailblazing Armorial III, who misjudged the fourth. Sundew was left in the lead and jumped Becher's far better than he had twelve months before. Cherry Abbot and the now fourteen-year-old Irish Lizard – ridden by future trainer David Nicholson – were not so fortunate and came down, while old Royal Tan was badly interfered with and did not jump the famous obstacle, ending his National adventures with a dull anti-climax.

The falls continued, with Sundew lucky not to join the number when clattering the tenth. The horse clearly enjoyed front-running, but Sundew was a far-from-convincing jumper of the big green fences, and Winter had to be at his best to keep the partnership intact. Much Obliged had been up with the pace, but he was to fall at the open ditch, the eleventh, frittering away another serious National chance, while three others, including the Irish hope Tutto, also departed at the fence.

Marching merrily back onto the racecourse proper, it was Sundew out in front from Athenian, The Crofter, ESB, Gentle Moya, Tiberetta and Goosander, with the likes of Four Ten, Rose Park, Wyndburgh and Glorious Twelfth further back. Goosander hit The Chair with a terrific crack and seemed certain to crumble, but the horse's strength shone through as he stood firm, while next to him, the mare Tiberetta stood right back from the enormous fence and put in a mighty leap.

Over half the field had gone by the water, while Rose Park had struggled to get near the leaders, and the horse was out of contention and pulled-up at the nineteenth as Sundew led on, his grinding gallop thieving the oxygen from the lungs of his rivals.

Throughout the second circuit, Winter kept the chestnut travelling strongly, despite the big horse consistently making errors. His nearest pursuers were ESB, The Crofter, Wyndburgh, Tiberetta and Glorious Twelfth, yet they were simply never able to lay up with Sundew, while Athenian was still in the hunt when falling four out, with the tiring Four Ten capsizing a fence later.

Sundew returned to the racecourse two lengths ahead of his rivals, of whom ESB was coming to the end of his tether, while The Crofter and Glorious Twelfth

Trainer Frank Hudson stands with two of his horses including the giant Sundew (right).

1957 GRAND NATIONAL RESULT

FATE	HORSE	AGE/WEIGHT	JOCKEY	ODDS
1st	SUNDEW	11.11.7	F.T. WINTER	20/1
2nd	WYNDBURGH	7.10.7	M. BATCHELOR	25/1
3rd	TIBERETTA	9.10.0	A. OUGHTON	66/1
4th	GLORIOUS TWELFTH	8.11.1	B. WILKINSON	100/8
5th	The Crofter	9.10.0	J. Power	66/1
6th	Goosander	9.11.7	H.J. East	5/1
7th	Sydney Jones	10.10.12	Mr M. Tory	25/1
8th	ESB	11.11.13	D.V. Dick	20/1
9th	Merry Throw	9.10.12	T. Brookshaw	40/1
10th	Sandy Jane II	10.10.2	H.R. Beasley	40/1
11th	Gentle Moya	11.10.6	G. Milburn	28/1
Fell	Four Ten	11.11.11	R. Morrow	50/1
Fell	Much Obliged	9.11.4	M. Scudamore	10/1
Fell	Armorial III	8.11.1	J.A. Bullock	50/1
Fell	Hart Royal	9.10.10	P. Pickford	100/7
Fell	Athenian	8.10.7	D. Ancil	66/1
Fell	Tutto	10.10.6	J. Lehane	100/6
Fell	China Clipper II	10.10.3	Major W.D. Gibson	66/1
Fell	Irish Lizard	14.10.2	D. Nicholson	66/1
Fell	Clearing	10.10.1	R. Curson	45/1
Fell	Morrcator	10.10.0	L. McMorrow	50/1
Fell	Red Menace	8.10.0	L. Wigham	33/1
Fell	Go-Well	9.10.9	Capt. P. Bengough	66/1
Fell	Fahrenheit	10.10.0	T. O'Brien	66/1
Fell	Waking	13.10.5	Capt. A.W.C. Pearn	66/1
Fell	Cherry Abbot	12.10.0	G. Underwood	66/1
Pulled-Up	Rose Park	11.11.13	G. Nicholls	28/1
Pulled-Up	Wild Wisdom	12.10.1	Mr L. Bridge	66/1
Pulled-Up	Monkey Wrench	12.10.0	R.J. Hamey	66/1
Brought Down	Icelough	11.11.3	P. Taaffe	28/1
Brought Down	Virginius	8.10.12	Mr A. Lillingston	50/1
Brought Down	Rendezvous III	9.10.6	A. Freeman	20/1
Brought Down	Felias	9.10.5	W. Rees	45/1
Refused	Carey's Cottage	10.10.6	T. Shone	50/1
Carried Out	Royal Tan	13.11.12	T. Taaffe	28/1

29 March 1957
Going – Good
Winner – £8,868
Time – 9mins 42 ⅖ secs
35 Ran
Favourite – Goosander
Top Weights – ESB and Rose Park
Winner trained by Frank Hudson at Henley-in-Arden, Warwickshire
Winner owned by Mrs G. Kohn
Sundew, chestnut gelding by Sun King – Parsonstown Gem.

could offer no more. Sundew cleared the last in far more convincing fashion than many of the previous twenty-nine fences and, although the hardy pair of Wyndburgh and Tiberetta were staying on stoutly to chase him home, Winter – who later revealed his great lack of confidence in Sundew's fencing – had driven a tired but game Sundew clear. Crossing the line to rich applause, he won by eight lengths and six, with the grey Glorious Twelfth taking fourth.

Sundew's win came for owner Mrs Geoffrey Kohn, who had previously owned National runners in Quite Naturally and Churchtown, and once owned a part share in ESB, relinquishing it to her friend Mrs Carver before that horse won the 1956 race. Sundew was trained by Frank Hudson, whose string totalled just eleven, and whose stables in Warwickshire were next door to the house of Mr and Mrs Kohn.

Sundew was far from the greatest jumper to win the Grand National, and much credit went to the Champion Jockey Winter, for whom it was a first victory over the National fences in any race, while the win was all the more unusual considering it was an extremely rare occurrence for a horse to win the race having fallen twice before in Nationals, although Sundew's victory was nothing compared to that of Grakle, who finally won on his fifth attempt in 1931. Grakle's record was a lesson in perseverance and, for the newest Grand National hero Sundew (one of the biggest horses in training at well over seventeen hands), third time was definitely lucky.

1958

MR WHAT

Sadly, the hero of the 1957 Grand National, Sundew, had lost his life when suffering a fatal fall at Haydock Park. Sundew had appeared well on course to defend his title at Aintree, and his unfortunate demise left the field of thirty-one with just one former winner, the declining force that was the veteran ESB, as the 1955 winner Quare Times was again absent through injury. It was, perhaps unfairly, labelled an inferior race in terms of quality, for the 1958 renewal was bereft of some of the true chasing superstars of the era, such as Mandarin, Kerstin and Linwell, but the field at Aintree could proudly boast some of the top stayers of the time, and some genuine Aintree horses.

Having run a bold race behind Sundew twelve months before, the Scottish-trained Wyndburgh was made favourite on the day. From the yard of Major Wilkinson, the horse had long been ante-post favourite for the Grand National, even though he was burdened with 10lbs more than in 1957. Wyndburgh was by no means the tallest of horses, yet had a strong frame and was a most clever jumper. In addition, he was a thorough stayer (as evidenced by his win during the season in the four-mile Eider Chase at Newcastle) and a genuine Aintree-type, having won the Grand Sefton in November.

Goosander, Eagle Lodge and Tiberetta all returned to Aintree having performed well the year before and, although Goosander was second favourite on account of the presence of his favoured soft going and Eagle Lodge was well-fancied due to five wins in moderate company during the season, Tiberetta was again largely unconsidered. It was difficult to see why the mare – trained by owner Mr Edward Courage – should not have been better supported, for she had a strong record in staying chases, was a true lover of the National fences (having won the Becher Chase earlier in the season to go with her 1957 National third), had a fair racing weight of 10st 6lbs and was partnered by George Slack, twice a Grand National runner-up aboard Tudor Line earlier in the decade.

Colledge Master (winner of the 1957 Aintree Foxhunters'), Hart Royal (who had over-jumped the first in 1957) and the large-framed and equally large-hearted Valiant Spark were all strongly tipped for glory while, in the absence of Quare Times, the Irish challenge was headed by the Duchess of Westminster's Cheltenham specialist Sentina, the chestnut Springsilver – partnered by Fred Winter – and the lightly built bay Mr What. An eight-year-old, Mr What had begun the season as a novice having fallen on his only start over fences the season before, but had shown rapid improvement, displaying increased confidence with each run, winning three-mile chases at Navan and Naas, and coming second in the big Leopardstown Chase. Mr What was trained by Tom Taaffe, yet neither of his sons, Pat or Tosse, was on board the horse in the National, with Pat on Sentina and Tosse on Brookling. Tosse could well have ridden Mr What, yet he had already committed to ride another smart Irish chaser, Sam Brownthorn, but when that horse was declared a non-runner, Arthur Freeman had already been summoned to partner Mr What. Freeman put up 6lbs overweight on the inexperienced horse, with Mr What starting at 18/1.

With the 1958 Grand National the first to be sponsored (by The Irish Hospital Sweepstakes), the race was by far the richest yet and, although it was a foggy March afternoon following a night of incessant rain, the usual roar erupted as the field were sent on their way.

On the soft turf no horse fell at the first fence, with the long-striding Longmead the first one to go at the second. Settling into a steady rhythm, it was Athenian that took the lead from Goosander, Never Say When, Wyndburgh and the northern raider Green Drill.

The fifth fence claimed its share of victims on this occasion as Rendezvous III, Princess Garter and Valiant Spark all fell, and it was here that Mr What had a lucky escape when he was knocked into by a loose horse that very nearly floored him. Surviving, however, Mr What came to a virtual standstill, resuming his race at the very back of the field.

Four more horses went at Becher's, with the outsider Frozen Credit refusing, 1956 favourite Must falling and bringing down Sentina, while Comedian's Folly was run out by a loose horse. Up front, Athenian and Goosander continued to dictate the pace, oblivious to the mishaps behind them.

The Irish chestnut Springsilver walloped the eleventh fence, taking a huge chunk out of the obstacle, yet miraculously survived intact, but further back the grey Glorious Twelfth refused and, heading back towards the racecourse, it was Athenian, Goosander, Green Drill, Never Say When and Tiberetta in the front rank, chased by Eagle Lodge, ESB, The Crofter, Wyndburgh and Colledge Master, while Mr What had made significant progress, closing on the leading bunch all the time and jumping beautifully. Brookling ended Tosse Taaffe's interest in the race by crashing at the thirteenth and, although the 40/1 shot Richardstown was a rare victim at the normally trouble-free water jump, eighteen horses set sail for glory with a circuit to run.

The pace had not been electric by any means, yet the soft going now proved taxing for many of the runners as the field gradually became depleted and strung out. Colledge Master waded through the seventeenth before being pulled-up,

Mr What wins easily in 1958.

pacemakers Athenian and Never Say When hit the deck at the big ditch second time round and, when Hart Royal refused at the second Becher's, there were only eight horses left.

Mr What had come through with such authority by Becher's that his magnificent jump there took him past Goosander – giving Tim Molony a splendid ride – and from there, Freeman sailed into an imperious-looking position, as Mr What continued to motor along like an Aintree natural, belying his relative inexperience over fences.

Green Drill was shaping as a potential danger to Mr What, but at the second Valentines, he made a crucial mistake that halted all his momentum and, although the much-loved veteran ESB had run gamely for a long distance and both Wyndburgh and Tiberetta were staying on in their usual admirable way, Mr What had drawn right away leaving the country, and was well clear by the time he reached the last fence.

At the final fence disaster very nearly struck. Freeman had glanced round to scout for what were non-existent dangers yet, in doing so, had slightly unbalanced his mount. Creeping a touch close to the fence, Mr What dived awkwardly at it, and Freeman did marvellously well to hold tight and stay on board. The crowd gasped at the incident, but once Mr What regained his composure, all in attendance were soon on their feet to applaud a very easy winner of the Grand National as Mr What romped home, totally deserving of his win, by a full thirty lengths and fifteen to Tiberetta and Green Drill, with the favourite Wyndburgh fourth.

Mr What had made a mockery of his inexperience and rubbished claims he was not physically robust enough to cope with the National fences, winning the race in as convincing a style as any winner in the modern era.

The horse was owned by County Wicklow businessman Mr David Coughlan and was a shining moment in the career of County Dublin trainer Taaffe. Proving his triumph was no fluke, Mr What would return to Aintree in future years to establish himself as one of the great Grand National competitors of his or any other era.

1958 GRAND NATIONAL RESULT

FATE	HORSE	AGE/WEIGHT	JOCKEY	ODDS
1st	MR WHAT	8.10.6	A. FREEMAN	18/1
2nd	TIBERETTA	10.10.6	G. SLACK	28/1
3rd	GREEN DRILL	8.10.10	G. MILBURN	28/1
4th	WYNDBURGH	8.11.3	M. BATCHELOR	6/1
5th	Goosander	10.11.7	T. Molony	100/7
6th	ESB	12.11.12	D.V. Dick	28/1
7th	Holly Bank	11.10.13	Mr P. Brookshaw	50/1
Fell	Longmead	8.11.1	G.W. Robinson	28/1
Fell	Athenian	9.10.11	D. Ancil	22/1
Fell	Valiant Spark	9.10.7	M. Scudamore	20/1
Fell	Rendezvous III	10.10.3	J.A. Bullock	45/1
Fell	Brookling	9.10.3	T. Taaffe	28/1
Fell	Never Say When	9.10.2	S. Mellor	50/1
Fell	Pippykin	10.10.5	T. Brookshaw	22/1
Fell	Princess Garter	11.10.3	Mr W. Roberts	66/1
Fell	Must	10.10.1	R. Morrow	50/1
Fell	The Crofter	10.10.0	J. Power	40/1
Fell	Richardstown	10.10.0	J. Morrissey	40/1
Pulled-Up	Wise Child	10.11.6	S. Hayhurst	45/1
Pulled-Up	Colledge Master	8.11.2	W. Rees	25/1
Pulled-Up	Ace Of Trumps	10.10.12	P.A. Farrell	40/1
Pulled-Up	Eagle Lodge	9.10.0	A. Oughton	18/1
Brought Down	Sentina	8.10.11	P. Taaffe	18/1
Brought Down	Sydney Jones	11.10.12	Mr M. Tory	28/1
Unseated Rider	Southerntown	12.10.1	P. Cowley	66/1
Refused	Glorious Twelfth	9.11.3	B. Wilkinson	28/1
Refused	Hart Royal	10.10.11	P. Pickford	18/1
Refused	Springsilver	8.10.4	F.T. Winter	18/1
Refused	Moston Lane	9.10.0	R.E. Jenkins	66/1
Refused	Comedian's Folly	10.10.0	Mr D. Scott	66/1
Refused	Frozen Credit	12.10.12	Mr P. Ransom	66/1

29 March 1958
Going – Soft
Sponsor – Irish Hospital Sweepstakes
Winner – £13,719
Time – 9mins 59⅘ secs
31 Ran
Favourite – Wyndburgh
Top Weight – ESB
Winner trained by Tom Taaffe at Rathcoole, County Dublin, Ireland
Winner owned by Mr D.J. Coughlan
Mr What, bay gelding by Grand Inquisitor – Duchess Of Pedulas.

1959

OXO

The quality of the 1959 Grand National received a terrific boost when the 1958 Cheltenham Gold Cup winner, Kerstin, was declared for the race. Kerstin rightfully topped the handicap on 12 stone, providing the rare occurrence of a mare heading the National weights. Trained by Verly Bewicke and ridden by Stan Hayhurst, Kerstin was one of the toughest horses in training, and her Gold Cup success had come at the expense of three former winners of that race, plus a future one in the top-class Mandarin. Although winless during the current season and with a hefty weight to carry, few doubted her ability to acquit herself admirably in her first Grand National.

Ireland again had high hopes of landing the prize through one of three fancied challengers, headed by the 1958 hero Mr What, as well as a pair of eight-year-old newcomers, Slippery Serpent and Nic Atkins. Despite having to carry an enormous 17lbs more than the year before, Mr What's destruction of the 1958 field had made a huge impression, and he was the clear 6/1 favourite in 1959, this time ridden by Tosse Taaffe for his father Tom. The Leopardstown Chase runner-up Nic Atkins was held in high regard on his Irish form, while the Tom Dreaper-trained chestnut Slippery Serpent had won four chases in succession earlier in the season before tipping up in that same Leopardstown Chase.

The home challenge included regulars Wyndburgh and Tiberetta, the Ryan Price-trained Done Up (winner of a recent four-mile chase at Hurst Park), and Oxo, a robust bay eight-year-old from the Hertfordshire yard of Willie Stephenson. With a background in the hunter field, the strong, compact Oxo had won four chases prior to the National, and was ridden by the fine Aintree jockey Michael Scudamore, placed twice before aboard Legal Joy and Irish Lizard.

On the wide outside of the field, the grand Aintree mare Tiberetta rose first at the opening fence from the 1958 Aintree Foxhunters' winner Surprise Packet, ridden by Gerry Scott. The Irish lost one of their big hopes when Nic Atkins hit the turf, joining the outsider Stop List on the ground.

The Welsh Grand National winner Oscar Wilde went at the fourth but, having figured rather tamely in recent Nationals, Becher's was to bare its teeth in fierce fashion on this occasion. Up front, Tiberetta, Surprise Packet, Turmoil and Kerstin all cleared the deadly fence well, but in behind, Valiant Spark, the big chestnut Eternal and Henry Purcell all fell (the lattermost sadly being killed), while The Crofter gave jockey Stan Mellor a horrible fall when the horse clattered into the fence and came down on his head. Amid the drama, Done Up was badly hampered and brought down, with the same happening to Glorious Twelfth, Mr Gay and Sundawn III. Those of the opinion that the stiff, upright style to the fences required modification certainly had fuel to add to their objective fires as Becher's emphatically claimed its prize.

Surprise Packet was travelling beautifully for Scott, as she and two other mares – Tiberetta and Kerstin – comprised the front rank. Having been behind early on, Oxo suddenly found himself in close proximity to the leaders following the carnage at Becher's. Belsize II, Dondrosa and Richardstown were all eliminated in the country and, returning to the racecourse, the trio of mares proudly led the way, with Kerstin taking splendidly to the Aintree fences.

Slippery Serpent crashed out at the thirteenth, causing frustrated sighs among the Irish support; while Tiberetta committed a rare blunder at The Chair, nearly resulting in a first-ever fall. But she survived, keeping her place among a hungry pack that began the second circuit, led by Surprise Packet and Kerstin with Oxo next.

No horse fell on the run to the second Becher's but, having given a bold account of herself, it was cruel luck on Surprise Packet that she nose-dived at the Brook when still leading. Kerstin too was put out at Becher's, still going strongly only to collide with Mainstown with such force that both horses ended up grounded. With Soltown, Kilballyown and Irish Coffee also coming to grief, no fewer than fourteen horses had fallen prey to Becher's in the 1959 Grand National.

Blissfully unaffected by the casualties, the old Aintree campaigner from Scotland, Wyndburgh, and the tough newcomer Oxo were left in the lead, and although still going just behind, Tiberetta, Mr What and Green Drill could not live with the front two and, by the second Canal Turn, Wyndburgh just held the lead.

It soon became apparent that, despite his significant Aintree experience, Wyndburgh was at a disadvantage. Having landed steeply at Becher's second time, one of jockey Tim Brookshaw's irons had snapped, so to equalise matters, Brookshaw kicked his other leg free, thus riding the rest of the Grand National with no stirrups.

Manfully, Brookshaw produced Wyndburgh with a series of glorious leaps as he engaged in a tremendous duel with Oxo coming back to the racecourse but, by the final fence, Oxo had surged into a five-length lead and Scudamore's long-standing dream of winning the National seemed certain to come true.

However, meeting the last fence wrong, Oxo lost momentum as well as some priceless energy and, tiring up the long run-in, the crowd rose to their feet as they realised the popular Wyndburgh was delivering one last brave challenge. But

Oxo holds off the late rally of Wyndburgh to win.

Oxo was gritty and resolute, Scudamore determined and, at the line they held Wyndburgh and the gallant Brookshaw by a length-and-a-half, with Brookshaw earning tremendous praise for his effort. Eight lengths back in third came Mr What with the game Tiberetta fourth in her final National, a retirement at stud looming.

Only four had finished, and the race again came in for its share of criticism, largely regarding the shape and size of the fences. Yet despite the concerns, it had been a National of real excitement and genuine sportsmanship and bravery. The courageous little Wyndburgh had finished second again, with plenty more Grand National adventure awaiting him.

Oxo, however, had triumphed at the first attempt, giving Stephenson the honour of training both a National winner and an Epsom Derby winner. He had won the Derby with Arctic Prince in 1951 to emulate both George Blackwell (Sergeant Murphy, 1923 National and Rock Sand, 1903 Derby) and Dick Dawson (Drogheda, 1898 National and Trigo and Blenheim, 1929 and 1930 Derbys).

Scudamore joined an illustrious list (that included Gerry Wilson, Tim Hyde, Dave Dick and Jimmy Power) of jockeys that had won both the Gold Cup and Grand National in modern times, with the newest Aintree hero winning at Cheltenham aboard Linwell in 1957. The Scudamore family held a rich reputation before Oxo's win, and continues in high standing to this day. Michael's father Geoffrey had won a Becher Chase over the National fences on Sawfish, his son Peter was a brilliant Champion Jockey who finished third in the 1985 National on Corbiere, while his grandson Tom is established as one of the top young jockeys at the beginning of the twenty-first century.

Michael Scudamore rode in sixteen consecutive Nationals between 1951 and 1966, his first ride coming on East A' Calling when only nineteen while, as a trainer, he saddled Charles Dickens to finish third to the great Red Rum in 1974.

1960

MERRYMAN II

1960 was a groundbreaking year at Aintree, for that year's Grand National was the first to be screened live to television audiences around the country. Having struggled through eight years of intense negotiations, the BBC was finally given permission from Mrs Topham to present live coverage of the race.

Unfortunately, the first televised Grand National featured a below-par turnout numerically, with only twenty-six runners facing the starter, although there was once more healthy competition among the principal contenders, with a number of quality Aintree types in the field, including the 1959 Aintree Foxhunters' winner Merryman II and the dual National runner-up Wyndburgh.

Scottish-bred and trained in Middleham, Yorkshire by the great Neville Crump, Merryman II was a big, attractive horse that had handled the National fences well in the Foxhunters'. As well as being a super jumper, Merryman II had also displayed his forte for stamina when ending the previous season with a win in the Scottish Grand National. Merryman II was made a warm 13/2 favourite on the day and was partnered at Aintree by Gerry Scott, having just his second National ride. Remarkably, Scott rode in the race with his collarbone strapped, having broken it at Doncaster shortly before the National meeting.

With Oxo an absentee, Michael Scudamore was given the honour of partnering the superb Aintree horse Wyndburgh who, although well-backed again, had 9lbs more to carry than when second in 1959. Wyndburgh had been placed in all three of his previous Grand National runs but, like the 1958 winner Mr What (a horse that had endured a poor season), was expected to find the going far tougher on this occasion having been raised in the handicap.

Of the newcomers, the most fancied were the diminutive Team Spirit and the admirable Dandy Scot. Trained in Ireland by Dan Moore, Team Spirit was a brave jumper and true stayer, indicating his love for extreme distances by winning most recently over four miles at Hurst Park. Team Spirit was the mount of Willie Robinson, and, despite worries that the horse was too small to cope with the big National fences, Team Spirit was well fancied, having also won the valuable Mildmay Memorial Chase at Sandown en route to Aintree. Fred Winter's mount,

Dandy Scot, was another with a big weight, having been allotted 11st 7lbs, yet the horse had enjoyed a marvellous season, winning four of five chases; his only defeat coming in the Mildmay Memorial when he fell at the last fence, and the Ryan Price-trained horse was tough and genuine with a fine temperament to cope with the hoopla of the big race.

As well as a large Aintree crowd, around 14 million people sat in their homes to watch the Grand National, glued to their screens as the action began to unfold. On good, quick ground, the runners were sensibly away, with Tea Fiend, Cannobie Lee and Green Drill the first to show. The stampede to the first lacked the cavalry charge approach of some of the previous Nationals, possibly due to the fact that Lord Sefton (mindful of the quick ground and some of the recent accidents) had advised the jockeys to restrain their normal cavalier approach to the first fence. As a result, only the outsider Lotoray came down at the opener, and with Tea Fiend out in front, there were no more casualties on the run to Becher's Brook.

The first shock lay in wait at the most famous fence as the benchmark of Grand National reliability, Wyndburgh, crashed out of the race, while amateur jockey Eddie Harty's first National adventure also ended with a fall from Knoxtown. Tea Fiend, with Gerry Madden on board, was showing up boldly in front, while Dandy Scot too was taking well to the National – until he made a mistake and went at the Canal Turn, with Pat Taaffe's mount Jonjo falling a fence later at Valentines.

The majority of the first circuit had passed without major incident, bar the unexpected fall of Wyndburgh at Becher's, but at The Chair (which had only claimed four fallers in the previous ten years), trouble was about to emerge. At the biggest fence on the course, the thirteen-year-old Holly Bank was a faller, and the obstacle also claimed Uncle Whiskers and Belsize II, the latter sadly fatally injured in front of the television cameras, dampening the mood at an important time for the race's reputation.

There were still seventeen left by the start of the second circuit, headed by Tea Fiend but being hunted up ominously by the smooth-travelling favourite Merryman II (who had survived a minor error at the seventh), with Badanloch, Green Drill, Cannobie Lee, Clear Profit, Eagle Lodge, Sabaria and Team Spirit all still in contention.

Becher's was to have a resounding impact second time round. Despite his burden of top weight, Mr What had gradually worked his way into a challenging position and, lying fourth at the Brook, he seemed sure to take a hand in the finish. But as shocking as Wyndburgh's exit had been on the first circuit, so was Mr What's on the second, as the 1958 winner was caught out on the landing side – skidding ungracefully along the ground and dumping Arthur Freeman to the turf. Pendle Lady, Aliform and Cannobie Lee also went (the latter straddling the fence and dropping jockey David Nicholson rudely over the other side), and suddenly the destiny of the 1960 Grand National lay between just a few horses.

Tea Fiend had run boldly, but his bid petered out by the Canal Turn, and the tired horse was passed by the strong-looking Merryman II and the improving

Merryman II jumps the final fence on his way to victory.

Badanloch. By the last open ditch, the twenty-seventh, the two had separated themselves by fifteen lengths from Tea Fiend and the stragglers.

It was Merryman II that made the first bid for glory, surging clear of Badanloch rounding the turn for home and, by two out, the favourite had opened up a five-length gap that showed no sign of shortening. Jumping the last with authority, Merryman II and Scott drew decisively clear and, crossing the line to the delight of favourite backers, won comfortably in grand style by fifteen lengths. Badanloch and jockey Stan Mellor had given a fine account of themselves but were no match for the winner, while the dour Clear Profit took third ahead of the gallant Tea Fiend, fourth of the eight finishers.

Miss Winifred Wallace, the owner of the winner, looked delighted in the winner's enclosure, calmly smoking a cigarette as Crump led Merryman II in. Miss Wallace had purchased the horse as a five-year-old and tutored him herself in the art of jumping, before sending him on to point-to-point success and then training.

It was a third success for Crump, who rated Merryman II better than his first winner Sheila's Cottage, although he refused to state whether the newest winner would have bettered Teal in 1952, while for Scott (who had ridden the horse brilliantly, taking the inside route the entire way), it was a most courageous effort given his injury. Scott's association with Aintree lasted long after he retired as a jockey, as he eventually became the official starter for the National.

The victory of Merryman II had been clear cut and utterly convincing, marking the first time an Aintree Foxhunters' winner had progressed to win the Grand National. He was also the first clear favourite to win since Sprig in 1927, and his success was enjoyed by the countless punters that had backed him before enjoying his victory in the comfort of their own homes, making the BBC's inaugural coverage of the race an overwhelming success.

1960 GRAND NATIONAL RESULT

FATE	HORSE	AGE/WEIGHT	JOCKEY	ODDS
1st	MERRYMAN II	9.10.12	G. SCOTT	13/2
2nd	BADANLOCH	9.10.9	S. MELLOR	100/7
3rd	CLEAR PROFIT	10.10.1	B. WILKINSON	20/1
4th	TEA FIEND	11.10.0	P.G. MADDEN	33/1
5th	Sabaria	9.10.3	M. Roberts	66/1
6th	Green Drill	10.10.3	G. Milburn	33/1
7th	Arles	8.10.4	Mr A. Moule	45/1
8th	Skatealong	12.10.0	R.R. Harrison	66/1
Fell	Mr What	10.11.11	A. Freeman	18/1
Fell	Wyndburgh	10.11.7	M. Scudamore	8/1
Fell	Dandy Scot	10.11.7	F.T. Winter	10/1
Fell	Holly Bank	13.10.12	Mr P. Brookshaw	50/1
Fell	Clanyon	12.10.8	R.E. Jenkins	50/1
Fell	Knoxtown	10.10.5	Mr E.P. Harty	45/1
Fell	Skipper Jack	8.10.4	D. O'Donovan	66/1
Fell	Pendle Lady	10.10.4	M. Towers	40/1
Fell	Jonjo	10.10.4	P. Taaffe	50/1
Fell	Uncle Whiskers	8.10.1	C. Finnegan	50/1
Fell	Belsize II	11.10.0	P. Shortt	66/1
Fell	Lotoray	10.10.6	M. Batchelor	66/1
Fell	Aliform	8.10.0	T.W. Biddlecombe	45/1
Pulled-Up	Irish Coffee	10.10.11	Mr W. St George Burke	66/1
Pulled-Up	Clover Bud	10.10.1	T. Taaffe	20/1
Pulled-Up	Eagle Lodge	11.10.1	W. Rees	45/1
Brought Down	Team Spirit	8.10.12	G.W. Robinson	9/1
Refused	Cannobie Lee	9.10.7	D. Nicholson	100/9

26 March 1960

Going – Good

Sponsor – Irish Hospital Sweepstakes

Winner – £13,134

Time – 9mins 26 1/5 secs

26 Ran

Favourite – Merryman II

Top Weight – Mr What

Winner trained by Neville Crump at Middleham, Yorkshire

Winner owned by Miss W.H.S. Wallace

Merryman II, bay gelding by Carnival Boy – Maid Marian.

1961

NICOLAUS SILVER

The 1961 Grand National promised to be the most interesting and captivating for years for a number of reasons. Aintree had finally bowed to public and media criticism regarding the structure of the fences and, while retaining the size of the obstacles, the take-off sides were now sloped to a fifty-degree angle to give horses a fairer idea of judging them. Previously, the stiff, upright fences had caused huge problems, and while their unique attributes were basically maintained, the move was seen as a step forward in putting the safety of horse and rider first, while the maximum weight was reduced from 12st 7lbs to 12 stone. In addition to the interest in the fence alterations, the field was one of the most competitive in years as three former winners lined up, headed by the brilliant Merryman II, while adding an Eastern flavour was the presence of two Russian challengers, Grifel (a chestnut ridden by Vladimir Prakhov) and Reljef (a bay ridden by Boris Ponomarenko), both prepared by the Russian trainer Alexiev and automatically allocated joint-top weight. Both were expected to achieve little at Aintree apart from improving frosty relations between East and West. The presence of the two Russian horses (a third, the promising Epigraf II, a three-time winner of Czechoslovakia's notorious Velka Pardubice, went wrong just days before the race) attracted much interest and certainly added extra spice to the 1961 National.

Ireland sent over a six-pronged attack for the 1961 race and one of these horses, Jonjo, displaced Merryman II (ridden this time by the capable Derek Ancil) as favourite. Jonjo had been most impressive when winning the Molyneux Chase over two-and-a-half miles of the National course in November, and a recent win in the big Leopardstown Chase had strengthened his National claims. While Pat Taaffe's mount was backed into 7/1 favouritism, other Irish raiders that stood out were the 1958 winner Mr What, little Team Spirit and the classy Hunter's Breeze.

Excluding the two Russian runners, Merryman II topped the weights, while also high in the handicap was the 1958 Hennessy Gold Cup winner Taxidermist,

partnered by amateur John Lawrence. Tim Brookshaw returned to ride the hardy perennial Wyndburgh, while Michael Scudamore was reunited with the 1959 winner Oxo, and the powerfully built Scottish Flight II – the mount of Bill Rees – was a popular selection on the day. Standing out in the paddock – if not the betting market – was the striking grey Nicolaus Silver, trained by Fred Rimell. A strong, compact nine-year-old ridden by twenty-five-year-old Irishman Bobby Beasley, Nicolaus Silver had most recently won the Kim Muir Memorial Chase at the Cheltenham Festival and had been impressing Rimell mightily in his work as the National drew near. A most attractive horse, Nicolaus Silver was owned by Mr Charles Vaughan, whose father, Major Douglas Vaughan, had owned the 1948 second First Of The Dandies.

With the going good to firm, a fast-run National was assured, but the drama began before the race even started. Waiting patiently at the start, Merryman II was kicked viciously by Lord Leigh's runner Jimuru and Ancil signalled for inspection. Happily the horse was sound and, returning to the line-up, the field soon broke away.

Scottish Flight II and Carrasco led them to the first on the inside, with Brian Oge, Floater and Taxidermist on the wide outside. Floater was the first to go, quickly joined on the ground by Tea Fiend and April Queen, with the Welsh Grand National winner Clover Bud brought down. The Russian horse Grifel had been up with the pace at the first, but jumped it tentatively, while Reljef appeared intimidated as he crawled over the fence at the back of the field.

Fresh Winds, locally owned and ridden by Roy Edwards, was dictating the gallop with a cavalier charge down towards Becher's, and the sheer pace with which the field met the mighty fence caused unsurprising grief. Brian Oge fell when well placed, and also coming down were Taxidermist, Carrasco, Kingstel and Grifel. Fresh Winds had opened up a sizeable lead jumping the Canal Turn and beyond but, when Reljef unseated Ponomarenko at Valentines, the Russian bid had come to an end – or so most thought.

Fresh Winds returned to the racecourse with a twenty-length advantage, sparking momentary hopes of a big-priced local winner but, in behind, the likes of Merryman II and Nicolaus Silver were travelling well within themselves, apparently unfazed by the leader's tactics. Indeed, it was after jumping The Chair and water that the chasing group began to reel in Fresh Winds like a pack of hungry wolves.

Having lost Vivant and Bantry Bay at The Chair, nineteen set out for the second circuit having survived one lap of the redesigned fences, with Wyndburgh, Badanloch and Jonjo creeping closer to the lead, but the race soon ended for the Irish fancy Hunter's Breeze as the horse fell at the seventeenth.

Having set a tremendous pace, Fresh Winds inevitably ran out of steam, and was an exhausted animal when crashing at the nineteenth while, back in front of the stands, a most extraordinary event occurred. With most of the field heading for Becher's again, a single rider crashed through The Chair, incredibly remaining

The grey Nicolaus Silver jumps the last fence clear of Merryman II.

aboard his horse. On closer view, the red silks of Grifel and jockey Prakhov could be identified, having remounted following their fall at Becher's. Receiving an encouraging roar from the crowd, the pair charged on independently, before Grifel banked the water jump, narrowly avoided a thorough soaking, and was then pulled-up.

Back at the head of affairs, the race was intensifying, with Merryman II and Nicolaus Silver taking up the running, tracked by Team Spirit, Scottish Flight II, Jonjo, Kilmore and O'Malley Point and, touching down at Becher's, Nicolaus Silver – who had taken off well back from the fence – pecked on landing, virtually scraping the ground with his nose, but his own strength together with the skill of Beasley helped the horse to recover without losing much ground.

The same group jumped the Canal Turn, Valentines and the remainder of the fences down the back, but as the favourite Jonjo and the others began to fade, it became a battle between Merryman II, Nicolaus Silver and the Fred Winter-ridden Kilmore from three out. Rounding the turn for home, hopes remained that Merryman II could become the first winner of successive Nationals since Reynoldstown, or that Winter could win a second National but, when the latter

gradually weakened and the weight pegged back Merryman II, it was the grey horse that took control.

Jumping the last two fences with purpose and precision, Nicolaus Silver drew clear of his rivals and, splendidly ridden by Beasley, stormed past the elbow and crossed the line to rich applause to win by five lengths. The volume of noise depicted a popular win, with the horse being the first grey to triumph since The Lamb in 1871. The gallant Merryman II had again displayed excellence over the National fences, and although the grey had triumphed on merit, the 25lbs Merryman was conceding proved a colossal gap to bridge. O'Malley Point and Scottish Flight II stayed on well to pass Kilmore, another to run admirably on his first attempt at the National, with Wyndburgh and Jonjo next to finish. In total, fourteen got round, the highest number since 1948, indicating – to an extent – that the fence alterations were successful.

At just over sixteen hands high, Nicolaus Silver was an endearing winner of the National. With the exception of his mistake at the second Becher's, the grey had jumped like a cat, delivering a second National success for Fred Rimell. Fred and Mercy Rimell had paid 2,500 guineas for the grey in 1960, knowing he had been entered for the 1961 Grand National. Formerly trained in Ireland, the horse had been running predominantly on unfavourable soft ground, but the quick ground at Aintree – thereafter considered essential for his best form – had brought the horse to life, and he was a good winner of the race.

Bobby Beasley hailed from a fine racing family that included his grandfather Harry and uncle Tom, two men that had between them recorded four Grand National victories between 1880 and 1891. Tom had won on Empress in 1880, Woodbrook in 1881 and Frigate in 1889, while Harry had triumphed aboard Come Away in 1891. Bobby, whose first National ride came on Sandy Jane in 1957, had previously won a Cheltenham Gold Cup on Roddy Owen and a Champion Hurdle on Another Flash, while further Gold Cup success awaited him through the brilliant Irish horse Captain Christy in 1974.

Nicolaus Silver had become the first grey to win the National for ninety years, and to date he remains the last of his colour to do so. Though never quite hitting the heights of 1961 again, the horse competed in two more Grand Nationals before an accident at home saw Nicolaus Silver put down having broken a leg.

1961 GRAND NATIONAL RESULT

FATE	HORSE	AGE/WEIGHT	JOCKEY	ODDS
1st	NICOLAUS SILVER	9.10.1	H.R. BEASLEY	28/1
2nd	MERRYMAN II	10.11.12	D. ANCIL	8/1
3rd	O'MALLEY POINT	10.11.4	P.A. FARRELL	100/6
4th	SCOTTISH FLIGHT II	9.10.6	W. REES	100/6
5th	Kilmore	11.11.0	F.T. Winter	33/1
6th	Wyndburgh	11.11.5	T. Brookshaw	33/1
7th	Jonjo	11.10.7	P. Taaffe	7/1
8th	Badanloch	10.10.11	S. Mellor	20/1
9th	Team Spirit	9.10.13	G.W. Robinson	20/1
10th	Siracusa	8.10.1	B. Wilkinson	100/7
11th	Mr What	11.11.9	D.V. Dick	20/1
12th	Ernest	9.10.1	H.J. East	33/1
13th	Sabaria	10.10.2	M. Roberts	100/1
14th	Irish Coffee	11.10.6	J. Magee	50/1
Fell	Taxidermist	9.11.4	Mr J. Lawrence	40/1
Fell	Hunter's Breeze	10.10.13	F. Carroll	100/7
Fell	Floater	8.10.11	E.P. Harty	50/1
Fell	Fresh Winds	10.10.10	R. Edwards	66/1
Fell	Brian Oge	10.10.10	J. Guest	100/1
Fell	Bantry Bay	10.10.7	Sir Wm. Pigott-Brown	40/1
Fell	Wily Oriental	9.10.6	P.G. Madden	40/1
Fell	Oscar Wilde	11.10.4	R.E. Jenkins	45/1
Fell	Jimuru	10.10.4	Mr J. Leigh	33/1
Fell	Carrasco	9.10.3	P. Pickford	40/1
Fell	Kingstel	9.10.0	G. Slack	50/1
Fell	Vivant	8.10.6	D. Nicholson	50/1
Fell	Tea Fiend	12.10.0	R.R. Harrison	40/1
Fell	April Queen	10.10.2	A. Biddlecombe	100/1
Pulled-Up	Grifel	8.12.0	V. Prakhov	100/1
Pulled-Up	Oxo	10.11.8	M. Scudamore	20/1
Pulled-Up	Imposant	9.10.13	Mr R. Couetil	100/1
Pulled-Up	Penny Feather	8.10.1	J. Lehane	66/1
Brought Down	Clover Bud	11.10.10	D. Mould	50/1
Unseated Rider	Reljef	7.12.0	B. Ponomarenko	100/1
Refused	Double Crest	9.10.7	A. Irvine	50/1

25 March 1961
Going – Good to Firm
Sponsors – Schweppes Limited and
   Irish Hospital Sweepstakes
Winner – £20,020
Time – 9mins 22 ⅗ secs
35 Ran

Favourite – Jonjo
Top Weights – Reljef and Grifel
Winner trained by Fred Rimell at
   Kinnersley, Worcestershire
Winner owned by Mr C. Vaughan
Nicolaus Silver, grey gelding by
   Nicolaus – Rays Of Montrose.

1962

KILMORE

The field assembled for the 1962 Grand National had an enticing blend of experience, youth and class, making the race one of the most fascinating of recent times. Favourite was the brilliant seven-year-old Frenchman's Cove, trained at Newmarket by Tom Jones. Frenchman's Cove was attempting the National fences for the first time, yet he had gained a reputation as a marvellous jumper, albeit around park courses, and his relentless galloping style had seen the chestnut compile some top-class form. Son of the 1946 Derby winner Airborne, Frenchman's Cove had finished fourth behind Saffron Tartan in an incredibly strong 1961 Cheltenham Gold Cup, a race in which the 1960 Gold Cup winner Pas Seul had finished second and the 1962 winner Mandarin third while, in the current season, Frenchman's Cove had disposed of the 1961 Grand National winner Nicolaus Silver in a Kempton Park chase and, at 7/1, was thought to have an outstanding chance of giving jockey Stan Mellor his first National win.

Another with a Classic-winning sire was Springbok. A stablemate of Merryman II at Neville Crump's yard, Springbok was a son of the 1932 Derby hero April The Fifth, and was considered to be a fast-improving horse. An eight-year-old bay, Springbok was also considered to be a fine jumper, possessing sufficient speed to win over two miles while having the stamina to serve as a chief contender in the top staying chases. Indeed, one of the horse's career highlights was winning the 1962 Hennessy Gold Cup at Newbury. Well weighted at Aintree with 10st 6lbs, Springbok became a first National ride for Pat Buckley.

Of the three former winners that lined up, Nicolaus Silver was thought to have the best chance of winning again, having won both the Grand Sefton Chase over the National fences and Doncaster's Great Yorkshire Chase since his finest hour in 1961, and was surprisingly allotted just 10st 10lbs. Merryman II was again top weight and had his third different Grand National partner in the form of Dave Dick – the 1956 victor replacing the injured Gerry Scott – while Mr What was still searching for his first victory since winning the Grand National in 1958.

Kilmore and jockey Fred Winter are led in.

Of the other veteran Aintree favourites, Wyndburgh – one of the finest Grand National horses in the race's history – was back for a sixth and final crack at glory, and he was joined in the field by Team Spirit, the Ryan Price-trained Kilmore and the former Hennessy and Whitbread winner Taxidermist, yet all four were considered to have had their best chance of Grand National glory. To the forefront of the betting were a host of horses running in the race for the first time, such as the Irish-trained pair of Solfen and Kerforo, the latter ridden by Pat Taaffe and a winner of two of Ireland's biggest chases, the Thyestes Chase and the Leopardstown Chase.

It was considered to be a fine Grand National field in 1962 but, as always, extra factors created a sense of unpredictability, and this time the chief ingredient was the weather. A chaotic blend of frost, rain, hail and snow had left Aintree with the heaviest ground since Quare Times had won in the bog of 1955, and the arts of survival as well as serious stamina were going to be needed to conquer the challenge.

Springbok, normally such an assured jumper, surprised many with his fall at the first as the outsider Fredith's Son proceeded to blaze a trail down to Becher's, and, on reaching the fence, the unconsidered Irish horse had carved open an eight-length gap to Duplicator, Dandy Tim, Siracusa, Clear Profit, Frenchman's Cove and Superfine.

The leader made his first mistake at the Canal Turn, momentarily surrendering his lead to the nine-year-old Duplicator while, at the eleventh, Josh Gifford – a jockey growing in reputation and status – saw his debut National ride end in a fall from Siracusa.

Taxidermist and jockey Mr John Lawrence.

Duplicator and Fredith's Son had set a brisk pace, despite the state of the ground and, at The Chair, a big pack in behind included Frenchman's Cove, Team Spirit, Mr What, Chavara, Cannobie Lee, Solfen, Gay Navaree and Nicolaus Silver, while Fred Winter was rooted to the rear of the field aboard the veteran Kilmore.

The pace quickened again at the start of the second circuit, with a large band of horses still in the hunt. Having jumped impeccably on his National debut, taking the fences with delightful grace, Frenchman's Cove was merely hacking along as the field headed for Becher's once more but, at the nineteenth, the race outlook changed drastically. Duplicator crashed out, as did Team Spirit and, with no chance of avoiding a collision, Frenchman's Cove was brought down, leaving Mellor understandably frustrated.

Two fences later, the Irish horse Kerforo fell when creeping into an ominous-looking position and, at Becher's second time, Fredith's Son was left in command from another Irish horse, the improving outsider Gay Navaree, then came Mr What, Clear Profit, Cannobie Lee, Wyndburgh and Nicolaus Silver, with Kilmore moving forward from a deeper position.

It was Gay Navaree, ridden by Mr A. Cameron, that swept forward to join Fredith's Son and, by Valentines, the two long shots held control, tracked by a quartet of proven Aintree veterans in Mr What, Wyndburgh, Nicolaus Silver and Kilmore, with the latter revelling in the heavy ground as he reeled the leaders into his sights.

Crossing the Melling Road and coming back to the racecourse, Gay Navaree had stolen possession of the lead as the game Fredith's Son began to tire, as did the 1961 hero Nicolaus Silver; the grey finding conditions far more distasteful than twelve months previously. Approaching two out, the three challenging the outsider were Mr What, Wyndburgh and Kilmore.

It was Kilmore that was finishing the strongest and, continuing his relentless drive that had begun at the second Becher's, he roared forward and jumped past the leader two out. Although Mr What and Wyndburgh were briefly able to stay with Kilmore, once over the last fence Winter's mount left them behind and, staying on resolutely he ran out a ten-length winner. Wyndburgh, the much-loved Aintree stalwart, had run another fine race to take second and, having finished in that position three times, as well as fourth and sixth, he ranks as one of the finest Aintree horses not to win the Grand National. Filling third place, Mr What proved that form over the big fences was perhaps the most important criteria when contesting the National. The first three horses home were true Aintree horses, all aged twelve, and only Chandler in 1848 had previously won the race at that age since records began, with the thirteen-year-old Sergeant Murphy in 1923 the only horse older than that to win. Having looked a potential winner for much of the second circuit, Gay Navaree faded to finish fourth, but received much credit, while the long-time leader Fredith's Son took fifth.

Captain Ryan Price.

Having placed Kilmore round the inner for the entire race, Winter's second National win very different to his first on Sundew in 1957. Sundew had boldly run from the front, yet Kilmore had been eased carefully into contention, hunting round for a circuit before making a decisive move at the second Becher's, relishing the ground as others began to tire. Kilmore's win highlighted the brilliance of Winter as a jockey and provided a glorious moment in the richly successful training career of the Findon-based Price.

1962 GRAND NATIONAL RESULT

FATE	HORSE	AGE/WEIGHT	JOCKEY	ODDS
1st	KILMORE	12.10.4	F.T. WINTER	28/1
2nd	WYNDBURGH	12.10.9	T.A. BARNES	45/1
3rd	MR WHAT	12.10.9	J. LEHANE	22/1
4th	GAY NAVARREE	10.10.0	MR A. CAMERON	100/1
5th	Fredith's Son	11.10.11	F. Shortt	66/1
6th	Dark Venetian	7.10.0	P. Cowley	100/1
7th	Nicolaus Silver	10.10.10	H.R. Beasley	100/9
8th	Cannobie Lee	11.10.1	E.P. Harty	40/1
9th	Ernest	10.10.0	A. Dufton	66/1
10th	Clover Bud	12.10.4	D. Nicholson	100/1
11th	Blonde Warrior	10.10.6	T.W. Biddlecombe	66/1
12th	Solfen	10.11.2	T. Taaffe	9/1
13th	Merryman II	11.11.8	D.V. Dick	20/1
14th	Colledge Master	12.10.13	Mr L.R. Morgan	33/1
15th	Fortron	9.10.0	R. Langley	100/1
16th	Politics	10.10.0	D. Bassett	100/1
17th	Clear Profit	12.10.0	T.J. Ryan	66/1
Fell	Superfine	9.10.6	Sir Wm. Pigott-Brown	100/6
Fell	Team Spirit	10.10.6	G.W. Robinson	22/1
Fell	Springbok	8.10.6	P. Buckley	100/8
Fell	Kerforo	8.10.3	P. Taaffe	100/9
Fell	Duplicator	9.10.2	G. Milburn	28/1
Fell	Siracusa	9.10.0	J. Gifford	33/1
Fell	Carraroe	10.10.0	Mr W. McLernon	66/1
Pulled-Up	Taxidermist	10.10.10	Mr J. Lawrence	20/1
Pulled-Up	Chavara	9.10.7	M. Scudamore	50/1
Pulled-Up	Clipador	11.10.4	P.A. Farrell	66/1
Pulled-Up	Vivant	9.10.0	R.J. Hamey	100/6
Pulled-Up	Melilla	8.10.0	G. Cramp	100/1
Pulled-Up	Seas End	10.10.5	J.H. Kempton	100/1
Brought Down	Frenchman's Cove	7.11.5	S. Mellor	7/1
Unseated Rider	Dandy Tim	9.10.0	R. Carter	50/1

31 March 1962
Going – Heavy
Sponsors – Schweppes Limited and Irish Hospital Sweepstakes
Winner – £20,238
Time – 9mins 50secs
32 Ran
Favourite – Frenchman's Cove
Top Weight – Merryman II
Winner trained by Ryan Price at Findon, Sussex
Winner owned by Mr N. Cohen
Kilmore, bay gelding by Zalophus – Brown Image.

1963

AYALA

Schweppes Limited had formed part of the sponsorship package for the previous two Grand Nationals yet, for the 1963 race, they decided to remove their name from the big event, opting for sole sponsorship of a new handicap Hurdle race at the same meeting. In their place came Vaux Limited, whose added prize money and bonus of the 'Vaux Gold Tankard' ensured the total value to the winner was the richest of any National yet.

With forty-seven horses in the field and no obvious market leader, the prospect of choosing the National winner was daunting, with the 1963 renewal one of the most open for some time. Previous winners Kilmore, Nicolaus Silver and Mr What returned, the lattermost now thirteen and competing in his sixth and final National, being ridden by the promising young Irish jockey Tommy Carberry.

Springbok, a first-fence faller in 1962, was made favourite at 10/1 having enjoyed a consistent season with two wins and two thirds, one win coming in the Hennessy Gold Cup at Newbury. Despite his untimely exit in the previous year's race, the horse was seen as a very good jumper, was well handicapped on his Hennessy form and had a National-winning jockey in Gerry Scott on board.

Catching the eye of both paddock spectators and racecourse punters were a pair of Irish-trained grey horses. Owen's Sedge was owned by Hollywood actor Gregory Peck, who cut a celebrity figure among the general public with his presence at Aintree to watch his horse run. Owen's Sedge was trained by Tom Dreaper and was an unusual colour, being a mix of chestnut and grey. However if his colouring was rare, his form was most encouraging, with a stylish win in the Leopardstown Chase following a third in Cheltenham's Mackeson Gold Cup. Even more fancied than Owen's Sedge was Loving Record, a big, rugged grey horse that had responded from a fall in the Leopardstown Chase to win over three miles at Navan. Partnered by Tom Taaffe, Loving Record was not among the incredible number of horses that had experienced the Grand National fences before, with twenty-nine having tackled the big green obstacles at some point.

Fulke Walwyn's Team Spirit had failed to complete twice in the Grand National but was again well backed, having recently won at Cheltenham. Frenchman's Cove lined up again having been most unlucky in 1962, but had disappointed bitterly in the recent Gold Cup, while newcomers Dagmar Grittell and Mr Jones had both won other chases over the National fences: the Topham Trophy and Becher Chase respectively. As one would expect with such a large field, many of the runners were considered to have little to no chance, including Ayala, bracketed with seventeen others on 66/1. Trained by Keith Piggott (whose father Ernie had won the 1912 National on Jerry M and the 1919 race aboard Poethlyn, and whose son Lester had quickly established himself as a Flat jockey of the highest standard with three Epsom Derby wins), Ayala was a lightly raced chestnut that had barely raised an eyebrow when winning a minor race at Worcester shortly before the National. Having his second ride in the race was nineteen-year-old Pat Buckley who, twelve months before, had fallen at the first on Springbok.

Though not as testing as when Kilmore had won, the ground was again on the soft side and, showing first as they broke away, was the 25/1 shot Out And About, ridden by Josh Gifford, and the horse would lead until deep onto the second circuit. French Lawyer, Chavara and the 1962 favourite Jonjo – ridden by Spanish amateur the Duque de Alburquerque – were also well to the fore as they hit the first, with Magic Tricks the only one to fall by the wayside while, as Out And About shot clear going down to Becher's, Look Happy, Wingless and Solonace all departed from the race. Out And About and Gifford flew Becher's like a bird, with Jonjo, French Lawyer and the Welsh Grand National winner Forty Secrets being the next over, while Good Gracious crashed out.

Out And About maintained the electric gallop, heading the thirty-two that swept back onto the racecourse and, in breathtaking fashion, the leader soared powerfully over The Chair tracked by a larger-than-normal band of runners. Although Mr Jones and jockey Paddy Farrell parted company at the water, the majority of horses were still very much alive heading for the second circuit.

Running down to the second Becher's, Out And About had been joined by another outsider in Loyal Tan, ridden by young Terry Biddlecombe, with French Lawyer still going strongly and the noseband-wearing Springbok beginning to lay down his challenge with an eyecatching forward move.

By Valentines, the serious challengers moved in for the kill as Out And About's game bid began to falter. French Lawyer remained among the leaders, but those looking the most menacing were Springbok, Ayala, Hawa's Song and the fast-improving Carrickbeg.

Ridden by racing journalist and the horse's part-owner, Mr John Lawrence, Carrickbeg was a big, bay seven-year-old with a thick white face. Crossing the Melling Road for the final time, the horse had moved through impressively and was now hot on the heels of French Lawyer and Springbok. With Ayala and Hawa's Song both still stalking those in front, a thrilling finish between these five appeared likely.

Ayala beats Carrickbeg in a tight finish.

French Lawyer was first to crumble as he tired rapidly from the second last, and soon Springbok too could offer no more as his three lighter-weighted rivals met the last fence almost in a line. Carrickbeg, easily identifiable with his big, white face, narrowly had the edge and was quickest away from Hawa's Song on the inside and Ayala on his outer.

Carrickbeg dug deep and pulled a couple of lengths clear, shaking off Hawa's Song in the process, and it looked for all the world as though Mr Lawrence would become the first amateur to win since Captain Petre in 1946. But sadly, despite still holding the lead at the elbow, Carrickbeg had broken down. Bravely soldiering on, the horse delivered a most courageous effort, but Ayala's finish came late and clinically. Forced home by Buckley, the bright chestnut got up to win, snatching victory by three-quarters of a length to the gallant Carrickbeg, with a further five lengths back to Hawa's Song. Team Spirit proved he could complete the course by staying on strongly in fourth, passing the weary favourite Springbok on the way to the line.

Carrickbeg received much sympathy for his noble effort, especially since Mr Lawrence had wasted doggedly to ride at the allotted weight. The seven-year-old had run his heart out and was the horse with whom the amateur – a lifelong lover of the race and a man given much credit in helping preserve the National in future years – came closest to winning the great race. Mr Lawrence (better known as Lord Oaksey) later became a well-recognised and much-loved racing analyst on television, and was one of the leading inspirations behind the efforts of the charity the Injured Jockeys Fund.

But it was to Ayala that Grand National glory went, resolutely sticking to his task to grab a pulsating victory at the death. The horse had jumped wonderfully well for a perceived 'no-hoper', with only one mistake at the first Canal Turn giving Buckley any concern. Ayala had been purchased by Piggott at the Epsom Sales three years previously and sold to well-known London hairdresser Mr Pierre 'Teasy-Weasy' Raymond, whose red and blue halved colours the horse ran in. Ayala too had proved his toughness through his National victory, for he had broken down in 1962 and had been pin-fired before recovering to carve his place in the Grand National's long and illustrious history.

1963 GRAND NATIONAL RESULT

FATE	HORSE	AGE/WEIGHT	JOCKEY	ODDS
1st	AYALA	9.10.0	P. BUCKLEY	66/1
2nd	CARRICKBEG	7.10.3	MR J. LAWRENCE	20/1
3rd	HAWA'S SONG	10.10.0	P. BRODERICK	28/1
4th	TEAM SPIRIT	11.10.3	G.W. ROBINSON	13/1
5th	Springbok	9.10.12	G. Scott	10/1
6th	Kilmore	13.11.0	F.T. Winter	100/8
7th	Owen's Sedge	10.11.6	P. Taaffe	20/1
8th	French Lawyer	9.10.0	T. Ryan	50/1
9th	Dark Venetian	8.10.2	D. Bassett	33/1
10th	Nicolaus Silver	11.11.0	H.R. Beasley	28/1
11th	Eternal	12.10.10	T. Brookshaw	25/1
12th	Chavara	10.10.2	R. Edwards	40/1
13th	Carraroe	11.10.1	Mr W. McLernon	33/1
14th	Siracusa	10.10.0	D. Mould	33/1
15th	Sham Fight	11.10.1	J. Fitzgerald	50/1
16th	Blonde Warrior	11.10.9	B. Lawrence	66/1
17th	Loyal Tan	8.10.5	T.W. Biddlecombe	66/1
18th	Woodbrown	9.10.0	J. Kenneally	66/1
19th	O'Malley Point	12.11.1	M. Scudamore	33/1
20th	Frenchman's Cove	8.12.0	D.V. Dick	100/6
21st	Forty Secrets	9.10.7	C. Chapman	50/1
22nd	Dandy Tim	10.10.0	L. Major	50/1
Fell	Mr Jones	8.10.10	P.A. Farrell	28/1
Fell	Out And About	8.10.7	J. Gifford	25/1
Fell	Good Gracious	9.10.7	P. Connors	66/1
Fell	Jonjo	13.10.6	Duque de Alburquerque	66/1
Fell	Peacetown	9.10.4	R. Langley	50/1
Fell	Gay Navaree	11.10.1	P. Cowley	50/1
Fell	Wingless	8.10.3	A. Biddlecombe	66/1
Fell	Avenue Neuilly	8.10.4	D. Nicholson	66/1
Fell	Connie II	11.10.0	J. Guest	50/1
Fell	Wartown	12.10.1	J. Gamble	66/1
Fell	Look Happy	10.10.0	J. Haine	40/1
Fell	Merganser	10.10.4	Mr J. Mansfield	66/1
Fell	Magic Tricks	9.10.0	O. McNally	66/1
Fell	Solonace	12.10.0	K.B. White	66/1
Pulled-Up	Loving Record	9.10.12	T. Taaffe	100/7
Pulled-Up	Dagmar Gittell	8.10.5	H.J. East	100/7
Pulled-Up	Moyrath	10.10.2	F. Carroll	33/1
Pulled-Up	Seas End	11.10.3	J.H. Kempton	66/1
Pulled-Up	College Don	11.10.0	B. Wilkinson	66/1
Pulled-Up	Reprieved	10.10.1	P. Pickford	50/1
Pulled-Up	Holm Star	9.10.0	E.F. Kelly	66/1
Pulled-Up	Capricorn	10.10.0	A. Major	66/1
Pulled-Up	Melilla	9.10.0	G. Cramp	66/1
Brought Down	Mr What	13.10.8	T. Carberry	66/1
Brought Down	Vivant	10.10.0	R.J. Hamey	40/1

31 March 1963

Going – Soft

Sponsors – Vaux Limited and Irish Hospital Sweepstakes

Winner – £21,315

Time – 9mins 35 ⅘ secs

47 Ran

Favourite – Springbok

Top Weight – Frenchman's Cove

Winner trained by Keith Piggott at Lambourn, Berkshire

Winner owned by Mr P.B. Raymond

Ayala, chestnut gelding by Supertello – Admiral's Bliss.

1964

TEAM SPIRIT

The triumph and disaster that goes hand in hand with racing – and particularly the Grand National – were illustrated in the boldest possible style in 1964. While the race was one of the most brilliantly exciting for many years, there was also an incident that cast a dark shadow over the event, bringing a chilling reminder of the dangers of the sport.

The high-class 1960 Cheltenham Gold Cup winner Pas Seul was among the thirty-three runners, yet even he could not crack the first eleven in the betting, all listed at 18/1 or lower in what was a most competitive renewal filled deep with talented newcomers. Most unusually, four horses shared favouritism on the day: Time, Pappageno's Cottage, Laffy and Flying Wild – none of whom had run in the National before.

Of the four, the classy grey mare from Ireland Flying Wild was second only to Pas Seul in the handicap, having raced in the highest company for some time. Her form was good, having won over two-and-a-half miles (thought to be her favoured distance) at Sandown during the season, and had also competed against the new superstar of National Hunt racing, Arkle, the winner of the Cheltenham Gold Cup. Having his third National ride was David Mould and, although Flying Wild was a super horse, there remained doubts over her stamina for the Grand National.

Like Flying Wild, the three other co-favourites had question marks against them. Pat Taaffe's mount Pappageno's Cottage had long been considered a National prospect but shouldered a hefty weight. Time had a low weight and the excellent Michael Scudamore on board but, despite winning a recent low-key race at Ludlow, had impressed few with his jumping; while Her Majesty Queen Elizabeth The Queen Mother's horse, the eight-year-old Laffy (trained by Peter Cazalet), had won twice during the season but had been injury plagued, losing his way the season before, and it was uncertain whether he would withstand the rigours of Aintree.

Two other newcomers that proved popular were Beau Normand and Purple Silk. A stablemate of Pas Seul at Bob Turnell's yard, Beau Normand was a most consistent chestnut owned by Mr Jim Joel and the horse had never finished outside the first three places in six runs during the season, three of which he won. Trained by George Vergette and ridden by Johnny Kenneally, the nine-year-old brown gelding Purple Silk had really come to hand as Aintree approached. During consecutive races in January, Purple Silk had fallen and refused, but had returned to sparkling form soon after by taking chases at Leicester and Wetherby, both times exhibiting a new zest for jumping, and with just 10st 3lbs to carry, was a hot fancy come National day.

The magnificent old warrior Kilmore, now fourteen, had rolled back the years during the season, displaying some fine form. The 1964 National would be the last for both Kilmore and his masterful jockey Fred Winter, while the surprise 1963 winner Ayala returned to Aintree with David Nicholson called up to ride, although the horse was out of form and was again unconsidered in the betting. Joining these Grand National veterans was the twelve-year-old Team Spirit, running in his fifth and final National. Team Spirit had enjoyed a season of consistency, and his strong finish to take fourth place in 1963 had not been forgotten by many shrewd judges. As in his previous four Grand National attempts, Team Spirit was partnered by Willie Robinson who, together with trainer Fulke Walwyn, was seeking an upturn in fortune having been left speechless by the defeat of their Champion Mill House to Arkle in the recent Gold Cup.

Fulke Walwyn, trainer of Team Spirit.

Purple Silk leads as Time goes down on his knees at Becher's. Just behind (right) is Team Spirit.

The day had begun on a tragic note with a terrible accident close to the Canal Turn, where a helicopter had crashed, killing the five people on board who were travelling to the race. Hoping to lift the spirits at Aintree were the thirty-three partnerships in the Grand National, each hungry for fortune, fame and glory, although disappointingly there was no sponsorship of the race on this occasion.

Merganser and Supersweet were the first to show from an even break and, although there were an unusually low number of fallers early on, the big Irish hope Flying Wild crashed out to the surprise of many at the opening fence, bringing dismay to the vast number that had backed the grey. There was further misery for favourite backers when Laffy came down at the fourth. Some horses take one look at the big green obstacles at Aintree and simply do not want anything to do with them and, according to jockey Bill Rees, Laffy loathed the fences.

It was the 1963 pacemaker Out And About and the locally trained outsider Peacetown that led the field to Becher's, and there Beau Normand made a

blunder that appeared to shake him to his roots, and he was to refuse at the eleventh, while the top weight Pas Seul came down at the twelfth.

Despite various high-profile early casualties, there remained plenty still in the running approaching The Chair, with a shocking episode lying in wait. The drama began when the majority of runners funnelled into the same take-off area. Though the leaders cleared the fence safely, there was considerable carnage in behind. Ayala fell when well placed, while Border Flight clubbed the fence with such ferocity that he flipped over in mid-air. Lizawake was unlucky to be brought down, although the game horse completed the course riderless in front of the field. Though Border Flight eventually walked away safely from his spectacular fall having remained on the ground for several minutes, his jockey, the leading northern rider Paddy Farrell, had suffered a far worse fate. It later emerged the rider had broken his back and would never walk again. It was a tragedy and one that followed soon after Tim Brookshaw, runner-up aboard Wyndburgh in 1959, had suffered the same injury in a Hurdle race at Aintree in December 1963. Still reeling from Brookshaw's injury, Farrell's injury sent shockwaves through the racing world and reminded everyone of the perils of National Hunt racing as well as the bravery of the competitors.

Wearing a sheepskin noseband, Peacetown led on at the start of the second circuit, enjoying himself in front, with Out And About next, followed by Team Spirit, Time, Reproduction, Pappageno's Cottage, Springbok and Purple Silk, while Kilmore remained in touch until departing at the fence before Becher's. Time was all but down at Becher's, seriously damaging his chance, and his challenge was totally extinguished when he fell at the twenty-sixth, while the outsider Reproduction, who had run above expectations, crashed out at the twenty-third, the smallest fence on the course.

Taking the Canal Turn for the second time, Peacetown seized a firm grip on the lead and, jumping down the back, his challengers emerged in a group of five consisting of Purple Silk, Springbok, Pontin-Go (formerly known as Gay Navaree, the 1962 fourth), Eternal and the rapidly improving Team Spirit. Coming back to the racecourse, the winner was sure to emerge from the six.

Peacetown had gone very wide at the last fence and was right over on the stands side on the run-in, displaying sudden signs of tiredness having given his all, and it was Purple Silk coming up the inner on the far side that was travelling the strongest. Purple Silk went clear passing the elbow and, with Peacetown beaten off, victory seemed certain. Motoring up the centre of the track was Team Spirit – yet even with just fifty yards to run, anything other than a Purple Silk win looked improbable.

It was not so much Purple Silk tiring as Team Spirit powering home with extra reserves of stamina; fighting back courageously under a determined and inspired Robinson ride, little Team Spirit caught Purple Silk just before the line to win by half a length, with Peacetown six lengths back in third, closely followed by the thirteen-year-old outsider Eternal, Pontin-Go and Springbok, the latter once more failing see out the National trip with conviction.

At just over fifteen hands high, Team Spirit was one of the smaller Grand National winners, and had incredibly won the race at his fifth attempt. The horse may have enjoyed Grand National success sooner, however, for Robinson felt that the horse would have gone extremely close in 1960 if not for being knocked over at the second Becher's.

Robinson had now added the Grand National to his 1963 Gold Cup success on Mill House and had also finished second in the 1958 Epsom Derby on Paddy's Point, while Walwyn now joined the select band of men to both ride and train National winners, having won aboard Reynoldstown as an amateur in 1936.

Team Spirit was owned by Americans Mr John K. Goodman, Mr Ron Woodard and Mr Gamble North from Tucson, Indianapolis and Chicago respectively, and the horse was given an honourable retirement after the race – one in which the highs and lows of racing were experienced in extreme measures.

1964 GRAND NATIONAL RESULT

FATE	HORSE	AGE/WEIGHT	JOCKEY	ODDS
1st	TEAM SPIRIT	12.10.3	G.W. ROBINSON	18/1
2nd	PURPLE SILK	9.10.4	J. KENNEALLY	100/6
3rd	PEACETOWN	10.10.1	R. EDWARDS	40/1
4th	ETERNAL	13.10.2	MR S. DAVENPORT	66/1
5th	Pontin-Go	12.10.0	P. Jones	66/1
6th	Springbok	10.10.11	G. Scott	100/6
7th	April Rose	9.10.0	E.P. Harty	22/1
8th	Baxier	8.10.0	Mr W. McLernon	40/1
9th	Crobeg	11.10.4	Mr J. Lawrence	50/1
10th	Pappageno's Cottage	9.11.0	P. Taaffe	100/7
11th	John O'Groats	10.10.3	P. Kelleway	22/1
12th	Supersweet	7.10.1	P. Broderick	40/1
13th	Claymore	11.10.0	Mr C. Davies	50/1
14th	Out And About	9.10.1	B. Gregory	33/1
15th	Sea Knight	9.11.0	Mr P. Nicholson	66/1
Fell	Pas Seul	11.12.0	D.V. Dick	22/1
Fell	Flying Wild	8.11.3	D. Mould	100/7
Fell	Laffy	8.10.8	W. Rees	100/7
Fell	Ayala	10.10.7	D. Nicholson	33/1
Fell	Kilmore	14.10.7	F.T. Winter	100/6
Fell	Border Flight	9.10.3	P.A. Farrell	100/6
Fell	Lizawake	11.10.4	H.R. Beasley	18/1
Fell	Dancing Rain	9.10.0	O. McNally	66/1
Fell	Centre Circle	9.10.0	J. Haine	40/1
Fell	Time	9.10.4	M. Scudamore	100/7
Fell	Reproduction	11.10.0	R. Langley	66/1
Fell	Merganser	11.10.0	J. Lehane	66/1
Fell	Gale Force X	7.10.0	R. Coonan	50/1
Fell	Groomsman	9.10.0	F. Shortt	66/1
Pulled-Up	Red Thorn	8.10.3	T.W. Biddlecombe	33/1
Pulled-Up	Reprieved	11.10.0	P. Harvey	66/1
Refused	Beau Normand	8.10.10	J. King	100/6
Refused	L'Empereur	10.10.5	J. Daumas	40/1

21 March 1964

Going – Good to Soft

Winner – £20,280

Time – 9mins 46 ⁴/₅ secs

33 Ran

Co-Favourites – Flying Wild, Pappageno's Cottage, Laffy and Time

Top Weight – Pas Seul

Winner trained by Fulke Walwyn at Lambourn, Berkshire

Winner owned by Mr J.K. Goodman

Team Spirit, bay gelding by Vulgan – Lady Walewska.

1965

JAY TRUMP

Although it was the richest Grand National to date, the 1965 renewal was dramatically and emphatically declared 'the last' at Aintree. Mrs Topham announced in the summer of 1964 that the racecourse was being sold to property developers. Although Mrs Topham secured the rights to the name 'Grand National Steeplechase' and claimed the event could be staged at another course if need be, it seemed the race in the form it had been established was doomed. Fortunately an injunction delayed the move, and no sale would take place for a number of years but, with Mrs Topham (now seen fairly or unfairly as the villain of the piece), the Grand National's future lay, each year, under a dark cloud of uncertainty. It would not be for many years that the safety and assured future of the race was cemented decisively.

If it had been the last National in 1965, the outcome could easily have resembled a heart-pounding western gunfight, with the victor strolling off proudly into the sunset. Mill House, the giant Gold Cup winner of 1963 and runner-up to Arkle in the same race in 1964 and 1965, had been allocated top weight by some margin, given his sky-high reputation, but when he was disappointingly withdrawn, the handicap became totally condensed, meaning the bottom weight – thirteen-year-old French Cottage – carried 10st 13lbs, with a tremendous advantage therefore going to those towards the top of the weights.

With Mill House absent, heading the field of forty-seven was the much-loved ex-hunter Freddie, who also happened to be favourite, albeit at tediously short odds of 7/2. Trained in Scotland by Reg Tweedie and ridden at Aintree by Pat McCarron, the eight-year-old brown gelding had won recent three-mile chases at Kelso and Sandown, beating heralded Grand National candidates Vultrix, The Rip and Kapeno in the latter contest. Freddie was a smart, polished jumper, and with form over extreme distances, he proved a most popular selection.

One of the classiest horses in the 1965 field was Rondetto, a beautifully built chestnut and one of the most popular horses of the decade. Aged nine, the 1965 race was to be the first of five Nationals Rondetto ran in, and he was a horse with enough speed to win over far shorter distances as well as stamina to win

top staying chases, such as the 1967 Hennessy. Trained by Bob Turnell, Rondetto won three chases before Aintree, most recently taking the National Hunt Handicap Chase at the Cheltenham Festival, beating future Gold Cup winner Fort Leney (considered inferior only to Arkle in Ireland) in the process. Rondetto was partnered by the ultra-tough Jeff King, having his second ride in the race following his mount on Beau Normand in 1964.

The likes of the giant Irish horse Quintin Bay and the seven-year-old stayers Leedsy and Vultrix (trained by Keith Piggott and Frank Cundell respectively), held sound claims, while other high-profile newcomers included the consistent Kempton specialist The Rip – owned by Her Majesty Queen Elizabeth The Queen Mother – and the intriguing American horse Jay Trump. The eight-year-old bay Jay Trump, bred in Pennsylvania, was twice a winner of America's toughest and most glorified steeplechase, the Maryland Hunt Cup, a race run over four miles, and he was ridden at Aintree by American amateur Tommy Crompton Smith, who had bought the horse for owner Mrs Mary Stephenson. On arrival in England, Jay Trump was sent into training with former Champion Jockey Fred Winter, enjoying his first season in his new profession, and his expertise helped guide the horse to three wins prior to the National, for which Jay Trump was priced at 100/6.

With such a large field hurtling towards the first on good ground, the surprise was that just one fell, that being the hopelessly out of form 1963 winner Ayala. Soon striding out in front were the 1964 third Peacetown and newcomer Phebu. The 100/1 shot Nedsmar had been right up there with them until coming down hard at Becher's, landing on his nose and sparking a mini pile-up, with the victims being the fancied Forgotten Dreams and the less well-backed trio of Barleycroft, Ruby Glen and the Mr Macer Gifford-ridden Crobeg.

Peacetown and Phebu continued to lead the way, and with the majority jumping well (although Groomsman gave his rider, the Spanish amateur the Duque de Alburquerque, a wicked fall at Valentines), the race was building up splendidly, with Brown Diamond, Pontin-Go, The Rip, Freddie, Kapeno and Leedsy just behind the leaders, while Jay Trump travelled sweetly up the inside.

Johnnie Haine had fallen from the Mr Paul Mellon-owned Red Tide early on the first circuit, and the loose horse was proving a real menace to quite a few. He had already interfered with Freddie, when he crossed in front of Phebu at the thirteenth, bringing down the unlucky leader. Rondetto had gradually crept into the race and took over the lead as he flew The Chair, and the horse received rich encouragement from the delighted crowds as he jumped the water.

Many had survived the first circuit but, as the imperious Rondetto increased the race tempo, some of the fancied horses lost their way. Leedsy was still in contention when crashing at the eighteenth while Kapeno and jockey Dave Dick had crept into a nice position when departing at the second Becher's to leave Rondetto travelling strongly in the lead from Freddie, Jay Trump and Vultrix, with a gap back to The Rip and the outsiders Mr Jones and Rainbow Battle, the early leader Peacetown having tired quickly.

Jay Trump holds Freddie to win.

There was still some way to go but, with weight a relative non-issue on this occasion for those at the top of the handicap, Rondetto must surely have held a serious chance. Yet, clipping the top of the twenty-sixth, he came down agonisingly, leaving Freddie and Jay Trump to dispute the lead. Drawing clear with decisive conviction, they soon had the race to themselves rejoining the racecourse.

Matching strides at the second last, Jay Trump appeared to be going marginally better on the outside of the favourite and held a slender lead at the last. Although Jay Trump dived somewhat at the final fence, Freddie similarly was far from fluent, jumping out to his left, and it was now down to finishing power as they battled to the line. The American horse was quickest away on the flat, carving out a two-length lead before switching to the inside at the elbow. But Freddie was one of the gamest horses in training and, battling back tenaciously, the favourite

looked sure to swallow up Jay Trump. Admirably ridden by his amateur jockey and showing a steely determination of his own, Jay Trump conjured one final surge, defiantly holding the Scottish horse by three-quarters of a length at the line in one of the most rousing finishes in National history. Nothing could be taken away from the runner-up, with his time worthy of winning many Nationals. Mr Jones was twenty lengths back in third with another 50/1 shot, Rainbow Battle, the Welsh Grand National winner, fourth. The Queen Mother's horse The Rip returned safely, seventh of the fourteen that finished.

It had been a most exciting National, with Freddie very nearly replicating the late finishes of Ayala and Team Spirit, but it was the courageous and classy Jay Trump that had won the day. Tommy Smith was the first amateur to win since 1946, with fellow amateurs Christopher Collins third on his Mr Jones and Mr Jon Ciechanowski sixth on L'Empereur. It was Smith's first ride in the National, and he admitted to being stunned at the chaotic and brutal nature of the race as it unfolded. His shock was no doubt eased with the knowledge that he had become the first American jockey to taste success in the National, giving Mrs Stephenson – from Cincinnati, Ohio – a marvellous moment with her very first racehorse. Amid all the pomp and pride of the American success was the mastery of Fred Winter. In his first season as a trainer he had guided a foreign horse to victory in the biggest race of them all. For Winter, it was the beginning of a very special 'second' career.

1965 GRAND NATIONAL RESULT

FATE	HORSE	AGE/WEIGHT	JOCKEY	ODDS
1st	JAY TRUMP	8.11.5	MR T.C. SMITH	100/6
2nd	FREDDIE	8.11.10	P. McCARRON	7/2
3rd	MR JONES	10.11.5	MR C.D. COLLINS	50/1
4th	RAINBOW BATTLE	9.10.13	G. MILBURN	50/1
5th	Vultrix	7.11.1	D. Nicholson	100/6
6th	L'Empereur	11.10.13	Mr J. Ciechanowski	100/1
7th	The Rip	10.11.5	W. Rees	9/1
8th	Loving Record	11.11.0	B. Hannon	33/1
9th	Tant Pis	10.10.13	Mr J. Alder	40/1
10th	Brown Diamond	10.10.13	Mr W. McLernon	50/1
11th	April Rose	10.10.13	Major P. Bengough	100/1
12th	Culleenhouse	11.10.13	T.W. Biddlecombe	25/1
13th	Peacetown	11.11.0	P. Pickford	25/1
14th	Moyrath	12.10.13	B. Richmond	100/1
Fell	Rondetto	9.11.6	J. King	100/8
Fell	Forgotten Dreams	11.11.0	R. Coonan	22/1
Fell	Kapeno	8.11.6	D.V. Dick	100/8
Fell	Ayala	11.10.13	S. Mellor	50/1
Fell	Time	10.10.13	Mr B. Scott	40/1
Fell	Dark Venetian	10.10.13	J. Renfree	100/1
Fell	Red Tide	8.10.13	J. Haine	33/1
Fell	Pontin-Go	13.10.13	J. Lehane	50/1
Fell	Leedsy	7.10.13	G.W. Robinson	18/1
Fell	Ronald's Boy	8.11.1	Mr G. Kindersley	100/1
Fell	Bold Biri	9.10.13	M. Scudamore	100/1
Fell	Groomsman	10.10.13	Duque de Alburquerque	100/1
Fell	Blonde Warrior	13.10.13	Mr D. Crossley-Cooke	100/1
Fell	Nedsmar	11.10.13	J. Hudson	100/1
Fell	Black Spot	8.10.13	J. Gamble	100/1
Pulled-Up	Lizawake	12.10.13	Mr G. Hartigan	100/1
Pulled-Up	Reproduction	12.10.13	R. Langley	40/1
Pulled-Up	Leslie	9.10.13	P. Jones	33/1
Pulled-Up	Sword Flash	12.10.13	T. Ryan	100/1

FATE	HORSE	AGE/WEIGHT	JOCKEY	ODDS
Pulled-Up	Vulcano	7.10.13	T. Carberry	50/1
Pulled-Up	Quintin Bay	9.10.13	P. Taaffe	25/1
Pulled-Up	Solonace	14.10.13	R.W. Jones	100/1
Pulled-Up	Cutlette	8.10.13	M. Roberts	50/1
Pulled-Up	Mr McTaffy	13.10.13	T. Jackson	100/1
Brought Down	Barleycroft	10.10.13	P. Harvey	100/1
Brought Down	Phebu	8.10.13	J. Morrissey	33/1
Brought Down	Ruby Glen	10.10.13	S. Davenport	33/1
Brought Down	Sizzle-On	9.10.13	P. Hurley	100/1
Brought Down	Crobeg	12.10.13	Mr M.C. Gifford	100/1
Refused	Coleen Star	11.10.13	J. Leech	100/1
Refused	Ballygowan	11.10.13	A. Redmond	66/1
Refused	Fearless Cavalier	14.10.13	R. West	100/1
Refused	French Cottage	13.10.13	Mr W.A. Tellwright	100/1

27 March 1965
Going – Good
Winner – £22,041
Time – 9mins 30³/₅secs
47 Ran
Favourite – Freddie
Top Weight – Freddie
Winner trained by Fred Winter at Lambourn, Berkshire
Winner owned by Mrs M. Stephenson
Jay Trump, bay gelding by Tonga Prince – Be Trump.

1966

ANGLO

For the second consecutive year, it was deemed that the imminent Grand National would be the last run at Aintree. Almost defiantly, a huge field of forty-seven turned out for the 1966 race, eager to play their part in the great race's history.

Favourite, as in 1965, was the star of Reg Tweedie's Scottish yard, Freddie. Again priced disgracefully short at 11/4, Freddie was one of the hottest favourites in National history, having won impressively at Doncaster in January, displaying his usual foot-perfect jumping. However, Freddie had a lot of weight to concede on this occasion, his 11st 7lbs less than only the 12 stone top weight allocated to the Japanese raider Fujino-O, a seven-year-old, stabled in England with Fulke Walwyn.

From the powerful Ryan Price yard (that had sent out Kilmore to win in 1962) came a most progressive and talented chestnut in What A Myth. A brilliant jumper with a striking white face, What A Myth had won all his five races during the season and his obvious class marked him out as a potential Gold Cup or Grand National winner. With excellent form over three miles and further and with a love for the soft ground present at Aintree in 1966, What A Myth was made 11/2 second favourite, with Paul Kelleway in the saddle.

Among those prominent in the betting were the Scottish Grand National winner Popham Down (whose place in National history would be assured twelve months later), the stamina-lacking grey Flying Wild (at the time, one of only two horses in training to have beaten the mighty Arkle, Mill House being the other) and the winner of the Grand Sefton Chase in November, The Fossa, ridden by Terry Biddlecombe.

In addition, two newcomers to the race, Highland Wedding and Forest Prince, were both highly regarded. Trained by Toby Balding, the lightly weighted Highland Wedding was a big, powerful brown horse, and one that seemed a step ahead of the handicapper – having won a number of chases since the publication of the weights, including the four-mile Eider Chase at Newcastle. Highland

Wedding was partnered by Owen McNally, whose previous two National rides had ended in falls from Magic Tricks in 1963 and Dancing Rain in 1964. The front-running Forest Prince also had struck a rich vein of form, winning four times during the season, and the horse represented a trainer/jockey combination that was successful with Merryman II in 1960, Neville Crump and Gerry Scott.

On form alone, the eight-year-old chestnut Anglo had no chance of winning the 1966 Grand National, having won just once from nine races during the season. But one important factor disassociated him from the large band of 100/1 shots in the field, this being that he came from the blossoming yard of second-season trainer Fred Winter, who had won so memorably with Jay Trump the year before and whose reputation continued to grow. Anglo's big-race jockey, Tim Norman, was involved in a much-publicised car accident forty-eight hours before the National. Travelling to Aintree with fellow jockeys Jeff King and Andy Turnell, their vehicle flipped over completely, causing slight concussion and a lacerated cheek for Norman. However, having been passed fit to ride, Norman took his place in the big field aboard the 50/1 shot.

Highland Wedding and jockey Owen McNally in action at Chepstow before the 1966 National, where they finished eighth. Highland Wedding won the race in 1969.

73

Anglo leads Forest Prince
over the final fence.

Jumping straight out into an early lead was Forest Prince and, with no fallers at the first two fences, Rough Tweed and jockey Pat Buckley became the first to go, falling at the gaping open ditch at the third.

Charging down to Becher's, Forest Prince led the large tribe, with Willow King, Quintin Bay, L'Empereur, Harry Black and Kapeno closest to him. At the awesome fence, Popham Down failed to recover from a bad mistake and fell, as did Packed Home, while Groomsman refused and Willow King blundered so badly that he lost a huge amount of ground, eventually pulling-up at the fourteenth.

With Forest Prince jumping magnificently, the leading group remained much the same coming back onto the racecourse, although Freddie had quietly moved into a leading position, while Michael Scudamore had rushed the seven-year-old Greek Scholar up to duel for the lead with Forest Prince. The intimidating sight of The Chair was simply too much for Fujino-O to stomach, and the horse bluntly refused, while of those that did attempt the jump, Black Spot, Game Purston and Irish Day came down on the landing side.

With plenty among the large field beginning to struggle, Forest Prince led out for the second circuit, with Kapeno challenging strongly (as he had the year before), while Norman had worked the chestnut Anglo into the race, with Greek Scholar, Freddie and Highland Wedding holding threatening positions as they jumped the fences going down to Becher's once more.

It was the second Becher's that seriously depleted the field, as the prominent Greek Scholar came down; Valouis found himself lodged between two fallen horses and was brought down when beginning to mount a challenge. In mid-division, What A Myth fell, Supersweet was baulked and fell while the 100/1 shot Leslie was brought down. Highland Wedding was very fortunate not to have joined the casualty list, narrowly avoiding the stricken Valouis, and the incidents left Forest Prince clear of Freddie, Anglo and Highland Wedding, with Quintin Bay, The Fossa and Loving Record next in line.

A rare mistake by Freddie at Valentines knocked the favourite back somewhat while, after clouting the last ditch four out, Highland Wedding's chance was ruined. From there on Forest Prince led Anglo back onto the racecourse. Coming clear, the winner was sure to emerge from the pair.

Having crossed the Melling Road for the final time, Forest Prince had still been travelling like a winner as he attempted to emulate the trailblazing exploits of Sundew in 1957. But approaching the second last, the leader suddenly began to waver, tiredness striking him at the worst moment as Anglo ranged upsides. In receipt of 8lbs from Forest Prince, Anglo – a flashy chestnut with a white face – quickly stole a two-length lead and, jumping the last well, stamped his authority on proceedings by shooting clear on the run-in, finishing extremely strongly and running out a comfortable twenty-length victor. Forest Prince had run with such energy and desire, yet he finished a shattered individual, passed on the run to the line by Freddie, who beat him by five lengths, with The Fossa fourth.

Anglo's win certainly came as a surprise. He was a relatively young horse and found a renewed enthusiasm at Aintree, a factor often associated with Grand National winners. Forest Prince, Freddie, Greek Scholar and Highland Wedding (each proving to be fine Aintree horses either in this or other Grand Nationals) had all held dominant positions on the second circuit, yet it was Anglo that had proved the best of them, and was a most deserved and rather clinical winner.

He may not have been as good as Jay Trump, but Anglo's Grand National win was more clear-cut, and his success poured more praise on the shoulders of Winter (one of a select few to have been Champion Jockey and then Champion Trainer), who maintained his 100 per cent training record in the race. Anglo had formerly been trained by Price, but switched to Winter's yard not long after Price lost his training license.

Anglo – originally named Flag Of Convenience – was perfectly ridden by twenty-two-year-old Norman, and the jockey who began as an amateur five years previously had impressed many with the stylish way he had brought Anglo through the field to win the biggest race of the year in thoroughly convincing style.

1966 GRAND NATIONAL RESULT

FATE	HORSE	AGE/WEIGHT	JOCKEY	ODDS
1st	ANGLO	8.10.0	T. NORMAN	50/1
2nd	FREDDIE	9.11.7	P. McCARRON	11/4
3rd	FOREST PRINCE	8.10.8	G. SCOTT	100/7
4th	THE FOSSA	9.10.8	T.W. BIDDLECOMBE	20/1
5th	Jim's Tavern	9.10.0	Mr N. Gaselee	100/1
6th	Quintin Bay	10.10.0	J. Cullen	100/1
7th	Norther	9.10.0	P. Jones	100/1
8th	Highland Wedding	9.10.0	O. McNally	15/2
9th	Vulcano	8.10.1	J. Gifford	25/1
10th	Gale Force X	9.10.0	R. Coonan	50/1
11th	Big George	11.10.0	J. Morrissey	33/1

FATE	HORSE	AGE/WEIGHT	JOCKEY	ODDS
12th	Loving Record	12.10.0	B. Hannon	50/1
Fell	What A Myth	9.11.4	P. Kelleway	11/2
Fell	Rough Tweed	12.10.7	P. Buckley	22/1
Fell	Kapeno	9.10.6	D. Mould	100/7
Fell	Packed Home	11.10.3	T. Carberry	33/1
Fell	Greek Scholar	7.10.4	M. Scudamore	50/1
Fell	Brown Diamond	11.10.0	F. Shortt	100/1
Fell	Popham Down	9.10.0	G.W. Robinson	22/1
Fell	Pontin-Go	14.10.0	T.M. Jones	100/1
Fell	Game Purston	8.10.0	P. Cowley	100/1
Fell	Supersweet	9.10.6	Mr D. Crossley-Cooke	100/1
Fell	Major Hitch	8.10.1	P. Broderick	50/1
Fell	Irish Day	10.10.0	J. Magee	40/1
Fell	Scottish Final	9.10.0	J. Gamble	100/1
Fell	Flamecap	9.10.0	F. Carroll	100/1
Fell	Black Spot	9.10.0	J. Speid-Soote	100/1
Fell	Harry Black	9.10.0	R. Court	100/1
Pulled-Up	Flying Wild	10.11.0	P. Taaffe	20/1
Pulled-Up	Stirling	10.10.11	H.R. Beasley	28/1
Pulled-Up	Vultrix	8.10.7	S. Mellor	100/7
Pulled-Up	Solimyth	10.10.1	Mr J. Lawrence	100/1
Pulled-Up	April Rose	11.10.7	Major P. Bengough	100/1
Pulled-Up	L'Empereur	12.10.2	Duque de Alburquerque	100/1
Pulled-Up	Willow King	11.10.0	L. McLoughlin	100/1
Pulled-Up	Royal Ruse	8.10.0	T. Hyde	100/1
Pulled-Up	Mac's Flare	10.10.0	R. Langley	100/1
Pulled-Up	King Pin	10.10.11	Mr T. Durant	100/1
Pulled-Up	In Haste	8.10.3	J. Leech	100/1
Pulled-Up	My Gift	10.10.0	A. Redmond	100/1
Pulled-Up	Bold Biri	10.10.0	J. Lehane	100/1
Brought Down	Valouis	7.10.0	E. Prendergast	50/1
Brought Down	Leslie	10.10.5	Mr J.M. Opperman	100/1
Unseated Rider	Dorimont	12.10.0	Mr W. Shand-Kydd	50/1
Refused	Fujino-O	7.12.0	J. King	100/1
Refused	Monarch's Thought	12.10.0	G. Cramp	100/1
Refused	Groomsman	11.11.0	Mr S. Roberts	100/1

26 March 1966

Going – Soft

Winner – £22,334

Time – 9mins 52 4/5 secs

47 Ran

Favourite – Freddie

Top Weight – Fujino-O

Winner trained by Fred Winter at Lambourn, Berkshire

Winner owned by Mr S. Levy

Anglo, chestnut gelding by Greek Star – Miss Alligator.

1967

FOINAVON

Every so often, an individual race comes along that will stand the test of time, being replayed and reviewed over and over again. This happens sometimes because of the quality of horses, sometimes the importance of the race – or a breathtaking finish. The Grand National, with its unique course and fences, as well as a worldwide status, has more opportunity than any other race to cause such excitement, but it also has by far the biggest chance of delivering the unexpected – drama that would be simply inconceivable anywhere else other than Aintree. The 1928 race, where Easter Hero had affected a race where every horse fell bar the winner was a case in point. But even that edition of the National paled in comparison to the stunning renewal in 1967. The Grand Nationals of 1956, 1977, 1981 and 1983 all rank among the most famous in the race's history for a variety of reasons, but it is hard to imagine a more emphatic, drama-laden Grand National than that of 1967.

With the injunction won by Lord Sefton two years previously now reversed, control and power of Aintree racecourse and its destiny had again swung back in favour of Mrs Topham, strengthening belief that the National's future was bleak, a fact emphasised by the reduction of fixtures at Aintree in the 1966/67 season.

Albeit hanging by a thread, the Grand National survived for the time being, and another huge field was assembled for a cracking 1967 race, with top weight the distinguished chaser What A Myth, fresh from finishing a good third to Woodland Venture in the Cheltenham Gold Cup. But it was another Ryan Price-trained inmate that held supremacy in the betting market, the Josh Gifford-ridden Honey End. The sparkling form of the ten-year-old brown gelding had encouraged a major rush of money for the horse, with his six wins during the season sending him to Aintree in red-hot form. Both Gifford and Price had the utmost confidence in Honey End's chance, and the horse began as 15/2 favourite.

Having finished second in the 1966 Topham Trophy, second-favourite Bassnet had already exhibited his beautiful jumping over the National fences. An eight-year-old partnered by David Nicholson, Bassnet had also claimed the scalp of Woodland Venture at Haydock in February.

The field of forty-four offered punters a plethora of serious candidates, with bold performers from 1966 Rondetto, Greek Scholar, Kapeno and Freddie again lining up, while Anglo returned to the scene of his greatest triumph in good form and reportedly fitter and stronger, according to Fred Winter, despite the fact he had risen 15lbs for his Grand National win.

Impressive fencers Red Alligator and Rutherfords both had their followers, as did the 1966 fourth The Fossa, while newcomers that gained much attention included Different Class and Kilburn. The Peter Cazalet-trained Different Class was a young horse very much on the rise, being a fine jumper and forceful galloper, and had shot to prominence by winning the National Hunt Handicap Chase at Cheltenham for his famous Hollywood owner Gregory Peck. The talented and consistent bay chaser Kilburn entered the race on the back of a convincing success at Sandown, and was partnered by the previous year's winning jockey Tim Norman, with Bobby Beasley taking the ride on Anglo.

Thirteen of the runners were priced at 100/1, among them Foinavon. Formerly trained by the great Tom Dreaper in Ireland, the horse had proved a disappointment and had been switched to the stable of John Kempton in Berkshire. Having run an incredible fifteen times during the season, his most notable achievement had been finishing a distant seventh in the Gold Cup. Kempton often rode the horse, but was unable to make the weight for the National and took up another engagement at Worcester instead, so in stepped John Buckingham for his first Grand National ride.

The going was good, the pace sure to be quick, and it was Johnny Lehane aboard 50/1 shot Penvulgo that galloped headstrong to the first fence with

Mayhem at the twenty-third fence.

Princeful and Barberyn in close attendance. Though not apparent at the time, the first fence would have a hugely significant bearing on the race. Although the fall of the well-backed Bassnet caused disappointment in the stands, neither the departure of the fallen Meon Valley or the brought-down Popham Down gained much attention.

For a race that was to prove so sensational, there were surprisingly few incidents on the first circuit, with only Bassnet's exit causing much of a stir, and all the fancied runners remained intact until Anglo met The Chair completely wrong, and was soon after pulled-up by Beasley.

Out in front, Rutherfords and the Stan Hayhurst-ridden Castle Falls had been jumping like a pair of bucks all the way round and, heading for the second Becher's, they led an enormous band of horses still in contention, with David Mould enjoying a fine ride aboard Different Class and each of Rondetto, Kirtle-Lad, Princeful, Greek Scholar, Kapeno, The Fossa, Quintin Bay and Norther directly in the hunt. The favourite Honey End was some way back but travelling strongly – Gifford slowly nudging him into the contest. It was noticeable that the big leading group had all jumped Becher's second time – most unusually – at the middle to inner portion of the fence, and the majority held these positions approaching the smallest fence on the course, the twenty-third, preceded by two loose horses.

One of those loose horses just happened to be the first-fence-faller Popham Down, and he was the catalyst for the drama that unfolded. With Rutherfords holding a tight position on the inside and Castle Falls running parallel to him, Popham Down swerved to the right at the last instant, running across the face of the fence and knocking Rutherfords sideways, blocking the take-off and hampering the rest of the field. A second loose horse hurtled Castle Falls through the fence while, immediately behind, Rondetto was struck as he took off, sending Johnnie Haine shooting over the fence. In behind the leaders, there was simply nowhere to go, and a mass pile-up ensued. Horses stacked into each other, jockeys were thrown over the fence without their mounts, some horses refused and some were stricken either in the fence or on the ground.

It was a scene of total destruction and mayhem yet, in the midst of the confusion, appeared Buckingham on Foinavon. The partnership had been well behind the main group at Becher's, but that was now to their advantage for, with slightly more time to plot their route, Buckingham steered Foinavon – who had been jumping safely but slowly – to the wide outside where, just managing to find enough of an opening, they chartered a path over the obstacle and emerged from the melee as the only tandem to negotiate the fence at the first time of asking.

Having parted company like so many, jockey Paddy Broderick found his mount Kirtle-Lad on the landing side of the fence, and promptly remounted and set off in pursuit of Foinavon. Not unfancied at 28/1, Kirtle-Lad could have been the one to ruin the Foinavon story, as although he was almost a fence down on the new leader coming to the Canal Turn, he had similarly broken free of the rest.

Foinavon is clear at the Canal Turn second time.

But, clearly affected by the events at the previous fence, Kirtle-Lad refused the Canal Turn and his race was over.

Foinavon was well clear of his pursuers and jumped Valentines in solidarity with magnificent grace. If he could stand up he was sure to win for, even though he was an undeniably slow horse, he was a fine jumper and the lead he now had was practically unassailable. In the event, it was the Denys Smith-trained pair of Greek Scholar and Red Alligator, together with the Tommy Carberry-ridden Packed Home and race favourite Honey End that set out in game pursuit of Foinavon although, jumping down the back, their cause seemed hopeless.

However, coming back onto the racecourse, Foinavon was, understandably, beginning to tire and it appeared it may yet be a race, as Greek Scholar and in particular Honey End were coming hard at him. Honey End had been marginally ahead of Foinavon at Becher's second time, slowly creeping into the race, but Gifford had been forced to put him to the twenty-third a number of times before finally negotiating the fence. Nevertheless, it was Honey End that was simply motoring towards the end, passing Greek Scholar and reducing Foinavon's lead to about twelve lengths by the last.

But, given a brisk reminder by Buckingham, Foinavon pulled clear again on the run-in, and with Honey End having used all his energy to get anywhere near the leader, the favourite could find no more. To applause acknowledging a colossal achievement, Foinavon crossed the line a fifteen-length winner for a delighted but very surprised Buckingham. Honey End had given his all in second, as had the fast-finishing third Red Alligator and the fourth Greek Scholar. Eighteen horses eventually completed, seventeen of which had suffered some sort of mishap at the twenty-third, or the 'Foinavon' fence, as it then became known.

Naturally, there were plenty of jockeys convinced they would have won. Gifford was adamant that Honey End would have emerged victorious despite being well back at the melee, while of the more prominent horses at the time of the pile-up, Hayhurst indicated Castle Falls was merely cantering, Paul Kelleway opinioned that What A Myth was in a tremendous position and Mould believed Different Class was travelling better than any. Castle Falls, among others, was one horse that needed assistance escaping the melee and, although he was fine having been pulled out of the fence and no other horse was seriously injured in the pile-up, the race did suffer a fatality, with Vulcano sadly dying from a fall at the third fence.

Obviously, Foinavon (named after a Scottish mountain and originally owned by Anne, Duchess of Westminster) was extremely fortunate to have won a Grand National, but his bizarre (he had to jump the final seven fences in the unusual position of having no other horses in the vicinity) and somewhat courageous win for Kempton, Buckingham and owner Mr Cyril Watkins did plenty to restore public interest in the Grand National. In an era of uncertainty for the National, Foinavon's win seemed to rekindle a waning interest in the event, and proved the race to be a national institution – a race where the unexpected can indeed happen, and dreams really can come true.

1967 GRAND NATIONAL RESULT

FATE	HORSE	AGE/WEIGHT	JOCKEY	ODDS
1st	FOINAVON	9.10.0	J. BUCKINGHAM	100/1
2nd	HONEY END	10.10.4	J. GIFFORD	15/2
3rd	RED ALLIGATOR	8.10.0	B. FLETCHER	30/1
4th	GREEK SCHOLAR	8.10.9	T.W. BIDDLECOMBE	20/1
5th	Packed Home	12.10.0	T. Carberry	100/1
6th	Solbina	10.11.2	E.P. Harty	25/1
7th	Aussie	10.10.0	F. Shortt	50/1
8th	Scottish Final	10.10.0	Mr B. Howard	100/1
9th	What A Myth	10.12.0	P. Kelleway	20/1
10th	Kapeno	10.11.1	Mr N. Gaselee	25/1
11th	Quintin Bay	11.10.0	J. Cullen	50/1
12th	Bob-A-Job	13.10.0	C. Young	100/1
13th	Steel Bridge	9.10.0	E. Prendergast	100/1
14th	Castle Falls	10.10.3	S. Hayhurst	50/1
15th	Ross Sea	11.10.3	J. Cook	66/1
16th	Rutherfords	7.10.11	J. Leech	28/1

FATE	HORSE	AGE/WEIGHT	JOCKEY	ODDS
17th	Freddie	10.11.13	P. McCarron	100/9
18th	Game Purston	9.10.0	K.B. White	66/1
Fell	Kilburn	9.11.0	T. Norman	100/8
Fell	Bassnet	8.10.11	D. Nicholson	10/1
Fell	Meon Valley	12.10.7	A. Turnell	66/1
Fell	Lucky Domino	10.10.5	J. Kenneally	66/1
Fell	Dorimont	13.10.0	R. Pitman	100/1
Fell	April Rose	12.10.8	Major P. Bengough	66/1
Fell	Vulcano	9.10.0	J. Speid-Soote	40/1
Fell	Ronald's Boy	10.10.13	Mr P. Irby	100/1
Fell	Border Fury	8.10.2	Mr D. Crossley-Cooke	100/1
Fell	Aerial III	11.10.9	Mr T. Durant	100/1
Fell	Tower Road	9.10.0	R. Williams	40/1
Pulled-Up	Anglo	9.11.1	H.R. Beasley	100/8
Pulled-Up	Forecastle	9.10.10	N. Wilkinson	50/1
Pulled-Up	The Fossa	10.10.2	S. Mellor	100/8
Pulled-Up	Norther	10.10.0	Mr J. Lawrence	50/1
Pulled-Up	Dun Widdy	11.10.10	Mr J. Edwards	100/1
Pulled-Up	Penvulgo	8.10.0	J. Lehane	50/1
Pulled-Up	Harry Black	10.10.0	R. Reid	100/1
Brought Down	Different Class	7.11.2	D. Mould	100/8
Brought Down	Limeking	10.10.13	P. Buckley	33/1
Brought Down	Popham Down	10.10.0	M.C. Gifford	66/1
Brought Down	Leedsy	9.10.5	T.S. Murphy	50/1
Brought Down	Princeful	9.10.2	R. Edwards	100/1
Refused	Rondetto	11.11.7	J. Haine	33/1
Refused	Kirtle-Lad	8.10.3	P. Broderick	28/1
Refused	Barberyn	12.10.1	N. Mullins	100/1

8 April 1967

Going – Good

Winner – £17,630

Time – 9mins 49³/₅ secs

44 Ran

Favourite – Honey End

Top Weight – What A Myth

Winner trained by John Kempton at Compton, Berkshire

Winner owned by Mr C.P.T. Watkins

Foinavon, brown gelding by Vulgan – Ecilace.

1968

RED ALLIGATOR

The Grand National was back for another year, despite the ever-lingering fears of extinction. Clouded in doubt the race may have been, but with another huge field doing it justice, it seemed absurd to think the National may be no more following the 1968 edition.

Dominating the betting market were horses that had been most unlucky in the mayhem of 1967 and were hungry for another chance. There was no Honey End or Greek Scholar on this occasion, but the likes of Different Class, Rutherfords and Red Alligator were most fancied to turn the tables in their favour. Below only the high-class What A Myth in the handicap, Different Class had again been in top form during the season, and film star Gregory Peck's horse had won over three-and-a-half miles at Sandown Park shortly before the National, a win that, coupled with his bold showing in the 1967 National, elevated him to race favourite. Rutherfords was back, this time with Pat Buckley on board, while Red Alligator had been a horse that had made up tremendous late ground the year before. Having been thrown over the fence at the twenty-third, jockey Brian Fletcher had scrambled back over the fence to retrieve the loose Red Alligator and, after a number of attempts at the fence, eventually set out in vain pursuit of Foinavon. Arguably, it was Red Alligator that finished strongest of any horse when taking third place. That effort, together with Red Alligator's good form over distances of three miles and beyond, mostly at northern tracks, saw the chestnut start co-third favourite of four, with twenty-year-old Fletcher again in the saddle for trainer Denys Smith.

Of the newcomers, two horses with eyecatching form were French Kilt and Moidore's Token. A lightly weighted eight-year-old trained by Frank Cundell and ridden by Stan Mellor, French Kilt had won his last three chases, all over three miles, winning at Chepstow, Sandown and Kempton. French Kilt was thought to have a definite chance if he could adapt to the big fences. Despite being an eleven-year-old, the Ken Oliver-trained Moidore's Token had been lightly raced down the years and was a magnificent jumper with no shortage of bravery. The mount of Barry Brogan, Moidore's Token had won his five previous races prior to Aintree.

Foinavon returned to defend his title, while old hands Rondetto (who had won the season's Hennessy Gold Cup), The Fossa and Kirtle-Lad were back, as was What A Myth – one of three trained by Ryan Price, the others being recent Wincanton winner the bay Master Of Art and the smallish Regal John, the mount of Josh Gifford. Trainer Toby Balding returned Highland Wedding to the race, having been forced to miss the 1967 contest, while a weak challenge from Ireland suggested Tommy Carberry's mount, the prolific mare Great Lark, would be their strongest contender. As well as the favoured horses, there was also great interest in 100/1 shot Highlandie, who was partnered by sixty-eight-year-old American amateur Tim Durant, the 'galloping grandfather'. Mr Durant had failed to complete the course aboard King Pin in 1966 and Aerial III in 1967, but stood to collect £500 if he could become the oldest man ever to complete the Grand National.

The sun shone ever so brightly as the field lined up and, away smoothly on good ground, The Fossa showed in front with Valouis, followed by Kirtle-Lad, Valbus, Rutherfords, Quintin Bay and Chamoretta, while the first to go were Fort Ord and jockey Tim Norman.

Jockey Brian Fletcher.

Beecham was the only other to drop out on the way down to Becher's, but the Brook was to claim its fair share of victims on this occasion. What A Myth, Go-Pontinental, Ross Four and Valouis all fell, sending chunks of the fence flying everywhere, while the amateur Nick Gaselee was brought down on Chu-Teh. Also falling (although later remounted then pulled-up) was Polaris Missile, the mount of Mr Nigel Thorne, who was the son of John Thorne – the horse's trainer and fine amateur, who would have a big part to play in a very emotional 1981 Grand National.

Valentines too ended the race for a number of runners, including Master Mascus and the refusing Great Lark, but two-thirds of the field remained coming back to the racecourse, with Rutherfords, The Fossa, Rondetto and Moidore's Token leading the way.

The Hennessy winner, the ever-popular Rondetto, sparked great cheers from the crowd as he sailed over The Chair in the lead but, most surprisingly, the normally innocuous water jump caused unexpected grief, with Foinavon out of luck on this occasion, crashing out as Bassnet, Champion Prince and Ronald's Boy were all brought down.

At the second Becher's, the leading group consisted of The Fossa, Rondetto, Rutherfords, Moidore's Token, Different Class, Princeful, Red Alligator and San Angelo, with one of the casualties being Highlandie and his veteran rider Mr Durant, although they were well to the rear when parting company. Just when it looked as though he would play a significant part in the finish of a Grand National, Rondetto's poor luck at Aintree surfaced again, coming down at the Foinavon fence, leaving jockey Jeff King very angry.

Jumping the Canal Turn with San Angelo, owned and trained by Mr Edward Courage (of Tiberetta fame), beginning to tire, it was a group of five that broke free, with Different Class offering huge encouragement to favourite backers as he hit the front at Valentines on the inside of the track. He was joined by Rutherfords in the centre and the improving Red Alligator towards the outside, then came The Fossa and the staying-on Moidore's Token. Jumping down the back for the final time, the race lay between the quintet.

Having guided Red Alligator clear on the wide outside for a circuit-and-a-half, Fletcher now put Red Alligator into the race with a serious challenge. David Mould remained ice cool on Different Class, giving the impression his mount had plenty in reserve. But as first The Fossa and then Rutherfords began to tire, Red Alligator leapt into the lead at the third last and, bounding across the Melling Road and back onto the racecourse, Fletcher suddenly had his rivals off balance.

Long-legged and spring-heeled, Red Alligator gained a lead of a number of lengths by the second last, with Different Class now off the bridle having looked so imperious a couple of fences earlier. Flying the last with an energetically high leap, Red Alligator was quickly away on the flat and, bouncing off the top of the ground, separated himself decisively from the tiring Different Class and the

Red Alligator jumps the last fence on his way to a comfortable success.

rallying Moidore's Token. Striding out confidently under Fletcher, Red Alligator ran out a most comfortable winner. While there were many hard luck stories in 1967, there were absolutely none on this occasion, the winner destroying the field and finishing as one of the most decisive Grand National victors. Twenty lengths was the winning margin, the exact same distance that Red Alligator's half-brother Anglo (they had the same dam, Miss Alligator) had won by in 1966. A dogged battle to the line saw Moidore's Token edge Different Class for second with Rutherfords fourth and The Fossa fifth. Moidore's Token became yet another Scottish-trained runner-up, following in the footsteps of Macmoffat, Wyndburgh and Freddie. Of the remainder, the well-fancied French Kilt had jumped poorly, never threatening in finishing fourteenth, but there was huge delight when it emerged that Mr Durant had remounted Highlandie and had managed to complete the course in fifteenth place. As well as achieving his place in history, Mr Durant generously donated his winning bet of £500 to the Injured Jockeys Fund.

Rarely had a Grand National win been as clear cut as that of Red Alligator, trained by Smith at Bishop Auckland in County Durham, and much credit went to the young Fletcher, who proved masterful in guiding the horse carefully round one circuit before playing his hand on the second. Time would reveal Fletcher to be one of the finest of all Grand National jockeys, with much success awaiting the rider during a glorious period in the 1970s.

1968 GRAND NATIONAL RESULT

FATE	HORSE	AGE/WEIGHT	JOCKEY	ODDS
1st	RED ALLIGATOR	9.10.0	B. FLETCHER	100/7
2nd	MOIDORE'S TOKEN	11.10.8	B. BROGAN	100/6
3rd	DIFFERENT CLASS	8.11.5	D. MOULD	17/2
4th	RUTHERFORDS	8.10.6	P. BUCKLEY	100/9
5th	The Fossa	11.10.4	R. Edwards	28/1
6th	Valbus	10.10.0	R. Langley	100/1
7th	Highland Wedding	11.11.0	O. McNally	18/1
8th	Reynard's Heir	8.10.4	T. Kinane	28/1
9th	Princeful	10.10.4	J. Leech	66/1
10th	Steel Bridge	10.10.4	E.P. Harty	100/1
11th	Manifest	10.10.0	R. Pitman	66/1
12th	San Angelo	8.10.10	W. Rees	25/1
13th	Some Slipper	11.10.0	R. Atkins	66/1
14th	French Kilt	8.10.0	S. Mellor	100/7
15th	Highlandie	11.10.12	Mr T. Durant (remounted)	100/1
16th	Dun Widdy	12.10.2	Mr A.P. Moore	100/1
17th	Quintin Bay	12.10.0	G.W. Robinson	66/1
Fell	What A Myth	11.12.0	P. Kelleway	28/1
Fell	Rondetto	12.10.12	J. King	33/1
Fell	Fort Ord	8.10.9	T. Norman	35/1
Fell	Vultrix	10.10.8	T.W. Biddlecombe	28/1
Fell	Quitte Ou Double L	8.10.8	Mr J. Ciechanowski	66/1
Fell	Master Mascus	9.10.6	Mr J. Lawrence	66/1
Fell	Master Of Art	8.10.2	Mr B. Hanbury	100/7
Fell	Go-Pontinental	8.10.0	M. C. Gifford	25/1
Fell	Ross Four	7.10.0	P. Jones	100/1
Fell	Fort Knight	9.10.0	R. Reid	40/1
Fell	Mixed French	9.10.0	G. Holmes	100/1
Fell	Kirtle-Lad	9.10.0	J. Enright	50/1
Fell	Polaris Missile	9.10.0	Mr N. Thorne	66/1
Fell	Beecham	9.10.0	B.R. Davies	100/1
Fell	Valouis	9.10.1	E. Prendergast	40/1
Pulled-Up	Phemius	10.10.8	G. Scott	50/1
Pulled-Up	Forecastle	10.10.8	Mr W. McLernon	50/1
Pulled-Up	Game Purston	10.10.0	D. Cartwright	100/1
Pulled-Up	Willing Slave	8.10.2	M.B. James	100/1
Brought Down	Bassnet	9.10.12	D. Nicholson	18/1
Brought Down	Foinavon	10.10.5	P. Harvey	66/1
Brought Down	Ronald's Boy	11.10.0	J. Harty	100/1
Brought Down	Champion Prince	9.10.12	Mr A. Wates	66/1
Brought Down	Chu-Teh	9.10.0	Mr N. Gaselee	33/1
Brought Down	Chamoretta	8.10.1	D. Elsworth	100/1
Refused	Regal John	10.10.8	J. Gifford	100/7
Refused	Great Lark	9.10.6	T. Carberry	100/6
Refused	Portation	10.10.0	G. Cramp	100/1

30 March 1968
Going – Good
Winner – £17,848
Time – 9mins 28⅘ secs
45 Ran
Favourite – Different Class
Top Weight – What A Myth
Winner trained by Denys Smith at Bishop Auckland, County Durham
Winner owned by Mr J. Manners
Red Alligator, chestnut gelding by Magic Red – Miss Alligator.

1969

HIGHLAND WEDDING

The Grand National field for the 1969 renewal was considerably smaller than most of the races in the 1960s, with just thirty facing the starter on this occasion. It was hotly anticipated that Red Alligator would become the first since Reynoldstown to record consecutive victories in the race, so well had the horse handled the big fences twelve months previously. An encouraging final run at Haydock sent Denys Smith's charge confidently to Aintree, for which the Grand National had been the horse's season-long target.

Bassnet, Rondetto, The Fossa and Moidore's Token were among the Aintree old hands reappearing in 1969, as was Toby Balding's Highland Wedding, a twelve-year-old now but arguably in the best form of his life. The brown gelding had won his last three races, including Newcastle's marathon Eider Chase for the third time in his career, illustrating his undoubted stamina. Highland Wedding – had been seventh in the 1966 National, despite spreading a plate at the fourth fence, and had been ante-post favourite in Foinavon's year before being withdrawn because of a late injury. His eighth behind Red Alligator in 1968 again proved the horse could handle the fences and, having dropped down the weights somewhat, he was again well-fancied on this occasion. One sad note regarding Highland Wedding's National raid was that his regular jockey, Owen McNally, had broken an arm so badly that his career had been ended but, in Eddie Harty (sixth aboard Solbina in 1967), the replacement in the saddle was a good one.

Of the newcomers, Fearless Fred, Arcturus and The Beeches all had their share of supporters. Fearless Fred and Arcturus sat at the top of the handicap and had both been placed in the season's Hennessy Gold Cup behind Man Of The West. Trained by Fred Rimell, Fearless Fred was considered to be a potential Cheltenham Gold Cup winner, although he was attempting to become the first seven-year-old to win the National since Bogskar in 1940. Together with Highland Wedding, the little grey. The Beeches had eyecatching form prior to Aintree. Trained by Bob Turnell, the consistent horse had won chases in excess of three miles at Windsor and Warwick and was a sure stayer.

Moidore's Token, a horse that had given such a good account of himself in the 1968 National, was noticeably sweating profusely before the race – a sign the occasion may have been getting to him. Charging to the first, all thirty horses survived the opening test, headed by a group consisting of Furore II, Limetra, Miss Hunter and Flosuebarb.

The second fence also failed to claim any victims, but the big ditch saw the end of Tudor Fort and, to the desperate disappointment of many in the crowd, Fearless Fred came tumbling down at the fourth, the groans ringing down from the stands.

One of the unlucky horses in Foinavon's year had been Castle Falls, and approaching Becher's, he had taken control of the lead, pursued by Miss Hunter, Furore II, Steel Bridge, Limetra, The Fossa and Flosuebarb. It was at Becher's that one of the two amateur American brothers riding in the race, Mr George Sloan, took a nasty fall as his grey horse Peccard came down, but the majority of runners survived the notorious Brook, as well as the Canal Turn and Valentines, the small field giving runners more space at the fences. With the beastly Chair also failing to claim any casualties, twenty-four remained in the race heading out for a second circuit, led now by the bottom weight Steel Bridge, ridden by Richard Pitman.

Despite the large number still travelling well, the previous year's first and second were not, and Red Alligator was a surprise faller at the nineteenth, ending hopes of a repeat victory, while Moidore's Token pulled-up lame at the twenty-first. Steel Bridge maintained his lead, with both Highland Wedding and the veteran Rondetto soon looming up as very real threats. Tommy Carberry had also driven Kilburn into a promising position, and the horse was still swinging along when he crashed out at the second Becher's.

Jockey Eddie Harty.

Trainer Toby Balding.

1969 GRAND NATIONAL RESULT

FATE	HORSE	AGE/WEIGHT	JOCKEY	ODDS
1st	HIGHLAND WEDDING	12.10.4	E.P. HARTY	100/9
2nd	STEEL BRIDGE	11.10.0	R. PITMAN	50/1
3rd	RONDETTO	13.10.6	J. KING	25/1
4th	THE BEECHES	9.10.1	W. REES	100/6
5th	Bassnet	10.10.12	J. Gifford	100/8
6th	Arcturus	8.11.4	P. Buckley	100/6
7th	Fort Sun	8.10.4	J. Crowley	28/1
8th	Kellsboro' Wood	9.10.10	A. Turnell	66/1
9th	Furore II	8.10.0	M.C. Gifford	20/1
10th	Miss Hunter	8.10.0	F. Shortt	50/1
11th	The Fossa	12.10.9	Capt. A.H. Parker-Bowles	33/1
12th	Limeburner	8.10.0	J. Buckingham	66/1
13th	Castle Falls	12.10.0	S. Hayhurst	66/1
14th	Limetra	11.10.9	P. Broderick	50/1
Fell	Fearless Fred	7.11.3	T.W. Biddlecombe	15/2
Fell	Red Alligator	10.10.13	B. Fletcher	13/2
Fell	Kilburn	11.10.9	T. Carberry	22/1
Fell	Hove	8.10.9	D. Nicholson	100/6
Fell	Tudor Fort	9.10.4	J. Haldane	50/1
Fell	Peccard	8.10.4	Mr G. Sloan	50/1
Fell	The Inventor	8.10.0	T. Hyde	33/1
Fell	Flosuebarb	9.10.0	J. Guest	100/1
Fell	Ballinabointra	10.10.1	P. Kelleway	100/1
Pulled-Up	Moidore's Token	12.10.9	B. Brogan	100/6
Pulled-Up	Villay	11.10.3	Mr D. Scott	100/1
Pulled-Up	Game Purston	11.10.0	S. Mellor	33/1
Brought Down	Tam Kiss	10.10.13	Mr J.R. Hindley	50/1
Refused	Terossian	9.11.3	Mr P. Sloan	50/1
Refused	Rosinver Bay	9.10.5	P. Taaffe	50/1
Refused	Juan	13.10.9	Mr P.J.H. Wills	100/1

29 March 1969
Going – Good
Winner – £17,849
Time – 9mins 30 ⅘ secs
30 Ran
Favourite – Red Alligator
Top Weight – Arcturus
Winner trained by Toby Balding at Weyhill, Hampshire
Winner owned by Mr T.H. McCoy jnr and Mr C.F.W. Burns
Highland Wedding, brown gelding by Question – Princess.

Eddie Harty made a decisive move at the Canal Turn, sending Highland Wedding into the lead and, with the Balding horse jumping and galloping with power and purpose, the remainder had to fight hard to even stay with him. Jumping the fences down the back, Highland Wedding galloped on confidently, the white star on his head shining out distinctively, while in behind, Steel Bridge, Rondetto, The Beeches and the fast-improving, tall figure of Bassnet tried to catch him. Ridden strongly by Josh Gifford, Bassnet appeared the likeliest danger to Highland Wedding yet, crossing the Melling Road and turning back on to the racecourse, he emptied alarmingly, and with the attractive grey The Beeches unable to quicken, Highland Wedding set about fending off his two remaining challengers, Steel Bridge and Rondetto.

Rondetto would have been a hugely popular winner of the National but, by the final fence, he was under heavy pressure to stay in contention as Jeff King asked the old warrior for one final effort. Try as he might, Rondetto had to give way as the noseband-wearing Steel Bridge came again to pose the biggest threat to Highland Wedding.

Kicked into the final fence by Pitman, it at first looked as though Steel Bridge would make a real race of the finish as he challenged on the outside of the leader. But Highland Wedding was a big, powerful horse with perhaps more stamina than any other in the race and, on the long run to the line, he asserted his authority, despite both Steel Bridge and Rondetto fighting on defiantly. The efforts of the chasing pair were to be in vain, however, and crossing the line Highland Wedding won the National by twelve lengths from Steel Bridge, with the gallant, thirteen-year-old chestnut Rondetto finally completing the course a length away in third. Then came The Beeches, Bassnet and a long gap back to the top weight Arcturus.

Highland Wedding became the third twelve-year-old of the 1960s to win the National following the successes of Kilmore and Team Spirit, proof that some horses show enough love for the specific demands of Aintree to return year after year and perform with credit. It was the first Grand National success for both Balding and Harty. While Highland Wedding was rewarded with a well-earned retirement in Canada by his owners, American Thomas McCoy jnr and Canadian Charles Burns.

1970

GAY TRIP

Irish challenger Vulture was runner-up in 1970.

From forty-five runners in 1968 to thirty the year before, the Grand National had its smallest field since 1960 as twenty-eight went to post for the 1970 renewal. With only two runners carrying in excess of 11 stone, it was perhaps not the classiest National either, but there was a decent influx of quality and plenty of interesting newcomers to the race.

At the top of the handicap was eight-year-old Gay Trip, formerly trained in Ireland by Dan Moore (who had recently sent out L'Escargot to win the Gold Cup) but now under the care of Fred Rimell, carrying the blue crossbelts of owner Mr Tony Chambers. At barely sixteen hands, Gay Trip was not as eyecatching an individual as the well-built ESB or the deeply attractive grey Nicolaus Silver, Rimell's previous National winners, but he was a tidy bay with spring-like jumping and speed to win over shorter distances. Indeed, the horse had never run over more than two-and-a-half miles. Gay Trip had been badly injured in the 1968 Mackeson Gold Cup at Cheltenham, requiring the next season off, but he had come back to form in the current campaign, winning the Mackeson and finishing sixth in the Gold Cup. Normally ridden by Terry Biddlecombe, an injury to that jockey allowed Pat Taaffe to come in for his final Grand National mount. At forty, Taaffe was the oldest professional rider in the race, yet his booking had come at the recommendation of Biddlecombe. As well as Gay Trip, Rimell sent the soft-ground-loving French Excuse to Aintree. The horse had won a Welsh Grand National and was actually more strongly fancied than Gay Trip, starting at 100/8.

There were few in the field with quality Grand National form but, as well as The Beeches, fourth in 1969, the veterans of seven Grand Nationals between them, Red Alligator and Rondetto, returned to Aintree. Rondetto was fourteen now, and his price of 22/1 seemed more to do with his huge army of followers, but Red Alligator had been in splendid recent form, winning three chases and finishing in the frame in three others.

Eddie Harty had a fair chance of another success aboard Dozo, and Vulture, a half-brother to Gay Trip, was considered the pick of the Irish, while Josh Gifford

was to have his last ever ride before taking over the Findon stables of Captain Ryan Price, partnering the chestnut Assad. The favourite was Two Springs ridden by Roy Edwards, the horse having enjoyed a consistent season, performing staunchly at courses such as Chepstow and Haydock Park.

As the race got underway on good ground, it was Gifford aboard Assad that led to the first, followed closely by Two Springs and the Irish raiders Miss Hunter and Vulture. Perry Hill's fall brought down Queen's Guide, but the other twenty-six survived intact. The first fence, Becher's, the Canal Turn and even the Foinavon fence had been the scenes of big pile-ups or large numbers of casualties in previous Nationals and, in 1970, the chief hazard was to prove the third fence. With an opening ditch as gaping as The Chair, the fence is an early indicator as to whether horses have the necessary stomach for the National and is a legitimate jumping test. Two Springs was first to capsize at the obstacle, with Rondetto and The Beeches also succumbing. Eight horses in total came to grief, including Racoon, who tragically broke his neck. In addition, Dessie Hughes' mount Persian Helen refused the fourth having been frightened by the incidents at the previous fence.

There was no respite in the action: French Excuse fell at the Canal Turn and the Bob Turnell-trained Bowgeeno went at the tenth, followed a fence later by the 1968 winner Red Alligator. It was a much-depleted field that returned to the racecourse, with Miss Hunter and Assad leading just eleven others.

Villay, ridden by his owner Mr Derek Scott, had proudly jumped to the front and led the field as they ran down towards Becher's for a second time. Villay was first over the daunting fence, with Gay Trip travelling imperiously well on his outside jumping Becher's with grace and perfection. Behind them, The Otter crashed heavily, bringing down the unlucky Specify in the process. Specify had been creeping into contention for jockey John Cook and was the hard-luck story of the race. The Fossa refused Becher's at the inside corner of the fence, and No Justice also refused further back. This left a band of eight to contest the remainder of the race.

Villay still led jumping Valentines, followed by Miss Hunter, Vulture, Gay Trip, Dozo, Ginger Nut, Assad and Mr Edward Courage's horse Pride Of Kentucky. The eight were grouped close enough together to suggest any of them could win, yet Vulture, Dozo and, in particular, Gay Trip appeared to travelling best.

With Villay a faller four from home, an exciting finish looked set to ensue and, by two out, Taaffe sent Gay Trip into the lead; his jumping looked glorious. Behind him, Gay Trip's closest rivals were faltering. Vulture suddenly came under pressure and Dozo began to get very tired. Displaying the class of a top weight, Gay Trip went clear after the last and, kept on strongly by Taaffe at the elbow, the horse went on to win very comfortably by twenty lengths. Vulture followed him home with another Irish runner, Miss Hunter, filling third ahead of the exhausted Dozo. On his final ride before starting out as a trainer, Josh Gifford guided Assad home safely, the last of seven to complete.

Pat Taaffe's final Grand National could not have gone any better, as Gay Trip jumped beautifully the entire way (after pitching on landing at the first), and was an excellent winner of the race. A third Grand National emphasised the expertise of Rimell in preparing horses for Aintree, while Gay Trip's win was also a third success for his sire Vulgan, who had also been responsible for Team Spirit in 1964 and Foinavon in 1967.

1970 GRAND NATIONAL RESULT

FATE	HORSE	AGE/WEIGHT	JOCKEY	ODDS
1st	GAY TRIP	8.11.5	P. TAAFFE	15/1
2nd	VULTURE	8.10.0	S. BARKER	15/1
3rd	MISS HUNTER	9.10.0	F. SHORTT	33/1
4th	DOZO	9.10.4	E.P. HARTY	100/8
5th	Ginger Nut	8.10.0	J. Bourke	28/1
6th	Pride Of Kentucky	8.10.0	J. Buckingham	13/1
7th	Assad	10.10.1	J. Gifford	28/1
Fell	Bowgeeno	10.10.13	J. Haine	22/1
Fell	Red Alligator	11.10.12	B. Fletcher	13/1
Fell	Two Springs	8.10.7	R. Edwards	13/2
Fell	Fort Ord	10.10.5	A. Turnell	50/1
Fell	French Excuse	8.10.2	K.B. White	100/8
Fell	The Otter	9.10.1	T.M. Jones	20/1
Fell	All Glory	9.10.0	A.L.T. Moore	50/1
Fell	The Beeches	10.10.0	S. Mellor	22/1
Fell	On The Move	8.10.1	G. Dartnall	100/1
Fell	Perry Hill	11.10.0	P. Kelleway	28/1
Fell	Racoon	8.10.3	D. Mould	33/1
Fell	Villay	12.10.0	Mr D. Scott	100/1
Brought Down	Specify	8.10.7	J. Cook	100/7
Brought Down	Battledore	9.10.5	T.S. Murphy	25/1
Brought Down	Permit	7.10.3	P. Buckley	35/1
Brought Down	Queen's Guide	9.10.0	Mr G. Wade	40/1
Unseated Rider	Rondetto	14.10.5	J. King	22/1
Unseated Rider	Game Purston	12.11.5	Mr M.C. Lloyd	100/1
Refused	The Fossa	13.10.0	G.W. Robinson	50/1
Refused	No Justice	9.10.0	J. Guest	50/1
Refused	Persian Helen	7.10.0	D.T. Hughes	35/1

4 April 1970
Going – Good
Winner – £14,804
Time – 9mins 38secs
28 Ran
Favourite – Two Springs
Top Weight – Gay Trip
Winner trained by Fred Rimell at Kinnersley, Worcestershire
Winner owned by Mr A.J. Chambers
Gay Trip, bay gelding by Vulgan – Turkish Tourist.

Eventual winner Gay Trip (2) follows The Otter (13) over the water jump.

1971

SPECIFY

Having jumped with such brilliance the year before, Gay Trip returned to Aintree for the 1971 race as favourite. Allotted top weight of 12 stone, the horse's form during the season had been patchy and he had fallen on his first run of the campaign. Despite a far stronger field than in 1970, Gay Trip had looked a superb winner the year before, and hopes were high he could become the first since Reynoldstown to record consecutive victories, this time with his regular rider Terry Biddlecombe aboard.

The high quality of the 1971 field was evident by the presence of former Gold Cup runner-up The Laird. Long envisioned as a National type, the brown ten-year-old was a top-class performer and had enjoyed a most fruitful season, winning his three most recent races at Ascot, Kempton and Cheltenham. Trained by Bob Turnell and ridden, as ever, by Jeff King, The Laird was owned by Mr Jim Joel, a man who craved a first National success despite a heavy weight burden, The Laird was considered to have a fine chance. The Laird was joined in the field by stablemate Charter Flight, a winner over the big fences in the Topham Trophy the year before.

Having chased home Gay Trip in 1970, Vulture and Miss Hunter formed a formidable challenge from Ireland – without a win in the race since Mr What's year. Included in their number were a cluster of interesting newcomers such as the recent Downpatrick winner King Vulgan and the talented seven-year-old Money Boat, both horses given live each-way chances. One most intriguing Irish runner was the improving young Black Secret, trained by Tom Dreaper and ridden by his son Jim, an amateur. The horse had run up a series of victories earlier in the season as he staked his Grand National claim although, probably because of his age, was generously priced at 20/1 on the day.

Recent Cheltenham Festival form was represented at Aintree by the well-backed, ultra-consistent Lord Jim, from the yard of Fulke Walwyn, while of those that had failed to complete in 1970, Two Springs was again a popular tip while The Otter's bid was backed by the extreme confidence of his stable. Specify

Specify (front right) beats Black Secret in an epic finish. Behind are Bowgeeno (on the rails) and Sandy Sprite.

had been the unlucky horse of the 1970 race, brought down at the second Becher's when going well. Although his recent form was poor, he was a former Cheltenham Festival winner (Mildmay of Flete Chase) and had clearly taken to Aintree the year before. Trained by John Sutcliffe in Surrey, the horse's intriguing run in 1970 was largely unconsidered by punters, as he was allowed to start at 28/1.

The anticipation was tremendous as the runners were dispatched and, thundering over the Melling Road, it was outsider Beau Bob that led the charge from Gay Buccaneer, Smooth Dealer, Flosuebarb and Limeburner. The first big shock of the race came when Gay Trip crashed out at the opening fence, as did outsider Craigbrock and, as the field raced on, it emerged that Twigairy, Brian's Best and Country Wedding had all been brought down.

The fall of Gay Trip had eliminated one major hope and another was out at the third as The Laird came down to the sound of discarded betting slips. Having swept over Becher's in the lead, Gay Buccaneer was carried extremely wide at the Canal Turn, relinquishing the lead to Miss Hunter, with Smooth Dealer too showing well, but more high-profile casualties were imminent as The Otter and Lord Jim bit the dust at fences ten and eleven respectively. The falls of those two meant the first four in the betting were now out of the race.

Miss Hunter held her advantage until The Chair, but there she misjudged her jump, taking off too early and paying the price. With the Irish mare failing to negotiate the beast of a fence, the white-faced chestnut Astbury was left in front, and he was soon joined by Beau Bob. Together they led the field out for a second circuit, tracked by The Inventor, John Buckingham's mount Limeburner and another mare, the chestnut Sandy Sprite.

Running down to Becher's again, Beau Bob struck the front, jumping boldly for jockey Richard Dennard. But the most famous of fences was to prove calamitous for the partnership as, having jumped it well, Beau Bob pecked slightly on landing, causing Dennard's saddle to slip. As the horse hurtled forward to the next fence, Dennard was unseated in the most frustrating fashion. In behind, Money Boat hit the deck as the fancied horses continued to fall by the wayside.

By the Canal Turn, ten horses had come clear of the rest, with the outsider Limeburner and the Welsh Grand National runner-up Sandy Sprite leading the way. Black Secret was going strongly, having survived a blunder at the Foinavon fence, then came Astbury, The Inventor, Bowgeeno, Specify, Regimental, Two Springs and Vichysoise.

Seven-year-old Sandy Sprite was travelling well for Ron Barry and, at the second last, looked the likely winner. Limeburner fell dramatically on the outside of the leaders when challenging, crumbling awkwardly and interfering with Astbury as he did so, but there were others left to challenge Sandy Sprite. Although Two Springs had run his race by the last, five horses stood a fine chance of winning. The mare touched down in front but was being chased relentlessly by Black Secret and Bowgeeno, with Astbury on the outside and Specify beginning a run up the inner.

At the elbow, the brave leader was engulfed cruelly and, in a scintillating finish (one of the finest ever witnessed at Aintree), John Cook rallied Specify, charging the horse through against the rails. At the death, the horse was able to hold the late thrust of Black Secret by a neck, emerging victorious from a classic, five-horse battle.

For Cook it was victory in his third National ride and for Sutcliffe a gigantic training achievement. Based in Epsom, Sutcliffe's team comprised just eight jumpers, yet Grand National glory was preceded by victory in the season's richest handicap Hurdle, the Schweppes Gold Trophy. Specify had been purchased for £13,000 by owner Mr Fred Pontin following a win at Windsor the season before, and the horse had made up for his unlucky run in the 1970 National by winning a thriller on this occasion.

Having been swamped in the closing stages and then gently eased home by Barry to finish fifth, the unlucky horse of the 1971 race was Sandy Sprite. Looking like becoming the first mare to win since Nickel Coin, it was later revealed she had broken down in the latter stages and it was only sheer bravery that had seen her finish. Her trainer John Edwards and jockey Barry were left pondering what may have been. For the connections of Specify, the celebrations could begin having secured their place in Grand National history.

1971 GRAND NATIONAL RESULT

FATE	HORSE	AGE/WEIGHT	JOCKEY	ODDS
1st	SPECIFY	9.10.13	J. COOK	28/1
2nd	BLACK SECRET	7.11.5	MR J. DREAPER	20/1
3rd	ASTBURY	8.10.0	J. BOURKE	33/1
4th	BOWGEENO	11.10.5	G. THORNER	66/1
5th	Sandy Sprite	7.10.3	R. Barry	33/1
6th	Two Springs	9.11.4	R. Edwards	13/1
7th	Vichysoise	9.10.3	P. Blacker	100/1
8th	King Vulgan	10.11.0	J. Crowley	16/1
9th	Regimental	8.10.6	Mr J. Lawrence	66/1
10th	Gay Buccaneer	10.10.0	P. Black	66/1
11th	Final Move	11.10.0	T. Stack	66/1
12th	Limeburner	10.10.0	J. Buckingham (remounted)	100/1
13th	Common Entrance	10.10.0	Mr M. Morris (remounted)	100/1
Fell	Gay Trip	9.12.0	T.W. Biddlecombe	8/1
Fell	The Laird	10.11.12	J. King	12/1
Fell	Cnoc Dubh	8.10.11	T. Carberry	20/1
Fell	Lord Jim	10.10.9	S. Mellor	9/1
Fell	Money Boat	7.10.7	R. Coonan	16/1
Fell	Soldo	10.10.7	D. Mould	66/1
Fell	The Otter	10.10.1	T.M. Jones	12/1
Fell	Copperless	10.10.1	M. Gibson	100/1
Fell	Craigbrock	12.10.1	P. Ennis	80/1
Fell	Indamelia	8.10.5	Mr P. Hobbs	100/1
Fell	Kellsboro' Wood	11.10.0	A. Turnell	100/1
Fell	Miss Hunter	10.10.0	Mr J. Fowler	33/1
Fell	Vulture	9.10.0	S. Barker	16/1
Fell	Zara's Grove	8.10.0	G. Holmes	66/1
Pulled-Up	Charter Flight	9.11.8	W. Rees	25/1
Pulled-Up	Flosuebarb	11.10.1	J. Guest	33/1
Pulled-Up	Highworth	12.10.5	Mr R.H. Woodhouse	100/1
Brought Down	Brian's Best	11.10.11	R. Evans	33/1
Brought Down	Twigairy	8.10.6	E.P. Harty	25/1
Brought Down	Country Wedding	9.10.0	R. Champion	50/1
Brought Down	Pride Of Kentucky	9.10.0	A. Mawson	50/1
Unseated Rider	Beau Bob	8.10.3	R. Dennard	40/1
Refused	The Inventor	10.10.7	B. Fletcher	20/1
Refused	Battledore	10.10.6	J. Enright	45/1
Refused	Smooth Dealer	9.10.3	A.L.T. Moore	33/1

3 April 1971
Going – Good
Winner – £15,500
Time – 9mins 34 1/5 secs
38 Ran
Favourite – Gay Trip

Top Weight – Gay Trip
Winner trained by John Sutcliffe at Epsom, Surrey
Winner owned by Mr F.W. Pontin
Specify, brown gelding by Specific – Ora Lamae.

1972

WELL TO DO

Since the announcement in 1965 that Mrs Topham intended to sell Aintree racecourse to property developers, the future of the Grand National had remained unresolved and apparently doomed. Although there was a ray of light in 1972 when the race received official commercial sponsorship for the first time since 1963, through BP Limited, the threat that the 1972 race would be the 'last' lingered, though the annual warning had now grown tiresome and almost tedious. Though the reality was that the great race was hanging by a thread, punters elected to focus their attention on the intriguing bounty of equine contestants for the 1972 renewal, an edition that promised a fine spectacle if the quality of the field was anything to go by.

Topping the handicap on 12 stone was the dual Cheltenham Gold Cup (1970, 1971) winner L'Escargot, a great Irish horse from the yard of Dan Moore. Hugely popular, full of class, a splendid jumper and with a history of competing against the best, the blinkered chestnut attracted huge interest on his first attempt at National glory, and was only the third Gold Cup winner of the last fifteen years to compete in the race. Indeed, having finished fourth in the most recent Gold Cup, L'Escargot's chance in the National seemed far stronger than that of Kerstin and Pas Seul in previous renewals, and at the ideal age of nine, the horse held every chance of fulfilling the dream of his owner (Mr Raymond Guest) of winning the race. L'Escargot was backed accordingly, and with his favoured soft ground present, he started the 17/2 favourite.

Returning to the scene of their epic duel of 1971 were Specify and Black Secret, as well as the third from that race, Astbury, and the 1970 winner Gay Trip. Having again fared disappointingly during the season, it was accepted that Specify now reserved his best for Aintree and, although his place in the betting was just outside that of the market leaders, Black Secret was well fancied to go one better than in 1971, and was one of ten Irish horses competing. Gay Trip had won another Mackeson Gold Cup during the season, had finished eighth in the Cheltenham Gold Cup and was again a most popular selection on the day.

Consistent chasers Fortina's Palace and Cloudsmere had their followers, as did the Eider Chase winner Fair Vulgan, while both Cardinal Error and Well To Do attracted plenty of support. Cardinal Error was a first Grand National ride for the blossoming talent of young John Francome, and the horse was noted as a very good jumper, having won four times on the road to Aintree. A strong-staying chestnut, Well To Do was bred by Mrs H. Lloyd Thomas, whose husband Hugh had owned the 1937 National winner Royal Mail. Well To Do was trained by Tim Forster and ridden by reigning Champion Jockey Graham Thorner, and the horse had enjoyed a steady season, winning once, but was running well enough to encourage a late surge of money, hacking his odds from 33/1 to 14/1.

A piercing Merseyside wind was accompanied by lashings of rain as the field of forty-two prepared for the start under drab, grey skies. From the off, it was Macer Gifford aboard Fair Vulgan that struck the front instantly and was the first to rise at the opening fence. The well-backed Gyleburn was a faller at the first, as was Saggart's Choice, the mount of Tommy Stack.

Two fences later, and favourite backers were cursing their luck asL'Escargot was knocked over in a typical twist of Grand National fate, while Cardinal Error, joint second in the betting, was so badly baulked that Francome soon pulled the horse up. With a bunch of the leading contenders already down and out, Fair Vulgan surged on towards Becher's, closely patrolled by Miss Hunter, General Symons, Astbury and Specify. Taking the sixth, Swan-Shot, Beau Parc and Lisnaree all came down as the most famous of hazards took its toll.

Some of the finest horsemen of the twentieth century. From left to right: Bob Davies, Terry Biddlecombe, Stan Mellor, Fred Rimell, Bryan Marshall, Graham Thorner, Jack Dowdeswell, Fred Winter, John Francome and Tim Brookshaw.

Above: Captain Tim Forster trained Well To Do.

Right: Well To Do (right) jumps the last fence with General Symons (25) and Gay Trip (hidden). Just behind is Black Secret.

Tenth the year before, Gay Buccaneer had fallen during the first circuit and, having cleared The Chair, the horse was running loose. Jumping the water, the riderless horse caused problems for the leader Fair Vulgan, interfering with him badly. Still in the lead but rattled, Fair Vulgan led on, but by the eighteenth his challenge had faltered badly and waiting to pounce were an abundance of contenders. Miss Hunter, Bright Willow, Black Secret, General Symons, Astbury, Rough Silk, Specify and Gay Trip were all right in contention on the second circuit, along with Well To Do, taken down the inside route by Thorner.

Rekindling Irish hopes still smarting from L'Escargot's premature departure, Black Secret hit the front at the second Becher's, once again relishing the challenge of the National, with his old adversary Specify again well positioned and four others – Gay Trip, Well To Do, Astbury and General Symons – going really well. The action was intensifying all the time, but as Black Secret took

Valentines, Astbury and Specify began to crack, and the race developed into a four-horse contest.

The outsider of the four gunning for glory, the chestnut General Symons landed in front two from home, his big, white face touching down ahead of Gay Trip, who had travelled down the outside for much of the way. Black Secret now came under extreme pressure to stay in touch, but it was Well To Do that was travelling best on the inside and, jumping the last, Thorner sent the rich chestnut clear.

Terry Biddlecombe had not given up on former winner Gay Trip and, passing General Symons, he rallied his horse for one last charge, coming on the stands side in search of better ground. Past the elbow, Gay Trip made his presence felt, but Well To Do was rugged and determined and, despite wavering slightly on the run-in, was in receipt of 22lbs. Sticking to the inside rails, he stayed on the stronger to win a fantastic race by two lengths from Gay Trip. Three lengths further back, Black Secret and General Symons flashed past the post, with a dead heat announced for third, with Astbury next followed by Specify, who despite not being able to stay with the leaders in the closing stages, had again run a fine race in the National.

It was a deeply personal victory for Tim Forster. The trainer had been bequeathed the horse in the will of the late Mrs Heather Sumner, who had bought him as a three-year-old, and Forster had endured a constant battle in his own mind as to whether to risk Well To Do at Aintree. Mrs Sumner had always desired a Grand National winner, yet even after the horse's final outing at Ludlow Forster was having his doubts. However, a late decision was made to send Well To Do to Aintree, and his Grand National victory was a most emotional one for all concerned. Well To Do never ran in the Grand National again, yet his win continued a remarkable pattern, as he was related to previous National winners Gregalach, Reynoldstown and Royal Mail.

1972 GRAND NATIONAL RESULT

1st	WELL TO DO	9.10.1	G. THORNER	14/1
2nd	GAY TRIP	10.11.9	T.W. BIDDLECOMBE	12/1
3rd =	BLACK SECRET	8.11.2	S. BARKER	14/1
3rd =	GENERAL SYMONS	9.10.0	P. KIELY	40/1
5th	Astbury	9.10.0	J. Bourke	25/1
6th	Specify	10.10.11	B. Brogan	22/1
7th	Bright Willow	11.10.1	W. Smith	28/1
8th	Money Boat	8.10.3	F. Berry	16/1
9th	Rough Silk	9.10.6	D. Nicholson	25/1
Fell	Fortina's Palace	9.10.7	J. King	16/1
Fell	The Pantheon	9.10.4	K.B. White	33/1
Fell	Swan-Shot	9.10.3	P. McCarron	33/1
Fell	Gyleburn	9.10.4	R. Barry	20/1
Fell	Saggart's Choice	9.10.1	T. Stack	28/1
Fell	Cloudsmere	8.10.4	D. Mould	18/1
Fell	Kellsboro' Wood	12.10.0	A. Turnell	100/1
Fell	Permit	9.10.0	R.R. Evans	100/1
Fell	Lime Street	8.10.1	R. Pitman	25/1
Fell	Just A Gamble	10.10.1	P. Buckley	100/1
Fell	Lisnaree	9.10.0	Mr F. Turner	100/1
Fell	Nom De Guerre	10.10.0	J. Haine	33/1
Fell	Gay Buccaneer	11.10.0	T. Hyde	33/1
Fell	The Otter	11.10.0	T.M. Jones	25/1
Fell	The Pooka	10.10.5	Mr C. Ross	50/1
Fell	Fair Vulgan	8.10.0	M. C. Gifford	14/1
Fell	Beau Parc	9.11.2	Mr A. Nicholson	50/1

FATE	HORSE	AGE/WEIGHT	JOCKEY	ODDS
Fell	Country Wedding	10.10.4	R. Champion	50/1
Pulled-Up	Rigton Prince	11.10.9	J. Enright	25/1
Pulled-Up	Twigairy	9.10.9	T.G. Davies	28/1
Pulled-Up	Pearl Of Montreal	9.10.4	R. Coonan	55/1
Pulled-Up	Deblin's Green	9.10.0	D. Cartwright	33/1
Pulled-Up	Nephin Beg	10.10.0	P. Morris	100/1
Pulled-Up	Miss Hunter	11.10.0	A.L.T. Moore	50/1
Pulled-Up	Even Delight	7.10.2	R. Dennard	40/1
Pulled-Up	Limeburner	11.10.0	W. Rees	100/1
Brought Down	Alaska Fort	7.10.13	H.R. Beasley	33/1
Refused	The Inventor	11.10.2	W. Shoemark	33/1
Refused	Cardinal Error	8.10.4	J. Francome	12/1
Refused	Vichysoise	10.10.3	P. Blacker	100/1
Refused	Bullocks Horn	9.10.0	Mr R. Smith	28/1
Refused	Vulture	10.10.2	P. Brogan	100/1
Knocked Over	L'Escargot	9.12.0	T. Carberry	17/2

8 April 1972
Going – Soft
Sponsor – BP Limited
Winner – £25,765
Time – 10mins 8secs
42 Ran
Favourite – L'Escargot
Top Weight – L'Escargot
Winner trained by Captain Tim Forster at Letcombe Bassett, Berkshire
Winner owned by Captain Tim Forster
Well To Do, chestnut gelding by Phebus – Princess Puzzlement.

1973

RED RUM

It is often the case in sport that the victorious are thrust into the spotlight, justifiably receiving their moments of glory. While the winners are showered with praise, the defeated are left to silently ponder what might have been, rarely given more than sympathetic recognition. This pattern is true for the Grand National, where every year a jubilant hero is led in by a swirl of cheering onlookers while all around beaten horses are returned to those associated with them, largely cast aside in the wake of another's triumph. However, the remarkable Grand National of 1973 is proof that, while winners will always be celebrated and ultimately remembered, those conquered should never be forgotten.

It had been announced by Mrs Topham shortly before the 1973 Grand National that she had reached an agreement for the sale of the racecourse and, although she stated she hoped the race would continue at Aintree, it was made clear that the 1973 renewal would be the last staged under her name. As if to prove categorically that the great race belonged at Aintree, a galaxy of star chasers graced the field in 1973, among them some of the finest horses ever to run in the National.

Having been bred in Australia by his owner Sir Chester Manifold, the ten-year-old Crisp had arrived in England two years previously having dominated the Australian chasing scene. Placed in the yard of Fred Winter, Crisp won his English debut race at Wincanton carrying the maximum 12st 7lbs in an absolute canter; thrilling Winter who soon realised the horse was something special. Over the next two seasons, Crisp firmly held his place among the best in the most dominant yard in the land, a yard that included such mighty horses as Champion Hurdlers Bula and Lanzarote and the magnificent chaser Pendil. Crisp won a Champion Chase at Cheltenham and was favourite for a Gold Cup, yet disappointed in the latter race only because of holding-up tactics that he despised. Nearly seventeen hands high, Crisp was a most imposing horse that loved to front run and both Winter and jockey Richard Pitman believed he was ideal for Aintree, where his jumping was expected to be a huge advantage. There

Crisp and jockey Richard Pitman.

were slight doubts surrounding his stamina, as well as the joint top weight of 12 stone he was allotted, yet this failed to deter punters, who sent the horse off 9/1 joint favourite.

Representing the form of the 1972 race were Black Secret and General Symons, while L'Escargot had escaped none the worse for his mishap the year before, having recently finished fourth in the Gold Cup, and had plenty of support despite being joint-top weight. Holding prominent positions in the betting market were newcomers Ashville and Princess Camilla. Ashville, trained in Newmarket by Tom Jones, had finished second in the National Hunt handicap Chase at the Cheltenham Festival, while the dour stayer Princess Camilla had won three times during the season, including over four miles at Warwick.

Adding a real touch of class to the race were Spanish Steps and Grey Sombrero. Owned and trained by Mr Edward Courage, Spanish Steps (whose dam was the fine Grand National mare Tiberetta) had won the 1969 Hennessy Gold Cup, been placed in a Cheltenham Gold Cup and was one of the most popular and consistent chasers in training, while the David Gandolfo-trained Grey Sombrero was expected to love the fast ground at Aintree in 1973, and was a horse that had previously won a Whitbread Gold Cup and a Midlands National.

But, unbeknown at the time, the most significant runner in the 1973 Grand National field was a horse trained closest to the course. Local trainer Donald 'Ginger' McCain had two prospects for the race, one of which was the white-faced Glenkiln, a winner over the big fences at Aintree's October meeting. But it was stablemate Red Rum that most captured the public attention. The eight-year-old had been laid out for the National and had won five consecutive races earlier in the season. Then given a winter break, Red Rum progressed significantly in three runs prior to Aintree to earn a share of favouritism with Crisp. Red Rum's partner in the National was Brian Fletcher, successful in the race five years previously.

Charging over the Melling Road, the thirty-eight runners made their way to the first fence. With a plan to bowl along in front, yet with sensible restraint, Crisp and Richard Pitman set off down the inside and, despite making a slight mistake at the first, were soon into a rhythm. In behind, 50/1 shot Richeleau suffered the first fall of his life, while at the third jockey Jeff King failed to survive the obstacle for the third time in four years as Ashville fell.

With Crisp already in control, Becher's Brook proved the downfall of outsiders Culla Hill, Beggar's Way and Mr Vimy. Jumping the Canal Turn and Valentines, Crisp set off down the back as if he had jumped Aintree a dozen times as Pitman gave up the plan to restrain Crisp and simply let the horse attack. The result was spectacular, with Crisp widening his advantage at every fence, with a series of fast, accurate leaps that were simply breathtaking.

Crisp held a lead of twenty lengths jumping The Chair, where he pecked briefly, but was at the water before the next horse had jumped the fifteenth. Jumping The Chair in second and clear of the pack himself, Grey Sombrero was about to suffer a terrible injury. Attacking the fence boldly, the grey landed awkwardly and appeared to stumble clumsily for a number of strides before capsizing. Although rising gingerly to his feet, the gallant horse had broken a shoulder and was later put down. This tragic twist left Crisp even further in front, as Glenkiln and Proud Percy also fell at The Chair and, heading out for the second circuit, Crisp was a huge distance clear of the chasing pack, led by Endless Folly, Red Rum, Rouge Autumn and Sunny Lad.

Crisp may have been a mere speck on the horizon, but Red Rum took the initiative, shaking off the pack at the big ditch. While Crisp flew Becher's and continued his exhibition of jumping over the Canal Turn and Valentines, Red Rum was beginning his move forward and had broken clear himself from Spanish Steps, Hurricane Rock, Rouge Autumn, Black Secret and Great Noise, yet had plenty to do to get anywhere near Crisp.

It had been so easy for Crisp, who had jumped with as much fluency and sense of style and purpose as any Grand National runner before him, literally toying with the giant fences. The horse had barely seen another in the race and, even rounding the turn for home and approaching two out, it seemed impossible for Crisp to be beaten. However, Crisp slowed going to the last, the first signs that he was beginning to tire, and once on the flat the picture changed instantly. Wandering out to his left, it appeared Crisp had suddenly reached his limit, and from striding along with such power, he now had to be cajoled, almost wrestled by Pitman to stay straight, and for one awful moment it seemed he would head, like a shattered athlete, straight for the bordered-off Chair.

Like a shark sensing blood, Red Rum was sent vigorously after the leader by Fletcher, eating into Crisp's lead all the time, yet even at the elbow a victory for Crisp looked possible. It was heartbreaking to watch, but as the big Australian horse began to shorten his stride, almost falling against the rails and clearly with nothing left yet desperately wanting to give more, Red Rum, coming down the centre of the track, cut him down and, giving 23lbs, Crisp could not hold him off. Getting up in the dying strides, Red Rum beat Crisp by three-quarters-of-a-length in one of the most enthralling of all Grand National finishes. The pair had basically been the only two in the race and, though he stayed on well, L'Escargot

Crisp (right) is overhauled at the death by Red Rum.

Red Rum and jockey Brian Fletcher are led back in.

1973 GRAND NATIONAL RESULT

FATE	HORSE	AGE/WEIGHT	JOCKEY	ODDS
1st	RED RUM	8.10.5	B. FLETCHER	9/1
2nd	CRISP	10.12.0	R. PITMAN	9/1
3rd	L'ESCARGOT	10.12.0	T. CARBERRY	11/1
4th	SPANISH STEPS	10.11.13	P. BLACKER	16/1
5th	Rouge Autumn	9.10.0	K.B. White	40/1
6th	Hurricane Rock	9.10.0	R. Champion	100/1
7th	Proud Tarquin	10.10.11	Lord Oaksey	22/1
8th	Prophecy	10.10.3	B.R. Davies	20/1
9th	Endless Folly	11.10.0	J. Guest	100/1
10th	Black Secret	9.11.2	S. Barker	22/1
11th	Petruchio's Son	10.10.5	D. Mould	50/1
12th	The Pooka	11.10.0	A.L.T. Moore	100/1
13th	Great Noise	9.10.2	D. Cartwright	50/1
14th	Green Plover	13.10.0	Mr M. Morris	100/1
15th	Sunny Lad	9.10.3	W. Smith	25/1
16th	Go-Pontinental	13.10.4	J. McNaught	100/1
17th	Mill Door	11.10.5	P. Cullis	100/1
Fell	Grey Sombrero	9.10.9	W. Shoemark	25/1
Fell	Glenkiln	10.10.7	J.J. O'Neill	33/1
Fell	Beggar's Way	9.10.1	T. Kinane	33/1
Fell	Ashville	8.10.4	J. King	14/1
Fell	Tarquin Bid	9.10.0	J. Bracken	100/1
Fell	Richeleau	9.10.0	N. Kernick	50/1
Fell	Fortune Bay II	9.10.3	Mr G. Sloan	66/1
Fell	Charley Winking	8.10.0	Mr D. Scott	100/1
Fell	Proud Percy	10.10.0	R.R. Evans	100/1
Fell	Culla Hill	9.10.7	Mr N. Brookes	100/1
Pulled-Up	General Symons	10.10.0	P. Kiely	33/1
Pulled-Up	Highland Seal	10.10.6	D. Nicholson	20/1
Pulled-Up	Mr Vimy	10.10.2	J. Haine	100/1
Pulled-Up	Astbury	10.10.2	J. Bourke	50/1
Pulled-Up	Beau Parc	10.10.1	A. Turnell	100/1
Pulled-Up	Rough Silk	10.10.0	T. Norman	66/1
Pulled-Up	Rampsman	9.10.0	D. Munro	100/1
Pulled-Up	Nereo	7.10.3	Duque de Alburquerque	66/1
Brought Down	Canharis	8.10.1	P. Buckley	16/1
Refused	Swan-Shot	10.10.0	M. Blackshaw	100/1
Refused	Princess Camilla	8.10.4	R. Barry	16/1

31 March 1973
Going – Firm
Sponsor – BP Limited
Winner – £25,486
Time – 9mins 1.9secs
38 Ran
Joint Favourites – Red Rum and Crisp

Top Weights – Crisp and L'Escargot
Winner trained by Donald McCain at
   Southport, Lancashire
Winner owned by Mr N.H. Le Mare
Red Rum, bay gelding by Quorum
   – Mared.

was twenty-five lengths back in third with Spanish Steps rounding out a first four of sheer class.

The crowd erupted having seen the local horse win and huge credit went to McCain for preparing Red Rum behind his used car showroom in Birkdale. Purchased on behalf of Mr Noel le Mare in August 1972, having previously been trained by former Champion Jockey Tim Molony, it was soon discovered that Red Rum was suffering from the crippling foot disease pedalostitis. Sending Red Rum (a well-built, beautifully balanced bay who stood just over sixteen hands high) into the salty waters of Southport Beach for a cooling walk, the horse amazingly emerged sound and ready to write his name into history.

The 1973 race brought together two tremendous heroes that fought out one of the most memorable Nationals ever, the race record time set by Golden Miller in 1934 shattered by nearly nineteen seconds in the process. Defeat for Crisp was a cruel price to pay for such an incredible performance, and he is generally considered the best Grand National horse not to have won the race. Although Crisp never ran in the race again, he did gain revenge over Red Rum when beating him at level weights at Haydock the following season. For Red Rum though, his performance had been equally impressive, fighting back from an impossible-looking position, jumping with rare precision and displaying the courage to wear down Crisp. Nobody knew it then but, for Red Rum, it was merely the beginning of a legendary era.

1974

RED RUM

True to her word, Mrs Topham sold Aintree racecourse in late 1973 to property developer Bill Davies and his Walton group for £3 million. In addition to purchasing the course, Mr Davies also bought the seven-year-old chaser Wolverhampton to represent him in the big race.

Carrying a featherweight 10 stone, a rush of late money made newcomer Scout favourite, the horse having won his last three races, but it was local star Red Rum who was the focus in the build up. Perhaps unfairly, Red Rum's win in 1973 had been somewhat overshadowed by the efforts of Crisp yet, since that thrilling win, four wins and a brave second in the Hennessy Gold Cup had seen Red Rum race to the top of the Aintree handicap. Statistics showed no horse since Reynoldstown had defied 12 stone to win the National, and that was the task facing Red Rum. Chiefly for this reason, Red Rum started only third in the betting at 11/1.

There was no Crisp on this occasion, but with L'Escargot and Spanish Steps running again, Red Rum had two class horses to contend with, now giving them both weight, with L'Escargot in particularly good form having run a fine race over the inadequate trip of the Cathcart Chase at Cheltenham prior to Aintree.

Of the forty-two runners, the majority were National newcomers. Former hunter-chaser Rough House was a strong fancy, as was the 1973 Welsh Grand National winner Deblin's Green and the improving eight-year-old Straight Vulgan. Royal Relief, who together with Spanish Steps and Quintus made up a trio of representatives for Mr Edward Courage, was twice a winner of the Champion Chase at the Cheltenham Festival and was a class horse, yet had never won beyond two-and-a-half miles, The field also contained a winner of Czechoslovakia's awesome steeplechase, the Velka Pardubice, in 40/1 shot Stephen's Society.

The race was delayed briefly through a display of bucking and kicking by the mare Princess Camilla yet, once sent on their way, the field received a huge roar. Ridden by Lord Oaksey, Royal Relief's Grand National was ended instantly when

the horse came down at the first. Following Mr Courage's horse out of the race was rank outsider Go-Pontinental at the third and Marshalla Salaman's mount Sixer a fence later.

Trained by the winning jockey in 1959, Michael Scudamore, the strongly built outsider Charles Dickens, ridden by Andy Turnell, headed the field during the early stages, while next came Sunny Lad, Pearl Of Montreal, Rough Silk, Rouge Autumn and Glenkiln and, in that order, they swept over Becher's. The famous fence failed to claim any victims, but the Canal Turn proved an unlucky trap for some, as Huperade and his owner-jockey John Carden succumbed, together with Argent, Karacola and Deblin's Green. Rough House too was a faller in the hands of promising amateur John Burke as the field tore on.

Charles Dickens led the survivors back on to the racecourse and, facing up to the mighty Chair, both Red Rum and Scout were making progress and easing into contention. A loose horse, which also cut right in front of L'Escargot on the inside, gave Turnell and Charles Dickens a momentary scare. Surviving the situation, the partnership cleared the huge fence and headed out for circuit two tracked by a large number of horses, most prominent of which were the eight-year-old Vulgan Town, Rough Silk, Red Rum, Scout, L'Escargot, Pearl Of Montreal and Sunny Lad.

Straight Vulgan had begun to challenge under Ron Barry when the fancied horse came down at the eighteenth and, displacing Charles Dickens in the lead, Red Rum found himself in control going back down to Becher's, with Scout moving up on the outside, L'Escargot and Spanish Steps sticking to the inner, and Vulgan Town and Charles Dickens in the centre making up the leading bunch. Red Rum was in front sooner than jockey Brian Fletcher ideally wanted, but the horse was jumping magnificently again, making light of his huge weight burden, and the rider elected to let Red Rum take the race to the rest, allowing him to stretch out in front. Of those in behind, Spanish Steps was pulling into contention and both L'Escargot and Scout remained dangerous propositions, while Charles Dickens continued to surprise with a maintained effort.

Five fences from home, Red Rum survived a scare, clipping the fence with his back legs in what would be an extremely rare error at Aintree, his nose brushing the ground on the landing side. But the mistake failed to stop him in his tracks and, with Scout coming off the bridle and beginning to struggle after Valentines, Red Rum was going by far the best. Racing back across the Melling Road for the final time, he had L'Escargot to beat, with Spanish Steps and Charles Dickens resigned to a fight for the minor places.

Jumping the second last four lengths ahead, Red Rum began to exhibit the same finishing power that had thwarted Crisp the year before and, clearing the last, he maintained a strong gallop all the way to the line, finishing to rapturous applause and winning by seven lengths from L'Escargot. True, L'Escargot had finished a lot closer than in 1973, but Red Rum was carrying 23lbs more now and the victory was totally convincing, with the manner in which Red Rum had performed at Aintree

Red Rum jumps the last fence on his way to consecutive victories.

FATE	HORSE	AGE/WEIGHT	JOCKEY	ODDS
1st	RED RUM	9.12.0	B. FLETCHER	11/1
2nd	L'ESCARGOT	11.11.13	T. CARBERRY	17/2
3rd	CHARLES DICKENS	10.10.0	A. TURNELL	50/1
4th	SPANISH STEPS	11.11.9	W. SMITH	15/1
5th	Rough Silk	11.10.0	M. Morris	66/1
6th	Vulgan Town	8.10.8	J. Haine	35/1
7th	Rouge Autumn	10.10.0	K.B. White	28/1
8th	Nereo	8.10.6	Duque de Alburquerque	100/1
9th	San-Feliu	11.10.3	P. Buckley	22/1
10th	Norwegian Flag	8.10.0	J. Bourke	50/1
11th	Scout	8.10.0	T. Stack	7/1
12th	Quintus	8.10.0	G. Thorner	33/1
13th	Dunno	10.10.1	Mr N. Mitchell	100/1
14th	Tubs VI	11.10.6	V. O'Brien	22/1
15th	Escari	8.10.2	P. Black	66/1
16th	Sunny Lad	10.10.4	D. Cartwright	20/1
17th	Princess Camilla	9.11.4	M. Blackshaw	28/1
Fell	Royal Relief	10.11.6	Lord Oaksey	18/1
Fell	Huperade	10.10.12	Mr J. Carden	100/1
Fell	Straight Vulgan	8.10.8	R. Barry	15/1
Fell	Rough House	8.10.6	Mr J. Burke	14/1
Fell	Glenkiln	11.10.2	R. Crank	50/1
Fell	Beau Bob	11.10.0	J. Glover	100/1
Fell	Culla Hill	10.10.8	Mr N. Brookes	100/1
Fell	Estoile	10.10.0	R. Hyett	66/1
Fell	Mill Door	12.10.2	J. McNaught	100/1
Fell	Go-Pontinental	14.10.0	J. Suthern	100/1
Pulled-Up	Roman Holiday	10.10.7	J. King	66/1
Pulled-Up	Bahia Dorada	9.10.2	J. Guest	100/1
Pulled-Up	The Tunku	8.10.1	R.R. Evans	100/1
Pulled-Up	Stephen's Society	8.11.5	Mr C.D. Collins	40/1
Pulled-Up	Pearl Of Montreal	11.10.0	T. Kinane	50/1
Pulled-Up	Astbury	11.10.0	Mr W. Jenks	66/1
Pulled-Up	Wolverhampton	7.10.0	R. Quinn	25/1
Brought Down	Argent	10.11.10	R. Coonan	50/1
Brought Down	Deblin's Green	11.10.0	N. Wakley	25/1
Brought Down	Sixer	10.10.0	M. Salaman	66/1
Brought Down	Karacola	9.10.0	C. Astbury	100/1
Unseated Rider	Shaneman	9.10.2	B. Hannon	50/1
Refused	Francophile	9.10.5	R. Pitman	16/1
Refused	Beggar's Way	10.10.2	V. Soane	66/1
Carried Out	Cloudsmere	10.10.4	P. Kelleway	100/1

on this occasion suggesting he had improved again from the year before. Charles Dickens finished a surprising third ahead of Spanish Steps, the latter again running so well in a big race to confirm himself as one of the most consistent chasers of his era. Of the remainder, the colourful Spanish amateur the Duque de Alburquerque rode his Nereo into eighth, while the disappointing Scout eventually struggled home in eleventh having looked a threat at the second Becher's – much to the relief of bookmakers Ladbrokes, who stood to lose £1 million on the horse.

His winning time had been eighteen seconds slower than in 1973, yet Red Rum emphatically underlined his status as a genuine Aintree horse, becoming the first since Reynoldstown to record consecutive victories and achieving the near-impossible by shouldering 12 stone in the process. In addition, Fletcher became only the second rider of the century to record three Grand National wins, emulating the great amateur Jack Anthony. Red Rum's performance in 1974 made many realise what a brilliant horse he was, with his victory exuding dominance, and it was now hotly anticipated that the horse could win for an unprecedented third time as he rapidly earned a place in the hearts of the nation's public.

30 March 1974
Going – Good
Winner – £25,102
Time – 9mins 20.3secs
42 Ran
Favourite – Scout

Top Weight – Red Rum
Winner trained by Donald McCain at
    Southport, Lancashire
Winner owned by Mr N.H. Le Mare
Red Rum, bay gelding by Quorum
    – Mared.

1975

L'ESCARGOT

Despite the prospect of local hero Red Rum making history as the only horse ever to win three Grand Nationals, the crowd on National day was worryingly sparse. It appeared the hike in admission prices was a major factor in the low turnout. All was not going well for new owner Bill Davies who, despite reaching an agreement with the *News of the World* to sponsor the Grand National (making it the richest to date), had received blunt criticism of his Aintree leadership. As well as those concerns, the chaser Davies had in training with Ginger McCain, Wolverhampton, collapsed and died while completing his preparation for a second crack at the National the day before the big race.

Emulating the disappointing crowd, the field for the 1975 race was on the small side, with only thirty-one going to post. However, those in attendance made sure their beloved Red Rum started as one of the hottest favourites of all time at 7/2. Red Rum had topped the ante-post lists ever since his brilliant win in 1974, and it was hard to imagine the horse not winning again. Red Rum had ended the previous campaign with a fine win in the Scottish National, enhancing his reputation still further, and his form was again good heading to Aintree in 1975. In contrast to his two Nationals wins, the ground was described as 'dead' for the 1975 race, a worry for a horse that loved good, quick ground yet, despite giving weight to all his rivals, Red Rum was once more expected to dominate at Aintree.

Receiving 11lbs from Red Rum was the now twelve-year-old L'Escargot, one of the best-loved chasers of the 1970s. It would be the horse's fourth run in the National and, despite being beaten easily by Red Rum in two of those races, the ground conditions favoured the Irish horse on this occasion. Although some of the speed that made L'Escargot a dual Gold Cup winner had evaporated, the horse retained much of his ability and had already proved he could handle Aintree. As usual, L'Escargot was partnered by Tommy Carberry, a man who had already won the Irish Grand National and the Cheltenham Gold Cup during the season.

Aintree veteran Spanish Steps, twice fourth in the race, had come down the weights somewhat yet retained plenty of support, while another of the older

horses in the field was The Dikler, a giant bay from Fulke Walwyn's yard and a horse running in the National for the first time. The Dikler had suffered from injury problems during the season but was a horse of unquestionable class. He had won the 1973 Cheltenham Gold Cup, had been runner-up in the same race in 1972 and had also won the King George VI Chase in 1971 and the Whitbread Gold Cup in 1974. A hard puller during his races but a horse with tremendous courage and determination, The Dikler was partnered at Aintree by Ron Barry and was grouped at 20/1 in the betting together with Spanish Steps, the Gold Cup fourth Glanford Brigg and newcomer Clear Cut, the mount of Tommy Stack.

Having bowed out early in the 1974 National, Rough House had enjoyed a fruitful year, winning the Great Yorkshire Chase, while Royal Relief was back and again ridden by Lord Oaksey. Of the newcomers, Graham Thorner's mount Land Lark was well-fancied and the big chestnut Rag Trade was a second National ride for John Francome, while Money Market attracted a swirl of late money having won the Mildmay/Cazalet Chase at Sandown and also finished fourth in the season's Hennessy Gold Cup.

The nerves of the participants were stretched to the limit when 18/1 shot Junior Partner spread a plate before the start, delaying the race by fifteen minutes. Having endured the agonising wait, the runners were finally sent on their way, with rank outsider Zimulator leading over the first fence. Among the early casualties was Junior Partner, who crashed out at the second. Zimulator's brief moment at the head of affairs was brought to a shuddering halt when he fell at the fourth, while a fence later, Rough House found himself on the deck for the second consecutive National.

Glanford Brigg and the veteran Beau Bob were right in the mix for the lead approaching Becher's the first time, but a pair of long shots, Barona and Spittin Image, failed to negotiate the famous fence, while Andy Turnell's mount

The great Irish chaser L'Escargot won the National with jockey Tommy Carberry.

April Seventh (a horse that would win the Whitbread and Hennessy Gold Cups before 1975 ended) suffered the misfortune of being brought down. Lord Oaksey had got six fences further than in 1974, but his luck did not hold as Royal Relief came down at the smallest fence, the seventh, while at the same Foinavon obstacle, a mistake by L'Escargot saw Carberry holding on to the horse's neck to remain intact.

Glanford Brigg and jockey Martin Blackshaw had assumed control of the race and they were going strongly heading for The Chair. As the course narrows, funnelling into the fence, there is no worse place to be preceded by loose horses, yet four ran in front of Glanford Brigg and the leading bunch prior to their take-off. Fortunately the riderless horses continued on their way, jumping the fence and avoiding a pile-up while, in behind, Blackshaw steered Glanford Brigg coolly over. Behind the leaders though, tragedy struck as Land Lark died instantly having collided awkwardly in mid-flight with another runner, Glen Owen.

With High Ken taking over from Glanford Brigg at the nineteenth, the race began to take shape, with Red Rum, L'Escargot and The Dikler hunting up the leader, while Southern Quest, Beau Bob, Manicou Bay and Money Market were all travelling well. High Ken's lead soon ended with a crashing fall at the fence before Becher's, and more tragedy lay in store at the Brook when Beau Bob plummeted head-first and broke his neck in a fatal fall.

As he had the year before, Red Rum jumped to the front, but this time it was apparent that L'Escargot was going equally as well, if not better, while The Dikler's long stride and effortless jumping kept him in contention together with Spanish Steps and Southern Quest. But the leading two began to draw away again, crossing the Melling Road in a rematch of the previous year.

Although the pair jumped the last fence together, Brian Fletcher was already hard at work on Red Rum while Carberry remained ice cool aboard the Irish horse. Presented with his best chance of finally conquering his Aintree nemesis, L'Escargot seized his opportunity, scooting clear of Red Rum and passing the post a fifteen-length winner in the light-blue and brown-hooped colours of his owner, Mr Raymond Guest, becoming the first Irish winner since Mr What. Spanish Steps ran his customary fine race, taking third, with Money Market edging out The Dikler for fourth. Although his followers were initially disappointed he had been beaten, the ground was certainly not to Red Rum's liking, and he had gone down to a fine horse in L'Escargot, one of the best chasers of the 1970s. Ginger McCain was quick to announce Red Rum would be back for another Grand National in twelve months time.

L'Escargot had beaten the champion and sealed a wonderful career, fully deserving his Grand National win. Twice a Gold Cup winner, the horse had now given Mr Guest the National win he so craved, having twice won the Epsom Derby in the 1960s with Larkspur and Sir Ivor. For Carberry, it crowned a splendid individual season and for County Kildare trainer Dan Moore, the victory atoned for finishing second as a jockey aboard Royal Danieli in the 1938 National. As for the great L'Escargot, his spectacular career was now at a close, and Mr Guest gave the chestnut as a present to Moore's wife in a fine, parting gesture.

1975 GRAND NATIONAL RESULT

FATE	HORSE	AGE/WEIGHT	JOCKEY	ODDS
1st	L'ESCARGOT	12.11.3	T. CARBERRY	13/2
2nd	RED RUM	10.12.0	B. FLETCHER	7/2
3rd	SPANISH STEPS	12.10.3	W. SMITH	20/1
4th	MONEY MARKET	8.10.13	J. KING	14/1
5th	The Dikler	12.11.13	R. Barry	20/1
6th	Manicou Bay	9.10.7	R. Champion	40/1
7th	Southern Quest	8.10.6	S. Shields	33/1
8th	Glanford Brigg	9.11.4	M. Blackshaw	20/1
9th	Hally Percy	11.10.0	M.C. Gifford	66/1
10th	Rag Trade	9.10.4	J. Francome	18/1
Fell	Clear Cut	11.11.1	T. Stack	20/1
Fell	High Ken	9.11.1	B. Brogan	28/1
Fell	Royal Relief	11.11.1	Lord Oaksey	22/1
Fell	Rough House	9.10.12	J. Burke	12/1
Fell	Barona	9.10.8	P. Kelleway	40/1
Fell	Land Lark	10.10.1	G. Thorner	14/1
Fell	Zimulator	8.10.0	Capt. D. Swan	100/1
Fell	Feel Free	9.10.0	M. Salaman	66/1
Fell	Glen Owen	8.10.0	D. Atkins	22/1
Fell	Junior Partner	8.10.0	K.B. White	18/1
Fell	Beau Bob	12.10.1	J. Glover	100/1
Fell	Kilmore Boy	9.10.2	P. Blacker	40/1
Fell	Spittin Image	9.10.0	M. Cummins	50/1
Pulled-Up	Even Dawn	8.10.4	D. Mould	50/1
Pulled-Up	Shaneman	10.10.8	Mr P. Greenall	100/1
Pulled-Up	Ballyath	9.10.0	J. Bourke	100/1
Brought Down	April Seventh	9.11.0	A. Turnell	28/1
Brought Down	Tudor View	9.10.0	G. McNally	100/1
Unseated Rider	Ballyrichard Again	10.10.1	A. Webber	40/1
Refused	Castleruddery	9.10.4	Mr T. Walsh	33/1
Refused	Rough Silk	12.10.8	Mr L. Urbano	28/1

5 April 1975
Going – Good
Sponsor – *The News Of The World*
Winner – £38,005
Time – 9mins 31.1secs
31 Ran
Favourite – Red Rum
Top Weight – Red Rum
Winner trained by Dan Moore at The Curragh, County Kildare, Ireland
Winner owned by Mr R.R. Guest
L'Escargot, chestnut gelding by Escart III – What A Daisy.

1976

RAG TRADE

In December 1975 Mr Davies, struggling to progress Aintree beyond its current flagging state, signed an agreement with Ladbrokes for the bookmakers to manage the course until 1978, after the Jockey Club had threatened to move the race to Doncaster. Almost instantly, Ladbrokes breathed fresh life into the racecourse, successfully restoring a large amount of enthusiasm for the Grand National through a series of innovations. One of the key areas management concentrated on was a larger focus on jump racing, limiting the amount of Flat races run at the National meeting. It was a credit to Ladbrokes that the Grand National crowd in 1976 was one of the biggest for years and a huge improvement over the disappointing attendance of 1975.

With three sterling efforts in the Grand National behind him, Red Rum again captured the public imagination. Top weight again, this time with 11st 10lbs, Red Rum returned to Aintree offering only marginal form and was without a win for fourteen months. He was, however, now considered the ultimate Aintree specialist and had firm ground to enhance his chance. Following a disagreement between Ginger McCain and Brian Fletcher earlier in the season, Red Rum had a new jockey in the form of Irishman and reigning Champion Jockey Tommy Stack, who had followed Red Rum home aboard the favourite Scout in 1974.

Red Rum had been favourite until a big gamble on the ten-year-old Barona saw the latter top the market at 7/1. A winner of the previous year's Scottish Grand National, Barona had fallen at the first Becher's in 1975, yet trainer Roddy Armytage had focused the horse's season on a return to Aintree. Stamina-rich and with a strong jockey in Paul Kelleway in the saddle, Barona had improved steadily through the season, with a fine performance behind the subsequent Gold Cup winner Royal Frolic at Haydock highlighting his Grand National chance.

When Rag Trade, then trained by Arthur Pitt, had jumped round Aintree to finish last of ten in the 1975 National, jockey John Francome had indicated the horse to be a most uncomfortable ride and declined to ride him again. A big, heavy chestnut, Rag Trade indeed could be difficult, but the horse had gone on

to land some decent prizes since that National. The horse (bred in Ireland by Ian Williams, whose father Evan had won the 1937 National on Royal Mail) had displayed fine stamina when winning both the Midlands National and the Welsh Grand National and was well backed at Aintree. Trained by Fred Rimell, Rag Trade and young John Burke had developed a promising partnership at Chepstow, and the jockey was again on board at Aintree.

Spanish Steps, Money Market and The Dikler were back having run well the year before, while newcomers Jolly's Clump, Tregarron and Prolan held prominent positions in the betting market. Both the Ian Watkinson-ridden Jolly's Clump and the nine-year-old Tregarron had been in prolific recent winning form, while the attractive grey horse Prolan appeared Ireland's top hope, having recently won the Kim Muir Chase at the Cheltenham Festival.

The excitement among the big crowd was palpable as the thirty-two runners charged towards the first fence. It was Spittin Image, a 66/1 outsider, that was first to rise, and here Ormonde Tudor and Huperade became the first of the National's inevitable victims.

Ridden by Andy Turnell, Spittin Image came to Becher's together with another long shot, Nereo, ridden by the fifty-seven-year-old Duque de Alburquerque, and the two soared the fence in tremendous style in the centre of the track. Tregarron was right on the heels of the leaders when he was caught out on the landing

Spanish amateur the Duque de Alburquerque took a crashing fall from Nereo in the 1976 race.

The strong chestnut Rag Trade won the 1976 National under jockey John Burke.

thick of the action, going well and holding every chance, yet there were others lining up to play a hand in the finish, among them Rag Trade, The Dikler, Ceol-Na-Mara, Sandwilan, Spanish Steps, with the favourite Barona last of the group but plugging on stoutly.

The noise level grew at every fence, especially when Red Rum went to dispute the lead five fences from home. Yet this exciting running of the race was clearly going to have a hectic finish, with no less than nine horses still within touching distance of the lead crossing the Melling Road for the final time.

side and became the first major casualty, very nearly rolling right into the path of The Dikler as he fell, though Ceol-Na-Mara was impeded and lost ground. Red Rum too had to be alert to sidestep the faller. Towards the inside, Glanford Brigg and Tudor View also came down as Money Market and Rag Trade followed the leaders to the seventh.

Nereo and his veteran rider were proudly disputing the lead when the Spanish amateur was unseated at the thirteenth, crashing down in a spine-chilling fall; the rest of the field galloping dangerously over the helpless jockey. The fall was so severe that the Duke remained unconscious for two days after the race and never rode in the National again. Nereo's exit left Spittin Image in the lead with Spanish Steps, Eyecatcher, Golden Rapper and Red Rum all in close attention.

With the exception of Tregarron, all the market leaders remained in the hunt for glory starting the second circuit and, by the twentieth fence, Francome's mount Golden Rapper had made significant progress up the inside to take hold of the lead. The little chestnut had been a recent addition to the Fred Winter stable and, heading down to Becher's, the horse was travelling very strongly. Holding a definite advantage and urged to attack the fence by Francome, Golden Rapper hit the obstacle hard and dived head-first to the ground in a spectacular fall, instantly changing the picture of the race. It looked bleak for the horse, such was the force with which he hit the turf, but fortunately Golden Rapper was swiftly to his feet, although Prolan and Boom Docker were brought down in the process. The events at Becher's left a clear-cut group of ten marching onwards and, taking the Canal Turn, Spittin Image just led and was joined by the mare Eyecatcher and also Churchtown Boy. Delighting the crowd, Red Rum was in the

Fred Rimell (right) holds Rag Trade at his stables the day after the horse's National win. Jockey John Burke is behind Rimell.

At the second last, four horses jumped in line. Eyecatcher on the inside moved up with purpose, while Ceol-Na-Mara, Red Rum and Rag Trade all battled for supremacy, with The Dikler trying desperately to stay with them just behind. Soon however, both The Dikler and Ceol-Na-Mara were left toiling as the three principals surged clear running to the last.

As Eyecatcher weakened, the crowd noise erupted like a volcano as Red Rum landed in front after jumping the last. Initially, Red Rum held the advantage on the flat but, on his outside, Rag Trade had been running a brilliant race, always in contention and, full of power, he quickly asserted himself over the Aintree legend. Burke's mount was finishing with admirable strength and, even though Red Rum and Stack pushed for one final effort after the elbow (bringing the crowd to their feet as the horse ate tantalisingly into Rag Trade's lead), it was to be Rag Trade's National, with the ten-year-old outlasting the two-time winner to triumph by two lengths. Red Rum had run his heart out again, and McCain insisted the horse would be back as a twelve-year-old to seek the elusive hat-trick. Fletcher again showed what a fine Grand National jockey he was, taking third on Eyecatcher, just in front of the dour Barona. Having almost been knocked out of the race at the first Becher's, Ceol-Na-Mara had responded gamely to take fifth with The Dikler belying his advancing years in sixth. Of the remainder, Jolly's Clump had disappointed, never threatening but returning home very lame while an exhausted Money Market collapsed having finished fourteenth, though he was thankfully revived with oxygen.

A fourth win in the race highlighted the skill of Kinnersley-based Fred Rimell, who had also won the season's Gold Cup with Royal Frolic, matching the feat last achieved by Vincent O'Brien in 1953. As a jockey, Rimell had been Champion four times, recovering from two broken necks, and now his four Grand National wins gave him more than any trainer in race history. Though nowhere near as graceful as his three previous National winners, Rag Trade had been trained to the minute by Rimell and was a deserving and convincing winner of a competitive 1976 race. Burke (who became the first jockey to win the Gold Cup and Grand National in the same year on different horses) had clearly given Rag Trade a fantastic ride, making up for a pair of falls from Rough House in his first two Nationals, while for winning owner 'Teasy Weasy' Raymond, it was the second taste of National success following Ayala's win in 1963.

1976 GRAND NATIONAL RESULT

FATE	HORSE	AGE/WEIGHT	JOCKEY	ODDS
1st	RAG TRADE	10.10.12	J. BURKE	14/1
2nd	RED RUM	11.11.10	T. STACK	10/1
3rd	EYECATCHER	10.10.7	B. FLETCHER	28/1
4th	BARONA	10.10.6	P. KELLEWAY	7/1
5th	Ceol-Na-Mara	7.10.6	J. Glover	22/1
6th	The Dikler	13.11.7	R. Barry	25/1
7th	Sandwilan	8.10.0	R. Hyett	100/1
8th	Spittin Image	10.10.0	A. Turnell	66/1
9th	Spanish Steps	13.10.2	J. King	22/1
10th	Black Tudor	8.10.0	G. Thorner	50/1
11th	Churchtown Boy	9.10.6	M. Salaman	33/1
12th	Highway View	11.10.10	P. Black	33/1
13th	Jolly's Clump	10.10.3	I. Watkinson	12/1
14th	Money Market	9.11.0	R. Champion	12/1
15th	Colondine	9.10.0	B. Forsey	60/1
16th	Indian Diva	9.10.3	Mr N. Henderson	100/1
Fell	Glanford Brigg	10.11.3	M. Blackshaw	28/1
Fell	High Ken	10.10.12	M. Dickinson	33/1
Fell	Roman Bar	7.10.10	G. Newman	33/1
Fell	Golden Rapper	10.10.8	J. Francome	28/1
Fell	Merry Maker	11.10.2	Mr A. Mildmay-White	50/1
Fell	Tregarron	9.10.1	C. Tinkler	12/1
Fell	Nereo	10.10.1	Duque de Alburquerque	100/1
Fell	Huperade	12.10.4	Mr J. Carden	100/1
Fell	Meridian II	9.10.0	J.J. O'Neill	33/1
Fell	Tudor View	10.10.0	C. Read	100/1
Fell	Ballybright	9.10.0	Mr S. Morshead	80/1
Fell	Ormonde Tudor	7.10.0	K. Bamfield	100/1
Pulled-Up	Perpol	10.10.6	K.B. White	66/1
Brought Down	Prolan	7.10.3	M. Morris	13/1
Brought Down	Thomond	11.10.3	Mr A.J. Wilson	100/1
Brought Down	Boom Docker	9.10.0	J. Williams	50/1

3 April 1976

Going – Firm

Sponsor – *The News Of The World*

Winner – £37,420

Time – 9mins 20.9secs

32 Ran

Favourite – Barona

Top Weight – Red Rum

Winner trained by Fred Rimell at Kinnersley, Worcestershire

Winner owned by Mr P.B. Raymond

Rag Trade, chestnut gelding by Menelek – The Rage.

1977

RED RUM

The 1977 Grand National meeting saw the transition from a mixed meeting to one purely comprised of jumping. With each race being generously sponsored, the main event itself would reward the winner with a prize of £41,000. These innovations paid off with a magnificent field for the Grand National, as forty-two lined-up, offering one of the finest collections of horses the race had ever witnessed.

Giving the race a tremendous boost in terms of form and class was the recent Cheltenham Gold Cup winner Davy Lad. Trained by Mick O'Toole, Davy Lad was a seven-year-old bay and, although somewhat fortunate to win at Cheltenham after his major rivals fell and a fourth, Summerville, broke down when travelling like the winner, the young horse obviously had plenty of improvement in him. Ridden, as at Cheltenham, by Dessie Hughes, Davy Lad had been merely a speculative entry for the National by O'Toole but, getting into the race with just 10st 13lbs, there were now high hopes the horse could become the first since Golden Miller to achieve the elusive Gold Cup/Grand National double.

If Davy Lad brought to Aintree the Cheltenham form, then the horse that had shown himself to be the most likely newcomer to win the National was Andy Pandy. A tall, athletic bay and a most clever jumper, Andy Pandy was another horse 'well-in' at the weights, having won four chases during the season and was clearly progressing. That Andy Pandy started favourite was no surprise, since he hailed from the most prolific of Grand National-winning yards, that of Fred Rimell and, like Rag Trade (missing through injury in 1977), Andy Pandy was partnered by John Burke. In searching for a fifth National winner, Rimell was represented by three others, including the big nine-year-old The Pilgarlic, a half-brother to L'Escargot.

Zeta's Son, Gay Vulgan and Winter Rain all shaped as possible winners of the National for a variety of reasons. Zeta's Son, a classy brown eight-year-old, had won the Hennessy Gold Cup in the mud for the small yard of Peter Bailey earlier in the season, while Gay Vulgan came in for much support having recorded a string of victories for trainer Fulke Walwyn, most notably over four miles at

Cheltenham in January. Having missed the previous season through injury, the talented Winter Rain had form over the National fences – having run well in the Topham Trophy two years previously – and had a more-than-capable jockey in Michael Dickinson, making the horse a popular each-way selection.

In a Grand National of multiple intriguing possibilities, Eyecatcher, Spittin Image and Churchtown Boy returned having run well the year before, the lattermost lining up a mere two days after bolting up in the Topham Trophy, a result that saw his National odds tumble to 20/1. In addition, the likes of Pengrail, Sage Merlin and War Bonnet were all in fine form, while Miss Charlotte Brew made race history by becoming the first female to ride in the National, partnering her own Barony Fort, much to the concern of Red Rum's trainer Ginger McCain, who believed the National was no place for female riders.

Red Rum himself was twelve now and again carried top weight. Having not won for over six months, Red Rum held a lofty place in the betting on past Grand National form alone. But the horse now reserved his best solely for Aintree and, quite rightly, was most respected on the day as well as attracting his usual large army of adoring followers. McCain predicted a bold run and, though the chance of the record-breaking third win remained alive, surely others had more serious designs on glory?

Sebastian V (light blue & yellow) and Boom Docker jump Becher's first time in the lead.

The Songwriter (44) and Churchtown Boy avoid the fallen Winter Rain after jumping Becher's.

The days preceding the National had been gloomy and wet, but the sun shone so brightly for the big race as the Scottish-trained Sebastian V led on the inside to the first with Duffle Coat up with the pace on the wide outside. Duffle Coat was first to go, closely followed by Spittin Image and, in total, seven horses came down at the first, including the fancied pair Pengrail and War Bonnet and the big, near-white outsider Willy What, who crashed in the centre. Gay Vulgan made a mistake that shook him severely and, apparently frightened by the fences according to jockey Bill Smith, was never going well thereafter.

The leaders had set off at a terrific pace and, even by the third fence, the field was well strung out, as Davy Lad saw his dreams end with a fall at the big ditch. By the fourth fence, thirteen had already departed. Sebastian V and Boom Docker came to Becher's in the lead in the centre of the track and, although he jumped the fence well, the landing side swept Sebastian V off his feet, while in behind came more grief. In the middle of the pack, Winter Rain nose-dived to the floor, tragically breaking his neck in a sickening fall and badly hampering Churchtown Boy and the rank outsider The Songwriter. Castleruddery and Lord Of The Hills were other casualties as Becher's again claimed a high toll.

All this had left Boom Docker and jockey John Williams in a clear lead and, running free, the horse widened his advantage from the Canal Turn, going further in front with every stride. With the chasing Prince Rock cannoning jockey Graham Thorner from the saddle out in the country, Boom Docker returned to the racecourse with a lead of twenty lengths.

Boom Docker sailed over The Chair with a huge lead but, in behind, Sage Merlin, who had himself come clear of the remainder, hit the top of the fence and crumpled on landing when going sweetly for Ian Watkinson. As Sage Merlin was falling, Boom Docker was already over the water, and not since Crisp had a

horse held such a lead going out for the second circuit, with Andy Pandy heading the chasing pack, followed by What A Buck, Brown Admiral, Sir Garnet, Forest King and Happy Ranger. At this stage Red Rum was well placed just behind these, with Churchtown Boy moving forward having been held up in the early stages.

With Boom Docker so far ahead approaching the seventeenth, the National again threw forward the unexpected. With no other horses for company, Boom Docker suddenly dug his feet in before the fence, grinding rudely to a halt in a blunt refusal. Frustrated, Williams had no choice but to turn the horse around and could only watch in agony as the rest of the field flew past him, capitalising on his misfortune. Dramatically, the race changed, and now Andy Pandy came clear himself in what appeared a decisive move. Hunted round for a circuit, Burke now attacked each fence and Andy Pandy responded stunningly by jumping like a stag on the way down to Becher's, pinging the big ditch in glorious style en route, and had carved an ominous twelve-length lead coming to the big fence. Behind him, Roman Bar crashed out when with the chasing pack. Jumping the fence well, Andy Pandy stumbled on landing and simply could not stay upright, and his chance evaporated in front of the disbelieving spectators, leaving Burke to thrust his whip to the turf in sheer frustration.

With Andy Pandy out, a most fascinating scenario arose as Red Rum then hit the front with the field totally strung out. Finding themselves in the lead, Tommy Stack allowed the horse to bowl along in front, a tactic the animal relished and, with the likes of What A Buck, Hidden Value, Forest King and Happy Ranger

Charlotte Brew, the first female jockey to compete in the National, jumps Becher's on her horse Barony Fort.

The favourite Andy Pandy comes down at Becher's second time when well clear.

Red Rum, What A Buck (blue cap) and Nereo (red cap) jump Becher's second time.

fading, it was Churchtown Boy that posed the chief threat to Red Rum as they jumped Valentines and beyond.

Crossing the Melling Road, the two had come well clear. Churchtown Boy, with Martin Blackshaw on board, was clearly travelling stronger but, tracking Red Rum, he clouted the second last, gifting Red Rum the edge. Unbelievably, history beckoned, as Red Rum began to come away from his rival, the crowd seemingly willing the great horse to the finish. He duly jumped the last and scorched up the run-in, flanked by a wall of noise unrivalled at Aintree as fans behind both inside and stand-side rails roared him home. Finishing with such purpose and strength, Red Rum crossed the line twenty-five lengths clear to take his place in history as a glorious, unique, three-time winner of the National. A tired Churchtown Boy had given everything and had run the perfect stalking race, yet his mistake two out had been crucial against the ultimate Aintree warrior, while Eyecatcher and The Pilgarlic had stayed on, though beaten horses, to grab the minor places. Back out on the course, Charlotte Brew had acquitted herself well, but Barony Fort had cried 'enough' four out and refused. Sadly, the National's darker side had surfaced twice in the race, with Zeta's Son a second fatality after breaking a leg at Valentines on the second circuit.

History had been made and Aintree, together with the whole country, hailed the horse as a hero. The bookmakers were hit as if by a truck by the result and, for the winner, even more fame followed, as he became a nationwide star, even featuring on the *BBC Sports Personality of the Year Awards* show. The achievement of McCain should not be underestimated, for he had now produced Red Rum in perfect order to compete in the Grand National five years consecutively, in which the horse had now jumped 150 of the biggest fences imaginable without mishap.

The 1977 National will always be remembered as the race that turned Red Rum into the all-time, undisputed Aintree King and a racing legend. Looking twelve months into the future, McCain envisioned his great horse attempting to win the race for an unthinkable fourth time.

1977 GRAND NATIONAL RESULT

FATE	HORSE	AGE/WEIGHT	JOCKEY	ODDS
1st	RED RUM	12.11.8	T. STACK	9/1
2nd	CHURCHTOWN BOY	10.10.0	M. BLACKSHAW	20/1
3rd	EYECATCHER	11.10.1	C. READ	18/1
4th	THE PILGARLIC	9.10.4	R.R. EVANS	40/1
5th	Forest King	8.10.2	R. Crank	33/1
6th	What A Buck	10.11.4	J. King	20/1
7th	Happy Ranger	10.10.5	P. Blacker	66/1
8th	Carroll Street	10.10.0	R. Linley	50/1

FATE	HORSE	AGE/WEIGHT	JOCKEY	ODDS
9th	Collingwood	11.10.0	C. Hawkins	50/1
10th	Hidden Value	9.10.4	J. Bourke (remounted)	40/1
11th	Saucy Belle	11.10.0	R.F. Davies (remounted)	200/1
Fell	Zeta' Son	8.11.4	M. Morris	18/1
Fell	Davy Lad	7.10.13	D.T. Hughes	10/1
Fell	Roman Bar	8.10.10	P. Kiely	25/1
Fell	Pengrail	9.10.8	R. Atkins	15/1
Fell	Andy Pandy	8.10.7	J. Burke	15/2
Fell	Prince Rock	9.10.6	G. Thorner	18/1
Fell	War Bonnet	9.10.6	T. Carberry	16/1
Fell	Winter Rain	9.10.6	M. Dickinson	16/1
Fell	Brown Admiral	8.10.1	S. Morshead	28/1
Fell	Duffle Coat	9.10.4	B.R. Davies	100/1
Fell	Nereo	11.10.0	R. Kington	100/1
Fell	Sage Merlin	9.10.5	I. Watkinson	20/1
Fell	Castleruddery	11.10.0	L. O'Donnell	40/1
Fell	Harban	8.10.0	F. Berry	66/1
Fell	Sebastian V	9.10.1	R. Lamb	22/1
Fell	Royal Thrust	8.10.0	C. Tinkler	100/1
Fell	Burrator	8.10.0	Mr J. Docker	50/1
Fell	Inycarra	10.10.0	S. Jobar	100/1
Fell	Spittin Image	11.10.5	R. Champion	50/1
Fell	Willy What	8.10.0	J. Glover	50/1
Fell	Huperade	13.10.7	Mr J. Carden	200/1
Pulled-Up	Gay Vulgan	9.10.8	W. Smith	9/1
Pulled-Up	Lord Of The Hills	10.10.1	D. Goulding	100/1
Pulled-Up	The Songwriter	8.10.0	B. Smart	200/1
Brought Down	High Ken	11.11.3	Mr J. Edwards	50/1
Brought Down	Fort Vulgan	9.10.0	N. Tinkler	50/1
Unseated Rider	Sir Garnet	8.10.3	J.J. O'Neill	20/1
Refused	Boom Docker	10.10.0	J. Williams	66/1
Refused	Sandwilan	9.10.0	R. Hyett	50/1
Refused	Foresail	10.10.0	G. Holmes	100/1
Refused	Barony Fort	12.10.1	Miss Charlotte Brew	200/1

2 April 1977

Going – Good

Sponsor – *The News Of The World*

Winner – £41,140

Time – 9mins 30.3secs

42 Ran

Favourite – Andy Pandy

Top Weight – Red Rum

Winner trained by Donald McCain at Southport, Lancashire

Winner owned by Mr N.H. Le Mare

Red Rum, bay gelding by Quorum – Mared.

1978

LUCIUS

The biggest of bombshells was dropped just days before the 1978 Grand National when it was announced that Red Rum had sustained an injury in his final piece of preparatory work and would miss the race. Now thirteen and having enjoyed a most distinguished career, where he became the most successful and famous of all Grand National horses, the decision was taken to retire the horse who had brought joy to so many. The news robbed the race of its star attraction and the ante-post favourite. Quite rightly, Red Rum was invited to lead the pre-race parade, where he enjoyed the applause and rich appreciation of the Aintree crowd one more time.

Although he was to live a long and happy retirement, Red Rum's absence cast a slightly sad atmosphere over National day and left a big hole to fill, yet there were plenty of interesting candidates ready to take up the mantle. Though the reformed betting market featured many new faces at the top end, a former winner returned from the sidelines to take his place as favourite. Since winning in 1976, the bulking chestnut Rag Trade had suffered a bad time with injury, had left Fred Rimell's yard and was now in training in the North with George Fairbarn. Rag Trade had won his most recent race to spark hopes he could rekindle former glories at Aintree. Partnered by the brilliant Irish jockey Jonjo O'Neill (who had failed to complete on three previous National rides), Rag Trade started the 8/1 favourite.

Most fancied of the National first-timers happened to be the Irish horse Tied Cottage. A natural front-runner, Tied Cottage was from the L'Escargot team of trainer Dan Moore and jockey Tommy Carberry and had finished second to Davy Lad in the 1977 Gold Cup, while another horse hotly tipped was the nine-year-old Master H. Trained in Worcestershire by Michael Oliver, Master H was a most consistent chestnut and three times a winner during the season, including recently at Worcester when carrying a big weight. Extremely confident, jockey Reg Crank indicated the horse had only once failed to complete a race in thirty-three starts.

The top weight Shifting Gold, Scottish Grand National winner Sebastian V, Irish raider So and 1977 runner-up Churchtown Boy all had their supporters, while also very popular was the northern hope Lucius. A bay nine-year-old from the yard of West Country native Gordon Richards (who trained at Greystoke Castle in the Lake District), Lucius was recognised as a solid stayer but a horse whose jumping would be put under the microscope at Aintree. A winner of three races in the run up to the National, Lucius was without regular jockey David Goulding because of injury, but had a fine replacement in multiple Champion Jockey Bob Davies.

As the thirty-seven runners were let go, it was Tied Cottage that instantly showed up boldly in front, followed by a thunderous procession of hooves pounding on the Aintree turf. As usual, the dash to the first fence brought about some grief, with the useful Otter Way coming down together with outsiders Cornish Princess and Teddy Bear II. In total contrast to the joy he had experienced on Red Rum the year before, Tommy Stack bore a glum expression following the fall of Hidden Value at the second, while Tied Cottage bounded on in front, throttling down towards Becher's.

With near reckless abandon, Tied Cottage jumped the monstrous fence alarmingly to his left and, failing to survive the perilous drop on the landing side, was promptly down on the floor. Henry Hall and Gleaming Rain also went at Becher's and, as Lucius and Double Bridal dictated the pace, more big fancies were soon to come a cropper. Darting swiftly to the right having jumped the Canal Turn, Crank's saddle slipped and he was most unluckily unseated while, following a mistake at Valentines, Shifting Gold fell at the tenth, as did the Irish challenger So; with Rag Trade toiling, a shock result appeared possible.

Returning to the racecourse, Lucius was jumping well in front and was accompanied in the leading group by Drumroan, Sebastian V, Double Bridal, Lean Forward, Harban, Mickley Seabright and Roman Bar. Again travelling well in the race was Churchtown Boy, but The Chair was to put paid to his chance and, following his fall, jockey Martin Blackshaw flung his whip to the ground in a show of frustration as another National-winning opportunity escaped.

Taking the water, a mini battle for the lead ensued between Lucius and Sebastian V, both horses clearly enjoying themselves and, heading out for the second circuit, they held command. One horse who had been struggling throughout, however, was Rag Trade and running down to Becher's again the brave old horse was pulled-up by O'Neill. It transpired that the injury plagued chestnut had broken down badly on his increasingly suspect legs, and it was now so serious that the horse was sadly put down.

Sebastian V led the survivors approaching Becher's, Lucius still right there with him. Drumroan and Roman Bar were both in contention, while making eyecatching progress was Fred Winter's recruit Lord Browndodd, together with The Pilgarlic. Harban was going nicely too but unseated his jockey at the big fence, while Graham Thorner performed miracles to stay on board the former

Irish hope Tied Cottage falls at Becher's when leading, followed by Double Bridal (yellow cap), Lucius (black and white) and Sebastian V (23).

Hennessy runner-up Tamalin after the horse made a dreadful blunder. With the leaders intact jumping Valentines and beyond, the bold fencing of Sebastian V had kept him in the lead and, as the race reached its final stages, there were many with their dreams still very much alive.

With proven stamina, Sebastian V showed no signs of stopping approaching two out, with Lucius fighting back and Lord Browndodd moving well for John Francome on the inside, while Coolishall was poised to challenge on the extreme

outside. Four others – The Pilgarlic, Drumroan, Mickley Seabright and The Songwriter – remained in contention with a frantic finish looming, although the last two were soon under heavy pressure.

Lord Browndodd had looked a real threat two out but, by the last, he had tired rapidly and it was the Martin O'Halloran-ridden Coolishall who looked the most dangerous as he came to challenge the long-time leaders Sebastian V and Lucius. As they flew over the last, five horses threw their hearts into a pulsating finish. With

Lucius (9) beats Sebastian V (noseband) and Drumroan.

1978 GRAND NATIONAL RESULT

FATE	HORSE	AGE/WEIGHT	JOCKEY	ODDS
1st	LUCIUS	9.10.9	B.R. DAVIES	14/1
2nd	SEBASTIAN V	10.10.1	R. LAMB	25/1
3rd	DRUMROAN	10.10.0	G. NEWMAN	50/1
4th	COOLISHALL	9.10.0	M. O'HALLORAN	16/1
5th	The Pilgarlic	10.10.1	R.R. Evans	33/1
6th	Mickley Seabright	10.10.3	Mr P. Brookshaw	33/1
7th	Lord Browndodd	10.10.7	J. Francome	16/1
8th	The Songwriter	9.10.0	B. Smart	50/1
9th	Roman Bar	9.10.8	P. Kiely	33/1
10th	Brown Admiral	9.10.0	J. Burke	33/1
11th	Golden Whin	8.10.4	S. Holland	50/1
12th	Tamalin	11.11.2	G. Thorner	25/1
13th	Lean Forward	12.10.0	H.J. Evans	33/1
14th	Nereo	12.10.0	M. Floyd	66/1
15th	Never Rock	9.10.0	K. Mooney	50/1
Fell	Shifting Gold	9.11.6	R. Champion	16/1
Fell	Tied Cottage	10.11.4	T. Carberry	9/1
Fell	Otter Way	10.10.10	J. King	16/1
Fell	War Bonnet	10.10.8	D.T. Hughes	50/1
Fell	So	9.10.4	Mr N. Madden	14/1
Fell	Hidden Value	10.10.0	T. Stack	25/1
Fell	Master Upham	10.10.0	P. Barton	25/1
Fell	Irish Tony	10.10.0	D. Atkins	33/1
Fell	Double Negative	8.10.0	C. Tinkler	33/1
Fell	Churchtown Boy	11.10.0	M. Blackshaw	14/1
Fell	Cornish Princess	10.10.1	R. Hoare	66/1
Fell	Henry Hall	9.10.0	F. Berry	66/1
Fell	Burrator	9.10.0	J. Suthern	66/1
Fell	Double Bridal	7.10.1	W. Smith	50/1
Fell	Teddy Bear II	11.10.4	P. Blacker	50/1
Fell	Silkstone	10.10.0	G. Graham	66/1
Fell	Gleaming Rain	10.10.0	S. Treacy	25/1
Fell	Sadale VI	11.10.1	C. Candy	66/1
Pulled-Up	Rag Trade	12.11.3	J.J. O'Neill	8/1
Unseated Rider	Master H	9.11.2	R. Crank	10/1
Unseated Rider	Harban	9.10.0	J.P. Byrne	66/1
Refused	April Seventh	12.10.11	A. Turnell	20/1

1 April 1978
Going – Firm
Sponsor – The *Sun*
Winner – £39,062
Time – 9mins 33.9secs
37 Ran
Favourite – Rag Trade

Top Weight – Shifting Gold
Winner trained by Gordon W. Richards
    at Greystoke, Cumbria
Winner owned by Mrs D.A. Whitaker
Lucius, bay gelding by Perhapsburg
    – Matches.

dogged determination, Lucius clawed his way back in front of Sebastian V and jockey Ridley Lamb, and as Coolishall failed to quicken on the outside and with The Pilgarlic unable to reach the front two down the inner, it was left to the dark-coloured gelding Drumroan to make a late charge at the leaders. Drumroan's challenge, however, was to be in vain, as Lucius proved strongest of all, holding off the ultra-game Sebastian V by half-a-length in a gripping conclusion to a most thrilling National. The late blitz by Drumroan had so nearly given trainer Peggy St John Nolan the honour of becoming the first female trainer to win the National, yet the horse had to settle for third in front of Coolishall and The Pilgarlic.

A fantastic, deeply competitive renewal of the race had been won by Lucius, purchased by Richards as an unbroken three-year-old and sold to Scottish owner Mrs Fiona Whitaker, whose black and white colours the horse ran in. Put up for sale for £2.5 million, Aintree's future was again uncertain, yet the 57,000 present on Grand National day proved that the race was as popular as ever. The biggest crowd since the early 1950s had been treated to a thriller, and many were on hand walking back to the winner's enclosure, cheering in Lucius, the newest hero of the great race.

1979

RUBSTIC

It was a huge relief when Ladbrokes agreed with Bill Davies to extend their management of the course until 1982, offering a sense of security – if only for the time being. After a year of sponsorship by the *Sun* newspaper, it was the turn of the Colt Car Company in 1979, sponsoring a Grand National that featured the newest Cheltenham Gold Cup winner.

Allotted a mere 10st 13lbs, the ultra-tough, uncompromising chestnut Alverton lined-up for the Grand National regarded as a near certainty if he jumped round. Trained in the North by Peter Easterby, Alverton had got the better of a tussle with Tied

Cottage in the snow at Cheltenham, and even though that rival had fallen at the final fence, Alverton was considered a horse at the peak of his powers – one that surely would have carried close to 12 stone in the following year's National. Slight doubts, including some harboured by his jockey Jonjo O'Neill, lingered regarding Alverton's jumping, but he appeared extremely 'well-in', and started the 13/2 favourite.

With the 1978 hero Lucius ruled out late on because of a cough, only eight of the thirty-four runners had run in the National before. Among these was The Pilgarlic, a big, strong individual forming a strong team representing Fred Rimell. The Pilgarlic had been sent hunting during the season and, having won his last race, was again a live each-way chance. Completing Rimell's team were the 1976 Gold Cup winner Royal Frolic, who carried top weight, nine-year-old Godfrey Secundus and outsider Double Negative.

With two of the first five in the betting, Captain Tim Forster had high hopes of adding to Well To Do's National success of 1972. Both Mr Snowman and Ben Nevis gave Forster a powerful duo to go to war with. The talented and consistent Mr Snowman, an impressive jumper, was a lightly raced ten-year-old and was a horse that on his previous six racecourse appearances had always made the frame. Bred in England, Ben Nevis had made his name in the United States, winning the respected Maryland Hunt Cup for his American owner. A rich chestnut, Ben Nevis had been sent to Forster's yard in preparation for the National, and his races preceding the big race showed improvement each time. American amateur Charlie Fenwick, a merchant banker, partnered Ben Nevis at Aintree.

Purdo falls at Becher's as Zongalero (red and white) leads from Alverton (3), Rubstic (light blue) and Kick On (30).

Jonjo O'Neill is sent flying as Alverton (3) crashes at Becher's second time.

An eyecatching run in the 1978 race saw Coolishall attract plenty of support, as did Drumroan, who returned to Aintree following a disappointing season. Having missed out on National glory with Lucius, David Goulding hoped for compensation aboard Rambling Artist, who had run well behind Alverton at Haydock Park recently, while Fred Winter's runner Rough And Tumble and the Midlands National winner Kick On were both lively tips. Among the dark horses was the near black Rubstic, trained in Scotland by John Leadbetter. Twice a runner-up in the Scottish National, Rubstic was a sure stayer while, in addition, the horse had never fallen, making him one of the safer bets to complete the daunting course.

A huge crowd of 66,000 cheered in anticipation as the runners came under starter's orders. Leading the charge away was Bob Champion on the chestnut Purdo and, reaching the first fence, the leader sailed over, though not so fortunate were Double Negative, Sandwilan, Wayward Scot and Vindicate, who all crashed out.

Bolting along in front, Purdo forced the pace from Jenny Pitman's runner Artistic Prince, together with Zongalero, Drumroan, Kick On and Ben Nevis – the next four fences passing without incident. Facing up to the mighty Becher's Brook, Purdo capsized at the fence while 100/1 shot Oskard also came down. At this stage, Alverton's jumping was holding up well and he travelled within

himself just behind the leaders, headed now by the red-and-white colours of Zongalero and the pale blue of Rubstic.

Crossing the Melling Road and returning to the racecourse (with Drumroan a faller out in the country), a pair of loose horses in Double Negative and Oskard were beginning to become a concern and, by the time the field approached the mighty Chair, the duo were harassing the leaders. The Swiss-owned horse Wagner, together with Zongalero and Rubstic, jumped The Chair safely but behind them, major destruction lay in wait, as The Chair took its largest ever toll. Narrowly missing the race favourite Alverton (who lay about fourth), the loose horses tore straight along the narrow take-off path before the fence, colliding with the chasing group and causing utter chaos. Seven horses – Rambling Artist, Ben Nevis, No Gypsy, Alpenstock, Kick On, Cartwright and Godfrey Secundus – were brought down, The Champ fell and, tragically, Kintai broke his back in the melee. With the field decimated in one fell swoop it was Wagner that led on for the second circuit, followed by Zongalero, Rubstic, Alverton, Rough And Tumble, Artistic Prince, Lord Browndodd and Coolishall.

It was becoming obvious how easily Alverton was going, hacking along sweetly on the wide outside. Despite making a small error at the twentieth, the race looked his for the taking as they approached Becher's again. But, in a cruel twist, Alverton altered his stride pattern running to the fence and never regained his rhythm. In one of the saddest moments in Grand National history, the Gold Cup winner went into the fence, hit the top with his chest and plunged to the ground, his neck broken. It was thought Alverton might have suffered a heart attack as the poor horse, most uncharacteristically, barely took off.

Leaving the dark scene at Becher's, where Mr Snowman had also come down, Lord Browndodd was next to depart when Andy Turnell pulled him up at the Canal Turn with blood pouring from his nose. Out in front, the survivors were still led by Wagner, Zongalero, Rubstic and Rough And Tumble, with The Pilgarlic making late ground as usual, though Coolishall came to grief when still with them at the twenty-seventh.

John Francome had never been placed higher in the National than the seventh he achieved aboard Lord Browndodd in 1978 but, as the plucky Rough And Tumble came to take the lead on the inside two out, it appeared now was his chance to win the great race. Rubstic was on the outside with Zongalero between the pair. The Pilgarlic was still in touch yet it seemed he did not have the finishing pace to win, although he always ran well in the four Nationals he contested. Wagner too had been left behind as the tempo increased and the race now lay between the front three.

Francome sent Rough And Tumble on jumping the last, and though his mount responded admirably, Rubstic and Zongalero came back for more and were staying on stronger. By the elbow, the two of them had collared Rough And Tumble and begun their own battle to the line. Inside the final hundred yards, Maurice Barnes urged Rubstic to find more, and the horse in the sheepskin noseband bravely obliged, outlasting Zongalero (considered a doubtful stayer beforehand) by a length-and-a-half. Bob Davies was narrowly denied a second National victory, but the courage of his horse Zongalero was soon evident as it emerged he returned lame. Rough And Tumble came home third and The Pilgarlic fourth. The National inevitably was subjected to a barrage of finger pointing following the deaths of two horses. This did little to raise the spirits of the unfortunate O'Neill, who was simply distraught following the tragic loss of Alverton. O'Neill had endured miserable luck for two consecutive years, having ridden the ill-fated Rag Trade in 1978, and the Grand National was not to be this great jockey's race, for he did not complete the course in eight attempts.

For Rubstic and connections though, it was a day to remember. The horse was the first ever Scottish-trained winner, and his victory was the pinnacle of John Leadbetter's training career. Leadbetter had only taken out a permit in 1975, his first season reaping just one winner. Rubstic had been seriously ill two years previously, nearly dying through dehydration. But the gallant horse recovered, and now presented owner Mr John Douglas with racing's most famous prize after a courageous display of staying power and fighting spirit.

1979 GRAND NATIONAL RESULT

FATE	HORSE	AGE/WEIGHT	JOCKEY	ODDS
1st	RUBSTIC	10.10.0	M. BARNES	25/1
2nd	ZONGALERO	9.10.5	B.R. DAVIES	20/1
3rd	ROUGH AND TUMBLE	9.10.7	J. FRANCOME	14/1
4th	THE PILGARLIC	11.10.1	R.R. EVANS	16/1
5th	Wagner	9.10.0	R. Lamb	50/1
6th	Royal Frolic	10.11.10	J. Burke	25/1
7th	Prime Justice	9.10.0	A.K. Taylor	200/1
Fell	Alverton	9.10.13	J.J. O'Neill	13/2
Fell	The Champ	11.10.12	W. Smith	25/1
Fell	Purdo	8.10.12	R. Champion	25/1
Fell	Mr Snowman	10.10.9	G. Thorner	10/1
Fell	Sandpit	9.10.7	T. Carmody	22/1
Fell	Wayward Scot	10.10.7	R.F. Davies	100/1
Fell	Drumroan	11.10.4	G. Newman	20/1
Fell	Coolishall	10.10.2	A. Webber	12/1
Fell	Double Negative	9.10.5	Mr E. Woods	66/1
Fell	Artistic Prince	8.10.3	P. Blacker	25/1
Fell	Oskard	10.10.0	M. Blackshaw	100/1
Fell	Sandwilan	11.10.0	Mrs J. Hembrow	100/1
Fell	Vindicate	12.11.8	Mr A. O'Connell	200/1
Pulled-Up	Lord Browndodd	11.10.3	A. Turnell	25/1
Pulled-Up	Red Earl	10.10.0	H.J. Evans	50/1
Pulled-Up	Dromore	11.10.10	Mr P. Duggan	50/1
Pulled-Up	Flitgrove	8.10.1	R. Linley	50/1
Brought Down	Ben Nevis	11.11.2	Mr C. Fenwick	14/1
Brought Down	Rambling Artist	9.10.6	D. Goulding	16/1
Brought Down	Godfrey Secundus	9.10.3	C. Tinkler	25/1
Brought Down	Kintai	10.10.0	B. Smart	100/1
Brought Down	No Gypsy	10.10.1	J. Suthern	66/1
Brought Down	Churchtown Boy	12.10.0	M. Salaman	25/1
Brought Down	Kick On	12.10.0	R. Hyett	50/1
Brought Down	Alpenstock	12.10.0	Mr D. Gray	100/1
Brought Down	Cartwright	10.10.0	A. Phillips	200/1
Unseated Rider	Brown Admiral	10.10.0	S. Morshead	100/1

31 March 1979
Going – Good
Sponsor – The Colt Car Co. Ltd
Winner – £40,506
Time – 9mins 52.9secs
34 Ran
Favourite – Alverton

Top Weight – Royal Frolic
Winner trained by John Leadbetter at Denholm, Roxburghshire, Scotland
Winner owned by Mr J. Douglas
Rubstic, brown gelding by I Say – Leuze.

1980

BEN NEVIS

With the *Sun* newspaper again sponsoring the Grand National in 1980, it was ironic that relentless rain in the days leading up to the race produced heavy ground on the big day. Originally, the talented grey horse from Gordon Richards' yard, Man Alive, was to run as joint-top weight with the 1976 Gold Cup winner Royal Frolic, but the former was withdrawn on the morning of the race due to the state of the ground, together with the 1979 fifth Wagner.

It was one of the poorest fields for a number of years in 1980, although the first three home in 1979 returned and dominated the betting market. Rubstic was favourite and was considered to have a super chance of recording consecutive victories. The horse had 11lbs more to carry than the year before but had won his two most recent races and had never fallen. Zongalero had a new jockey in Aintree debutant Steve Smith-Eccles while John Francome was again booked to ride Rough And Tumble, though the lhorse was without a win for sixteen months.

Together with the three principals from 1979, the most popular selections were nine-year-old newcomer Jer and Fred Rimell's horse Another Dolly. Partnered by another Aintree first-timer in Phil Tuck, the consistent Jer had won three recent races, including the Great Yorkshire Chase at Doncaster, often seen as a useful guide for the National, and had beaten Rubstic in the process. Another Dolly was perhaps the most intriguing runner in the National. Not renowned for his stamina but a high-class individual nonetheless, the horse had recently finished second in the two-mile Queen Mother Champion Chase at Cheltenham, though he would eventually be awarded the race when the winner was later disqualified. Riding Another Dolly was Jonjo O'Neill, hoping to change the wretched luck that had haunted him in recent Nationals.

Again in the field were the likes of Grand National veterans Prince Rock, Coolishall, Drumroan, Churchtown Boy and The Pilgarlic while, having been thwarted by the mayhem at The Chair in 1979, Ben Nevis also returned. In contrast to the year before, Ben Nevis was largely unfancied on this occasion

and was still to win a race in England since joining Captain Tim Forster's stable following a stellar career in the States. With a history of loathing heavy ground and with the Forster yard hampered by coughing, it was with extreme pessimism from the trainer that the horse was allowed to take his chance, again ridden by American amateur Charlie Fenwick, whose grandfather, Mr Howard Bruce, had owned the 1928 runner-up Billy Barton.

With conditions underfoot so testing, the jockeys wisely opted for a far steadier approach to the first fence, knowing that only the hardiest of competitors would complete the course. It was newcomer Delmoss that was first of the thirty runners to the fence and even the slower pace brought about the downfall of Salkeld and Mannyboy. The open ditch at the third caused the fall of the fancied Jer, with the Aintree stalwart Churchtown Boy brought down. Coolishall was next to depart a fence later when a broken iron caused the unseating of his rider, Mr Munro-Wilson.

Out in front and jumping extravagantly, Delmoss led down to Becher's Brook, tracked by Rubstic, So And So, Zongalero, Levanka, Kininvie and Sandwilan, ridden by Mrs Jenny Hembrow. Delmoss had quickened the pace by Becher's, and the famous drop caught out the prominent So And So, who crumpled on landing while, towards the rear, O'Neill again saw his hopes dashed as Another Dolly plunged to an ugly looking fall. Last over Becher's first time was Ben Nevis, seemingly going nowhere on the rain-soaked ground.

Returning to the racecourse, Delmoss had carved open a useful lead from Rubstic, Levanka, Sandwilan, Kininvie and Rough And Tumble, but the white face of Ben Nevis could be seen making rapid progress through the pack on

Jonjo O'Neill falls at Becher's again, this time from Another Dolly.

Ben Nevis (6) and Delmoss are well clear by Becher's second time.

the inside. The loose Coolishall threatened to hamper Delmoss approaching The Chair but, fortunately, there was no repeat of the chaos of 1979. There was a shock, however, when Rubstic, miscalculating the gaping ditch, clouted the top of the fence and suffered his first ever fall, drawing disbelieving gasps from the stands.

Delmoss continued his strong gallop, but the exertions were becoming too much for many. The Vinter pulled-up at the beginning of the second circuit, while

Even Up – badly hampered by Rubstic's fall at The Chair – refused soon after. The nineteenth claimed Casamayor and Drumroan, while Prince Rock, Sandwilan, Godfrey Secundus and Kininvie all cried enough and Zongalero refused a fence later having nearly fallen, clearly an exhausted animal.

With the field greatly depleted and the survivors strung out like washing, Delmoss had been joined by Ben Nevis and the two were well clear facing up to Becher's again. Delmoss made a terrible mistake and came crashing down while,

Three To One and Royal Stuart (11) give chase behind the leaders.

in behind, the drop caught out Three To One. This left Ben Nevis with a strong advantage at the Foinavon fence and, with only a few still continuing, including Rough And Tumble, The Pilgarlic and Royal Stuart, the American horse suddenly had the race at his mercy.

Jumping down the back, no horse could get close enough to challenge Ben Nevis and, although the game Rough And Tumble reduced the lead to four lengths at the last, Ben Nevis had plenty in reserve. Galloping clear in fine style, the horse drew right away passing the elbow, crossing the line with jubilant American applause ringing in his ears as he became a comfortable twenty-length winner. In the slowest-run race since 1955, only four horses completed the war of attrition, with the front two followed home by The Pilgarlic (who had now finished third, fourth twice and fifth) and the New Zealand-bred Royal Stuart, ridden by Philip Blacker.

A surprise winner for both connections and the bookmakers, the twelve-year-old had achieved the dream of his American owner Mr Red C. Stewart jnr. Ben Nevis was a first winner in the country for Charlie Fenwick, the owner's son-in-law, and the thirty-two-year-old banker from Baltimore had given the horse a fine ride, presenting Captain Forster with his second National victory. Having fulfilled the task set for him on leaving the United States, the gutsy, wholehearted Ben Nevis was then given a most honourable retirement in America.

1980 GRAND NATIONAL RESULT

FATE	HORSE	AGE/WEIGHT	JOCKEY	ODDS
1st	BEN NEVIS	12.10.12	MR C. FENWICK	40/1
2nd	ROUGH AND TUMBLE	10.10.11	J. FRANCOME	11/1
3rd	THE PILGARLIC	12.10.4	R. HYETT	33/1
4th	ROYAL STUART	9.10.10	P. BLACKER	20/1
Fell	Casamayor	10.10.12	J. King	50/1
Fell	Rubstic	11.10.11	M. Barnes	8/1
Fell	Another Dolly	10.10.10	J.J. O'Neill	12/1
Fell	So And So	11.10.10	R. Linley	28/1
Fell	Flashy Boy	12.10.8	C. Grant	50/1
Fell	Our Greenwood	12.11.6	Mr A. O'Connell	100/1
Fell	Jimmy Miff	8.10.5	A. Brown	50/1
Fell	Drumroan	12.10.5	T. McGivern	22/1
Fell	Jer	9.10.4	P. Tuck	10/1
Fell	Delmoss	10.10.2	G. Newman	25/1
Fell	Salkeld	8.10.0	C. Hawkins	20/1
Fell	Three To One	9.10.2	Mr T.G. Dun	25/1
Pulled-Up	The Vinter	9.10.8	B.R. Davies	16/1
Pulled-Up	Levanka	11.10.4	F. Berry	100/1
Pulled-Up	Dromore	12.10.8	Mr P. Duggan	100/1
Pulled-Up	Godfrey Secundus	10.10.0	S. Morshead	20/1
Pulled-Up	Sandwilan	12.10.0	Mrs J. Hembrow	100/1
Pulled-Up	Kininvie	11.10.0	J. Williams	100/1
Brought Down	Churchtown Boy	13.10.0	A. Turnell	50/1
Unseated Rider	Coolishall	11.10.10	Mr B. Munro-Wilson	40/1
Unseated Rider	Mannyboy	10.10.2	R. Rowe	33/1
Refused	Royal Frolic	11.11.4	J. Burke	16/1
Refused	Prince Rock	12.11.0	T. Carmody	12/1
Refused	Zongalero	10.10.13	S. Smith-Eccles	11/1
Refused	Even Up	13.10.6	A. Webber	50/1
Refused	Rathlek	10.10.0	P. Barton	35/1

29 March 1980

Going – Heavy

Sponsor – The *Sun*

Winner – £45,595

Time – 10mins 17.4secs

30 Ran

Favourite – Rubstic

Top Weight – Royal Frolic

Winner trained by Captain Tim Forster at Letcombe Bassett, Oxfordshire

Winner owned by Mr R.C. Stewart jnr

Ben Nevis, chestnut gelding by Cashiri – Ben Trumiss.

1981

ALDANITI

If Foinavon's Grand National had been the most sensational and Red Rum's third win the most historically significant, then the biggest human interest story associated with the race came from the unforgettable 1981 renewal. Not a soul present at Aintree was unaware of the struggles that had befallen one of the competing partnerships and seldom, if ever, could a story be more suitable for a fairytale ending than the defiant and often distressing episode portrayed by Bob Champion and his mount Aldaniti.

Champion, a veteran jockey, had first ridden in the National in 1971, with sixth-place finishes aboard Hurricane Rock in 1973 and Manicou Bay in 1975 his best results. A few months after partnering Purdo in the 1979 race, Champion was diagnosed with cancer and a challenge far more treacherous than any of the fearsome Aintree fences lay ahead. For his part, the burly chestnut Aldaniti had suffered a series of severe leg injuries that would have left most horses declared as invalids. Having broken down badly in November 1979, trainer Josh Gifford had been virtually advised to have the horse put down. Instead, Gifford sent Aldaniti to the home of his owner, Mr Nick Embiricos, where he was gradually eased back to fitness before returning to Gifford's Findon stables.

Often inspired by the goal of riding Aldaniti in the National (a race for which Champion had always believed Aldaniti had the ideal credentials), Champion won his personal battle and, building up his fitness in America, returned to partner his old friend in a trial race at Ascot in February 1981, which they won convincingly to book a date at Aintree. Aldaniti had been a very good horse in his younger days and had been placed in each of a Cheltenham Gold Cup, Hennessy Cognac Gold Cup and Scottish Grand National, and had the heart and determination to match any in the 1981 field. Obviously, the horse's injury problems and lack of races were worries before a race such as the National, but with a jockey ultra-confident the pair would win, a momentous wave of public support saw the eleven-year-old Aldaniti start as 10/1 second favourite.

With thirty-nine runners in 1981, the opposition to Aldaniti was extremely strong, with a worthy favourite in the form of the big chestnut Spartan Missile. Owned, trained and bred by his fifty-four-year-old jockey, Mr John Thorne, Spartan Missile was a proven performer over the big fences having twice won the Aintree Foxhunters'. Spartan Missile was more than just a good hunter: he belonged in top-class company and had proved this by finishing fourth to Little Owl in the recent Gold Cup and had also been runner-up in a Whitbread. Another to attract tremendous interest because of his jockey, Spartan Missile posed as a real live threat, starting 8/1 favourite.

Rubstic was back having won well at Doncaster recently, as was Zongalero – but the latter had been disappointing prior to Aintree and seemed a shadow of his former self. The tough little youngster Senator Maclacury had the top Aintree jockey John Burke on board and was the main hope of Ireland, having won the Punchestown National Trial, while top weight was Royal Mail, the most recent Whitbread winner and runner-up to Alverton in the 1979 Gold Cup. Of the remainder, Fred Winter's veteran Royal Exile was expected to go well for youngster Ben De Haan, while the consistent Royal Stuart was fancied to improve on his fourth place in 1980.

Aintree was lit up to glorious effect by bright sunshine, and leading to the first fence was the outsider Kininvie, who landed safely over the obstacle. Not so fortunate were Barney Maclyvie and Another Captain, who both departed the race, while Aldaniti made a mistake that almost rendered his hard work in recovery ruined. But, surviving the error, Aldaniti continued towards the back of the field as Kininvie and Carrow Boy set the pace heading for Becher's, with the usually trouble-free fourth fence claiming Delmoss, Kilkilwell, Chumson and Bryan Boru.

Aldaniti jumps the Canal Turn second time.

Aldaniti and jockey Bob Champion emotionally win the 1981 race from Spartan Missile, Royal Mail and Three To One (left).

In a glorious spectacle, the entire field streamed over Becher's safely, led by Kininvie, Carrow Boy, Tenecoon, Lord Gulliver and Choral Festival, but Another Prospect came down at the Canal Turn, and early pacesetters Carrow Boy and Tenecoon were also casualties out in the country.

By the thirteenth, the thick white face of Aldaniti had come through to raise the spirits of his followers, sitting just behind the new leader Zongalero, but the fence caught out Lord Gulliver and, as the large number still standing soared The Chair to the roar of the crowd, the second circuit looked sure to provide an exciting finish.

Having been patient and hunted round for a circuit, Champion now sent Aldaniti to the front jumping the seventeenth, taking each fence with accuracy and authority on the way down to Becher's, his legs coping admirably with the drop landings. The mare Kylogue Lady was an early departure on the second circuit as Champion began to call the shots. Sticking to the inside as they met the big ditch, the challengers were bunching up behind Aldaniti, most prominent of which were Rubstic, Pacify, Royal Mail, Senator Maclacury and Spartan Missile. Royal Stuart had shaped as a real danger as he stalked the leaders, but a bad blunder at the twentieth stopped his momentum, and the frustrated Welsh jockey Hywel Davies was unseated a fence later with his leathers broken.

Aldaniti proudly cleared Becher's with a slim edge over his pursuers while, on the outside, 50/1 shot Pacify had really travelled well until brushing through the top of the fence and crumbling on landing when lying second. After jumping the Canal Turn, Aldaniti and Royal Mail broke free from Three To One, Senator Maclacury, Spartan Missile, Royal Exile, Might Be, Rathlek and the toiling Casamayor as the race approached boiling point.

Aldaniti and Royal Mail found themselves in a private duel. Both were jumping beautifully and, crossing the Melling Road, the race looked between the pair as they surged on. In behind, only Senator Maclacury, Three To One, Rubstic and the rallying Spartan Missile could smell the leaders, the lattermost being very nearly taken out by two loose horses that broke through the inside running rail trying to rejoin the race.

The class horse of the race, Royal Mail, loomed as a real danger to Aldaniti two out but made a total mess of the fence, almost sending Philip Blacker to the floor, and now it was advantage Aldaniti. Though getting tired, Aldaniti was quickly away after the last, finding extra reserves as he battled bravely for his jockey. Royal Mail was now struggling to respond to the leader and began to weaken but, coming from off the pace under an inspired ride by Thorne was the favourite Spartan Missile. Flashing past Royal Mail at the elbow, Spartan Missile set about reeling in Aldaniti and, such was the drive of his finish, he initially looked like doing so. But Aldaniti was a battler, full of courage and staying power and, responding to Champion's urges, he found extra reserves, striding out to win

Bob Champion overcame cancer to win the National.

1981 GRAND NATIONAL RESULT

FATE	HORSE	AGE/WEIGHT	JOCKEY	ODDS
1st	ALDANITI	11.10.13	R. CHAMPION	10/1
2nd	SPARTAN MISSILE	9.11.5	MR M.J. THORNE	8/1
3rd	ROYAL MAIL	11.11.7	P. BLACKER	16/1
4th	THREE TO ONE	10.10.3	MR T.G. DUN	33/1
5th	Senator Maclacury	7.10.12	J. Burke	20/1
6th	Royal Exile	12.10.0	B. De Haan	16/1
7th	Rubstic	12.10.7	M. Barnes	11/1
8th	Coolishall	12.10.3	W. Smith	25/1
9th	Rathlek	11.10.1	P. Barton	50/1
10th	So	12.10.8	J. Francome	40/1
11th	Sebastian V	13.10.2	R. Lamb	33/1
12th	Cheers	9.10.0	P. Scudamore	20/1
Fell	Carrow Boy	9.11.6	G. Newman	33/1
Fell	Chumson	10.11.7	Mr A. O'Connell	50/1
Fell	Zongalero	11.10.11	S. Smith-Eccles	14/1
Fell	Barney Maclyvie	10.10.8	M. Lynch	33/1
Fell	Martinstown	9.10.7	Mr M. Batters	33/1
Fell	Kilkilwell	9.10.6	N. Madden	33/1
Fell	Another Prospect	9.10.8	Mr A.J. Wilson	40/1
Fell	Delmoss	11.10.1	F. Berry	50/1
Fell	Drumroan	13.10.6	Mr M. Graffe	50/1
Fell	Kylogue Lady	9.10.0	T. Quinn	100/1
Fell	Lord Gulliver	8.10.0	C. Brown	50/1
Fell	Might Be	10.10.0	A. Webber	50/1
Fell	Pacify	11.10.0	S. Jobar	50/1
Fell	Another Captain	9.10.0	C. Hawkins	40/1
Fell	Tenecoon	12.10.0	C. Mann	100/1
Fell	Choral Festival	10.10.2	Mr M.J. Low	66/1
Fell	No Gypsy	12.10.0	J. Suthern	100/1
Fell	Three Of Diamonds	9.10.4	P. Leach	100/1
Fell	Kininvie	12.10.0	P. Hobbs	100/1
Pulled-Up	My Friendly Cousin	11.10.2	A. Brown	100/1
Unseated Rider	Royal Stuart	10.10.2	H. Davies	16/1
Refused	The Vintner	10.10.8	C. Grant	20/1
Refused	Casamayor	11.10.6	Mr P. Webber	100/1
Refused	Bryan Boru	10.10.0	Mr J. Carden	100/1
Refused	Son And Heir	11.10.0	S. Morshead	100/1
Refused	Dromore	13.10.8	Mr P. Duggan	100/1
Refused	Deiopea	10.10.0	Mrs L. Sheedy	100/1

4 April 1981
Going – Good
Sponsor – The *Sun*
Winner – £51,324
Time – 9mins 47.2secs
39 Ran

Favourite – Spartan Missile
Top Weight – Royal Mail
Winner trained by Josh Gifford at Findon, Sussex
Winner owned by Mr S.N.J. Embiricos
Aldaniti, chestnut gelding by Derek H
   – Renardeau.

by four lengths to the thunderous applause and emotional delight of the crowd. In a genuine example of true sportsmanship, Thorne was first to congratulate Champion moments after Aldaniti crossed the line. Thorne had also endured hard times for he had lost his son Nigel – who had ridden Polaris Missile in the 1968 National – in a motorcycle accident, and here he concluded his race had been lost when Spartan Missile was hampered at the Canal Turn and that he hoped to ride the horse to victory in 1982. Having run out of steam under his big weight, Royal Mail (trained by former jockey Stan Mellor) emerged with great credit in third ahead of Three To One and the Irish horse Senator Maclacury.

The scenes that followed were understandably filled with emotion as it became apparent just what had been achieved. Josh Gifford received much praise for bringing Aldaniti to his peak for Aintree, and the trainer in turn designated credit to the Embiricos family for their part in the horse's recovery and the willingness to run him in the National having lost the promising Stonepark over the big fences two days before.

But without doubt the day belonged to Bob Champion and Aldaniti, who had both met the challenge of the toughest steeplechase on earth with the same dedication and strength they had shown in their previous battles in life, winning endless admirers in the process. On a day when hope was handed out to thousands through their accomplishments, the 1981 victors could truly be described as heroes.

1982

GRITTAR

A cloud of sadness hovered over the 1982 Grand National. John Thorne, noble runner-up the year before on Spartan Missile, had tragically lost his life following a fall in a point-to-point race just weeks prior to the race. Thorne's loss was a bitter blow to the racing world and, although insignificant in comparison, further problems lay ahead for Aintree. Now in the final year of the Ladbrokes agreement, Bill Davies had opted to price the racecourse at £7 million, a huge increase on his original purchase. It was the Jockey Club who then responded by launching the 'Aintree Grand National Appeal', hoping to raise the necessary money to save the race. It seemed most unrealistic and slightly farcical that such an important event should resort to this, yet the deadline was set for November 1982, with failure to find the required funds offering the old fear that there would be no more Aintree Grand Nationals.

Once more, an amateur had the ride on the Grand National favourite. At forty-eight years of age, Mr Dick Saunders, a close friend of the late John Thorne, partnered Grittar, a brilliant jumper who, at nine, was at the peak of his powers. Like the sidelined Spartan Missile, Grittar had made his name as an outstanding hunter-chaser, winning both Foxhunter races at Cheltenham and Aintree the previous year. Trained in Leicestershire by permit-holder Mr Frank Gilman, Grittar had recently finished sixth behind the ultra-talented Silver Buck in the Gold Cup in preparation for the National and, despite a big weight of 11st 5lbs, the horse was a strong favourite at 7/1.

Royal Mail was again top weight and now had Bob Davies on board, while Aldaniti returned to defend his crown, although he now had 10lbs extra to carry and had failed to sparkle in his most recent run at Haydock. Three To One was also present – meaning that three of the four placed horses from 1981 ran again. Three To One had won well at Hexham prior to the National, fuelling hopes of a win for trainer Ken Oliver, who had sent out Wyndburgh and Moidore's Token to be second in previous editions.

Plenty of newcomers flocked the field of thirty-nine; among their number was a belated National appearance for the grey Man Alive, while the each-way hope

Deep Gale was the first of many Grand National runners for the major Irish punter J.P. McManus. The 1979 Welsh Grand National winner Peter Scot was a rock-solid jumper and the mount of Paul Barton, while both the well-fancied Tragus and the stamina-rich grey Loving Words came into the race in fine form, the latter having won a four-mile chase at Warwick earlier in the season. Of the others, the sure-footed bay Again The Same at least provided Jonjo O'Neill with hope of completing the course, while of the two female riders competing, Mrs Geraldine Rees was doing so for the first time, riding the bay Cheers, a horse that had plugged round to finish last of twelve in 1981.

Led by the trailblazing Delmoss, the big field set off at a lightning pace and were already well spaced out at the first, with the leaders going far too quickly. From such a fierce gallop, the carnage that occurred was inevitable. Disputing the lead with Delmoss, Deep Gale was the first to go as he crashed face-first into the turf. A plethora of spectacular tumbles quickly followed, including the grey Man Alive, who skidded for a number of yards before dislodging Andy Turnell. Capsizing towards the back, there would be no fairytale ending on this occasion for Aldaniti – Bob Champion's smile from 1981 was replaced with a disgusted frown as Aldaniti cantered away loose. In total ten horses went at the first, the highest total since 1951, with speed again undoing the majority. The others to go were Mullacurry, Jimmy Miff, Three To One, Rambling Jack, Cold Spell, Artistic Prince and Rathlek.

With the big ditch claiming another quartet, the field was radically depleted heading for Becher's. Delmoss, Carrow Boy, Saint Fillans and Grittar were first

Grittar and jockey Dick Saunders were winners of both the Aintree and Cheltenham Foxhunters' before landing the 1982 National.

Cheers and Mrs Geraldine Rees (left) collide with Coolishall and Ron Barry early on in the 1982 race. Mrs Rees survived and became the first female jockey to complete the National.

over the monster fence, but Peter Scot suffered a rare fall as did Royal Mail and, with Again The Same's mistake enough to continue O'Neill's dreadful luck at the fence, many of the fancied runners were out of the race by the Canal Turn.

Settling down into some sort of normality, Delmoss led the sparse band of survivors back onto the racecourse. Severely interfered with by the riderless Jimmy Miff approaching the thirteenth it was a miracle Delmoss was not carried out but with a great display of horsemanship, jockey Bill Smith gathered Delmoss and managed to get him to jump the fence, albeit in a wild, exaggerated manner. Fortunately, Delmoss had escaped the incident intact and, jumping The Chair and water, led out for a second circuit in a clear lead from Carrow Boy, St Fillans and Good Prospect.

Delmoss had set off at such a hectic pace that it was no surprise when he began to tire, and Carrow Boy took up the running from Saint Fillans, Grittar, Loving Words, Tragus and the chestnut outsider Hard Outlook: these would be the key players for the conclusion of the race.

A bad blunder at the second Becher's by Saint Fillans had allowed Grittar to take over from Phil Tuck's mount on the inside, and the favourite began a strong, relentless gallop from Valentines that had his rivals under heavy pressure. When Saint Fillans and Carrow Boy crashed out four from home, causing Loving Words to swerve violently and unship Richard Hoare, only a fall looked likely to stop Grittar winning.

Only Hard Outlook remained in the hunt and, although the chestnut got close to Grittar at the last, where the favourite made a rare blunder by going right through the fence, Saunders always appeared in total command and, coming well clear passing the elbow, the cheers ran out to acclaim Grittar as the new hero of Aintree. Despite the heavy burden on his back and the fact Hard Outlook only carried 10st 1lb, Grittar galloped on defiantly, becoming one of the easiest winners in modern times. Hard Outlook had run above expectations and tried hard, but was no match for the winner, and it was testament to how dominating Grittar's performance had been when Loving Words, remounted by Hoare, was third past the post and a long way back, edging out Delmoss. It was some time later when Mrs Geraldine Rees achieved the milestone of becoming the first female jockey to complete the Grand National. Having been roared on by the crowd and coaxed over the last few fences by amateur Pat O'Connor on fellow back-marker Three Of Diamonds, Rees came home in eighth and last place aboard the thoroughly exhausted Cheers. Having sadly fallen at the first fence, Aldaniti was graciously retired, his place in Aintree folklore assured, and both he and Bob Champion then set about raising huge amounts of money for the Bob Champion Cancer Research Trust.

At forty-eight, Saunders (a Northamptonshire farmer and Jockey Club member) became the oldest rider to win the National, graciously pinning all the praise on the majestic Grittar. As he had vowed to do beforehand, Saunders promptly retired from race riding, bowing out in the most perfect of ways. Frank Gilman also made history by becoming the first permit holder to win the National and, in Grittar, he had an exceptional Aintree horse – one young enough to return for (as everyone hoped) future Aintree Grand Nationals.

Rough And Tumble's refusal at Becher's sends John Francome flying over the fence.

The victorious Grittar is led back to the racecourse stables.

1982 GRAND NATIONAL RESULT

FATE	HORSE	AGE/WEIGHT	JOCKEY	ODDS
1st	GRITTAR	9.11.5	MR C.R. SAUNDERS	7/1
2nd	HARD OUTLOOK	11.10.1	A. WEBBER	50/1
3rd	LOVING WORDS	9.10.11	R. HOARE (remounted)	16/1
4th	DELMOSS	12.10.3	W. SMITH	50/1
5th	Current Gold	11.10.8	N. Doughty	25/1
6th	Tragus	10.11.4	P. Scudamore	14/1
7th	Three Of Diamonds	10.10.7	Mr P. O'Connor	100/1
8th	Cheers	10.10.0	Mrs Geraldine Rees	66/1
Fell	Royal Mail	12.11.10	B.R. Davies	17/2
Fell	Aldaniti	12.11.9	R. Champion	12/1
Fell	Carrow Boy	10.11.7	G. Newman	40/1
Fell	Peter Scot	11.11.5	P. Barton	16/1
Fell	Deep Gale	9.11.2	T.J. Ryan	22/1
Fell	Rambling Jack	11.11.1	T.G. Dun	16/1
Fell	Man Alive	11.11.0	A. Turnell	33/1
Fell	Mullacurry	10.10.12	Mr T.J. Taaffe	16/1
Fell	Saint Fillans	8.10.11	P. Tuck	33/1
Fell	Gandy VI	13.10.8	N. Madden	50/1
Fell	Old Society	8.10.8	P. Walsh	33/1
Fell	Three To One	11.10.3	R. Lamb	12/1
Fell	Sun Lion	12.10.3	S. Smith-Eccles	50/1
Fell	Coolishall	13.10.3	R. Barry	33/1
Fell	Senator Maclacury	8.10.0	P. Kiely	20/1
Fell	Artistic Prince	11.10.0	C. Brown	50/1
Fell	Jimmy Miff	10.10.1	Mr M. Williams	50/1
Fell	This Way	11.10.2	C. Candy	100/1
Fell	Deermount	8.10.0	J.P. Byrne	100/1
Fell	Rathlek	12.10.12	Mr J. Carden	100/1
Pulled-Up	Again The Same	9.11.8	J.J. O'Neill	16/1
Brought Down	Royal Stuart	11.10.4	Mr D. Gray	40/1
Brought Down	Cold Spell	10.10.0	S. Jobar	40/1
Unseated Rider	The Vintner	11.10.7	Mr D. Browne	50/1
Unseated Rider	Martinstown	10.10.3	Miss Charlotte Brew	100/1
Unseated Rider	Choral Festival	11.10.4	Mr M.J. Low	100/1
Refused	Rolls Rambler	11.10.12	Mr A.J. Wilson	20/1
Refused	Good Prospect	13.10.12	R. Linley	50/1
Refused	Rough And Tumble	12.10.8	J. Francome	16/1
Refused	Tiepolino	10.10.4	H. Davies	50/1
Refused	Monty Python	10.10.0	B. De Haan	66/1

3 April 1982
Going – Good
Sponsor – The *Sun*
Winner – £52,507
Time – 9mins 12.6secs
39 Ran

Favourite – Grittar
Top Weight – Royal Mail
Winner trained by Frank Gilman at
    Morcott, Leicestershire
Winner owned by Mr F.H. Gilman
Grittar, bay gelding by Grisaille – Tarama.

1983

Delmoss leads at the fourteenth fence from Corbiere (right), Hallo Dandy (24) and Colonel Christy.

CORBIERE

The Grand National Appeal had been put back to later in the year when the funds raised were estimated to be some £3 million short of the required total. For now, the attention turned to the National itself, although the whole process of securing the future of Aintree had long become pathetically tedious – perhaps lending to the reason why the money raised through the support of the general public had proved insufficient.

With Geraldine Rees having made the breakthrough for female jockeys in the 1982 National by completing the course, the stage was set for another historic achievement, as three women trainers held very realistic chances of winning the big race. The Helen Hamilton-trained Peaty Sandy and Pilot Officer, trained by the late Fred Rimell's wife Mercy, both had strong claims having been placed in the season's Welsh Grand National. But it was with Lambourn trainer Jenny Pitman that a lot of the attention focused. Mrs Pitman had once been married to Richard Pitman, runner-up aboard the gallant Crisp in 1973, and she had built-up the run-down Weathercock House stables from virtually nothing into one of the finest establishments in the land. Pitman saddled outsiders Artistic Prince and Monty Python, but it was with the broad chestnut Corbiere that her best chance lay. A fearless worker in all conditions on the gallops and splendid jumper and resolute galloper on the racecourse, Corbiere was a horse of immense heart and determination and, while not possessing the speed of a Gold Cup candidate, was a match for any horse in the land in staying handicap chases,. He had risen to Grand National prominence with a gutsy win in the Welsh Grand National the previous December. With 11st 4lbs to carry, the young Corbiere found his favoured soft ground present at Aintree, where he was partnered by twenty-three-year-old Ben De Haan, who had previously finished sixth aboard Royal Exile in 1981.

Race favourite was the 1982 hero Grittar, who by Frank Gilman's own admission had not had the ideal preparation for the race and possibly lacked the element of sharpness on this occasion. Nevertheless, Grittar had jumped so well

in 1982 that it was hard to imagine the horse failing to play a serious part and, with Paul Barton in the saddle, started a warm market leader at 6/1.

Those rivalling Grittar in the market were plentiful, with Fulke Walwyn's soft ground-loving Bonum Omen (a winner of marathon chases at Cheltenham and Warwick) proving particularly popular given the state of the going while, having missed the previous season through injury, Spartan Missile returned to the scene of his near miss behind Aldaniti in 1981. Now trained by the up-and-coming Nicky Henderson, Spartan Missile was a most popular chaser – although he was now eleven – a recent win at Newbury together with his previous Aintree exploits guaranteed a wave of support.

Venture To Cognac was a former Cheltenham Festival winner and had come seventh in the 1982 Gold Cup, while the talented Mid Day Gun had been carefully brought back to fitness and winning form by trainer John Webber, the horse having broken a bone in his knee earlier in his career. Mid Day Gun was a first National ride for Graham McCourt, while the 1982 Topham Trophy winner Beacon Time was the final ride in the race for Jonjo O'Neill. Of the remainder, there was sustained each-way support for the Michael Cunningham-trained Irish stayer Greasepaint, while the former Irish Grand National winner King's Spruce was ridden by Mrs Joy Carrier and, at 28/1, appeared the most worthwhile challenger yet of all female-ridden horses in the National.

Led by the now customary charge from Delmoss, the big field of forty-one thundered towards the first fence. Joined by the striking white face of Corbiere at the opening obstacle, Delmoss was first over but, for the well-backed Mid Day Gun and outsiders Tower Moss and Midday Welcome, the race was over in a heartbeat, the lattermost horse unceremoniously depositing the previous year's heroine Geraldine Rees to the turf.

Becher's second time; stumbling on landing is Spartan Missile as Peaty Sandy (9) jumps the fence beautifully.

Yer Man, with a big break to the likes of Peaty Sandy, Political Pop and Venture To Cognac and, having lost the disappointing Bonum Omen (who was never in contention when refusing), the field faced up again to Becher's, with the leaders taking the fence admirably. Towards the rear, a mistake by Spartan Missile unseated Hywel Davies when the horse was down on his knees while, at the next, Greasepaint survived a bad blunder to stay in contention.

Over the Canal Turn and Valentines, both Hallo Dandy and Corbiere turned on the pressure with some stunning jumps; as Colonel Christy and Grittar tired, only Yer Man and Greasepaint could live with the two leaders crossing the Melling Road for the final time.

As Keengaddy and Beacon Time joined the leading group, long shots That's It and Mender fell away at fences three and four, as Becher's lay in wait for the remainder. For the second consecutive year Royal Mail failed to survive the fence, with the second female rider departing as King's Spruce was badly hampered and unable to avoid a fall, while Beech King and the veteran Three To One also came down at the most feared of the obstacles.

It was Keengaddy and jockey Steve Smith-Eccles that now took the field along, but the horse lost a lot of ground when carried wide at the Canal Turn, a fence that saw the sad demise of outsider Duncreggan, who fell fatally back in the field. Out of position and with his momentum badly interrupted, Keengaddy crashed out at Valentines as Delmoss again took up the running, joined up front by another outsider in Hallo Dandy, ridden by Welshman Neale Doughty.

In the distance waited the monster Chair fence, and it was here that the next wave of victims were claimed. Delmoss, Hallo Dandy, Corbiere, Greasepaint and Grittar were jumping well and dominating at the head of affairs, the quintet landing safely over the fifteenth, but behind them there was chaos. Pilot Officer's fall brought down Williamson, while 300/1 shot Sydney Quinn obviously took a serious dislike to the vast trench before the fence, landing straight inside it. Canford Ginger and O'er the Border both departed and Arrigle Boy shot his jockey over the fence having refused, as another of the Grand National's most notorious fences made an impact.

Despite the casualties, most of the big guns were still standing at the start of the second circuit, where the veteran Delmoss began to fade, relinquishing the lead to the surprising Hallo Dandy on the outside, with another outsider Colonel Christy running smoothly in the centre and Corbiere jumping magnificently on the inner. Behind these came Grittar, Greasepaint and the improving chestnut

Corbiere gets a kiss from Jenny Pitman, the first woman to train a National winner.

Striding to two out, Corbiere was still going in relentless style as Hallo Dandy began to weaken on softer-than-ideal ground. The blinkered Yer Man was still in touch on the outside but, at this stage, nothing was going better than the white-faced chestnut Greasepaint for amateur jockey Colin Magnier.

Again Corbiere showed his rugged determination, however, clearing the last well and setting off for the final drive to the line. He had shaken off all but Greasepaint by the elbow. Three lengths down in the closing stages, Greasepaint suddenly began a charge that cut down the leader's advantage with every stride. To a thunderous crescendo of noise, Greasepaint looked to be reeling in Corbiere and reached his quarters fifty yards from the line but, as Mrs Pitman had indicated to all beforehand, Corbiere was as hard a fighter as there was and, sensing the Irish horse's advance, found the extra strength needed to hold off Greasepaint by three-quarters of a length in a most dramatic finish. Yer Man and Hallo Dandy had both done themselves proud in claiming the minor places, while Grittar was fifth home.

As the television cameras focused on Jenny Pitman, the emotional trainer could be seen with tears in her eyes, scarcely able to believe her achievement. Having held a licence since 1975, Pitman had trained Corbiere from a three-year-old and the chestnut she called 'Corky' had a very special place in her heart. In becoming the first lady to train the Grand National winner, Pitman set the standards for all women in racing and, up until she retired in the late 1990s (handing over the duties at Weathercock House to son Mark and becoming a writer of racing-themed thrillers), her engaging, colourful personality made her both respected and popular at every race meeting she attended, especially the Grand National. In a highly successful career that would include another Grand National success in the 1990s, Pitman trained two Gold Cup winners, three Welsh Grand Nationals winners, multiple Cheltenham Festival winners and winners of the Hennessy, King George VI, Scottish National and Irish National. As for the equine hero of the hour, Corbiere would establish himself as an Aintree legend, proving to be one of those rare horses that simply thrived in the race and rose – for the next four years – to the unique challenge of the event.

1983 GRAND NATIONAL RESULT

FATE	HORSE	AGE/WEIGHT	JOCKEY	ODDS
1st	CORBIERE	8.11.4	B. DE HAAN	13/1
2nd	GREASEPAINT	8.10.7	MR C. MAGNIER	14/1
3rd	YER MAN	8.10.0	T.V. O'CONNELL	80/1
4th	HALLO DANDY	9.10.1	N. DOUGHTY	60/1
5th	Grittar	10.11.12	P. Barton	6/1
6th	Peaty Sandy	9.11.3	T.G. Dun	12/1

FATE	HORSE	AGE/WEIGHT	JOCKEY	ODDS
7th	Political Pop	9.11.3	G. Bradley	28/1
8th	Venture To Cognac	10.11.12	Mr O. Sherwood	28/1
9th	Colonel Christy	8.10.0	P. Hobbs	66/1
10th	Delmoss	13.10.3	W. Smith	50/1
Fell	King Spruce	9.11.4	Mrs J. Carrier	28/1
Fell	Royal Mail	13.11.4	Mr T. Thomson Jones	50/1
Fell	Carrow Boy	11.10.12	G. Newman	33/1
Fell	Mid Day Gun	9.10.8	G. McCourt	14/1
Fell	Pilot Officer	8.10.7	S. Morshead	22/1
Fell	Beech King	9.10.8	Mr P. Duggan	60/1
Fell	Hot Tomato	11.10.2	J. Burke	100/1
Fell	Three To One	12.10.2	P. Tuck	25/1
Fell	Duncreggan	10.10.0	G. McGlinchey	75/1
Fell	Keengaddy	10.10.0	S. Smith-Eccles	15/1
Fell	Mender	12.10.1	A. Webber	50/1
Fell	Midday Welcome	12.10.0	Mrs G. Rees	500/1
Fell	Sydney Quinn	11.10.0	P. Double	300/1
Fell	That's It	9.10.0	G. Holmes	200/1
Fell	Tower Moss	10.10.1	R. Rowe	300/1
Pulled-Up	Tacroy	9.11.9	F. Berry	33/1
Pulled-Up	Beacon Time	9.10.6	J.J. O'Neill	25/1
Pulled-Up	Fortina's Express	9.10.3	P. Scudamore	20/1
Pulled-Up	Oakprime	8.10.5	R. Linley	66/1
Pulled-Up	Canford Ginger	8.10.0	J.H. Davies	33/1
Brought Down	Williamson	9.10.0	C. Mann	100/1
Unseated Rider	Spartan Missile	11.11.7	H. Davies	9/1
Refused	Bonum Omen	9.10.9	K. Mooney	15/2
Refused	Menford	8.10.0	M. Perrett	100/1
Refused	The Vintner	12.10.0	C. Grant	66/1
Refused	Arrigle Boy	11.10.1	C. Pimlott	100/1
Refused	Artistic Prince	12.10.0	C. Brown	66/1
Refused	O'er The Border	9.10.12	Mr P. O'Connor	200/1
Refused	Monty Python	11.10.2	P. O'Brien	150/1
Refused	Never Tamper	8.10.0	J. Williams	500/1
Ran Out	The Lady's Master	12.11.2	Mr W.P. Mullins	200/1

9 April 1983
Going – Soft
Sponsor – The *Sun*
Winner – £52,949
Time – 9mins 47.4secs
41 Ran
Favourite – Grittar
Top Weight – Grittar
Winner trained by Mrs Jenny Pitman at Upper Lambourn, Berkshire
Winner owned by Mr B.R.H. Burrough
Corbiere, chestnut gelding by Harwell – Ballycashin.

1984

HALLO DANDY

It was with enormous delight and a huge sense of relief when whisky distillery giants Seagram, led by Major Ivan Straker, stepped in to rescue the Grand National. Outgoing chief Bill Davies accepted an eventual sum of £3.4 million for the racecourse, with the Grand National to be controlled totally by the Jockey Club. Through an Aintree Racecourse Company, new rules were introduced that improved the quality of entrants, while the safety limit for the race was set at forty runners. Seagram agreed to sponsor the race for the next five years, with an option for five more and, with plans for reconstruction to the grandstand in full flow and with the richest prize yet on offer to the winner, the new hierarchy had provided the solid future the race had been in need of for too long.

No doubt influenced by the considerable and most welcome changes, a massive entry of one hundred and forty-one was received for the 1984 Seagram Grand National and, with the going on the day good, a maximum field turned out for the first National in Aintree's new era. Having fought out a dramatic finish to the 1983 race, both Corbiere and Greasepaint returned to clash heads. Jenny Pitman's Corbiere had been allotted top weight of 12 stone by race handicapper Captain Christopher Mordaunt – a weight that infuriated the trainer, who made no hesitation in writing off the horse's winning chance. In addition, Corbiere's season had been blighted by injury and, despite Mrs Pitman landing the recent Gold Cup with the exceptional Burrough Hill Lad, there were others preferred in the market to the courageous winner of the year before.

Like Mrs Pitman, Dermot Weld, new trainer of the favourite Greasepaint, was unhappy with the big weight his horse was burdened with. Nevertheless, the Irish chestnut's gallant run the year before had endeared him to many, and a return to Aintree had long been the horse's seasonal target. Running into form at Navan prior to the race, Greasepaint was sent off the market leader on 9/1 for new owner Mr Michael Smurfit and jockey Tommy Carmody.

It promised to be a deeply competitive renewal, as both Yer Man and Hallo Dandy returned from the year before. An athletic, sound-surface loving, dark bay horse formerly trained by Ginger McCain, Hallo Dandy was another whose season-long aim had been the National. Trained in Cumbria by Gordon Richards, the horse (like the 1976 winner Rag Trade, by the sire Menelek) had been kept to the northern tracks during the season, protecting his handicap mark and, having been given a midwinter break, Hallo Dandy had reappeared at Ayr three weeks prior to the National, where he tuned up for the big race in promising style. Far better supported than in 1983, Richards declared himself more confident with Hallo Dandy than he had been before Lucius had triumphed in 1978.

Old favourites Grittar and Spartan Missile returned with decent chances, but both were now advanced in years and again had big weights. There were many others ready to stake their claims for a place in history. Among these were the lightly raced Irish hunter Eliogarty, a previous winner of the Cheltenham Foxhunters', and the big bay horse Lucky Vane, the winner of the season's Eider Chase and hailing from the yard of Toby Balding. The John Edwards-trained Broomy Bank was a hot tip, having won the Kim Muir at Cheltenham, while recent Haydock Park winner Midnight Love represented Red Alligator's trainer Denys Smith. Of the outsiders, there was a first National ride for Miss Valerie Alder on Bush Guide, while a win for the eleven-year-old bay Silent Valley would have been highly admirable, considering the horse – twice placed in the Hennessy Cognac Gold Cup – had recovered from a broken leg two seasons before.

Earthstopper rises magnificently at Becher's from the grey Two Swallows.

Fourteenth fence: Broomy Bank (red and yellow) tracks the leaders together with Canford Ginger (blue and white) and the hidden Lucky Vane.

An excited crowd settled down to watch the first National under the Seagram banner, as the David Nicholson-trained Burnt Oak set off an explosive pace. Despite the terrific gallop, no horse fell until the third fence, when Golden Trix came a cropper, but the rest of the field survived to face Becher's Brook. Burnt Oak took the famous fence fully ten lengths ahead while, behind him, Midnight Love, Hazy Dawn, Clonthturtin and Three To One (running in his fifth National) all fell.

Miss Alder's race was over when Bush Guide went at the Canal Turn, as Burnt Oak continued to blaze along out in the country, being tracked by Greasepaint, Imperial Black, Corbiere and Tacroy. The leader plunged dramatically through the twelfth, but somehow survived to lead back onto the racecourse.

The Chair claimed the Michael Dickinson-trained pair of former Gold Cup fifth Ashley House and the chestnut Carl's Wager, but thirty-one had survived a circuit. With a tremendous finish in prospect, Burnt Oak, though showing signs of weariness, led a glory-hungry pack out for the second circuit, with Greasepaint, Earthstopper, Grittar, Two Swallows, Tacroy, Spartan Missile and Corbiere close behind.

Burnt Oak had burned out by the eighteenth, as the chestnut Earthstopper and race favourite Greasepaint came through to lead. Two that had made progress through the field were Hallo Dandy and Eliogarty, and the pair were starting to make rapid ground on the leaders. The crowd looked on in awe at Becher's as Eliogarty moved up on the outside to dispute the lead with Greasepaint and the grey horse Two Swallows, while Earthstopper delivered a mighty leap towards the inner. It was here that Hallo Dandy jumped right into contention as the race began to heat up considerably.

An atrocious mistake at Valentines by Eliogarty robbed him of vital momentum as old rivals Greasepaint and Hallo Dandy began a procession over the next line of fences. Crossing the Melling Road, the pair, still on the bridle, had developed a clear lead over Earthstopper, with Two Swallows, Lucky Vane, Corbiere and Eliogarty struggling to catch them.

With the race to themselves by two out, Greasepaint suddenly came under pressure for the first time while Hallo Dandy appeared full of running. Relishing the good ground, Hallo Dandy out-jumped his Irish opponent at the last two to open up what appeared a decisive advantage. Hallo Dandy was away quickly on the flat but began to wander sharply over to the stands side, allowing Greasepaint back into the race coming down the inner. The crowd rose to their feet, roaring on another great finish as Greasepaint battled back – as he had done the year before. But with a touch more speed and considerably less weight, it was Hallo Dandy that won the duel and, pulling away again at the end, won by four lengths. The gallant Greasepaint had run his heart out and looked the most likely winner, as Carmody remained motionless crossing the Melling Road for the final time. But he had to settle for second again, ahead of the fast-finishing Corbiere and the dour Lucky Vane. In total, a record twenty-three got round, but sadly Earthstopper collapsed and died having finished fifth. This was a cruel end for a horse that had run so well for a long way, serving to illustrate the enormous effort Grand Nationals horses deliver – each and every one as gallant as the next.

Fulfilling the promise he had shown the year before, Hallo Dandy provided a second winner for the highly respected Gordon Richards and continued a streak

Above: Hallo Dandy and jockey Neale Doughty lead the Irish chaser Greasepaint at the last fence.

Left: Gordon Richards, trainer of Hallo Dandy.

1984 GRAND NATIONAL RESULT

FATE	HORSE	AGE/WEIGHT	JOCKEY	ODDS
1st	HALLO DANDY	10.10.2	N. DOUGHTY	13/1
2nd	GREASEPAINT	9.11.2	T. CARMODY	9/1
3rd	CORBIERE	9.12.0	B. DE HAAN	16/1
4th	LUCKY VANE	9.10.13	J. BURKE	12/1
5th	Earthstopper	10.11.1	R. Rowe	33/1
6th	Two Swallows	11.10.0	A. Webber	28/1
7th	Fethard Friend	9.10.12	G. Newman	22/1
8th	Broomy Bank	9.10.12	Mr A.J. Wilson	12/1
9th	Jivago De Neuvy	9.11.0	Mr R. Grand	50/1
10th	Grittar	11.11.10	J. Francome	12/1
11th	Hill Of Slane	8.10.2	S. Smith-Eccles	33/1
12th	Tacroy	10.10.7	F. Berry	28/1
13th	Doubleuagain	10.10.5	T. Morgan	100/1
14th	Beech King	10.10.1	P. Kiely	66/1
15th	Eliogarty	9.11.5	Mr D. Hassett	16/1
16th	Spartan Missile	12.11.4	Mr J. White	18/1
17th	Yer Man	9.10.2	T.V. O'Connell	25/1
18th	Fauloon	9.10.13	W. Smith	50/1
19th	Another Captain	12.10.1	A. Stringer	66/1
20th	Mid Day Gun	10.10.3	G. McCourt	40/1
21st	Poyntz Pass	9.10.5	H. Rogers	100/1
22nd	Jacko	12.10.4	S. Morshead	66/1
23rd	Canford Ginger	9.10.1	C. Brown	100/1
Fell	Ashley House	10.11.13	G. Bradley	20/1
Fell	Midnight Love	9.11.4	C. Grant	28/1
Fell	Hazy Dawn	9.10.9	Mr W.P. Mullins	100/1
Fell	Imperial Black	8.10.7	C. Hawkins	50/1
Fell	Bush Guide	8.10.5	Miss Valerie Alder	33/1
Fell	Door Step	8.10.2	Mr J. Queally	100/1
Fell	Carl's Wager	9.10.2	Mr R.J. Beggan	28/1
Fell	Three To One	13.10.2	P. Tuck	66/1
Fell	Fortune Seeker	9.10.0	P. Barton	100/1
Fell	Golden Trix	9.10.1	K. Mooney	50/1
Fell	Clonthturtin	10.10.0	T.J. Taaffe	100/1
Fell	Kumbi	9.10.0	K. Doolan	100/1
Pulled-Up	Silent Valley	11.10.8	T.G. Dun	33/1
Pulled-Up	Burnt Oak	8.10.7	P. Scudamore	25/1
Pulled-Up	The Drunken Duck	11.10.3	A. Brown	100/1
Unseated Rider	Roman General	11.10.3	Major M. Wallace	100/1
Refused	Pilot Officer	9.10.2	Mr A. Sharpe	33/1

31 March 1984
Going – Good
Sponsor – Seagram
Winner – £54,769
Time – 9mins 21.4secs
40 Ran
Favourite – Greasepaint

Top Weight – Corbiere
Winner trained by Gordon W. Richards
   at Greystoke, Cumbria
Winner owned by Mr R. Shaw
Hallo Dandy, bay gelding by Menelek
   – Dandy Hall.

that would make jockey Neale Doughty one of the most successful Aintree riders of the modern era. The Welshman had ridden a perfect tactical race, keeping Hallo Dandy towards the rear before launching his challenge at the second Becher's. The win came for insurance broker Mr Richard Shaw, who had purchased the horse shortly before the 1983 race. Hallo Dandy competed in two more Grand Nationals and was a fine example of a horse that, although fairly innocuous on other courses, came alive around Aintree.

As another epic contest came to a close, those that truly loved the Grand National could now look forward to the following year's edition with a heart-warming feeling of security, safe in the knowledge that the great race was here to stay.

1985

LAST SUSPECT

The form of the 1984 Grand National was proudly represented when the first four home from that race lined-up again in 1985. Given another light campaign by Gordon Richards, the title-holder Hallo Dandy was back to defend his crown, this time with Gold Cup-winning jockey Graham Bradley replacing the injured Neale Doughty, but the horse had risen 10lbs since the year before and was without his favoured good ground on this occasion. Greasepaint was as popular as ever, his whole season again dedicated to burying the ghosts of Nationals past and, having pleased trainer Dermot Weld in the build-up to Aintree, held a share of favouritism at 13/2. Having enjoyed a spell hunting during the winter months, another bold show was expected from top weight Corbiere, the chestnut fresh from a recent victory at Chepstow, while Lucky Vane again had his supporters, really shaping like a Grand National contender when winning over four miles at Cheltenham in January.

Joining Greasepaint atop the betting market was one of the most rapidly improving chasing prospects in the land, ridden by one of the hottest properties to emerge on the jumps scene for many a year. The horse was the bay eight-year-old West Tip and the jockey the rising young star from Northern Ireland, Richard Dunwoody, competing in his first National. West Tip had won four races in a row prior to Aintree, including the big three-mile handicap chase at the Cheltenham Festival, and was a superb jumper that looked tailor made for the National. West Tip was a tough, hardy customer too, as he had survived an horrific collision with a lorry early in life that had left behind a huge scar on his quarters. With West Tip well weighted and possessing a terrific chance, it was with keen interest that the watching world waited to see how the natural talents of Dunwoody would cope with his first National experience.

The Irish bay Drumlargan, a former Whitbread Gold Cup winner, toyed with favouritism during much of the pre-race build-up, while both the 1984 seventh Fethard Friend and Classified, the two-and-a-half-mile specialist from Nicky Henderson's yard, attracted plenty of each-way support. Of the remainder, the strapping bay from Mick Easterby's northern yard, Mr Snugfit, appeared something of a dark horse – having compiled a string of staying-chase wins since the publication of the weights, in which he was set to carry the minimum 10 stone. Carrying the colours of Anne, Duchess of Westminster, made so famous by the legendary Arkle, was the Captain Tim Forster-trained Last Suspect. The inconsistent and somewhat temperamental brown eleven-year-old, though clearly possessing talent somewhere in his make-up, had proved both disappointing and decidedly moody of late, and a typically pessimistic Forster had been reluctant to even run him in the National. But run he did, predominantly on the advice of jockey Hywel Davies, with the horse starting at 50/1.

Seagram added a fitting tribute to the heroes of the past and present by holding a commemoration before the race where the surviving National-winning jockeys were given replica trophies to mark their achievements, presented to them by HRH Princess Anne. It was a further sign of the new-found commitment to the great race and its traditions and, with major construction to the grandstand and general complex in place under the new management (including former National jockeys Chris Collins and Peter Greenhall), the sense of progress at the racecourse was fully evident.

Once underway, the maximum field was soon led by the familiar big white face of Corbiere on the inside, but Hallo Dandy evoked memories of Gay Trip and Aldaniti as he fell hard at the first, joined unceremoniously on the ground by Talon, Solihull Sport and Bashful Lad.

Two-time winning jockey Pat Taaffe receives a commemorative honour from HRH Princess Anne at the 1985 Grand National meeting.

Becher's first time: Hill Of Slane hits the deck surrounded by, among others, Scot Lane (12), Mr Snugfit (36) and Our Cloud (42).

Broomy Bank. With Dudie falling at the nineteenth, the field faced up to Becher's again.

With Dunwoody enjoying a dream ride, West Tip looked certain to go extremely close, but the picture changed completely at Becher's. Getting too close and knocking the top branches off the top of the fence, West Tip had no chance of staying on his feet on the landing side, coming down when clearly holding every chance. Peter Scudamore, who had replaced the sidelined Ben De Haan on Corbiere, now sensed his chance of a first National success and drove Corbiere on, the horse responding with a series of amazing jumps from Valentines and beyond, his nearest challengers being Rupertino, Last Suspect, Greasepaint, Classified and the steadily improving Mr Snugfit.

Corbiere seemed set to win for a second time crossing the Melling Road as Rupertino faded, Greasepaint came under pressure and Last Suspect struggled to stay on terms, having made mistakes. But having quietly crept into the race on the second circuit, Phil Tuck was edging the lightly weighted Mr Snugfit ever closer and, by two out, the big bay loomed as a real danger.

Sailing past the heavily burdened Corbiere, Mr Snugfit came to the last full of running and, with his long stride taking him clear of his rivals on the run in, he looked sure to provide a National win for the North. Mr Snugfit held a distinct advantage at the elbow, but the power that had sent him past Corbiere soon drained from within the big horse and suddenly he was one-paced, Tuck praying for the line to arrive. Having only been fourth jumping the last, the tail-swishing Last Suspect came with a devastating final burst, forced forward vigorously by Davies. Right against the stand-side rails, Last Suspect flashed home, getting up on the line to deny Mr Snugfit by a length-and-a-half. The winner had produced an awesome finishing thrust having looked dead and buried at the final fence, and the result was one of the most thrilling conclusions ever witnessed in the

Recent Cheltenham Festival winner Northern Bay (with excellent trainer-of-the-future Philip Hobbs on board) went at the second while the outsider Crosa demolished the third, with Knockawad and Shady Deal also going at the big ditch. The seven-year-old Dudie, a notoriously sketchy jumper, had raced headstrong into the lead, and it was he that met Becher's in front, followed by Corbiere, Roman Bistro (also ridden by a future training great in Paul Nicholls) and Glenfox, partnered by New Zealand jockey Mr Denis Gray. The leaders cleared the fence well but, in behind, Tacroy and Hill Of Slane were out of the race.

Dudie survived an untidy jump at Valentines to hold his lead from Glenfox, Corbiere, Roman Bistro, Classified, Imperial Black, Greasepaint and Musso but, breaking down unfortunately at the tenth, Lucky Vane's Grand National ended prematurely. Dudie continued to make errors yet, having led back onto the racecourse, he was foot perfect at the biggest fence on the course, The Chair, but Greasepaint lost valuable ground with a dreadful blunder. Conversely, West Tip joined the leaders for the first time, putting in a splendid leap to announce his challenge.

The erratic Dudie ploughed over to the far side of the course beginning the second circuit, losing much ground and, over the next line of fences, an established order emerged as Corbiere – jumping as well as ever on the inside – was joined by the strong-travelling West Tip and the surprising Robert Stronge-ridden chestnut Rupertino in the centre, all three vying for the lead in a breathtaking spectacle. Next came Greasepaint, Scot Lane, Last Suspect and

Last Suspect (11) mounts his challenge on the second circuit with Greasepaint (red and white) on his inside.

Anne, Duchess of Westminster, the owner of Last Suspect, after the horse's win.

1985 GRAND NATIONAL RESULT

FATE	HORSE	AGE/WEIGHT	JOCKEY	ODDS
1st	LAST SUSPECT	11.10.5	H. DAVIES	50/1
2nd	MR SNUGFIT	8.10.0	P. TUCK	12/1
3rd	CORBIERE	10.11.10	P. SCUDAMORE	9/1
4th	GREASEPAINT	10.10.13	T. CARMODY	13/2
5th	Classified	9.10.7	J. White	20/1
6th	Imperial Black	9.10.1	C. Hawkins	66/1
7th	Rupertino	10.10.0	R. Stronge	33/1
8th	Scot Lane	12.10.1	C. Smith	28/1
9th	Glenfox	8.10.0	Mr D. Gray	50/1
10th	Blackrath Prince	9.10.0	B. Reilly	66/1
11th	Captain Parkhill	12.10.0	C. Grant	100/1
Fell	Hallo Dandy	11.10.12	G. Bradley	14/1
Fell	Tacroy	11.10.3	A. Stringer	33/1
Fell	West Tip	8.10.1	R. Dunwoody	13/2
Fell	Kumbi	10.10.0	K. Doolan	25/1
Fell	Dudie	7.10.0	A. Mullins	50/1
Fell	Shady Deal	12.10.3	R. Rowe	50/1
Fell	Talon	10.10.0	A. Webber	33/1
Fell	Knockawad	8.10.0	K. O'Brien	66/1
Fell	Hill Of Slane	9.10.2	S. Smith-Eccles	25/1
Fell	Royal Appointment	10.10.0	P. Gill	66/1
Fell	Solihull Sport	11.10.0	S. Morshead	100/1
Fell	Fauloon	10.10.2	K. Mooney	66/1
Fell	Bashful Lad	10.10.3	G. McCourt	50/1
Fell	Crosa	10.10.0	S. Moore	100/1
Fell	Leney Dual	10.10.8	Mr D. Pitcher	100/1
Fell	Immigrate	12.10.0	J. Hansen	100/1
Fell	Northern Bay	9.10.1	P. Hobbs	66/1
Pulled-Up	Drumlargan	11.11.8	J. Francome	8/1
Pulled-Up	Lucky Vane	10.10.13	J. Burke	10/1
Pulled-Up	Fethard Friend	10.10.7	P. Barton	16/1
Pulled-Up	Musso	9.10.0	Mr S. Sherwood	50/1
Pulled-Up	Onapromise	9.10.5	A. Brown	100/1
Pulled-Up	Clonthturtin	11.10.5	Mr T. Thomson Jones	50/1
Pulled-Up	Never Tamper	10.10.3	C. Brown	200/1
Pulled-Up	Greenhill Hall	9.10.0	D. Wilkinson	200/1
Refused	Broomy Bank	10.10.7	Mr A.J. Wilson	33/1
Refused	Tubbertelly	8.10.1	T.J. Taaffe	50/1
Refused	Roman Bistro	9.10.3	P. Nicholls	150/1
Refused	Our Cloud	9.10.0	Mr J. Queally	150/1

National. Mr Snugfit and Phil Tuck had been left heartbroken by their narrow defeat, while National stalwarts Corbiere and Greasepaint had again run most admirable races to take the minor places, Corbiere in particular proving what a force he was at Aintree. Of the leading fancies, the Irish stayer Drumlargan was pulled-up during the race having broken a blood vessel.

The outcome could have been much different but for Davies. Neither the Duchess of Westminster nor Forster wished to run Last Suspect at Aintree and only an encouraging telephone call made by the jockey to the owner prevented the horse from being withdrawn. It was Davies' finest moment, made all the more special considering the jockey had nearly lost his life in a fall at Doncaster the year before. For Captain Forster, Last Suspect's victory came as even more of a surprise than that of Ben Nevis, but he had now achieved the monumental feat of training three Grand National winners. Generally unconsidered beforehand, the National inspired Last Suspect, the horse whose late run earned him a place on Aintree's prestigious roll of honour.

30 March 1985

Going – Good to Soft

Sponsor – Seagram

Winner – £54,314

Time – 9mins 42.7secs

40 Ran

Joint Favourites – Greasepaint and West Tip

Top Weight – Corbiere

Winner trained by Captain Tim Forster at Letcombe Basset, Oxfordshire

Winner owned by Anne, Duchess of Westminster

Last Suspect, brown gelding by Above Suspicion – Last Link.

1986

WEST TIP

Last Suspect had been retired shortly after his 1985 Grand National win, but had subsequently come back into training with Captain Forster for another season, with another crack at the National his main aim. Last Suspect won both his races prior to Aintree and joined fellow former winners Corbiere and Hallo Dandy, as well as perennial challenger Greasepaint, in another maximum field.

But it was to be the two horses that caught the eye most in defeat the previous year – Mr Snugfit and West Tip – that headed the betting. Purchased after the 1985 race by Mr Terry Ramsden for the sole purpose of winning the Grand National, Mr Snugfit had been the subject of a huge ante-post gamble. Trainer Mick Easterby had total confidence in his horse following an encouraging performance on his latest start and, despite drifting in price shortly before the start, Mr Snugfit was sent off the 13/2 favourite. Unlike Mr Snugfit, West Tip had failed to complete the year before, but had looked arguably the most likely winner when he capsized at the second Becher's. However, that fall had done little to deter the horse's spirit, and a recent win over the useful Beau Ranger at Newbury indicated a horse primed for a big run. The form of that race was franked considerably when Beau Ranger beat the excellent Gold Cup runner-up Wayward Lad two days before the National. With Richard Dunwoody again on board, West Tip looked totally relaxed in the paddock, and eventually started a point behind the favourite at 15/2.

Though horses with previous National experience dominated the betting market, the handsome chestnut Door Latch figured among the fancied newcomers. Door Latch had finished third in the season's Hennessy Cognac Gold Cup and had also won at Ascot, offering a strong belief that the horse was ninety-one-year-old owner Mr Jim Joel's best chance yet of landing the great race. Trained by Josh Gifford, Richard Rowe wore the owner's famous black-and-scarlet silks, the jockey's best National performance so far coming aboard Earthstopper in 1984.

With Greasepaint considered by many to have missed his chance of National glory and Drumlargan now twelve, the possibility of an Irish win leaned towards

West Tip and jockey Richard Dunwoody were partners in five Grand Nationals.

two horses new to the race. The striking chestnut Monanore had won three times in his last four races, most recently at Gowran Park, bringing Tom Morgan's mount into the reckoning at 22/1, while Tom's brother Ken had a first National ride aboard the big brown horse Kilkilowen. Trained by Jim Dreaper, Kilkilowen was considered a magnificent jumper, and a stream of support on the morning of the race saw his odds tumble to 25/1.

It was certainly one of the deepest Nationals for many years, with trainer Nicky Henderson saddling both the 1985 fifth Classified and the recent winner of Cheltenham's Mildmay of Flete Chase, The Tsarevich, owned by Seagram's Major Ivan Straker. Both horses were more noted for running over shorter distances, yet Henderson believed both would stay and was unable to pick his preferred candidate. Classified was one of two horses (Northern Bay was the other) purchased shortly before the National by Cheveley Park Stud owners David and Pat Thompson.

Of the other interesting runners, automatic top weight was the Hungarian-bred stallion Essex, owned and trained in Czechoslovakia by Vaclav Chaloupka, while Mark Dwyer's mount Knock Hill, American-owned, was a thorough stayer that had won at both Cheltenham and Warwick in January. Imperial Black and Rupertino both ran again having showed boldly the year before, while the injury-plagued Young Driver (trained in Scotland by John Wilson), had been trained specifically for the National and ranked among the race's dark horses.

An early life collision with a lorry that left an horrific scar on his hindquarters failed to stop West Tip winning the 1986 National.

An inch of snow had fallen on the track overnight and, with National day overcast, the ground turned lifeless, cutting up noticeably in places. Not surprisingly for an entire, Essex was extremely lively in the preliminaries, bucking spectacularly, anxious to begin the race and, when the field were let go, the customary roar greeted the forty runners as the Czech raider pulled his way to the front, joined by rank outsider Doubleuagain as they met the first fence. Port Askaig was first to go but, in behind and towards the wide outside, Door Latch provided the first shock, hitting the ground after a clumsy take-off.

With outsider Lantern Lodge falling at the second, a pattern quickly emerged up front with Tacroy and Doubleuagain bowling along in the centre from the hard-pulling Essex on the outside. The Ginger McCain-trained Dudie unseated young Kevin Doolan at the third but was remounted to continue someway in arrears, while gasps of shock were reserved for Corbiere at the fourth when the Aintree stalwart hit the top of the fence and plunged to the ground when travelling down his usual inside route.

The leaders approached Becher's in the same order, with the white face of The Tsarevich emerging just behind together with Kilkilowen, as both Greasepaint and West Tip cruised through smoothly to take prominent positions. It was a glorious sight as the tightly bunched field swept over Becher's without a single casualty until the back-marker Dudie fell when hopelessly tailed-off, this time calling it a day.

Jumping Valentines and beyond, the leaders managed to stay out of trouble but, behind them, the grief was mounting up as both Tracys Special and Mount Oliver fell, while the tenth fence proved particularly troublesome as Ten Cherries brushed through the spruce and plummeted to the turf when on the heels of the leaders. Both Master Tercel and Another Duke (owned by BBC presenter Des Lynam) came down, while the unlucky Acarine collided with a loose horse and was brought down.

Jumping beautifully, Kilkilowen had come through on the inside to dispute the lead with Tacroy and Doubleuagain and, as the twenty-eight survivors crossed the Melling Road, plenty were still in contention, although Mr Snugfit was towards the rear with Hallo Dandy and Little Polveir, while Last Suspect was clearly not enjoying himself on this occasion and, receiving reminders from Hywel Davies, had only one behind him as they returned to the racecourse.

A dreadful blunder by Knock Hill at the thirteenth saw Dwyer lucky to stay in the saddle, badly denting the horse's chance while, having run far too free, Essex was pulled-up before the fourteenth with a broken girth. West Tip delivered the most stunning jump at The Chair, standing right off the fearsome fence, while Classified quietly moved into a leading position under Steve Smith-Eccles – just one of a huge number of horses that held strong prospects starting out for the second circuit. With ground on the soft side of good, Hallo Dandy was struggling at the back, while even further off the pace was Last Suspect, and the disappointing 1985 hero was soon pulled-up.

The Czech stallion Essex leads Kilkilowen (nearside) and The Tsarevich over Becher's first time.

Doubleuagain had jumped for fun for a circuit, but his reward for such a bold display was to be knocked over by a loose horse at the seventeenth when disputing the lead, while Tacroy soon began to tire and a sloppy jump at the nineteenth ended his run. The major players were now starting to emerge and, negotiating Becher's again without trouble, a leading group comprising of Kilkilowen, Classified, Northern Bay, The Tsarevich, West Tip, Young Driver, Sommelier and the rapidly improving Monanore began to assert themselves, pulling clear of the remainder jumping the fences down the back.

Rounding the turn for home, an exciting finish looked assured, as Scotland's Young Driver rushed past the tiring Kilkilowen, Northern Bay and Monanore, and he took the lead at the second last from Classified, Sommelier and The Tsarevich, with Dunwoody poised on the inner aboard West Tip.

Jockey Chris Grant jumped the last clear on Young Driver but, with the others beaten off, it was West Tip that came to challenge the outsider at the elbow. Supremely confident, Dunwoody glanced across at his opponent passing the

elbow, and then released West Tip for his run to the line. Despite pricking his ears and idling in front, West Tip had plenty in reserve and was always holding the Scottish horse. Crossing the line, West Tip won by a comfortable two lengths as Dunwoody punched the air in triumph. There was no doubt that the best horse had won the National, as West Tip had always been jumping and travelling extremely well, being always in the front rank before coming to play his hand two out. With his history of injuries, Young Driver was game in defeat, with the training achievement of Wilson admirable, while Classified had again run an excellent race, despite weakening from two out having shaped as a serious threat turning for home. Having never threatened the leaders, Mr Snugfit came from a long way back to take fourth ahead of Sommelier, the latter ridden by Pat Taaffe's son Tom.

An ultra-tough horse, West Tip had made amends for the previous year's disappointment by winning in convincing style for his Worcestershire trainer Michael Oliver. Battle-hardened not only on the racecourse, but in life itself,

Becher's second time: The Tsarevich (mauve cap) leads Northern Bay (39), Monanore (27) and West Tip.

West Tip had very nearly lost his life in a collision with a lorry in his earlier days and had been eased back to health through the dedicated care of the trainer's wife. After the race, the soft-speaking Dunwoody thanked his retainer Captain Forster and owner Lord Chelsea for releasing him from the mount of first-fence faller Port Askaig, and the win emphatically announced the jockey's arrival as a major force on the jumps scene. For Dunwoody, becoming Champion Jockey was now the target and, while he would achieve that honour with flying colours, further Grand National stardom awaited both he and the newest hero of Aintree, West Tip.

1986 GRAND NATIONAL RESULT

FATE	HORSE	AGE/WEIGHT	JOCKEY	ODDS
1st	WEST TIP	9.10.11	R. DUNWOODY	15/2
2nd	YOUNG DRIVER	9.10.0	C. GRANT	66/1
3rd	CLASSIFIED	10.10.3	S. SMITH-ECCLES	22/1
4th	MR SNUGFIT	9.10.7	P. TUCK	13/2
5th	Sommelier	8.10.0	T.J. Taaffe	50/1
6th	Broomy Bank	11.10.3	P. Scudamore	20/1
7th	The Tsarevich	10.10.7	J. White	16/1
8th	Monanore	9.10.0	T. Morgan	22/1
9th	Little Polveir	9.10.3	C. Brown	66/1
10th	Greasepaint	11.10.9	T. Carmody	16/1
11th	Northern Bay	10.10.0	P. Hobbs	33/1
12th	Hallo Dandy	12.10.8	N. Doughty	16/1
13th	Kilkilowen	10.11.3	K. Morgan	25/1
14th	Imperial Black	10.10.0	R. Crank	66/1
15th	Rupertino	11.10.0	G. Charles-Jones	66/1
16th	Why Forget	10.10.7	R. Lamb	35/1
17th	Gayle Warning	12.10.9	Mr A. Dudgeon	50/1
Fell	Corbiere	11.11.7	B. De Haan	14/1
Fell	Drumlargan	12.11.6	T.J. Ryan	40/1
Fell	Door Latch	8.11.0	R. Rowe	9/1
Fell	Ballinacurra Lad	11.10.8	G. Bradley	22/1
Fell	Lantern Lodge	9.10.7	A. Mullins	100/1
Fell	Tracys Special	9.10.6	S.C. Knight	150/1
Fell	Another Duke	13.10.4	P. Nicholls	200/1
Fell	Plundering	9.10.1	S. Sherwood	25/1
Fell	Dudie	8.10.0	K. Doolan	100/1
Fell	Master Tercel	10.10.7	D. Browne	150/1
Fell	Port Askaig	11.10.5	G. McCourt	35/1
Fell	Ten Cherries	11.10.0	A. Sharpe	66/1
Fell	Mount Oliver	8.10.0	J. Bryan	500/1
Pulled-Up	Essex	8.12.0	Mr V. Chaloupka	100/1
Pulled-Up	Last Suspect	12.11.2	H. Davies	14/1
Pulled-Up	Knock Hill	10.10.1	M. Dwyer	18/1
Pulled-Up	Fethard Friend	11.10.2	P. Barton	35/1
Pulled-Up	Late Night Extra	10.10.2	Mr T. Thomson Jones	500/1
Brought Down	Acarine	10.10.13	R. Stronge	33/1
Brought Down	St Alezan	9.10.2	C. Smith	150/1
Unseated Rider	Tacroy	12.10.1	A. Stringer	200/1
Unseated Rider	Ballymilan	9.10.0	C. Hawkins	50/1
Knocked Over	Doubleuagain	12.10.0	C. Mann	500/1

5 April 1986
Going – Good to Soft
Sponsor – Seagram
Winner – £57,254
Time – 9mins 33secs
40 Ran
Favourite – Mr Snugfit

Top Weight – Essex
Winner trained by Michael Oliver at
   Droitwich, Worcestershire
Winner owned by Mr P. Luff
West Tip, bay gelding by Gala
   Performance – Astryl.

1987

MAORI VENTURE

Before the main event in 1987, the courageous 1981 winning partnership of Bob Champion and Aldaniti again lit up Aintree. Galloping proudly in front of a packed grandstand, the duo had completed a sponsored walk from Buckingham Palace to Aintree Racecourse on behalf of the Bob Champion Cancer Trust Fund. Joined on their travels by a vast array of personalities, they achieved another memorable goal by raising a considerable amount of money, and their return provoked a rapturous reception from all those present on the day.

Many of the old favourites from recent Nationals had run in the race for the last time as a largely new cast emerged for the 1987 renewal. Greasepaint had been withdrawn at the four-day stage, while Hallo Dandy and Last Suspect had now been retired. However, Corbiere ran again as a twelve-year-old and the Nicky Henderson-trained pair, Classified and The Tsarevich, were once more fancied after impressing in 1986.

Favourite though was the most recent winner West Tip, who had won with such authority under Richard Dunwoody the year before. Slightly disappointing during the season, West Tip appeared to be coming good at just the right time when finishing a staying-on fourth behind The Thinker (a late withdrawal from the National field) in the recent Cheltenham Gold Cup. If not for a fall in 1985, West Tip may have been going for a hat-trick in 1987 and, despite having 10lbs more to carry now, the horse was a red-hot favourite at 5/1.

Extremely well handicapped with a mere 10st 2lbs was the dashing, deeply attractive grey horse Dark Ivy. Reckoned to be every bit as good as Lucius and Hallo Dandy by his trainer Gordon Richards, Dark Ivy had been lightly raced during the season having switched to Greystoke Stables from the Irish yard of Bunny Cox, but a recent win at Ayr on the back of a second in Newcastle's marathon Eider Chase highlighted the horse's chance. Both Richards and jockey Phil Tuck were particularly bullish over Dark Ivy's prospects of becoming the first grey since Nicolaus Silver to win the National and, having won the best-turned-out in the paddock, a flood of money for the horse saw him go off 11/2 second favourite.

Plundering, having fallen in the 1986 race, had gone on to win the Whitbread Gold Cup carrying the pink colours with cherry hearts of American Mrs Miles Valentine and the Fred Winter-trained horse was a popular selection, as was the recent winner of Cheltenham's Kim Muir Chase, The Ellier. Bewley's Hill and Valencio, although big outsiders, provided the international interest, representing the United States and Czechoslovakia respectively – the former being a winner of the 1984 Maryland Hunt Cup. Towards the top of the handicap but largely unconsidered was Maori Venture, a strong, compact chestnut. Bred in Wales, Maori Venture had some quality form to his name, winning the Mandarin Chase at Sandown in 1984 and finishing third in the season's Hennessy Cognac Gold Cup. However, prone to jumping errors, Maori Venture was considered a risky bet to complete the course, and even his trainer Andy Turnell admitted to having a stronger fancy for the horse's stablemate Tracys Special.

As an excited crowd watched on a misty afternoon, it was young Guy Landau, having his first National ride, that sent the front-running chestnut Lean Ar Aghaidh straight into the lead, and he rose at the first together with Insure, Valencio and Plundering, with Corbiere compassing his usual inside route. Bad mistakes saw the departures of Lucky Rew and Smartside at the first while Mr David Pitcher – who had bought the outsider Brown Trix so he could have a ride in the race – was unseated at the big ditch.

Heading for Becher's, Lean Ar Aghaidh had pulled into a clear lead in the centre of the track with the Irish Grand National winner Insure, Northern Bay, Classified and You're Welcome all going smoothly on the leader's heels. In behind though, the runners were bunching up and, as the majority of the field met the fence, a

Loose horse Lucky Rew clips the first chunks of spruce off the immaculately dressed Becher's Brook, followed by Lean Ar Aghaidh.

The race heats up at Becher's second time with Maori Venture (scarlet cap) making ground. Others in contention include You're Welcome (25) and The Tsarevich (black and mauve cap).

desperate tragedy occurred. With the Irish horse Attitude Adjuster (the youngest horse in the field) appearing to change direction at the last moment, the grey Dark Ivy was squashed for room with Why Forget on his inside. Unsighted meeting Becher's, Dark Ivy had no room for a clean jump, hit the fence hard and ghosted to the ground, breaking his neck in a cruel, disheartening fatal fall. Jumping without concern to that point, Dark Ivy's fall was as ridiculous as it was unfortunate and came as if the gods had singled out his fate for that precise moment. Bewley's Hill was brought down directly behind and, as the mist thickened, the field continued, leaving behind them a most sombre atmosphere at Becher's.

With the majority of the field intact, it was a well-stocked group that returned to the racecourse. Outsider Big Brown Bear was running a tremendous race on the inside and was accompanied by Lean Ar Aghaidh and Northern Bay taking The Chair, with Miss Jacqui Oliver moving up on the outside aboard Eamon's Owen to make a line of four. However, Eamon's Owen lunged extravagantly at the gaping ditch, landing hard on the other side and unseating Miss Oliver, the jockey sent sprawling over the horse's neck and spilling on to the ground. Little Polveir also clipped the fence and unseated Colin Brown, but the remainder streamed over, receiving great vocal encouragement as they took the water and set out for the second circuit.

Lean Ar Aghaidh and Big Brown Bear immersed themselves in a fascinating duel on the run down to Becher's again, both jumping with relish, while making steady progress towards the outside was Steve Knight on Maori Venture. A slight mistake at Becher's by Lean Ar Aghaidh sent Landau's arms shooting for the sky, but he recovered quickly and continued his powerful march, as West Tip too began to make his presence felt. Having been among the leaders, Northern Bay began to tire and, at the Canal Turn, a slipped saddle caused the unseating of Steve Smith-Eccles from Classified.

Big Brown Bear's gallant run began to falter on the run to two out, but plenty remained in contention with Lean Ar Aghaidh doing his utmost. Attitude Adjuster, Maori Venture, You're Welcome and The Tsarevich loomed as potential dangers, although West Tip was caught flat-footed as the leaders took the second last, and there would be no repeat success for the 1986 hero.

Incredibly, Lean Ar Aghaidh found another burst of energy, and a huge roar went up as he touched down in front jumping the last. Having run with enthusiasm and jumping with electricity the entire way, it was only approaching the elbow that the leader was finally swallowed up. Lean Ar Aghaidh was engulfed by the powerful, surging runs of Maori Venture on the outside and The Tsarevich on the inner and these two then battled out the finish. With the white faces of both horses matching each other in a rousing conclusion, it was Maori Venture that proved the stronger, his class ultimately telling as he found a little extra in the final fifty yards to beat The Tsarevich by five lengths in a thrilling finish. The gutsy Lean Ar Aghaidh took third in front of West Tip, whose determination grabbed fourth place from You're Welcome (carrying the Aldaniti colours). The Ellier made up a lot of late ground to take sixth with Corbiere

Pictured later in 1987 are the National-winning team of trainer Andy Turnell and jockey Steve Knight (wearing the colours of Turnell's other National runner, Tracys Special).

1987 GRAND NATIONAL RESULT

FATE	HORSE	AGE/WEIGHT	JOCKEY	ODDS
1st	MAORI VENTURE	11.10.13	S.C. KNIGHT	28/1
2nd	THE TSAREVICH	11.10.5	J. WHITE	20/1
3rd	LEAN AR AGHAIDH	10.10.0	G. LANDAU	14/1
4th	WEST TIP	10.11.7	R. DUNWOODY	5/1
5th	You're Welcome	11.10.2	P. Hobbs	50/1
6th	Tracys Special	10.10.0	S. McNeill	50/1
7th	The Ellier	11.10.0	F. Berry	18/1
8th	Attitude Adjuster	7.10.6	N. Madden	25/1
9th	Northern Bay	11.10.1	R. Crank	50/1
10th	Monanore	10.10.3	T. Morgan	20/1
11th	Smith's Man	9.10.0	M. Perrett	14/1
12th	Corbiere	12.10.10	B. De Haan	12/1
13th	Big Brown Bear	10.10.2	R. Stronge	200/1
14th	Cranlome	9.10.0	M. Richards	500/1
15th	Colonel Christy	12.10.0	S. Moore	300/1
16th	Plundering	10.10.11	P. Scudamore	16/1
17th	Preben Fur	10.10.0	A. Stringer	66/1
18th	Bright Dream	11.10.2	R. Rowe	50/1
19th	Why Forget	11.10.0	C. Grant	40/1
20th	Gala Prince	10.10.0	T. Jarvis	500/1
21st	Brit	8.10.1	A. Jones	500/1
22nd	Insure	9.10.10	Mr C. Brooks	45/1
Fell	Valencio	10.12.0	R. Rowell	500/1
Fell	Glenrue	10.10.3	B. Powell	33/1
Fell	Dark Ivy	11.10.2	P. Tuck	11/2
Fell	Smartside	12.10.0	P. Gill	100/1
Fell	Marcolo	10.10.0	P. Leech	66/1
Fell	Lucky Rew	12.10.0	C. Mann	500/1
Pulled-Up	Drumlargan	13.11.2	Mr G. Wragg	66/1
Pulled-Up	Daltmore	9.10.0	A. Mullins	100/1
Pulled-Up	Run To Me	12.10.2	Mr N. Mitchell	150/1
Pulled-Up	Brown Veil	12.10.1	Mr M. Armytage	200/1
Pulled-Up	Le Bambino	10.10.2	C. Warren	500/1
Brought Down	Bewley's Hill	10.12.0	Mr W.B. Dixon Stroud jnr	100/1
Unseated Rider	Classified	11.10.3	S. Smith-Eccles	9/1
Unseated Rider	Brown Trix	9.10.8	Mr D.F. Pitcher	100/1
Unseated Rider	Little Polveir	10.10.2	C. Brown	33/1
Unseated Rider	Eamon's Owen	10.10.0	Miss Jacqui Oliver	200/1
Refused	Hi Harry	9.10.0	M. Flynn	100/1
Knocked Over	Spartan Orient	11.10.0	L. Harvey	500/1

4 April 1987
Going – Good
Sponsor – Seagram
Winner – £64,710
Time – 9mins 19.3secs
40 Ran
Favourite – West Tip

Top Weights – Bewley's Hill and
 Valencio
Winner trained by Andrew Turnell at
 East Hendred, Oxfordshire
Winner owned by Mr H.J. Joel
Maori Venture, chestnut gelding by
 St Columbus – Moon Venture.

returning safely in what would be his final National, finishing twelfth, one place ahead of the surprising Big Brown Bear. The sad and much-publicised demise of Dark Ivy at Becher's led to RSPCA members calling for the fence to be altered. Racecourse manager John Parrett reassured all concerned parties that every angle of race safety would be reviewed and, although no alterations were installed before the next National, the cries of displeasure over the make-up of the fences were becoming increasingly loud and more determined.

Maori Venture had dismissed fears over his suitability for the National by winning the race in fine style. Able to bide his time, the horse was able to jump with great care and precision, before being put into the race by Knight on the second circuit. The victory came as a surprise for his ninety-two-year-old owner Jim Joel, who had at last achieved Grand National glory having tried for many years without success. Mr Joel had won the Epsom Derby with his Royal Palace in 1967 and was on a plane on the way back from South Africa when being informed of the news. Maori Venture's win provided a major spark to the troubled start to the training career of Andy Turnell. The trainer had prematurely taken over for his late father Bob two years previously and had been forced to vacate their stables near Marlborough, Wiltshire. Setting up again at East Hendred, Oxfordshire, the first season there had been curtailed badly by a virus. Now Maori Venture had provided Turnell with the ideal boost and, for Knight, the horse was to be left to him in the will of the most grateful owner.

1988

RHYME 'N' REASON

Favourite for the 1988 Grand National was the eight-year-old Sacred Path, a lightly raced bay from the yard of Oliver Sherwood. As a jockey, Sherwood had partnered Venture To Cognac into eighth place behind Corbiere in 1983 and now he had a terrific chance with his first National runner as a trainer. Sacred Path had never finished out of the first three in ten completed chases and was considered a reliable jumper and certain stayer. The horse had won his only race of the season over three-and-a-half miles at Warwick to ignite a wave of support, while riding the horse would be Clive Cox, also having his first experience of the National.

Although Maori Venture had since been retired, the three placed horses from 1987 returned. West Tip was now a veteran, at home over the big fences, and he arrived at Aintree in much the same form as the previous year, having run encouragingly in the Gold Cup. West Tip carried top weight on this occasion and was as popular as ever while the 1987 runner-up The Tsarevich, again with John White on board, was fancied to go well once more, despite his advancing years. After such a bold and gallant run the year before, Lean Ar Aghaidh had then won the Whitbread Gold Cup, again giving a fine, front-running exhibition, and was subsequently installed among the ante-post favourites for the 1988 National. Having headed the market for much of the previous twelve months, the chestnut lost that position on the day of the race after a deluge of rain hit the course forty-eight hours beforehand, robbing Lean Ar Aghaidh of the fast ground he adored.

It was jockey Brendan Powell's belief that his horse Rhyme 'N' Reason would have won the recent Cheltenham Gold Cup if not for falling late on when making a menacing forward move. In a way, the horse's disappointment at Cheltenham was in keeping with his career in general. Rhyme 'N' Reason had won an Irish Grand National as a six-year-old when trained by David Murray-Smith, but had then been plagued by serious jumping problems for the next two seasons. Transferring to the yard of David Elsworth, the horse rocketed back to form, winning four races before Cheltenham, his career revitalised. Had he won the Gold Cup, Rhyme 'N' Reason would have started one of the shortest-priced

favourites of all time, for he was a class horse and still only nine. Even so, the horse was well weighted with 11 stone and had plenty of support, starting joint-second favourite at 10/1 with Lean Ar Aghaidh.

The two leading Irish candidates were Hard Case and Lastofthebrownies, the former a two-an-a-half-mile specialist trained by Jim Dreaper and the latter a multiple winner during the season for his trainer Mouse Morris, while the 1987 Aintree Foxhunters' winner Border Burg and the J.P. McManus-owned Bucko – a recent winner at the Cheltenham Festival – had their followers. Quietly fancied for the North was the strapping chestnut Durham Edition. Normally kept to lesser company at the Northern tracks by his trainer Arthur Stephenson, Durham Edition had proved his worth in a quality field by finishing third to the high-class Playschool in the season's Hennessy. A grand jumper and sure stayer, the horse was partnered by Chris Grant, runner-up aboard Young Driver in 1986.

Rushing the start, a number of over-eager runners snapped the tape causing a delay but, once on their way, it was the favourite Sacred Path that showed first in the centre of the track from Insure on the inside and Gee-A – ridden by top female jockey Gee Armytage – on the wide outside. To agonising groans, Sacred Path put in an over-zealous leap at the first, and landed steeply on the landing side in a typical early Grand National fall. Further back, outsiders Tullamarine and the abysmal jumper Hettinger also came to grief, the latter taking half the fence with him as he crashed out.

Landing awkwardly over the second, the injury-riddled grey Smith's Man pulled-up lame, while another grey, Brass Change, was lucky to survive a bad

The unveiling of former jockey Philip Blacker's sculpture of three-time winner Red Rum in 1988. Right to left are: Major Ivan Straker, Blacker, HRH Princess Anne, Ginger McCain and Red Rum.

Big Brown Bear leads the riderless favourite Sacred Path and Lean Ar Aghaidh (3) at Becher's first time.

mistake at the big ditch and Lucisis found himself hopelessly tailed-off, having jumped the opening fences alarmingly out to his right. A slipped saddle forced Peter Hobbs to pull-up You're Welcome before Becher's, as Big Brown Bear forged to the front on the inside from Gee-A on the outside.

As the leaders sailed over Becher's without incident, Rhyme 'N' Reason took the fence boldly on the wide outside but was caught out by the famous drop. Sliding onto his belly, the horse seemed certain to topple over, yet amazingly Powell stayed on board and the horse rose to his feet. Almost from a standstill, the horse set off in pursuit of the main pack following one of the most dramatic recoveries in Grand National history, yet he had lost a huge amount of ground. Marcolo also gave future trainer Miss Venetia Williams a shocking fall at the back of the field and, even though he was a long way last jumping the fence, Lucisis was brought down by the faller.

Slightly bothered by a loose horse, Lean Ar Aghaidh had come to dispute the lead with his old rival Big Brown Bear jumping down the back, and they were followed closely by Gee-A, Kumbi and Eton Rouge as they came out of the country and back onto the racecourse. Course Hunter and Little Polveir had made eyecatching progress coming towards The Chair and, almost unbelievably, Rhyme 'N' Reason now showed up on the outside, moving into the leading dozen.

A slow jump at The Chair cost Big Brown Bear ground he was never able to make up, and it was Lean Ar Aghaidh that led out for the second circuit from an extremely packed group consisting of Gee-A, Course Hunter, Little Polveir, Kumbi, Eton Rouge, The Tsarevich, West Tip, Bucko, Strands Of Gold, Border Burg, Rhyme 'N' Reason, Durham Edition and the retreating Big Brown Bear, while struggling towards the rear were Preben Fur, Midnight Madness, Tracys Special and the well-backed Repington.

With ground softer than ideal, Lean Ar Aghaidh began to lose his place jumping the big ditch, where the fancied Hard Case fell, as Little Polveir – running in his third National – took control in the centre from Gee-A and Rhyme 'N' Reason on the outside, with West Tip and Course Hunter improving on the inner.

However, it was the Peter Scudamore-ridden Strands Of Gold that had made the most significant progress and, heading for Becher's again, the pair had rushed through on the inside to snatch a clear lead. Travelling ominously well at the time, Strands Of Gold attacked Beachers with ferocity but, clouting the top of the fence, the horse had no chance of staying upright, coming down at the drop's steepest point, as Scudamore was left to rue a missed opportunity. Perhaps distracted by Strands Of Gold's fall, Course Hunter slipped down on his knees, but jockey Paul Croucher managed a fine recovery, though The Tsarevich was badly hampered in the process.

Becher's had drastically altered the race outlook, and six now broke free, with the winner sure to come from within the group. Little Polveir led, tracked by Rhyme 'N' Reason, Durham Edition and Lastofthebrownies, with Aintree veterans West Tip and Monanore next, the latter having made up a lot of ground

Rhyme 'N' Reason is down on his knees at Becher's first time, followed by Hard Case (4).

Strands Of Gold about to fall at the second Becher's as Little Polveir (8) takes control.

Monanore (14) on his way to third place in 1988, preceded by Lean Ar Aghaidh (3). The faller is Kumbi.

FATE	HORSE	AGE/WEIGHT	JOCKEY	ODDS
1st	RHYME 'N' REASON	9.11.0	B. POWELL	10/1
2nd	DURHAM EDITION	10.10.9	C. GRANT	20/1
3rd	MONANORE	11.10.4	T.J. Taaffe	33/1
4th	WEST TIP	11.11.7	R. DUNWOODY	11/1
5th	Attitude Adjuster	8.10.6	N. Madden	33/1
6th	Friendly Henry	8.10.4	N. Doughty	100/1
7th	The Tsarevich	12.10.10	J. White	18/1
8th	Course Hunter	10.10.1	P. Croucher	20/1
9th	Lean Ar Aghaidh	11.11.0	G. Landau	10/1
Fell	Hard Case	10.10.12	K. Morgan	13/1
Fell	Strands Of Gold	9.10.3	P. Scudamore	20/1
Fell	Sacred Path	8.10.0	C. Cox	17/2
Fell	Kumbi	13.10.0	C. Llewellyn	100/1
Fell	Lastofthebrownies	8.10.0	T. Carmody	25/1
Fell	Marcolo	11.10.0	Miss V. Williams	200/1
Fell	Smartside	13.10.4	Mr A. Hambly	100/1
Fell	Brass Change	10.10.0	M. Kinane	100/1
Fell	Tullamarine	11.10.0	M. Bowlby	200/1
Fell	Hettinger	8.10.0	Miss Penny Ffitch-Heyes	200/1
Pulled-Up	Border Burg	11.10.7	S. Sherwood	16/1
Pulled-Up	Midnight Madness	10.10.5	M. Richards	25/1
Pulled-Up	Bucko	11.10.5	M. Dwyer	16/1
Pulled-Up	Gee-A	9.10.3	Gee Armytage	33/1
Pulled-Up	You're Welcome	12.10.1	P. Hobbs	33/1
Pulled-Up	Tracys Special	11.10.0	S.C. Knight	33/1
Pulled-Up	Memberson	10.10.3	R.J. Beggan	33/1
Pulled-Up	Northern Bay	12.10.4	H. Davies	50/1
Pulled-Up	Smith's Man	10.10.0	M. Perrett	50/1
Pulled-Up	Eton Rouge	9.10.5	D. Browne	25/1
Pulled-Up	Preben Fur	11.10.0	S.J. O'Neill	100/1
Brought Down	Lucisis	9.10.6	Mr J. Queally	40/1
Brought Down	Bright Dream	12.10.2	R. Rowe	66/1
Brought Down	Polly's Pal	10.10.0	J.K. Kinane	100/1
Unseated Rider	Little Polveir	11.10.7	T. Morgan	33/1
Unseated Rider	Insure	10.10.0	B. De Haan	80/1
Refused	Repington	10.10.1	C. Hawkins	16/1
Refused	Sir Jest	10.10.2	K. Jones	22/1
Refused	Big Brown Bear	11.10.2	R. Stronge	66/1
Refused	Seeandem	8.10.0	P. Leech	100/1
Refused	Oyde Hills	9.10.0	M. Brennan	100/1

9 April 1988
Going – Good to Soft
Sponsor – Seagram
Winner – £68,740
Time – 9mins 53.5secs
40 Ran
Favourite – Sacred Path

Top Weight – West Tip
Winner trained by David Elsworth at Whitsbury, Hampshire
Winner owned by Miss Juliet E. Reed
Rhyme 'N' Reason, bay gelding by Kemal – Smooth Lady.

on the second circuit. But when Little Polveir cannoned Tom Morgan into the sky five from home and Lastofthebrownies crashed out rudely a fence later, only four remained in the hunt, with West Tip weakening as Rhyme 'N' Reason led them round the home turn.

Striding clear of Monanore, Rhyme 'N' Reason led to the second last, but stalking the leader on his outside was the big chestnut Durham Edition, who was merely cruising under Grant. Smoothly, the giant Northern chaser swept into the lead and, jumping the last in fine style three lengths ahead, was away quickly on the flat. Victory for Durham Edition looked a certainty, but approaching the elbow, Powell conjured Rhyme 'N' Reason for one final challenge. Battling like a tiger, class told on the final run to the line and, with Durham Edition unable to shake off his pursuer after the elbow, Rhyme 'N' Reason wore the Northern horse down, sweeping past on the wide outside to win by four lengths. It was cruel luck on Grant, who had ridden a beautiful race only to be denied victory once more in the final strides. Monanore was fifteen lengths back in third with West Tip fourth yet again, enhancing his Aintree reputation with another faultless round, only tiring late on under a big weight.

Rhyme 'N' Reason completed one of the finest comebacks in race history. Virtually down and out at the first Becher's, he had then shown a never-say-die attitude to haul in Durham Edition. Twenty-seven-year-old Powell had suffered a broken arm in a fall from Glenrue in the 1987 race, and not even a summons to the steward's office to explain his apparently excessive use of the whip during the closing stages could curtail his euphoric joy. Elsworth had worked hard to convince owner Miss Juliet Reed to run the horse she adored in the toughest race of all, but now all concerned could celebrate the win, particularly the trainer, who had backed Rhyme 'N' Reason at twice his starting odds.

1989

LITTLE POLVEIR

It is often the case that the Cheltenham Festival, which precedes the Grand National meeting normally by three weeks, unveils or highlights potential challengers for the big race at Aintree. To conquer the tough, punishing final hill at Cheltenham requires real stamina, especially in the staying chases, and horses that can cope there are often thought to have the necessary reserves for the National, although Aintree of course is an entirely different challenge, being a fast, flat track that can take slow-footed stayers off their feet in the early stages of the National. Having missed the best part of two years with leg injuries, the lightly raced Dixton House had run just twice during the season but, on his latest start in the Ritz Club Handicap Chase at Cheltenham, he showed just what a fine horse he was on his day. Destroying a good field that included fellow National aspirants Gala's Image, Smart Tar and Gainsay, the horse won by twelve lengths and was immediately installed as favourite for Aintree. The horse, although a ten-year-old, had the potential to improve even further, especially considering the heavy going at Aintree was in his favour (certainly benefiting his suspect legs), and Dixton House began as the 7/1 favourite for trainer John Edwards and jockey Tom Morgan.

Arthur Stephenson sent four runners to the National from his Bishop Auckland yard, spearheaded by the ultra-tough chestnut The Thinker, winner of the Cheltenham Gold Cup in the snow in 1987. While The Thinker carried top weight of 11st 10lbs, it was the 1988 runner-up Durham Edition that was the public fancy, duelling for favouritism with Dixton House before the off. Up only a couple of pounds for his effort behind Rhyme 'N' Reason, Durham Edition had been aimed all season at the National, although the heavy ground was not in his favour. Completing the Stephenson team were the Eider Chase winner Polar Nomad and the consistent Sir Jest, carrying the yellow-and-blue colours of owner Mr Peter Pillar.

Arguably the best form belonged to the tiny brown horse Bonanza Boy, trained by Martin Pipe and ridden by Peter Scudamore. Bonanza Boy had easily won the

season's Welsh Grand National in the mud at Chepstow, and had then finished a respectable fourth behind the great grey Desert Orchid in the Cheltenham Gold Cup. Bonanza Boy relished testing conditions and, despite his small stature, the horse was a fine jumper.

A big, workmanlike black horse trained by Jenny Pitman, Stearsby too was a former Welsh National winner, while Dermot Weld's charge Perris Valley had won the previous season's Irish Grand National. Veteran West Tip returned for his fifth Grand National, having recently won a hunter-chase at Hereford, while Mark Wilkinson's first National runner, Smart Tar, carried the famous yellow-and-red Courage colours previously carried to such effect over the National fences by the likes of Spanish Steps. With conditions underfoot suiting, some late money came for Little Polveir, having his fourth run in the race and now trained by Toby Balding. The horse had not enjoyed the best of luck in the race before, but was a previous Scottish Grand National winner, and those shrewd punters who recalled how well the horse was travelling until unseating Tom Morgan five out in 1988 gobbled up the 50/1 on the morning of the race, sending Little Polveir off a 28/1 chance for race debutant Jimmy Frost.

The rank outsider Hettinger was the subject of an interesting challenge on this occasion. A first-fence faller in 1988, the horse was a risky jumper but, ridden by Ray Goldstein, Hettinger stood to earn £200 from bookmakers Victor Chandler if he survived the first and £100 for every fence thereafter. All proceeds would be presented to the Leukaemia Research Fund.

Jenny Pitman meets the Duke of York in a special ceremony for National-winning trainers in 1989. Also in shot, from left to right: David Elsworth, Andy Turnell (hidden), Michael Oliver, Frank Gilman, Josh Gifford, John Leadbetter and Gordon Richards.

Tom Morgan (light-blue sleeves) can only watch as favourite Dixton House (far left) gallops away riderless from his fall at Becher's.

Although the ground was heavy, the sun shone vibrantly as the runners were called into line, only for a frustrating delay to ensue. First, Memberson spread a plate and, when the start appeared imminent, the temperamental ten-year-old Bob Tisdall surged through the tape. To a belated roar, the field was finally released, although the shabby-looking tape appeared to get caught among the runners on the outside. It was a situation that needed reviewing, as Aintree found out to its cost four years later. Having ruined one start, Bob Tisdall whipped round and refused to take part as the runners galloped away. Although he eventually got going, the horse only did so as the field met the first fence.

With Cerimau and Cranlome the early casualties, Dixton House, jumping fast and accurately in the centre, led the field to Becher's with Newnham, Mithras and West Tip going strongly on the inside from Stearsby on the outer. Becher's first time perhaps made more impact on this occasion than any time in the past, and the consequences were far reaching. Dixton House rose to take the monstrous fence well but, losing his footing on the landing side, crumbled agonisingly to the ground. Further back, two horrific accidents occurred. With many of the runners fanning to the outside to avoid the big drop on the inner, Brown Trix found himself right against the outside rail, hit the top of the fence and plunged to the sloping ground, ending up in the ditch. Towards the centre, Seeandem totally misjudged his take-off and dived head-first into the Brook, fatally injured. Amid the drama, Hettinger's run came to an end, the grey Sergeant Sprite fell and Sir Jest was brought down.

Racing away from the vicious incidents, Stearsby and West Tip thrilled the crowds with an exhibition of spectacular jumping racing down the back, until Stearsby bluntly refused the eleventh, catapulting Brendan Powell to the other side. Left in the lead, West Tip proudly led a tightly bunched group over the Melling Road, with Newnham, Team Challenge, Little Polveir, Mr Chris, Smart Tar, Kersil and Mithras the most prominent.

In a perfect line over The Chair, Little Polveir, West Tip, Mithras and Kersil colourfully led onwards as the veteran Smartside departed back in the field while, at the water, the outsider Mr Chris somersaulted out of the race having appeared to clip the heels of the preceding Mithras.

As in the year before, Little Polveir began his charge at the start of the second circuit, jumping splendidly in the centre, while moving up on the outside was the big bay Smart Tar, his white face showing prominently as he came through to challenge for the lead. But Smart Tar's run ended with a bad mistake at the twentieth that sent Carl Llewellyn flying and, as Little Polveir led West Tip, Lastofthebrownies, Monanore, Team Challenge, Bonanza Boy and Durham Edition into Becher's, the field were flagged away from the outside corner where the injured Brown Trix remained stricken.

Little Polveir took every fence down the back with increased confidence but, as he came back across the Melling Road, there were still nine horses in contention, with Lastofthebrownies and Durham Edition going particularly well and, for the first time, The Thinker was getting involved, beginning a late run from off the pace having been down on his back legs at the second Becher's.

By the final fence Durham Edition looked a real danger as Little Polveir brushed through the spruce, but Chris Grant's mount found nothing once on the flat, and Little Polveir surged again, taking a lead of two lengths to the elbow as West Tip, The Thinker and Lastofthebrownies emerged from the pack to offer a serious challenge. The riderless Smart Tar almost wiped out Little Polveir as he passed the elbow and straightened for the line, but the loose horse was a blessing in disguise, inspiring one last burst from the leader and, to enormous applause, Little Polveir crossed the line a most deserving winner by seven-and-a-half lengths to the relentless West Tip and The Thinker, both running mighty races. Lastofthebrownies took fourth, with Durham Edition finishing a tame fifth having failed to quicken on the heavy ground.

Little Polveir, named after a salmon pool on the river Dee, had squandered a winning opportunity in 1988 but had now made up for it in brilliant style with a brave display of front-running and glorious jumping to beat a highly competitive field. Frost had studied footage of the 1988 race to plot Little Polveir's route, and his homework was rewarded with a stunning victory, the second for trainer Toby Balding, twenty years after Highland Wedding's win. Little Polveir was previously owned by Mike Shone, who also owned the fast-ground-loving Castle Warden, a one-time National contender. Mr Ted Harvey had approached Shone about buying one of his horses for his son David to ride in amateur events and, with the going normally good or better at Aintree, Shone elected to sell Little Polveir. When Castle Warden was withdrawn from the National, Shone could only ponder what might have been as Little Polveir won for his new owner and Balding – the trainer giving much credit for the horse's win to previous trainer John Edwards, ironically out of luck with the favourite Dixton House.

Balding suffered the misfortune of later losing his other runner Brown Trix, who was put down having broken a shoulder at Becher's, and the sad death of he and Seeandem, coupled with recent tragedies involving the likes of Dark Ivy, saw the calls for radical changes to Becher's more intense than ever. A proposal was put forward in the House of Commons for the race to be banned and, while that cry was clearly exaggerated, it was near impossible for the Grand National to justify the loss of two more brave horses this time. The Jockey Club's response was to conduct a full investigation into race safety. As a result, Becher's was drastically altered some months later, with the notorious Brook filled in and the slope on the landing side levelled off considerably.

Little Polveir takes Becher's second time in the lead. A groundsman stands atop the fence, bordering off the outside as Brown Trix remained stricken on the landing side having fallen first time round.

1989 GRAND NATIONAL RESULT

FATE	HORSE	AGE/WEIGHT	JOCKEY	ODDS
1st	LITTLE POLVEIR	12.10.3	J. FROST	28/1
2nd	WEST TIP	12.10.11	R. DUNWOODY	12/1
3rd	THE THINKER	11.11.10	S. SHERWOOD	10/1
4th	LASTOFTHEBROWNIES	9.10.0	T. CARMODY	16/1
5th	Durham Edition	11.10.11	C. Grant	15/2
6th	Monanore	12.10.6	G. McCourt	20/1
7th	Gala's Image	9.10.3	N. Doughty	18/1
8th	Bonanza Boy	8.11.1	P. Scudamore	10/1
9th	Team Challenge	7.10.0	M. Bowlby	30/1
10th	Newnham	12.10.5	Mr S. Andrews	50/1
11th	The Thirsty Farmer	10.10.2	L. Kelp	100/1
12th	Attitude Adjuster	9.10.6	N. Madden	25/1
13th	Sidbury Hill	13.10.0	K. Mooney	100/1
14th	Mr Baker	11.10.0	M. Moran	100/1
Fell	Smart Tar	8.10.3	C. Llewellyn	18/1
Fell	Dixton House	10.10.3	T. Morgan	7/1
Fell	Perris Valley	8.10.0	B. Sheridan	16/1
Fell	Gainsay	10.10.6	M. Pitman	25/1
Fell	Cranlome	11.10.0	K. O'Brien	66/1
Fell	Sergeant Sprite	9.10.2	T.J. Taaffe	50/1
Fell	Brown Trix	11.10.5	Mr D.F. Pitcher	300/1
Fell	Seeandem	9.10.0	L. Cusack	100/1
Fell	Cerimau	11.10.0	P. Hobbs	80/1
Fell	Friendly Henry	9.10.4	H. Davies	66/1
Fell	Hettinger	9.10.0	R. Goldstein	300/1
Fell	Mr Chris	10.10.0	B. Storey	200/1
Pulled-Up	Memberson	11.10.2	Mr G. Upton	33/1
Pulled-Up	Beamwam	11.10.6	Mr D. Naylor-Leyland	100/1
Pulled-Up	Bartres	10.10.3	G. Bradley	33/1
Pulled-Up	Mithras	11.10.1	R. Stronge	66/1
Pulled-Up	Polar Nomad	8.10.0	A. Merrigan	80/1
Pulled-Up	Numerate	10.10.0	Miss Tarnya Davis	100/1
Pulled-Up	Kersil	12.10.0	A. Orkney	300/1
Pulled-Up	Mearlin	10.10.0	S. McNeill	300/1
Brought Down	Sir Jest	11.10.1	M. Hammond	40/1
Refused	Stearsby	10.10.9	B. Powell	14/1
Refused	Bob Tisdall	10.10.7	J. White	25/1
Refused	Queensway Boy	10.10.0	A. Webb	50/1
Refused	Rausal	10.10.0	D. Tegg	50/1
Refused	Smartside	14.10.5	Mr A. Hambly	300/1

8 April 1989
Going – Heavy
Sponsor – Seagram
Winner – £66,840
Time – 10mins 6.9secs
40 Ran
Favourite – Dixton House

Top Weight – The Thinker
Winner trained by Toby Balding at Fyfield, Hampshire
Winner owned by Mr E. Harvey
Little Polveir, bay gelding by Cantab – Blue Speedwell.

1990

MR FRISK

The 1990 Grand National was thrust forcefully into the spotlight due to the much-publicised changes made to the famous Becher's Brook, as critics waited to assess the effect of the alterations. Although still presenting a most formidable challenge, gone was the treacherous slope on the landing side, replaced with a more even, gradual descent to the now filled-in brook. The idea was to stop horses rolling back into the ditch and to provide less of a punishing impact on landing and, while taking away somewhat from the tradition and history of the race, it was generally agreed that, with the safety of the horses a priority, the changes were for the better.

An extended dry spell resulted in lightning-fast ground for the 1990 race and, while former race favourite Sacred Path and outsider Why So Hasty were withdrawn in the morning when conditions proved unsuitable, there were plenty left among the thirty-eight runners that were poised to relish the going.

Perhaps no race during the season provided more clues for the Grand National than the Hennessy Cognac Gold Cup in November. With the ground at Newbury that day similar to Aintree, the first four home in a brilliant race had been Ghofar, Brown Windsor, Mr Frisk and Durham Edition. Of the four, it was the Nicky Henderson-trained Brown Windsor that most captured the public imagination, rapidly developing into one of the best young chasers in the land. The eight-year-old had dismantled the Whitbread Gold Cup field the season before when still a novice and had won the Cathcart Chase at the Cheltenham Festival since the Hennessy. Brown Windsor was an exceptional jumper, had never fallen and had a fine Aintree jockey in John White in the saddle, all factors helping the horse start 7/1 favourite.

The David Elsworth-trained Ghofar had won the Hennessy as a six-year-old and was also considered a fine jumper, while the veteran Durham Edition had won the Charlie Hall Chase at Wetherby earlier in the year, performed admirably at Newbury and had been given a nice break by Arthur Stephenson in preparation for his speciality race, the Grand National, for which the fast ground was definitely in his favour. Mr Frisk, a tall, athletic, bright chestnut by the

Charlie Parkin and sister Nicola, children of photographer Bernard, stand in Becher's Brook in 1977, illustrating the enormity of the fence before its modifications in 1990.

Aintree punter William Martin stands in the modified Becher's Brook, now levelled off considerably on the landing side.

temperamental sire Bivouac, had been among the favourites for the 1989 race but had been a late withdrawal due to unsuitable heavy ground. Trained by Kim Bailey, the horse was a natural front-runner who Bailey had long believed could win a National. Owned by American Mrs Harry Duffey, Bailey had fought hard to persuade the owner to allow the horse to run, and with conditions ideal for him, Mrs Duffey relented and gave permission for Mr Frisk to take his chance. Partnering the horse was the stylish amateur Marcus Armytage, whose sister Gee had ridden Gee-A in the 1988 race.

Richard Dunwoody deserted old favourite West Tip (running in his sixth and final National) to ride Cheltenham's Ritz Club Chase winner Bigsun, while both the lightly raced Gordon Richards entrant Rinus and the Aintree and Cheltenham Foxhunters' winner Call Collect attracted support, although trainer John Parkes expressed concerns over the fast ground for the latter. Ireland was represented chiefly by Lastofthebrownies and the heavily weighted chestnut Hungary Hur, while one of the dark horses was the talented Uncle Merlin, trained by Captain Tim Forster and naturally drawing comparisons to the 1980 hero Ben Nevis – for Uncle Merlin too had been sent over from America to train for the National having previously won a Maryland Hunt Cup.

For the second straight year, Aintree bathed in glorious sunshine and, although the young chaser Polyfemus spread a plate at the start causing a delay, the field soon charged away at a terrific pace. Leading at the first fence was the grey two-mile specialist Star's Delight on the wide outside from Polyfemus on the

The grey Pukka Major, Polyfemus (25), Durham Edition (5) and Course Hunter (33) give chase at the start of the second circuit.

A view from the stands. The crowd cheer as the runners take the first fence in 1990. Among the leaders are the grey Star's Delight, Mr Frisk (6), Bob Tisdall (7), Gee-A (green and white), Brown Windsor (4) and Uncle Merlin (blue, white disc).

inside and Bob Tisdall, Gee-A and Brown Windsor in the centre, with Gala's Image the only one to drop out. Uncle Merlin and Charter Hardware joined the leaders jumping the big ditch while, back in the field, Thinking Cap and Conclusive fell.

Mr Frisk came to match Uncle Merlin up front and, heading to Becher's for the first time, there was a huge sense of anticipation. As the leaders swept stylishly over, the fence retained some of its bite by claiming Lanavoe yet, more importantly, the veteran Young Driver – who had gone lame jumping the fence – avoided more serious injury due to the decreased risks of the fence on the landing side, for which his jockey Jimmy Duggan was particularly grateful. Sadly, with Becher's behind them, tragedy lay in wait at the Canal Turn as Mr Frisk and Uncle Merlin continued their awesome gallop. In mid-division, the previous year's Scottish Grand National winner Roll-A-Joint plunged head-first to the ground and broke his neck in an horrific fall.

Marching down the back, Uncle Merlin had taken to the big fences in spectacular fashion, blatantly enjoying the experience as he led with Mr Frisk. Coming back onto the racecourse, the duo were tracked closely by Brown Windsor, Polyfemus and the quirky grey Pukka Major, with Mick's Star, Hungary Hur, Charter Hardware and Rinus next, although Star's Delight – who had jumped extremely wide at the Canal Turn – was pulled up before the thirteenth while, at the same fence, Gainsay came down in an ugly fall and, on struggling to his feet, collided with the Aintree veteran Monanore and sent him through the protective barriers.

Polyfemus ploughed through the top of The Chair and knocked the stuffing out of himself, while Hungary Hur made a dreadful mistake on the outside but survived, unlike Huntworth, who clipped the fence with his back legs and came down. The pace set by Uncle Merlin and Mr Frisk had been electric, and many runners were beginning to tire at the start of the second circuit, while others – most notably Bonanza Boy, West Tip and Call Collect – had been taken off their feet in the early stages and were struggling to get involved.

But Uncle Merlin and Mr Frisk were relishing the battle, jumping like a pair of stags and matching each other stride for stride heading down to Becher's. In behind them, Hungary Hur sadly had gone wrong, shattering a leg running to the nineteenth and becoming the second fatality. It was a cruel blow for the National and bitterly upsetting for connections, but Hungary Hur's demise was a reminder that accidents sadly happen to horses, and not always jumping fences.

Of the two leaders, Uncle Merlin was skipping along under a light weight and appeared to be getting the upper hand. A magnificent jump at the twenty-first gave the American horse a slight lead coming to Becher's. Sailing over in grand fashion, Uncle Merlin landed steeply and toppled over, dislodging a distraught Hywel Davies. It was a long way from the finish, but Uncle Merlin's exit was agonisingly similar to the likes of Andy Pandy, West Tip and Strands Of Gold in previous Nationals: horses meeting the second Becher's in a winning position only for the great fence to catch them out. Even though the fence had been altered, Becher's had again significantly shaped the outcome of the Grand National.

None of this mattered to Mr Frisk and the chestnut was sent clear in front, taking each fence on the run back to the racecourse in tremendous style, as only Rinus, Sir Jest, Brown Windsor and Durham Edition gave meaningful chase. By two out, only Rinus and Durham Edition were left to challenge but, with the former tiring, it was again the big Northern horse that came to the last fence poised to mount a winning bid.

As in 1988, Chris Grant had coasted through on Durham Edition to throw down his challenge and, when Mr Frisk belted the last fence, victory finally seemed Durham Edition's for the taking. Even at the elbow it looked only a

Uncle Merlin (36) and Mr Frisk lead at Becher's second time, but the former would capsize on landing.

Kim Bailey, trainer of Mr Frisk.

1990 GRAND NATIONAL RESULT

FATE	HORSE	AGE/WEIGHT	JOCKEY	ODDS
1st	MR FRISK	11.10.6	MR M. ARMYTAGE	16/1
2nd	DURHAM EDITION	12.10.9	C. GRANT	9/1
3rd	RINUS	9.10.4	N. DOUGHTY	13/1
4th	BROWN WINDSOR	8.10.10	J. WHITE	7/1
5th	Lastofthebrownies	10.10.0	C. Swan	20/1
6th	Bigsun	9.10.2	R. Dunwoody	15/2
7th	Call Collect	9.10.5	Mr R. Martin	14/1
8th	Bartres	11.10.0	M. Bowlby	66/1
9th	Sir Jest	12.10.0	B. Storey	66/1
10th	West Tip	13.10.11	P. Hobbs	20/1
11th	Team Challenge	8.10.0	B. De Haan	50/1
12th	Charter Hardware	8.10.0	N. Williamson	66/1
13th	Gallic Prince	11.10.4	Mr J.F. Simo	100/1
14th	Ghofar	7.10.0	B. Powell	14/1
15th	Course Hunter	12.10.0	G. Bradley	66/1
16th	Bonanza Boy	9.11.9	P. Scudamore	16/1
17th	Solares	10.10.0	Mr P. McMahon	150/1
18th	Gee-A	11.10.2	D. Murphy	66/1
19th	Mick's Star	10.10.1	S.J. O'Neill	66/1
20th	Bob Tisdall	11.10.5	K. Mooney	66/1
Fell	Gainsay	11.10.7	M. Pitman	66/1
Fell	Gala's Image	10.10.0	J. Shortt	66/1
Fell	Roll-A-Joint	12.10.0	S. McNeill	28/1
Fell	Conclusive	11.10.4	S. Smith-Eccles	28/1
Fell	Lanavoe	11.10.0	P. Leech	100/1
Fell	Huntworth	10.10.9	Mr A. Walter	66/1
Fell	Thinking Cap	9.10.0	P. Malone	100/1
Pulled-Up	Hungary Hur	11.11.2	T. Carmody	50/1
Pulled-Up	Star's Delight	8.10.0	J. Lower	50/1
Pulled-Up	Torside	11.10.3	J. Frost	66/1
Pulled-Up	Polyfemus	8.10.2	R. Rowe	18/1
Pulled-Up	Against The Grain	9.10.0	J. Osborne	25/1
Pulled-Up	Young Driver	13.10.4	J. Duggan	150/1
Unseated Rider	Pukka Major	9.10.4	M. Richards	100/1
Unseated Rider	Joint Sovereignty	10.10.1	L. Wyer	50/1
Unseated Rider	Nautical Joke	11.10.0	Mr K. Johnson	66/1
Unseated Rider	Uncle Merlin	9.10.3	H. Davies	16/1
Carried Out	Monanore	13.10.5	T.J. Taaffe	100/1

7 April 1990
Going – Firm
Sponsor – Seagram
Winner – £70,870
Time – 8mins 47.8secs
38 Ran
Favourite – Brown Windsor

Top Weight – Bonanza Boy
Winner trained by Kim Bailey at Upper
   Lambourn, Berkshire
Winner owned by Mrs H.J. Duffey
Mr Frisk, chestnut gelding by Bivouac
   – Jenny Frisk.

matter of time before the horse would pull clear to win. However, Armytage rallied Mr Frisk again on the inside and the two horses engaged in a pulsating duel to the line. Coaxed home masterfully by his amateur rider in a finish worthy of any top professional, it was Mr Frisk that found extra, displaying resilience and courage to deny the luckless Durham Edition by under a length. Armytage punched the air in triumph, the first amateur to win since Dick Saunders on Grittar and, on blazing-fast ground, the course record set by Red Rum in 1973 had been shattered by over fourteen seconds. Great sympathy went out to Grant, now three times an agonising second, as Durham Edition had again been outbattled up the long Aintree run-in. Rinus came home third ahead of Brown Windsor, who just edged Lastofthebrownies for fourth. West Tip jumped round as safely as ever, finishing tenth, and departed the race a true Grand National legend. Naturally, there was further disapproval following the loss of two more brave horses, although Becher's this time avoided any controversy.

Mr Frisk had won the National on ground he adored, justifying Bailey's faith in him. A few weeks later, Mr Frisk confirmed himself a fantastic horse by winning the Whitbread Gold Cup at Sandown Park to crown an unforgettable season.

1991

SEAGRAM

Not since Golden Miller in 1934 had a Cheltenham Gold Cup winner arrived at Aintree and won the Grand National in the same season. L'Escargot had won both, but four years apart, while Alverton would surely have gone close but for his accident. With the changes at Becher's and a general move towards greater horse safety, the 1990s saw a number of Gold Cup winners take their chance in the National, and it was in 1991 that Jenny Pitman saddled a contender primed to capture the elusive 'double'.

Mrs Pitman had taken great care to guide the dark bay Garrison Savannah through an injury-plagued campaign. Having won the Sun Alliance Chase at Cheltenham the year before, Garrison Savannah was to be aimed at the Cheltenham Gold Cup. But, after his first run of the season at Haydock, the horse was found to be lame in his shoulder and was then treated with acupuncture all the way through to Gold Cup day. Repelling the late challenge of the French horse The Fellow, Garrison Savannah won a thrilling Gold Cup and then had his focus switched to the Grand National, where his allotted weight of 11st 1lb now looked extremely lenient. The horse was as graceful a jumper as could be found and, as at Cheltenham, had the trainer's son Mark aboard; the jockey having recovered bravely from a broken pelvis sustained shortly after the Gold Cup win. Garrison Savannah was a horse that benefited from a sound surface, so the rain that fell at Aintree during National week was of some concern. It was not enough, however, to deter the majority of punters and, with the Pitman connection attracting many, Garrison Savannah began as the 7/1 second favourite.

Because of the rain, Martin Pipe's dual Welsh Grand National winner Bonanza Boy started favourite, the horse having recently won over four miles at Uttoxeter. But Bonanza Boy had failed at Aintree when conditions were really testing in 1989, and plenty of other horses were fancied to take the honours on this occasion. Among them were Kempton's *Racing Post* Chase winner Docklands Express – a most consistent horse from Kim Bailey's yard – and the hardy New

Zealand-bred chestnut Seagram (no connection to the race sponsors), a winner of the Ritz Club Chase at Cheltenham, trained by David Barons in Devon.

Bailey also saddled the 1990 winner Mr Frisk but, with the absence of fast ground, the horse drifted out to 25/1 on the day, with the likes of Bigsun, the talented but error-prone Ten Of Spades and the previous year's third Rinus (who had long been the ante-post favourite for the race) all more fancied. Ballyhane, third in the *Racing Post* Chase, spearheaded a strong team for Josh Gifford that included Foyle Fisherman, Envopak Token and Golden Minstrel, all winners at the Cheltenham Festival in their time, while no horse deserved a National win more than Aintree veteran Durham Edition, who was now thirteen. A win for the veteran horse would have provided a major boost for trainer Arthur Stephenson, who had lost his star chaser and leading Grand National candidate The Thinker in a freak work accident just days before the race.

The start was delayed when Nicky Henderson's horse Ten Of Spades spread a plate, and the horses were irritated further when some inconsiderate animal rights demonstrators decided it would be wise to hold up proceedings by running onto the course brandishing abusive banners. They may have believed their intentions were worthy, but it merely served as a nuisance to the horses, some of which were already on edge in the preliminaries. Again, it would take the 1993 race to finally eliminate these particular stunts for good.

With the path cleared for the runners to finally begin the race, the field of forty – including the Czechoslovakian mare Fraze – began the trail to the first fence, led by the French-trained Oklaoma II, who thundered down the inside. Having never finished outside the first three in fourteen chases, Docklands Express crashed abruptly on the outside, handing a rude introduction to the National to jockey Anthony Tory, while the veteran Run And Skip (winner of the 1985 Welsh National) came down at the second.

Golden Freeze, also trained by Jenny Pitman, emerged on the inner to lead at Becher's with Oklaoma II, while Mr Frisk and the outsider Over The Road were showing well on the outside. Taming Becher's in great style, Golden Freeze led further out into the country, where Rinus leapt into prominence for the first time at Valentines. Although Joint Sovereignty capsized at the eleventh, the large field remained virtually intact swinging back onto the racecourse, with the Gold Cup winner Garrison Savannah moving through sweetly on the inside to join his stablemate Golden Freeze.

By time they reached The Chair, Team Challenge made it three Pitman-trained horses among the leading places and, receiving the usual enthusiastic showering of applause and encouragement, the order beginning the second circuit was: Golden Freeze, Team Challenge, Oklaoma II, Rinus, Garrison Savannah, General Chandos, Ballyhane and Over The Road. Bonanza Boy had a lot of ground to make up on the leaders, while Mr Frisk (who had disappointed in his final race before the National) was clearly struggling on the ground and started to retreat.

In the centre of the track, Neale Doughty was constructing his challenge aboard Rinus, with the horse beginning to shape up as a real contender. Tanking to the head of affairs, Rinus came to the twentieth full of running, but agonisingly brushed the top of the fence and came down, giving Doughty his first fall in eight National rides, having completed each of the previous seven. In an instant, the race changed, as a group of seven began to separate themselves from the pack, with Golden Freeze still leading from the cruising Garrison Savannah and sticking to the inside, while the white-faced Seagram was improving all the time together with New Halen, Auntie Dot, Over The Road and Durham Edition. The 50/1 outsider New Halen had made eyecatching progress running to Becher's, but a mistake at the big fence left the horse with spruce hanging from his saddle and his chance diminished, while further back Blue Dart unseated Hywel Davies and Bigsun was down on his nose and soon pulled-up by Richard Dunwoody.

Garrison Savannah had merely hunted round for a circuit-and-a-half, but a tremendous roar echoed round Aintree as the horse jumped to the front at the Foinavon fence, taking control over the Canal Turn and Valentines. Jumping every obstacle with perfect precision, the Gold Cup winner exuded class as he led back towards the racecourse. In behind, the surprising mare Auntie Dot was still only cantering under Mark Dwyer, and then came the resilient Seagram, Durham Edition and Over The Road – but all were struggling to stay with the leader at this stage.

Having shaken off all but Seagram, Garrison Savannah jumped the last fence four lengths ahead and quickly stretched the advantage to ten lengths reaching the elbow, seemingly destined for a place in history. But it was here that the going possibly sapped the stamina away from Garrison Savannah, as Seagram came with a renewed effort under race debutant Nigel Hawke. Charging down the outside, Seagram was cutting down the leader's advantage with every menacing stride and, finishing like a train, the chestnut stormed past the beleaguered Garrison Savannah to win by five lengths, Hawke flinging his arm towards the sky in delight crossing the line. The runner-up had given his all, had jumped beautifully and had been given a wonderful ride by Pitman, but the late burst by Seagram had denied Mark in much the same way Red Rum's relentless drive edged the jockey's father Richard aboard Crisp in 1973. Auntie Dot had travelled exceptionally well for a long way, looking a serious contender on the second circuit until fading into third, ahead of Over The Road, the fast-finishing Bonanza Boy and the gallant Durham Edition. The one sad note was the loss of

New Halen (22) makes a mistake at Becher's second time as Garrison Savannah (orange) leads. Jumping the fence are Over The Road (29), Seagram (11) and the hidden Auntie Dot.

Trainer David Barons cracks open the champagne to celebrate Seagram's win.

the game Ballyhane, who finished eleventh but suffered a haemorrhage shortly after the race.

Major Ivan Straker, the British-based chief of sponsors Seagram, had been offered Seagram the horse to buy on two occasions but declined, and it was for Sir Eric Parker that the chestnut triumphed. David Barons (who also owned a half share in the winner) had been visiting New Zealand for some time to purchase young horses and his wife had bought Seagram as a three-year-old for just under £4,000. Seagram had broken down earlier in his career but, as an older horse, had established himself as one of the toughest and most consistent chasers in the land. Showing all his qualities at Aintree in 1991, Seagram provided his trainer with the biggest moment of his career, which had previously included saddling Broadheath and Playschool to consecutive Hennessy victories in the 1980s.

1991 GRAND NATIONAL RESULT

FATE	HORSE	AGE/WEIGHT	JOCKEY	ODDS
1st	SEAGRAM	11.10.6	N. HAWKE	12/1
2nd	GARRISON SAVANNAH	8.11.1	M. PITMAN	7/1
3rd	AUNTIE DOT	10.10.4	M. DWYER	50/1
4th	OVER THE ROAD	10.10.0	R. SUPPLE	50/1
5th	Bonanza Boy	10.11.7	P. Scudamore	13/2
6th	Durham Edition	13.10.13	C. Grant	25/1
7th	Golden Minstrel	12.10.2	T. Grantham	50/1
8th	Old Applejack	11.10.1	T. Reed	66/1
9th	Leagaune	9.10.0	M. Richards	200/1
10th	Foyle Fisherman	12.10.0	E. Murphy	40/1
11th	Ballyhane	10.10.3	D. Murphy	22/1
12th	Harley	11.10.0	G. Lyons	150/1
13th	Mick's Star	11.10.0	C. Swan	100/1
14th	Ten Of Spades	11.11.1	J. White	15/1
15th	Forest Ranger	9.10.0	D. Tegg	100/1
16th	Yahoo	10.11.1	N. Williamson	33/1
17th	Golden Freeze	9.11.0	M. Bowlby	40/1
Fell	Rinus	10.10.7	N. Doughty	7/1
Fell	Docklands Express	9.10.3	A. Tory	20/1
Fell	Southernair	11.10.1	Mr J.F. Simo	100/1
Fell	Run And Skip	13.10.0	D. Byrne	66/1
Fell	Joint Sovereignty	11.10.0	L. O'Hara	100/1
Pulled-Up	Fraze	8.11.10	V. Chaloupka	100/1
Pulled-Up	Mr Frisk	12.11.6	Mr M. Armytage	25/1
Pulled-Up	Oklaoma II	11.10.7	R. Kleparski	66/1
Pulled-Up	Master Bob	11.10.5	J. Osborne	20/1
Pulled-Up	Bigsun	10.10.4	R. Dunwoody	9/1
Pulled-Up	Solidasarock	9.10.4	G. Bradley	50/1
Pulled-Up	Huntworth	11.10.8	Mr A. Walter	50/1
Pulled-Up	Envopak Token	10.10.0	M. Perrett	28/1
Pulled-Up	General Chandos	10.10.3	Mr J. Bradburne	150/1
Pulled-Up	Bumbles Folly	10.10.5	J. Frost	150/1
Pulled-Up	Mister Christian	10.10.0	S. Earle	100/1
Pulled-Up	Hotplate	8.10.2	P. Niven	80/1
Pulled-Up	Abba Lad	9.10.0	D. Gallagher	250/1
Unseated Rider	Crammer	11.10.2	Mr J. Durkan	28/1
Unseated Rider	New Halen	10.10.0	S.J. O'Neill	50/1
Unseated Rider	The Langholm Dyer	12.10.6	G. McCourt	100/1
Unseated Rider	Blue Dart	11.10.2	H. Davies	80/1
Refused	Team Challenge	9.10.0	B. De Haan	50/1

6 April 1991
Going – Good to Soft
Sponsor – Seagram
Winner – £90,970
Time – 9mins 29.9secs
40 Ran
Favourite – Bonanza Boy

Top Weight – Fraze
Winner trained by David Barons at
   Woodleigh, Devon
Winner owned by Sir Eric Parker and
   Mr D.H. Barons
Seagram, chestnut gelding by Balak
   – Llanah.

1992

PARTY POLITICS

With Seagram, fittingly, winning the last Seagram-sponsored Grand National in 1991, the hugely successful sponsors passed the torch to subsidiary product Martell. With their committed backing running all the way through to the 2004 race, the Grand National went from strength to strength with every Martell-sponsored contest that passed.

Once more, the recent Cheltenham Gold Cup winner was in the field. Having emerged victorious from a titanic struggle with The Fellow and Docklands Express, the combative chestnut Cool Ground had been a surprise but deserving winner of chasing's Blue Riband. Trained by two-time National winner Toby Balding, the former Irish point-to-pointer had won the Welsh National in 1990 and had a reputation as a stout stayer with drive and determination, though with a preference for soft ground. With the same weight as Garrison Savannah carried in 1991, Cool Ground's chance was obvious if recovered sufficiently from his exertions in the Gold Cup. Having won on the horse at Cheltenham, the brilliant young jockey Adrian Maguire missed Aintree through injury, thus a dream spare ride was handed to Martin Lynch, the horse starting at 10/1.

The diminutive bay Docklands Express had quickly developed into one of the most consistent chasers in training. Having fallen at the first in the 1991 National, the horse had gone on to win the Whitbread Gold Cup on a disqualification and, in the current season, had been placed in the Hennessy, King George and Gold Cup. With Peter Scudamore – the finest jockey in the field not to have won the National – booked to ride, Docklands Express started favourite over Brown Windsor, a horse returning from a season missed through injury and partnered by Richard Dunwoody.

At the head of the handicap were Twin Oaks and Seagram. A big, old-fashioned type of chaser trained by Gordon Richards, Twin Oaks was a specialist over the tricky Haydock Park fences, winning six times at the course, and was a powerful horse used to carrying big weights. Seagram had endured a disappointing season and had 12lbs more to carry than in 1991. Now a twelve-year-old, the game winner of the year before was largely unfancied on this occasion, starting 33/1.

The giant Party Politics (right) edges Romany King to win in 1992.

The mare Auntie Dot had long been an ante-post fancy for the National, while the grey Stay On Tracks had been third in the Eider Chase at Newcastle and was a popular selection to give trainer Arthur Stephenson and jockey Chris Grant a long overdue National victory. Two owners that, as the years progressed, would enter an endless stream of horses in their quest for a National win, J.P. McManus and Trevor Hemmings, were represented by the Irish-trained Laura's Beau and Rubika respectively, while the ultra-consistent Romany King gave Balding another outstanding representative. The most topical selection (with the country in an election year) was the Nick Gaselee-trained Party Politics. The horse was an absolute giant, standing over eighteen hands high, and had finished runner-up in both the season's Hennessy and Welsh National. Acquired shortly before the National (together with outsider Roc De Prince) by Cheveley Park Stud owners David and Patricia Thompson, Party Politics was ridden by Welshman Carl Llewellyn, replacing the injured regular Andy Adams.

It was Josh Gifford's veteran runner Golden Minstrel that led on the inside as they came to the first from Ghofar in the centre. The field were travelling at a sensible, even pace, and the only casualty was the Irish runner Rawhide, unseating the unlucky Kevin O'Brien. Ghofar was lucky to survive a shocking mistake at the big ditch as Golden Minstrel led down to Becher's from Forest Ranger, Brown Windsor and the Jenny Pitman-trained Willsford, the latter being easy to identify as he was wearing light-blue blinkers.

Golden Minstrel stood a mile off Becher's, delivering a mighty leap but, in behind, Brown Windsor took a stride too many, got in close and brought groans

A casualty during the race, Aintree veteran Bonanza Boy is caught having run loose.

horses were in touching distance of the lead, with horses such as Docklands Express, Cool Ground and Stay On Tracks coming through strongly to challenge. But, as long-time leaders Willsford and Golden Minstrel began to fade, it was Party Politics and Romany King that emerged from the vast pack to take command. Party Politics in particular was travelling extremely smoothly, his giant frame towering over his rivals as he danced over the huge fences with the minimum of fuss. Increasing the pace rounding the turn for home, Party Politics used his raking stride to break away from Romany King, and together the two pulled right away from the chasing group – consisting predominantly of Stay On Tracks, Docklands Express, Ghofar, Cool Ground, Hotplate, Old Applejack and the staying-on top weight Twin Oaks.

Jumping the last two fences cleanly, Party Politics began to devour the ground once on the flat, being driven relentlessly by Llewellyn. Richard Guest had refused to give in aboard Romany King, however, and challenged bravely at the elbow, charging frantically at the big horse. But Party Politics' gallop was resolute and, pulling clear in the final run to the line, the giant recorded a mightily impressive win by two-and-a-half lengths. Romany King had himself finished well clear of a large group that had stayed competitive for far longer than in most Nationals, the runner-up finishing fifteen lengths ahead of the staying-on Laura's Beau, with Docklands Express fourth ahead of Twin Oaks who, although never seriously threatening, had finished strongly under his hefty burden. In a race that proved a real spectacle with the large number of challengers on the second circuit, twenty-two horses completed, with no serious injuries for any of the runners.

from the crowd as he came down in a rare but spectacular fall. Immediately behind him, Party Politics belied his size to demonstrate some nifty footwork to clear the fallen horse, while Romany King also had to be alert to avoid being brought down.

Both Golden Minstrel and Willsford were jumping boldly out in front as they raced down the back and, returning to the racecourse, they led Ghofar, Hotplate, Forest Ranger and Party Politics. With Rowlandsons Jewels the only one to depart at The Chair, over thirty horses streamed by the stands to begin the second circuit, with the Gold Cup winner Cool Ground well in touch, but Seagram struggling towards the rear.

The Ginger McCain-trained outsider Hotplate was starting to run a very big race for Graham McCourt and, at the seventeenth, the horse jumped up to dispute the lead. With the riderless New Halen situated in the ditch having just refused, Bonanza Boy unseated Steve Smith-Eccles at the nineteenth, but a large number of horses remained in the hunt approaching Becher's again. Hotplate had surged into a clear lead, with Willsford still there on the inside, Golden Minstrel on the outside and Ghofar in the centre. A great jump at the fence sent Romany King into the leading places, with Party Politics hunting this group up cunningly. Golden Minstrel stumbled on the landing side, losing momentum and, further back, both Mister Ed and Cloney Grange crashed out as Becher's displayed its uncanny ability to catch horses out.

As the field jumped Valentines, an incredible number of horses still had a chance of victory, with a real bunch finish a possibility. No fewer than eighteen

Nick Gaselee,
trainer of Party Politics.

The massive Party Politics had beaten them all and gave the impression that, avoiding injury, he could return to Aintree to compete in many more Nationals. Certainly he was young enough at eight. The victory was a crowning moment for Nick Gaselee and all the more pleasing considering the horse had suffered from wind problems, undergoing two operations to correct this. For the Cheveley Park Stud owners Mr and Mrs Thompson, their late purchase had proved inspired. The owners had also bought Classified and Northern Bay before the 1986 race, and Party Politics had now bettered the third-place finish of Classified in that edition. Llewellyn had orchestrated a wonderful ride on the winner, maximising the big horse's power over the final fences to win with authority. Llewellyn had failed to get round aboard Kumbi and Smart Tar in his previous rides, but he would develop into one of the finest Grand National jockeys of the modern era. In the aftermath of his glory, Llewellyn graciously made sure nobody forgot the unlucky situation of his stricken colleague Andy Adams, sidelined from the ride on Party Politics having fractured a leg at Doncaster six weeks before the race.

1992 GRAND NATIONAL RESULT

FATE	HORSE	AGE/WEIGHT	JOCKEY	ODDS
1st	PARTY POLITICS	8.10.7	C. LLEWELLYN	14/1
2nd	ROMANY KING	8.10.3	R. GUEST	16/1
3rd	LAURA'S BEAU	8.10.0	C. O'DWYER	12/1
4th	DOCKLANDS EXPRESS	10.11.2	P. SCUDAMORE	15/2
5th	Twin Oaks	12.11.7	N. Doughty	9/1
6th	Just So	9.10.2	S. Burrough	50/1
7th	Old Applejack	12.10.0	A. Orkney	35/1
8th	Over The Road	11.10.0	R. Supple	22/1
9th	Stay On Tracks	10.10.0	C. Grant	16/1
10th	Cool Ground	10.11.1	M. Lynch	10/1
11th	Ghofar	9.10.3	H. Davies	25/1
12th	Forest Ranger	10.10.0	D. Tegg	200/1
13th	What's The Crack	9.10.0	J. Osborne	20/1
14th	Rubika	9.10.2	P. Niven	28/1
15th	Golden Minstrel	13.10.0	E. Murphy	150/1
16th	Auntie Dot	11.10.7	M. Dwyer	12/1
17th	Roc De Prince	9.10.9	C. Swan	40/1
18th	Mighty Falcon	7.10.0	P. Holley	80/1
19th	Radical Lady	8.10.0	J. Callaghan	80/1
20th	Willsford	9.10.0	M. Bowlby	16/1
21st	Team Challenge	10.10.0	B. De Haan	100/1
22nd	Sirrah Jay	12.10.0	R.J. Beggan	100/1
Fell	Brown Windsor	10.10.8	R. Dunwoody	8/1
Fell	Cloney Grange	13.10.0	D. O'Connor	100/1

FATE	HORSE	AGE/WEIGHT	JOCKEY	ODDS
Fell	Mister Ed	9.10.0	D. Morris	100/1
Pulled-Up	Seagram	12.11.4	N. Hawke	33/1
Pulled-Up	Omerta	12.10.4	L. Wyer	33/1
Pulled-Up	Huntworth	12.10.0	M. Richards	66/1
Pulled-Up	Karakter Reference	10.10.1	D. O'Sullivan	50/1
Pulled-Up	Hotplate	9.10.5	G. McCourt	50/1
Pulled-Up	Royal Battery	9.10.0	R. Greene	80/1
Pulled-Up	Why So Hasty	11.10.0	W. Worthington	250/1
Unseated Rider	Bonanza Boy	11.10.11	S. Smith-Eccles	25/1
Unseated Rider	Rawhide	8.10.0	K. O'Brien	50/1
Unseated Rider	Rowlandsons Jewels	11.10.3	G. Bradley	60/1
Unseated Rider	Honeybeer Mead	10.10.0	N. Mann	100/1
Refused	New Halen	11.10.0	R. Bellamy	66/1
Refused	Golden Fox	10.10.0	S. Earle	200/1
Refused	Stearsby	13.10.6	S. Mackey	250/1
Refused	Kittinger	11.10.0	I. Lawrence	200/1

4 April 1992
Going – Good to Soft
Sponsor – Martell
Winner – £99,943
Time – 9mins 6.4secs
40 Ran
Favourite – Docklands Express
Top Weight – Twin Oaks
Winner trained by Nick Gaselee at Upper Lambourn, Berkshire
Winner owned by Mrs D. Thompson
Party Politics, brown gelding by Politico – Spin Again.

(Race void)

Throughout its history, the Grand National had witnessed thrills and spills, high drama, excruciating tension, marvellous excitement and fabulous competitors. Above all, it is recognised as the world's greatest steeplechase. The 1993 version certainly provided moments of unforgettable action, stocked with the usual collection of magnificent horses primed to the minute, and probably provided more drama than any National run before. However, without doubt, the 1993 Grand National turned out to be the most chaotic, laughable and depressing running of the proud event ever staged. For the name of the sport and the great race, it was a disaster, heaping mockery on a national institution steeped in tradition and sporting excellence.

The day of the race brought with it the usual unique sense of expectation and optimism as people all over the country scoured the morning's newspapers for tips and advice on where to place their money. National day, like no other sporting day of the year, unites the nation, and 1993 was no different. Certainly on paper it appeared one of the hardest Nationals to predict for some time and, although many of the horses at the bottom of the betting were of poor quality, the top half was packed with some fine horses, with a plethora of big race winners among them.

Both Party Politics and Romany King were back to renew their rivalry. After a disappointing start to the season, the giant Party Politics had been fitted with a special tube in his neck to aid his breathing, and the operation paid instant dividends as the horse won his preparatory race at Haydock Park. With Carl Llewellyn winning his fitness battle having been injured at the Cheltenham Festival, late money was poured on the strapping nine-year-old, who started the 7/1 favourite. Romany King had long been ante-post favourite having run so well in 1992, and the horse now had a new owner in the form of Urs Schwarzenbach, a Swiss banker. Trained to the second by Toby Balding, the one concern, despite late rain, was the good-to-firm ground, as Romany King preferred it far softer.

There was no doubt that the form horse of the race was the ten-year-old chestnut Zeta's Lad. The horse was unbeaten during the season, improving with

every race as he won five consecutive chases. Trained by John Upson, the horse's victories had included Gowran Park's Thyestes Chase and Kempton's *Racing Post* Chase, and it was after the latter that Upson decided the National was the race for Zeta's Lad. With a light weight and looking a picture in the paddock, Upson revealed his total confidence that the horse would win, calmly smoking a cigar as Zeta's Lad cantered down to the start under jockey Robbie Supple.

Jenny Pitman's strong hand included the 1991 runner-up Garrison Savannah, who had stayed clear of the injuries that had dogged him in the past, and the high-class chestnut Royal Athlete, another injury-prone chaser that had run the race of his life to finish third in the recent Cheltenham Gold Cup. Also representing Pitman was the ten-year-old bay Esha Ness, a horse that had started favourite for the Kim Muir at Cheltenham, only to finish fifth. Mrs Pitman had warned that Esha Ness was no forlorn hope, with the gelding partnered by the very capable John White.

Captain Dibble was the thirteenth and final National ride for Peter Scudamore and the horse had won the previous year's Scottish National, while David Nicholson's runner Givus A Buck had won the Ritz Club Chase at Cheltenham. The Committee, from the Irish yard of Homer Scott, had run well in the Kim Muir. With plenty of very good horses, longer odds were available for the likes of the 1992 third Laura's Beau, trained in Ireland by Frank Berry, the 1991 Hennessy winner Chatam, the Midlands National winner Mister Ed, the quirky chestnut Riverside Boy – a winner over four-and-a-quarter-miles and from the family of Spanish Steps – and one-time leading Gold Cup candidate Kildimo, now a veteran at thirteen and the winner of the Becher Chase in November and a half-brother to the 1979 hero Rubstic.

The grey Howe Street and Sure Metal avoid the prohibitive cones placed in front of The Chair.

Just So was ruled out in the morning because of the going, and the day was grey, with strong winds and driving rain. The crowd were warmed considerably when the twenty-eight-year-old Red Rum enthusiastically led the parade, but what happened next could only be described as a shambles. As millions the world over tuned in to watch the famous race, an already late start was delayed further by the usual suspects of protestors and demonstrators. Their exhibition was conducted in front of the first fence, and concerned jockeys pointed this out to starter Keith Brown, as the increasingly frustrated horses were asked to take a turn and wait.

With some horses becoming especially quarrelsome, particularly Chatam and Royle Speedmaster, the runners were belatedly called into line. Eager to begin the race, the starter released the tape, only for the feeble-looking device to rise slowly, clobbering a number of runners – including New Mill House on the inside – resulting in a false start. The flagman in front of the first fence, Ken Evans, signalled to the charging runners, and they quickly retreated to try again. With the crowd too becoming loud and impatient, the confusion was mounting and, getting back in line, the stubbornness of some of the horses was reaching crisis levels. Some were sweating profusely and some were getting mulelish as the delay and general fuss took its toll.

After what seemed like an eternity, the tape went up again as the majority of the field got away successfully, but on the wide outside, the slow-rising tape had first caught the head of young Judy Davies' mount Formula One and then curled round the neck of Richard Dunwoody, giving him no chance of continuing on Wont Be Gone Long, with eight others stopped in their tracks. Shouting frantically as thirty of the field hurtled unknowingly away in the distance, Keith Brown tried in vain to recall the field, the crowd booing relentlessly. However, the flagman on this occasion was missing in action, as the majority began the most surreal of journeys.

To a stunned silence, Sure Metal, Rowlandsons Jewels and Cahervillahow jumped the first in the lead, and mercifully there were no fallers until the grey Farm Week capsized at the fourth. All those running jumped Becher's in great style, with David's Duky – who had been baulked by Farm Week's tumble – tailed-off. As they reached the Canal Turn, a chorus of disapproval echoed down from the spectators. Royal Athlete was next to go at the tenth and outsider Senator Snugfit a fence later and, as Sure Metal and the near-white Howe Street led back onto the racecourse, an eerie silence ghosted over the tannoy commentary.

Waiting at The Chair were a number of cones randomly placed in front of the fence, with a flag-bearing official desperately trying to attract the attention of the runners. But, with the memory of the demonstrators fresh in their minds, the jockeys could hardly be blamed for thinking this was another mindless attempt to stop the National and, as they jumped the mighty fence, the grandstand erupted with a vicious assault of booing.

Esha Ness (yellow), The Committee (centre) and Romany King take the last fence believing there is a race to be won.

It was only upon returning to the start (where nine runners stood innocently watching proceedings), that many who had completed a circuit saw their own trainers and colleagues waving at them to stop, and duly reacted by pulling-up. Among these were fancied horses Party Politics, Zeta's Lad, Captain Dibble and Garrison Savannah. But for those out in front and not sure of what was happening, how could they give up a chance of winning the Grand National? Although a number of jockeys looked round, no doubt stunned as to why so many were dropping out, they carried on their quest amid deafening silence.

When disputing leaders Sure Metal and Howe Street plunged out simultaneously in cruel fashion at the twentieth, and with the Irish horse The Gooser crumbling a fence later, eight horses were left to endure an arduous battle over the remaining fences and, with Romany King and The Committee striking the front jumping the Canal Turn (where Interim Lib unseated), they marched on for home.

With the two leaders beginning to come under pressure at the last, John White steered Esha Ness through to take it up and, staying on strongly, galloped to the line to faint applause, edging the fast-finishing Cahervillahow. Romany King, The Committee, Givus A Buck, On The Other Hand and Laura's Beau followed them home having completed the most demanding of steeplechases for nothing.

Within seconds of crossing the line, White was informed the race would not count; the heartbroken look on the jockey's face explaining all, his dreams crushed and a brilliant ride aboard a most game horse rendered meaningless. Fortunately, no horses were killed, but Travel Over sustained a serious injury

Peter Scudamore, who pulled-up after a circuit on Captain Dibble, explains his version of events to the gathered listeners.

1993 GRAND NATIONAL RESULT

FATE	HORSE	AGE/WEIGHT	JOCKEY	ODDS
1st	ESHA NESS	10.10.0	J. WHITE	50/1
2nd	CAHERVILLAHOW	9.10.11	C. SWAN	25/1
3rd	ROMANY KING	9.10.7	A. MAGUIRE	15/2
4th	THE COMMITTEE	10.10.0	N. WILLIAMSON	25/1
5th	Givus A Buck	10.10.0	P. Holley	16/1
6th	On The Other Hand	10.10.3	N. Doughty	20/1
7th	Laura's Beau	9.10.0	C. O'Dwyer	20/1
Fell	Royal Athlete	10.10.4	B. De Haan	17/2
Fell	Sure Metal	10.10.0	S.J. O'Neill	50/1
Fell	The Gooser	10.10.0	K. O'Brien	50/1
Fell	Howe Street	10.10.0	A. Orkney	66/1
Fell	Paco's Boy	8.10.0	M. Foster	100/1
Fell	Senator Snugfit	8.10.0	Peter Hobbs	200/1
Fell	Farm Week	11.10.1	S. Hodgson	200/1
Pulled-Up	Quirinus	11.11.10	J. Brecka	300/1
Pulled-Up	Garrison Savannah	10.11.8	M. Pitman	10/1
Pulled-Up	Party Politics	9.11.2	C. Llewellyn	7/1
Pulled-Up	Captain Dibble	8.10.8	P. Scudamore	9/1
Pulled-Up	Zeta's Lad	10.10.4	R. Supple	15/2
Pulled-Up	Riverside Boy	10.10.0	M. Perrett	28/1
Pulled-Up	Rowlandsons Jewels	12.10.0	D. Gallagher	50/1
Pulled-Up	New Mill House	10.10.0	T. Horgan	66/1
Pulled-Up	David's Duky	11.10.0	M. Brennan	100/1
Pulled-Up	Travel Over	12.10.2	Mr M. Armytage	100/1
Pulled-Up	Stay On Tracks	11.10.0	K. Johnson	50/1
Pulled-Up	Mister Ed	10.10.0	D. Morris	25/1
Pulled-Up	Direct	10.10.3	P. Niven	100/1
Unseated Rider	Interim Lib	10.10.4	Mr J. Bradburne	200/1
Refused	Joyful Noise	10.10.1	T. Jarvis	150/1
Refused	Bonanza Boy	12.10.0	S. McNeill	100/1
Left	Chatam	9.11.7	J. Lower	28/1
Left	Roc De Prince	10.10.6	G. McCourt	66/1
Left	Latent Talent	9.10.2	J. Osborne	28/1
Left	Kildimo	13.10.0	L. Wyer	40/1
Left	Wont Be Gone Long	11.10.1	R. Dunwoody	16/1
Left	Nos Na Gaoithe	10.10.2	R. Garritty	66/1
Left	Formula One	11.10.0	Judy Davies	200/1
Left	Tarqogans Best	13.10.0	B. Clifford	500/1
Left	Royle Speedmaster	9.10.5	Mr J. Durkan	200/1

3 April 1993
Going – Good to Firm
Sponsor – Martell
Winner – £102,495
Time – 9mins 1.4secs
39 Ran
Favourite – Party Politics

Top Weight – Quirinus
Esha Ness trained by Mrs Jenny Pitman
   at Upper Lambourn, Berkshire
Esha Ness owned by Mr P. Bancroft
Esha Ness, bay gelding by Crash
   Course – Beeston
RACE VOID.

following the commotion at the start and never raced again, while others, such as the spirited Sure Metal and Howe Street, had needlessly fallen.

It was originally suggested that the nine that did not jump a fence – Wont Be Gone Long, Chatam, Tarqogan's Best, Nos Na Gaoithe, Kildimo, Formula One, Roc De Prince, Royle Speedmaster and Latent Talent – be allowed to race, but after much discussion and a great deal of dissatisfaction, the 1993 Grand National was declared void with all bets refunded.

The reactions of the jockeys and trainers included anger, frustration and sadness, with the Jockey Club receiving much of the blame, being branded unprofessional in their approach. Keith Brown incurred the wrath of racegoers, yet of all involved, he perhaps was least to blame, for the starting tape was pathetic, the horses and jockeys understandably on edge and the volume of the crowd fierce. Both times Brown successfully called for a false start, but the second time the flagman was apparently nowhere to be seen. The contributions of the demonstrators must also not be forgotten, for their part in unsettling the horses was major, with racecourse security similarly to blame for failing to stop the protestors breaching the course.

It was clear that if the Grand National was to reclaim its place as a great and respected event in the sporting calendar, drastic and thorough changes would have to take place to ensure that what happened to the disastrous 1993 race never occurred again.

1994

MIINNEHOMA

The changes made at Aintree to eradicate the problems that had ruined the 1993 race were both sensible and effective. Over £1 million had been spent on overall security, with perimeter fences erected to stop demonstrators rushing onto the course. The much maligned, lever-operated starting tape was replaced by a considerably faster electronic gate, raised by a simple push of a button. To eliminate confusion and crowd noise for the starter, nobody was allowed within fifty yards of his rostrum, while three new flagmen, all former jockeys, were positioned further down the course to provide added assistance.

With relentless heavy rain and snow on the Friday throwing the running of the race into doubt, Aintree first had to pass an early morning inspection before racing went ahead. With such heavy ground, clearly the National was going to emphasise stamina, with conditions deemed unacceptable for Bishops Hall, Windy Ways and Rifle Range – all of whom were withdrawn on the morning of the race.

Included in the field of thirty-six were some brilliant individuals, the most striking being the immensely popular French horse The Fellow, trained by Francois Doumen and the recent winner at the fourth time of asking of the Cheltenham Gold Cup. A brilliant jumper, The Fellow had been a raider on British shores from a young age, finishing runner-up in the Gold Cup in both 1991 and 1992. The horse had won a pair of King George VI Chases as well as a Grand Steeplechase de Paris, but it was his recent Gold Cup success that meant so much to his trainer and confirmed the horse as one of the greats of the modern era. Owned by Marquesa de Moratalla and ridden by Polish-born jockey Adam Kondrat, it was with some surprise that the French horse was allowed to take his chance in the National, for he had a dislike of softer conditions. But his presence brought a huge element of class to the race, and he carried an enticing weight of 11st 4lbs, behind the Slovakian raider Quirinus and the former Welsh and Scottish National winner Run For Free.

Most fancied in the betting were two horses familiar with the hunter-chase scene, Moorcroft Boy and Double Silk. Trained by David Nicholson, the bright chestnut Moorcroft Boy had adjusted well to handicap chases and had developed into a worthy National candidate during the season, winning over four miles at Cheltenham, taking the Warwick National and then finishing second in the Greenalls Gold Cup at Kempton Park. Tough and courageous, Moorcroft Boy was by that excellent sire of stayers Roselier, and started 5/1 favourite. The nine-year-old Double Silk was thrust into handicap company for the first time at Aintree having taken all before him in the hunter-chase sphere, winning nine in a row including the Aintree and Cheltenham Foxhunters'. Trained by Mr Reg Wilkins and ridden by amateur Ron Treloggen, Double Silk's front-running, bold-jumping style was considered ideal for the National and he began at 6/1.

Having broken blood vessels earlier in his career, it had only been in the current season that the eight-year-old chestnut Master Oats had begun to impact the chasing scene, rising steadily through the ranks armed with a relentless galloping style that wore opponents down, particularly on softer surfaces. A graceful, fluent jumper, Master Oats had destroyed Moorcroft Boy in the Greenalls Gold Cup and, with just 10 stone to carry, shaped as a serious threat for trainer Kim Bailey and jockey Norman Williamson.

One of the class horses in the field having won the 1992 Sun Alliance Chase, the brown gelding Miinnehoma had suffered from poor form and injury in the interim period, but had returned from a long lay off to win at Newbury before finishing an encouraging seventh in the Gold Cup for Martin Pipe. Lightly raced for an eleven-year-old, Richard Dunwoody took the ride at Aintree, while the Gold Cup third Young Hustler was also popular as he looked to become the first seven-year-old since Bogskar in 1940 to win. Zeta's Lad, Romany King and Garrison Savannah all ran again, while among the newcomers were dual Whitbread Gold Cup winner Topsham Bay, Cheltenham's Mildmay of Flete winner Elfast, former Hennessy Cognac Gold Cup favourite Black Humour and Fiddlers Pike, the mount of fifty-one-year-old Mrs Rosemary Henderson, who had gained special permission from the Jockey Club to participate.

As the runners paraded in front of the grandstand, Aintree was pleasantly illuminated by bright sunshine and, with the new starting tape working exactly as planned, it was with renewed spirit that the 1994 National began. Immediately Double Silk pulled to the front and, together with the chestnut Young Hustler, met the first in the lead in the centre of the track. In behind them, Henry Mann, Fourth Of July and the fancied Elfast crashed out, while the giant Ushers Island – a former Cheltenham Festival winner over four miles – and Aintree veteran Romany King hit the boggy turf at the third and fourth fences respectively.

The pace was noticeably slower than normal approaching Becher's, with some of the field already well detached, such as Roc De Prince, Southern Minstrel, the Irish runner Captain Brandy and the tailed-off Quirinus. But Double Silk put in a mighty leap at Becher's, and he led on from Riverside Boy, Garrison Savannah, Young Hustler and the improving Master Oats on the wide outside while, towards the rear, Laura's Beau, It's A Cracker and New Mill House fell.

Riderless Double Silk is brought down by the fall of Black Humour at The Chair. Jumping the fence are Channels Gate (37) and Into The Red.

A loose horse hampered Garrison Savannah at the seventeenth, causing him to refuse and similarly cause the refusal of Run For Free in behind and, when Riverside Boy decided he had had enough a fence later, there were very few left heading for Becher's again, with Fiddler's Pike suddenly beginning to get into the action. The Fellow was all but down at Becher's and, at the Canal Turn, the French horse was tiring badly as he came down before being rudely struck by Mister Ed as he struggled to his feet.

With the Gold Cup winner out of the picture, just five horses were left in contention as the gruelling race neared its conclusion, with Ebony Jane, Miinnehoma, Just So, Moorcroft Boy and Into The Red making their way bravely back onto the racecourse, with Miinnehoma under tight restraint from Dunwoody and travelling imperiously. Moorcroft Boy had come to take it up by the final fence, with the riderless Young Hustler running dangerously loose just ahead, and a thunderous roar went up as the favourite touched down in front and scooted away from Miinnehoma and the one-paced Just So.

However, Dunwoody had remained calm aboard Miinnehoma and, on the run to the elbow, it was clear he was merely waiting to unleash his horse past Moorcroft Boy. Sweeping by the favourite, a comfortable victory looked likely for Miinnehoma but, coming with a renewed effort was Simon Burrough on the tall brown horse Just So. Often referred to as 'Just Slow', the horse loved the going and was a thorough stayer. Rising up to challenge, his dark frame reached Miinnehoma's girth fifty yards from the line, trying mightily to overhaul the leader. But Dunwoody would not be denied and, as Miinnehoma found vital reserves, the pair held on in a rousing finish to win by a length-and-a-quarter.

Double Silk continued to jump energetically, but the eleventh fence claimed the unlucky Young Hustler when the riderless Ushers Island crashed right in front of him, bringing the chestnut down. That incident was merely a prelude for the drama that unfolded at the normally incident-free thirteenth. Double Silk had settled into a beautiful rhythm, jumping really well with Riverside Boy on his outside but, possibly distracted by a loose horse jumping and stumbling directly in front of him, Double Silk brushed the top of the fence and came down in his first ever fall. On his outside, Master Oats had been travelling as well as any, but he too seemed to lose concentration, falling heavily and giving Topsham Bay nowhere to go, the big bay horse unseating Jimmy Frost. In addition, outsider Mighty Falcon cannoned into Double Silk as he rose to his feet, unseating Paul Holley, and Mr Boston also fell, as the fence decimated the field, changing the race outlook dramatically. With loose horses running free, more drama followed at The Chair when Black Humour – who had been progressing quietly through the field – landed on top of the fence and was subsequently hit by the trailing Double Silk, both horses ending up on the ground in a tangled mess.

A vastly reduced field began the second circuit, the horses being totally strung out with many pulling-up. Garrison Savannah now led on the inside from the erratic Riverside Boy, who had drifted all the way over to the extreme outside, clearly becoming disenchanted with the race, while Miinnehoma, Ebony Jane and The Fellow were prominent in the centre, with Moorcroft Boy and the improving slogger Just So in behind.

Richard Dunwoody is poised on Miinnehoma (8) at the last fence as they prepare to challenge the favourite Moorcroft Boy. The loose horse is Young Hustler.

Simon Burrough brought Just So (right) with a late rally to challenge Miinnehoma. Ebony Jane (left) was fourth.

Just So had given his all, yet had been beaten by a horse of higher class and great resolve. Moorcroft Boy came home third some twenty lengths back having run a great race. The horse broke his neck in the Becher Chase later that year, but recovered to prove his toughness by winning the 1996 Scottish National. Ebony Jane was fourth and Mrs Henderson proudly finished higher than any woman before her in fifth with Roc De Prince the only other to complete in what had been a war of attrition and a National run on the most testing of conditions. Thankfully no horses were killed, although the unlucky Double Silk had cracked nine ribs, but lived to fight another day.

Not surprisingly, it was the slowest National since 1955. Back in the winner's enclosure, an interview was conducted via telephone with winning owner Freddie Starr, the Liverpool-born comedian who was not present at Aintree. It was a first Grand National success for Martin Pipe and a second for Dunwoody. Miinnehoma's victory illustrated the unbelievable talent of Dunwoody, the jockey steering the 'forgotten' horse home with unrivalled coolness, patiently holding on to his horse, preserving his stamina right to the very end. After such a disappointing episode in 1993, the thrilling 1994 National went a long way to restoring the race to its proud and lofty position in the sporting world.

1994 GRAND NATIONAL RESULT

FATE	HORSE	AGE/WEIGHT	JOCKEY	ODDS
1st	MIINNEHOMA	11.10.8	R. DUNWOODY	16/1
2nd	JUST SO	11.10.3	S. BURROUGH	20/1
3rd	MOORCROFT BOY	9.10.0	A. MAGUIRE	5/1
4th	EBONY JANE	9.10.1	L. CUSACK	25/1
5th	Fiddlers Pike	13.10.0	Mrs R. Henderson	100/1
6th	Roc De Prince	11.10.0	J. Lower	100/1
Fell	The Fellow	9.11.4	A. Kondrat	9/1
Fell	Zeta's Lad	11.10.13	R. Supple	16/1
Fell	Black Humour	10.10.12	G. Bradley	33/1
Fell	Double Silk	10.10.4	Mr R. Treloggen	6/1
Fell	Romany King	10.10.1	R. Guest	22/1
Fell	Rust Never Sleeps	10.10.0	P. Carberry	66/1
Fell	Henry Mann	11.10.0	C. Swan	50/1
Fell	Mr Boston	9.10.2	P. Niven	16/1
Fell	Master Oats	8.10.0	N. Williamson	9/1
Fell	Gay Ruffian	8.10.0	R. Farrant	150/1
Fell	Elfast	11.10.4	G. McCourt	18/1
Fell	Laura's Beau	10.10.0	B. Sheridan	40/1
Fell	Fourth Of July	10.10.0	J.P. Banahan	50/1
Fell	New Mill House	11.10.0	T. Horgan	150/1
Fell	It's A Cracker	10.10.0	C. O'Dwyer	33/1
Pulled-Up	Southern Minstrel	11.10.1	M. Dwyer	50/1
Pulled-Up	Paco's Boy	9.10.0	M. Foster	200/1
Pulled-Up	He Who Dares Wins	11.10.0	C. Grant	66/1
Brought Down	Young Hustler	7.10.12	D. Bridgwater	16/1
Brought Down	Mister Ed	11.10.0	D. Morris	50/1
Brought Down	Mighty Falcon	9.10.0	P. Holley	250/1
Unseated Rider	Quirinus	12.11.10	J. Brecka	250/1
Unseated Rider	Topsham Bay	11.10.11	J. Frost	25/1
Unseated Rider	Ushers Island	8.10.0	A. Dobbin	66/1
Unseated Rider	Into The Red	10.10.0	J. White	25/1
Unseated Rider	Captain Brandy	9.10.0	K. O'Brien	50/1
Refused	Run For Free	10.11.7	M. Perrett	25/1
Refused	Garrison Savannah	11.10.3	J. Osborne	25/1
Refused	Riverside Boy	11.10.0	M. Richards	33/1
Refused	Channels Gate	10.10.0	T. Jenks	100/1

9 April 1994
Going – Heavy
Sponsor – Martell
Winner – £115,606
Time – 10mins 18.8secs
36 Ran
Favourite – Moorcroft Boy

Top Weight – Quirinus
Winner trained by Martin Pipe at
    Nicholashayne, Wellington, Somerset
Winner owned by Mr Freddie Starr
Miinnehoma, bay or brown gelding by
    Kambalda – Mrs Cairns.

1995

ROYAL ATHLETE

The most improved horse in training, Master Oats, become the fourth horse in the 1990s to try and win both the Gold Cup and Grand National in the same season. Having begun to show his potential before a fall at Aintree in the 1994 race, Master Oats had progressed mightily, winning four chases, including the rerouted Welsh Grand National at Newbury and culminating with a destruction of a high-class field in the Cheltenham Gold Cup. A relentless galloper and a horse at the absolute peak of his career, the key to Master Oats' success was soft ground or heavier, for he was able find his rhythm and bury his opponents in these conditions – as he had so ruthlessly in the Gold Cup. There were lingering doubts over his jumping, as he had made a few early errors at Cheltenham, and jockey Norman Williamson planned to give Master Oats plenty of daylight on the wide outside at Aintree to settle the horse. With the ground rapidly drying out, Kim Bailey inspected the course on the morning of the race before giving the all clear for the chestnut to run and, despite carrying top weight of 11st 10lbs, Master Oats started a rock-solid 5/1 favourite.

Among the opposition to Master Oats were a number of the horses he had beaten at Cheltenham, including Dubacilla, Miinnehoma, Young Hustler and Nuaffe. The David Nicholson-trained mare Dubacilla, runner-up at Cheltenham, was a thorough stayer and a half-sister to Just So, while Miinnehoma had again had a light campaign, finishing third in the Gold Cup, but had 9lbs more to carry than for his National win in 1994, with conditions completely different. Young Hustler had run consistently well all season for his trainer Nigel Twiston-Davies while Nuaffe, from the Irish yard of Pat Fahy, was something of a chancy jumper, but had won well over Haydock Park's stiff fences in the Greenalls Gold Cup.

As well as former winner Party Politics, the Andy Turnell-trained chestnut Country Member (extremely well backed having won the Grand Military Gold Cup at Sandown) and the Flat-bred Crystal Spirit (born to win a Derby but now a high-class jumper having finished third in a Sun Alliance Chase), Jenny Pitman saddled no fewer than six runners. Among them were Garrison Savannah,

Esha Ness – the winner of the 'National that never was' – and Lusty Light, carrying the Corbiere colours of owner Mr Bryan Burrough. Also representing Mrs Pitman was the chestnut Royal Athlete, a good-class horse formerly placed in a Gold Cup but with a history of leg trouble. Ridden by Grand National debutant Jason Titley, Royal Athlete was one horse expected to thrive on the drying ground but, even so, his odds of 40/1 rendered him something of a forgotten runner.

With Aintree radiant beneath beaming sunshine, only thirty-five horses faced the starter. Away to a quick start, Josh Gifford's runner Topsham Bay and the outsider Over The Deel set a cracking pace to the first fence. With most of the runners from the centre to inner of the course jumping the fence well, it was towards the outside where the grief occurred. Country Member's white face was first to hit the floor and Lusty Light, The Committee (ridden by Japanese jockey Mr Tanaka), Tinryland and Bishops Hall all fell, while Errant Knight unseated Mark Perrett and the giant chestnut Jumbeau was unluckily brought down having cleared the obstacle well. In total, a fifth of the field had been wiped out and further grief arrived when Young Hustler blundered and unseated Carl Llewellyn at the third when disputing the lead. In behind, Zeta's Lad and General Pershing both crashed out, the former leaving Graham Bradley unconscious.

Two of the Pitman team, Superior Finish and Do Be Brief, held the lead at Becher's from the fast-ground-loving Topsham Bay. Williamson had taken Master Oats down the outside, and the Gold Cup winner had quickly found his rhythm, jumping gloriously and well in contention. As the main pack streamed over Becher's, Miinnehoma was struggling badly at the rear, and Dunwoody was forced to give the horse some stiff reminders.

The big brown gelding Superior Finish appeared to be relishing his task out in front, delivering a huge jump at Valentines before stumbling at the tenth and unseating Peter Niven while, two fences later, both Chatam and Esha Ness came down. Do Be Brief led back onto the racecourse from Crystal Spirit, Camelot Knight, Garrison Savannah, Ebony Jane, Royal Athlete and Master Oats. Although there were many loose horses accompanying the main group, including three tearing away at the head of affairs approaching The Chair, they did not prove to be a problem for the remainder of the race.

Having kept out of trouble for a circuit, Master Oats really got into the race at the start of the second. Still being kept very wide by Williamson, the horse took each fence in his stride coming back to Becher's, jumping the big ditch at the nineteenth with power and purpose. Enjoying an equally fine ride was Titley on Royal Athlete and he had come through on the inside to dispute the lead with the Gold Cup winner at the famous fence, with Topsham Bay and the 100/1 outsider Over The Deel well placed in the centre.

Racing down the back, Royal Athlete and Master Oats engaged in a dual. Both were jumping exceptionally well, yet there was a feeling that it was Royal Athlete that was travelling the easier and, when he out-jumped the Gold Cup winner at the twenty-seventh, it was clear Master Oats had a real fight on his hands.

Left: Gold Cup winner Master Oats (1) is well placed jumping The Chair, with Over The Deel (34) and Topsham Bay (14) also in contention.

Below: Royal Athlete and jockey Jason Titley jump the last on their way to a memorable win.

Rounding the turn for home, the leading two had been joined by a whole host of pursuers, headed by old adversaries Party Politics and Romany King, as well as the Becher Chase winner Into The Red and the surprising Over The Deel. It was here that Master Oats came under pressure as Royal Athlete surged on. Taking the final fence, the leader was away quickly as Master Oats faded, and first Romany King then the long-striding Party Politics went in pursuit. Hitting the elbow, Royal Athlete was clear – now the only threat was the giant Party Politics, who chased him the best he could. But Royal Athlete was not to be denied and, staying on strongly, he sprinted up the run in, crossing the line seven lengths ahead of Party Politics, who had delivered another fine Aintree performance. Six lengths back came Over The Deel for jockey Mr Chris Bonner and trainer Howard Johnson – just getting the best of a bunch finish that included the fast-finishing Dubacilla, Into the Red and Romany King – with Master Oats a valiant seventh but having run perhaps an even better race than at Cheltenham, for he had given considerable weight to all those involved in the finish on ground that had not favoured him.

Jenny Pitman's affiliation with the Grand National had now grown even stronger with the hugely impressive success of Royal Athlete and, even though the horse she called 'Alfie' had been the longest-priced winner since Last Suspect,

The connections of Royal Athlete receive the winning trophy – the Philip Blacker Bronze.

he was a classy individual who was confirming the promise of his early career, which had been curtailed by injury. On this occasion, Mrs Pitman had Royal Athlete's owners, Garry and Libby Johnson, to thank, for they had requested the horse run at Aintree in preference to the Scottish National. The victory was also a most welcome success for Jason Titley. The Irishman had ridden a mere seven winners during the season, yet had constructed the perfect ride down the inside as Royal Athlete won a Grand National to savour, with a dominant display over the most famous fences in the world.

1995 GRAND NATIONAL RESULT

FATE	HORSE	AGE/WEIGHT	JOCKEY	ODDS
1st	ROYAL ATHLETE	12.10.6	J.F. TITLEY	40/1
2nd	PARTY POLITICS	11.10.2	M. DWYER	16/1
3rd	OVER THE DEEL	9.10.0	MR C. BONNER	100/1
4th	DUBACILLA	9.11.0	D. GALLAGHER	9/1
5th	Into The Red	11.10.0	R. Guest	20/1
6th	Romany King	11.10.0	Mr M. Armytage	40/1
7th	Master Oats	9.11.10	N. Williamson	5/1
8th	Riverside Boy	12.10.0	C. Swan	40/1
9th	Garrison Savannah	12.10.0	W. Marston	16/1
10th	Topsham Bay	12.10.0	P. Hide	20/1
11th	Cool Ground	13.10.0	P. Holley	50/1
12th	Ebony Jane	10.10.0	A. Maguire	20/1
13th	Gold Cap	10.10.6	G. McCourt	50/1
14th	Crystal Spirit	8.10.4	J. Osborne	12/1
15th	For William	9.10.0	C. O'Dwyer	100/1
Fell	Chatam	11.10.6	A.P. McCoy	25/1
Fell	Lusty Light	9.10.2	R. Farrant	12/1
Fell	Nuaffe	10.10.0	S. O'Donovan	20/1
Fell	General Pershing	9.10.0	D. Bridgwater	20/1
Fell	Country Member	10.10.0	L. Harvey	11/1
Fell	Bishops Hall	9.10.0	C. Maude	66/1
Fell	Tinryland	11.10.2	M.A. Fitzgerald	50/1
Fell	The Committee	12.10.0	T. Tanaka	75/1
Fell	Esha Ness	12.10.0	J. White	50/1
Fell	Desert Lord	9.10.0	F. Woods	100/1
Fell	Do Be Brief	10.10.0	B. Powell	66/1
Fell	Camelot Knight	9.10.2	Mr M. Rimell	66/1
Pulled-Up	Miinnehoma	12.11.4	R. Dunwoody	11/1
Brought Down	Jumbeau	10.10.0	S. McNeill	100/1
Unseated Rider	Young Hustler	8.11.2	C. Llewellyn	10/1
Unseated Rider	Zeta's Lad	12.10.3	G. Bradley	50/1
Unseated Rider	Dakyns Boys	10.10.0	T. Jenks	50/1
Unseated Rider	Errant Knight	11.10.0	M. Perrett	75/1
Unseated Rider	Superior Finish	9.10.3	P. Niven	33/1
Unseated Rider	It's A Snip	10.10.0	J.R. Kavanagh	200/1

8 April 1995
Going – Good
Sponsor – Martell
Winner – £118,854
Time – 9mins 4.1secs
35 Ran
Favourite – Master Oats
Top Weight – Master Oats

Winner trained by Mrs Jenny Pitman at
 Upper Lambourn, Berkshire
Winner owned by Gary Johnson and
 Libby Johnson
Royal Athlete, chestnut gelding by
 Roselier – Darjoy.

1996

ROUGH QUEST

Red Rum, the most celebrated Grand National winner of all time and three times the champion during the 1970s, passed away before the 1996 Grand National. Fittingly, the great warrior was laid to rest near the winning post at Aintree, as the racecourse honoured the horse that had captured the hearts and imaginations of sporting fans everywhere during his illustrious career.

Continuing a worrying trend, only twenty-seven runners went to post for the 1996 race and, in all honesty, there were only a handful of horses that appeared to possess the necessary quality of a National winner. True, the extremely well weighted Gold Cup runner-up Rough Quest was a very worthy favourite and Young Hustler, Life Of A Lord, Deep Bramble, Son Of War and Party Politics all rightly deserved strong consideration, but the overall standard of the 1996 race was poor. The situation of attracting better quality together with the maximum quantity was in need of serious attention.

The ten-year-old bay Rough Quest had enjoyed a breakout season, establishing himself as one of the best chasers in the land for Irish trainer Terry Casey, whose base was in Surrey. Rough Quest had won the Ritz Club Chase at the 1995 Cheltenham Festival and, in the current campaign, had finished second in top chases such as the Hennessy Cognac Gold Cup at Newbury and Betterware Cup at Ascot before winning the *Racing Post* Chase at Kempton. It was in the Gold Cup at Cheltenham that Rough Quest truly earned his place among the best in the land, running a splendid race and going down by a mere four lengths to the brilliant young Irish chaser Imperial Call. Immediately earning a quote of just 4/1 for Aintree, Casey initially ruled out the National and it was revealed Rough Quest was suffering from a condition affecting his muscle enzymes. But as the National grew closer, Rough Quest was found to be in the form of his life, convincing Casey to send the gelding to Aintree. With just 10st 7lbs to carry and with rising star Mick Fitzgerald in the saddle, the horse started 7/1 favourite.

Ireland provided a powerful challenge in 1996 with the fast-ground-loving big brown horse Life Of A Lord running for brilliant young trainer Aiden

O'Brien, Thyestes Chase winner Wylde Hide competing for leading Irish owner J.P. McManus and the grey horse Son Of War, a former Irish National winner, representing trainer Peter McCreery. Party Politics ran again and the strong-staying chestnut Deep Bramble – winner of two good chases at Sandown the season before – was well fancied for the up-and-coming duo of trainer Paul Nicholls and jockey Tony McCoy. Among the dark horses were Jenny Pitman's Superior Finish, who had shown boldly on the first circuit in 1995, and the consistent Encore Un Peu, a flashy chestnut from Martin Pipe's yard.

With no delay, Gerry Scott – jockey of the 1960 winner Merryman II and starting his first National – called in the runners, and soon the field were on their way to a roar of excitement in the glorious sunshine. The fast-breaking Captain Dibble was soon joined up front by Young Hustler and Superior Finish as they met the first fence. Over-jumping, the chestnut Bavard Dieu gave the previous year's winner Jason Titley a nasty fall, while Bishops Hall went at the first for the second consecutive year.

It was a pair of outsiders, Three Brownies and Sure Metal (the latter ridden by Ginger McCain's son Donald) that set the pace, the pair jumping for fun and setting a searching gallop. Towards the rear, Party Politics shocked the crowd with an uncharacteristic fall at the third and, with the temperamental Chatam refusing at the fifth, the field faced up to Becher's. It was noticeable how the smaller-than-normal field did not fan towards the outside as in previous Nationals, the majority not being intimidated to attack the middle to inner, as Sure Metal, Three Brownies, Sir Peter Lely and Greenhill Raffles – trained in Scotland by Lucinda Russell – led on.

Rough Quest (noseband) parades before the 1996 race followed by Chatam and Superior Finish.

Mick Fitzgerald is all smiles as Rough Quest jumps the last ahead of Young Hustler.

Cantering beautifully under Chris Maude, the top weight Young Hustler joined the leaders coming back onto the racecourse, where sadly the first fatality since 1991 occurred when poor Rust Never Sleeps fractured a shoulder on the run to the thirteenth. The majority of the field, well bunched, were jumping magnificently – none more so than the surprise package Three Brownies, with the talented Paul Carberry on board – and all the survivors cleared The Chair with no problems. Heading out for a second circuit, Three Brownies still led with Sure Metal, followed closely by Young Hustler, Over The Deel, Sir Peter Lely, Greenhill Raffles, Superior Finish, Riverside Boy, Life Of A Lord, Son Of War and Rough Quest.

On the march down to Becher's again, many of the fancied runners began their challenges. Hacking along, Young Hustler hit the front, while Life Of A Lord and Rough Quest moved forward smoothly on the outside, with Deep Bramble well positioned on the heels of the leaders alongside with Son Of War – though the latter pair were down on their noses at Becher's. Thirteen-year-old Riverside Boy

was giving the youngest rider in the race, David Walsh, a fabulous ride, and Sir Peter Lely continued to impress with his jumping.

The Canal Turn ruined a large portion of the Irish raid, with first Son Of War and then Wylde Hyde unseating their riders at the sharp, ninety-degree turn. Up front, Young Hustler and Three Brownies continued to jump from fence to fence as they began to work their way back to the racecourse, closely marshalled by Sir Peter Lely and the rapidly improving Encore Un Peu.

Coming back over the Melling Road for the final time, Life Of A Lord began to run out of steam and, before two out, Deep Bramble sadly broke down – so badly in fact that the horse was unable to run again. It was a shame considering that the chestnut was starting to pick up the leaders in eyecatching style and may well have been placed. It was Rough Quest that loomed as the main challenger over the final fences, as a mistake two out by Three Brownies saw his gallant run deteriorate, while both Young Hustler and Sir Peter Lely began to tire.

Encore Un Peu jumped the last in front and set off fast up the long run-in under David Bridgwater, but it was clear that Fitzgerald was merely biding his time on the favourite, who was notorious for idling in front. Rounding the elbow and having ridden a race of outstanding patience and timing, Fitzgerald played his hand, coming on the outside of Encore Un Peu and asking Rough Quest to quicken. Decisively, the favourite accelerated past his rival and, although cutting across him slightly, took a decisive lead that he kept until the line, winning to rapturous applause by a length-and-a-quarter. Superior Finish was sixteen lengths away in third, with Sir Peter Lely edging Young Hustler for fourth. Three Brownies had run a blinder to take sixth, while Life Of A Lord, who later won the Whitbread Gold Cup, finished seventh.

Immediately, a steward's enquiry was called to discuss Rough Quest's apparent impeding of Encore Un Peu. A reversal of the result would have been extremely harsh as the best horse in the field had clearly won; for fifteen agonising minutes, the connections of Rough Quest sweated over the outcome. Finally it was called and, after a faultless round of jumping and a masterful ride from Fitzgerald, Rough Quest had won the National. For Casey it was the proudest moment of his training career, and it was a bitter blow to racing when the trainer sadly died a few short years later following a long illness. Owner Mr Andrew Wates had won the 1970 Foxhunter's at Aintree and had also ridden in the National itself in 1968 on Champion Prince, being brought down at the water. But it was left to jubilant jockey Mick Fitzgerald to put the magical triumph into words. 'After this', suggested Fitzgerald, 'sex is an anti-climax!'

Mick Fitzgerald (left), trainer Terry Casey (centre) and owner Andrew Wates, connections of Rough Quest.

1996 GRAND NATIONAL RESULT

FATE	HORSE	AGE/WEIGHT	JOCKEY	ODDS
1st	ROUGH QUEST	10.10.7	M.A. FITZGERALD	7/1
2nd	ENCORE UN PEU	9.10.0	D. BRIDGWATER	14/1
3rd	SUPERIOR FINISH	10.10.3	R. DUNWOODY	9/1
4th	SIR PETER LELY	9.10.0	MR C. BONNER	33/1
5th	Young Hustler	9.11.7	C. Maude	8/1
6th	Three Brownies	9.10.0	P. Carberry	100/1
7th	Life Of A Lord	10.11.6	C. Swan	10/1
8th	Antonin	8.10.0	J. Burke	28/1
9th	Over The Deel	10.10.0	Mr T. McCarthy	33/1
10th	Vicompt De Valmont	11.10.1	P. Hide	22/1
11th	Captain Dibble	11.10.0	T. Jenks	40/1
12th	Riverside Boy	13.10.0	D. Walsh	66/1
13th	Over The Stream	10.10.0	A. Thornton	50/1
14th	Greenhill Raffles	10.10.0	M. Foster	100/1
15th	Into The Red	12.10.0	R. Guest	33/1
16th	Lusty Light	10.10.11	W. Marston	14/1
17th	Sure Metal	13.10.1	D. McCain	200/1
Fell	Party Politics	12.10.11	C. Llewellyn	10/1
Pulled-Up	Deep Bramble	9.11.5	A.P. McCoy	12/1
Pulled-Up	Chatam	12.10.3	J. Lower	40/1
Pulled-Up	Rust Never Sleeps	12.10.0	T. Horgan	20/1
Pulled-Up	Far Senior	10.10.0	T. Eley	150/1
Unseated Rider	Son Of War	9.11.0	C. O'Dwyer	8/1
Unseated Rider	Bishops Hall	10.10.1	Mr M. Armytage	22/1
Unseated Rider	Wylde Hide	9.10.0	F. Woods	12/1
Unseated Rider	Bavard Dieu	8.10.1	J.F. Titley	50/1
Unseated Rider	Brackenfield	10.10.0	Guy Lewis	100/1

30 March 1996
Going – Good
Sponsor – Martell
Winner – £142,534
Time – 9mins 0.8secs
27 Ran
Favourite – Rough Quest
Top Weight – Young Hustler
Winner trained by Terry Casey at Beare Green, Surrey
Winner owned by Mr A.T.A. Wates
Rough Quest, bay gelding by Crash Course – Our Quest.

1997

LORD GYLLENE

The 1997 Grand National marked the 150th anniversary of the world's most famous steeplechase. With fantastic organisation and solid, generous sponsorship, the event had certainly come a long way from those early adventures over ploughed fields and stone walls, and the race was now so popular that an estimated 500 million people worldwide were expected to tune in to watch live action of the latest renewal. Yet the 1997 Grand National experienced drama that no other edition of the race could relate to and, in its aftermath, left the spirit of the Grand National as strong as ever.

A pleasant rise in numbers from 1996 saw thirty-eight horses declared for the big race, with former Gold Cup winner Master Oats heading the handicap on 11st 10lbs, giving enormous amounts of weight away to every other runner. There was plenty of potential among the fancied horses, of which the majority were newcomers but, again, the overall quality was sub-standard. With the horses being saddled shortly before the race and some already walking round the paddock, the excitement, as always, was starting to grow to meteoric proportions. To describe what happened next as a let-down is a severe understatement. Although it was definitely that, it also illustrated the extremities of cowardice and spite some people will demonstrate to instil fear and panic in fellow human beings, while at the same time ruining one of the most loved spectacles in the sporting calendar and a national institution.

About an hour before the start, a pair of coded telephone messages were received by Merseyside police, threatening that bombs had been placed on the racecourse. Naturally, with the dangers of the warnings, the only feasible action was taken. The stands were evacuated and, as the giant screen facing the grandstand displayed, all persons in all areas were requested to leave immediately. Within an hour, the racecourse was desolate, as the bomb squad set about the task of securing the area. With the safety of the public a priority and with damage done to parts of the running rails and a number of the fences, the race was forced into postponement, with thousands left stranded on the streets without belongings that were left behind in the abrupt and mandatory exit. There were many heroes that weekend, not least the brave stable lads who defiantly refused to leave the helpless horses, and the generous people of Merseyside who rallied round to assist the wandering masses.

It was testament to the courage of Aintree, racing and the British public as a whole that, at five o'clock on Monday afternoon, the race was finally run, sending the most emphatic message to terrorists that the 'show must go on'. There was no charge for entry, with around 20,000 people attending, many of them youngsters. Although no cars were allowed on the course and everyone was thoroughly searched on admission, the general atmosphere was magnificent.

The disturbances of Saturday had proved tough on the horses, some of which had been adversely affected, and both Belmont King and Over The Stream were withdrawn from the rescheduled race. Although he had finished third in the previous season's King George VI Chase, Master Oats had failed to recapture the form of his scintillating Gold Cup season, with injury hampering much of the previous year. The horse had been pulled-up on his only run of the season in the Ericsson Chase at Leopardstown, and it was to the eight-year-old Go Ballistic that favouritism went. Trained by John O'Shea, the consistent performer had won the Betterware Cup at Ascot, but had impressed most of all when finishing a staying-on fourth in the Cheltenham Gold Cup behind the blazing chestnut Mr Mulligan. Go Ballistic was partnered by Mick Fitzgerald, whose 1996 winning mount Rough Quest was absent with injury.

The 'voice' of Aintree, Sir Peter O'Sullevan, commentated on his last Grand National in 1997.

The 1996 Sun Alliance Chase winner Nahthen Lad and the lightly raced Smith's Band were both well fancied to give Jenny Pitman a third winner, while Captain Tim Forster's Scottish Grand National runner-up General Wolfe and former Irish National winner Feathered Gale, from Arthur Moore's yard, were both lively each-way selections. The most striking horse in the field though was the athletic Suny Bay, a big grey that had won the Greenhalls Grand National Trial at Haydock Park. Trained by Charlie Brooks, Suny Bay had been really well fancied on the Saturday when conditions more closely resembled his favoured soft going but, by Monday, the ground had dried out considerably. Even so, Suny Bay – a fine jumper – was considered to be a horse with considerable talent, perhaps even Gold Cup class, and drew plenty of support, starting at 8/1.

Among the dark horses was the New Zealand-bred stayer Lord Gyllene, trained in Shrewsbury by Steve Brookshaw, nephew of Tim Brookshaw, the gallant runner-up on Wyndburgh in 1959. A well-built, nine-year-old bay, Lord Gyllene had emerged during the season as a long-distance chase specialist, winning three times at Uttoxeter, including the marathon Singer & Friedlander National Trial. The horse then finished second to the equally progressive Seven Towers in the Midlands National to book his Aintree ticket. A fleet-footed jumper, Lord Gyllene was outside the handicap proper, yet had shown the progression to warrant a place towards the head of the market and was ridden by Tony Dobbin, who had won over the big fences aboard Into The Red in November's Becher Chase.

As the thirty-six runners lined-up in heart-warming defiance beneath a drab, late afternoon sky, the race marked the fiftieth and final National commentary for 'The Voice', Sir Peter O'Sullevan – whose legendary callings of the race brought with them emotion, detail and the ability to inspire anyone who heard them. Among the first names described in that unmistakable tone in 1997 were Lord Gyllene and Suny Bay, who shot off at a cracking pace on the inside with Smith's Band out wider and the other grey runner, Dextra Dove, out widest of all. Suny Bay met the first with a tremendous leap while, towards the back, the outsider Full Of Oats was the only one to come down.

Indeed, there were no other casualties running down to Becher's, by which time Paul Holley's mount Northern Hide had joined the leaders. Streaming over the big fence, all the field were closely bunched and jumping well, Lord Gyllene setting the standard at the head of affairs. With Becher's tamed, it was the Foinavon fence that claimed the next victims, with Back Bar falling and Glemot rudely unshipping Simon McNeill with an angry buck. While Nahthen Lad and Dextra Dove moved forward to track the leaders on the inside and outside respectively, Nuaffe crashed out at the eleventh and Master Oats had to carefully hurdle the fallen horse.

Returning to the racecourse, a series of dramatic events unfolded in front of the stands. First the fancied Irish runner Wylde Hyde made a mess of the thirteenth, falling to his knees yet recovering admirably under top Irish jockey Charlie Swan and then, a fence later, Straight Talk, partnered by young Joe Tizzard,

With a loose horse to his left and the grey Suny Bay behind, Lord Gyllene leads the 1997 Grand National.

tragically suffered a fatal, leg-breaking fall. Creeping into contention, Celtic Abbey unseated Richard Johnson after a terrible blunder at The Chair and, when approaching the water, the leader Lord Gyllene was inches away from being wiped out by the riderless Glemot, Dobbin snatching up his mount skilfully to avoid a collision before continuing without mishap. Swinging out for another circuit and getting tremendous encouragement from the crowd, they led from Smith's Band, Suny Bay, Northern Hide, Nahthen Lad, Avro Anson, Dextra Dove, Valiant Warrior, Master Oats and Buckboard Bounce.

So far Lord Gyllene, Smith's Band and Suny Bay had filled the leading three positions the entire way, and the race continued in the same fashion racing down to Becher's again, with all three travelling well, particularly Lord Gyllene. But the National's darker side surfaced again at the twentieth, as Smith's Band got the fence completely wrong, hit it sideways and came down hard, breaking his neck in a terribly sad fatal fall, leaving Richard Dunwoody bruised and distraught as the rest of the field galloped on.

By the time Lord Gyllene cleared Becher's again, the field was breaking up noticeably as only Suny Bay and the improving Master Oats were able to stay with the leader. Go Ballistic had never got into the race, and the favourite was some twenty lengths behind when a bad mistake at the second Valentines sent him down on his knees, and he was soon pulled-up by Fitzgerald.

But Lord Gyllene was not stopping in front and, jumping like a cat, skipped back onto the racecourse as Master Oats, having moved into second, began to run out of steam, the big grey Suny Bay plugging past him in pursuit of the leader. However only a fall could now deny Lord Gyllene and, when he jumped the final two fences as cleanly as the previous twenty-eight, Dobbin had the simplest of tasks in guiding home the horse to a most impressive win by twenty-five lengths. Suny Bay took second place, and would go on to prove himself a horse of high class. Camelot Knight and the Gordon Richards-trained Buckboard Bounce stayed on to take the minor places, the latter the first placed horse in the National for leading owner Sir Robert Ogden. A weary Master Oats came next, having run with courage and class. Although returning to a high level of form, he was ultimately outdone by weight and some most progressive rivals in the first two home.

Lord Gyllene had led from start to finish, readily disposing of his opposition with a ruthless display of jumping and fast front-running, clearly appreciating the good ground. The winner was owned by Mr Stan Clarke, chairman of both Uttoxeter and Newcastle racecourses and a staunch supporter of National Hunt racing. Mr Clarke had purchased Lord Gyllene having seen footage of the horse running in New Zealand, anticipating he could one day prove to be a National horse, for which Brookshaw (who had only taken out a licence two years previously) developed him perfectly.

As another Grand National drifted into the horizon, there was an enormous sense of achievement. Everyone associated with the race could be proud that the 1997 renewal was safely on record as complete. Under the most extreme circumstances, the spirit of the National had come shining through, setting an example to all, and further enhancing the lofty status of one of sport's great events.

1997 GRAND NATIONAL RESULT

FATE	HORSE	AGE/WEIGHT	JOCKEY	ODDS
1st	LORD GYLLENE	9.10.0	A. DOBBIN	14/1
2nd	SUNY BAY	8.10.3	J. OSBORNE	8/1
3rd	CAMELOT KNIGHT	11.10.0	C. LLEWELLYN	100/1
4th	BUCKBOARD BOUNCE	11.10.1	P. CARBERRY	40/1
5th	Master Oats	11.11.10	N. Williamson	25/1
6th	Avro Anson	9.10.2	P. Niven	12/1
7th	Killeshin	11.10.0	S. Curran	33/1
8th	Dakyns Boy	12.10.0	T.J. Murphy	100/1
9th	Nahthen Lad	8.10.9	J.F. Titley	14/1
10th	Valiant Warrior	9.10.3	R. Garritty	50/1
11th	Antonin	9.10.0	C. O'Dwyer	14/1
12th	Northern Hide	11.10.1	P. Holley	66/1
13th	Turning Trix	10.10.0	J.R. Kavanagh	25/1
14th	Pink Gin	10.10.0	Mr C. Bonner	100/1
15th	New Co	9.10.0	D.J. Casey	40/1
16th	General Wolfe	8.10.0	L. Wyer	16/1
17th	Evangelica	7.10.0	R. Supple	33/1
Fell	Smith's Band	9.10.2	R. Dunwoody	12/1
Fell	Straight Talk	10.10.3	Mr J. Tizzard	50/1
Fell	Nuaffe	12.10.0	T. Mitchell	100/1
Fell	Back Bar	9.10.0	T.P. Treacy	100/1
Fell	Full Of Oats	11.10.0	J. Culloty	33/1
Fell	Don't Light Up	11.10.0	Mr R. Thornton	100/1
Pulled-Up	Lo Stregone	11.10.4	G. Bradley	14/1
Pulled-Up	Feathered Gale	10.10.3	F. Woods	16/1
Pulled-Up	Bishops Hall	11.10.1	M. Richards	50/1
Pulled-Up	Dextra Dove	10.10.0	C. Maude	33/1
Pulled-Up	Go Ballistic	8.10.3	M.A. Fitzgerald	7/1
Pulled-Up	River Mandate	10.10.1	A. Thornton	50/1
Pulled-Up	Scribbler	11.10.2	D. Fortt	100/1
Pulled-Up	Mugoni Beach	12.10.0	G. Tormey	100/1
Unseated Rider	Wylde Hide	10.10.0	C. Swan	11/1
Unseated Rider	Glemot	9.10.0	S. McNeill	50/1
Unseated Rider	Celtic Abbey	9.10.0	R. Johnson	66/1
Unseated Rider	Spuffington	9.10.2	P. Hide	100/1
Refused	Grange Brake	11.10.4	D. Walsh	100/1

7 April 1997
Going – Good
Sponsor – Martell
Winner – £178,146
Time – 9mins 5.9secs
36 Ran
Favourite – Go Ballistic

Top Weight – Master Oats
Winner trained by Steve Brookshaw at Shrewsbury, Shropshire
Winner owned by Sir Stanley Clarke
Lord Gyllene, bay gelding by Ring The Bell – Dentelle.

1998

EARTH SUMMIT

After the events of 1997, security at Aintree was extremely tight for the 1998 Grand National meeting, with no cars allowed on the premises and every individual subjected to a thorough check before entering the course. Although it took longer than usual to get in, the racing public were fully co-operative, with the extra lengths taken in increasing security being a small price to pay for safety and peace of mind. One thing that could not be controlled, however, was the weather. When torrential rain hit Aintree during the days before the race, another heavy-ground National lay in store.

After two weaker Nationals in terms of overall quality in 1996 and 1997, 1998 was probably the weakest overall in recent times. Only seven runners were in the handicap proper, with thirteen of the thirty-seven runners listed at 100/1 or higher. It is hard to criticise any Grand National field, considering the almighty test the race provides for horse and rider, but, although Suny Bay carrying 12 stone kept the weights down considerably, many in the race would not have got anywhere near the final forty in 2004 or 2005, for example.

Undoubtedly the class horse of the race, the grey Suny Bay returned to Aintree an even better prospect than when chasing home Lord Gyllene, having enjoyed a fine season. After a dominating display winning the Edward Hamner Memorial Chase at Haydock, Suny Bay headed to Newbury where he became one of the most convincing winners of the Hennessy Cognac Gold Cup for many a year and set alight talk of a possible Cheltenham Gold Cup bid. Unfortunately for Suny Bay, he suffered a slight setback that, by trainer Charlie Brooks' own admission, left the horse a little short of peak fitness at Cheltenham. Still, Suny Bay ran with credit to come fifth and headed to Aintree in prime condition, partnered on this occasion by the veteran Graham Bradley, starting at 11/1.

Although Lord Gyllene was sadly absent this time through injury, one former National winner in the field was Rough Quest, a horse that had missed the bulk of the previous season when injuring himself in the King George. Rough Quest was one of three horses to carry in excess of 11 stone, the other being the quirkiest of

eight-year-olds, Challenger Du Luc, from the Martin Pipe stable. Unquestionably talented, Challenger Du Luc had won the Cathcart Chase at the Cheltenham Festival as a six-year-old and the 1996 Murphys Gold Cup (formerly the Mackeson) at Cheltenham, but had since developed a reputation for being something of a devil. This was most apparent in the season's King George when, cruising on the bridle after the last fence, he found nothing, being seemingly unwilling to battle and gifting the race to See More Business. Despite his reputation, many believed the big Aintree fences could bring Challenger Du Luc to life as they did Last Suspect in 1985 and, with the brilliant Tony McCoy aboard, the horse started at 12/1.

The mare Dun Belle was the pick of a weak Irish challenge, having finished second to the excellent Doran's Pride in the Irish Hennessy, and the French horse Ciel De Brion was seen as a lively outsider having finished fourth in the Hennessy at Newbury for Francois Doumen and jockey son Thierry. The conditions were deemed most suitable for the progressive stayer Him Of Praise, a lazy but sure-footed bay from the Oliver Sherwood yard that had won four times earlier in the season, including the Mildmay-Cazalet Memorial Chase at Sandown Park. But it was a horse that had already won two 'Nationals' that started favourite. With stamina his absolute forte, the heavy ground thrust Earth Summit to the head of the market for trainer Nigel Twiston-Davies. Owned by The Summit Partnership (that included Aintree press officer Nigel Payne and former footballer Ricky George), Earth Summit had won the Scottish National at Ayr as a six-year-old and a highly promising career looked likely. However, two years later at Haydock, Earth Summit suffered a serious tendon injury, which was feared to be career-ending. But, under the care of his trainer and assistant

Carl Llewellyn won his second Grand National in 1998.

Earth Summit goes clear of the gallant Suny Bay at the final fence.

Peter Scudamore, the former Champion Jockey, Earth Summit slowly but surely regained fitness and returned to the racecourse. Two runs in the early part of the season proved disappointing, but the horse stayed on in testing conditions to win the season's Welsh Grand National at Chepstow. Always regarded as a super jumper, the heavy ground was directly in Earth Summit's favour and, as a further twist, riding him would be Carl Llewellyn, replacing the unfortunate broken-leg victim Tom Jenks. Llewellyn, of course, had replaced an injured Andy Adams before partnering Party Politics to success in 1992.

The sun arrived on National day but it was clear that conditions were treacherous out on the course, with the turf looking even heavier than in Miinnehoma's year. With no delay the field were sent on their way. Making a surprisingly brisk charge to the first fence, Him Of Praise was among the first to rise in the centre of the track together with the Irish mare Dun Belle, while Scotton Banks, Go Universal and Greenhill Tare Away headed those going down the inner. Dun Belle clipped the first fence but got away with it, but not so fortunate was Challenger Du Luc, who crashed awkwardly, while Pashto, Banjo, What A Hand and the blinkered grey Diwali Dancer all came to grief.

The pace travelling down to Becher's was fairly strong given the conditions and there were plenty of mistakes and fallers. The reluctant Fabricator came down at the third and the white-faced chestnut Do Rightly fell hard at the fourth having clouted the fence. With Griffins Bar another casualty at the fifth, the field was already considerably reduced before Becher's. Him Of Praise led at the fence with Greenhill Tare Away, Decyborg, Dun Belle and Ciel De Brion, as both Court Melody and Choisty tumbled out of the race towards the inside. A mistake by Dun Belle unseated Tommy Treacy at Valentines and, with Nahthen Lad, General Crack and the tailed-off Damas all out of the contest as they crossed the Melling Road for the first time, the conditions and fences had already taken a heavy toll.

Coming back onto the racecourse the two leaders – Greenhill Tare Away and the attractive chestnut Decyborg – had opened up a clear lead, but now slowed the pace down somewhat as The Chair lay in wait. Both jockeys in the leading duo – Simon McNeill and Paul Carberry – were enjoying terrific rides but, approaching the fourteenth, they received a scare that almost ruined their respective races. From out of nowhere, a loose horse charged across the face of the leaders and looked likely to cause a pile up, only to have a change of heart at the last moment and jump the fence with the field. Even so, both leaders were interfered with somewhat, allowing Ciel De Brion to come through and join them for the first time.

Having received a huge roar from the crowd jumping the water, many tired runners had already cried enough before the start of the second circuit, while many of those that continued began making weary mistakes. Decyborg had already faded as Ciel De Brion and Greenhill Tare Away led on from the improving Earth Summit on the outside, with Rough Quest, Suny Bay and Brave Highlander quietly hunting these up further back. Ciel De Brion made a mistake at the eighteenth and Earth Summit an uncharacteristic one a fence later, but both survived heading for Becher's again, with only thirteen left in the race.

With Becher's negotiated safely, it was the Canal Turn that ended Brave Highlander's promising run, as the horse wearing the Aldaniti colours put in a bad jump that unseated Philip Hide, while Rough Quest too began to tire soon after. Even though the former National winner preferred softer going, he was struggling in conditions too severe for him. With very few left, Ciel De Brion plunged out of contention five out. When Greenhill Tare Away's brave run ended a fence later, when he nearly refused and subsequently unseated McNeill, Earth Summit and Suny Bay were left well clear with the race to themselves.

Bradley wore a broad smile as the two matched strides crossing the Melling Road for the final time. The big grey did seem to be travelling smoothly but, taking the second last, it was clear that the battle was an uneven one. A fine horse in his own right, Earth Summit was in receipt of 23lbs from Suny Bay, and the blinkered bay began to edge ahead. Jumping the last, the final stages appeared to go in ultra-slow motion as Earth Summit dug deep into his stamina reserves, holding his slim lead rounding the elbow. Suny Bay, who had been as white as the beard of Father Christmas before the race, was now chocolate coloured and, bravely as he tried, he simply could not force his way past Earth Summit. Grinding home in the gruelling conditions, Earth Summit crossed the line an eleven-length

Grand National winner Earth Summit parades at Chepstow racecourse, where he had previously won a Welsh National.

1998 GRAND NATIONAL RESULT

FATE	HORSE	AGE/WEIGHT	JOCKEY	ODDS
1st	EARTH SUMMIT	10.10.5	C. LLEWELLYN	7/1
2nd	SUNY BAY	9.12.0	G. BRADLEY	11/1
3rd	SAMLEE	9.10.1	R. DUNWOODY	8/1
4th	ST MELLION FAIRWAY	9.10.1	A. THORNTON	20/1
5th	Gimme Five	11.10.0	K. Whelan	25/1
6th	Killeshin	12.10.0	S. Curran (remounted)	25/1
Fell	Challenger Du Luc	8.11.3	A.P. McCoy	12/1
Fell	Banjo	8.10.7	R. Johnson	14/1
Fell	Nahthen Lad	9.10.3	R. Farrant	13/1
Fell	Ciel De Brion	8.10.0	T. Doumen	16/1
Fell	Court Melody	10.10.0	T.J. Murphy	25/1
Fell	Celtic Abbey	10.10.0	N. Williamson	33/1
Fell	What A Hand	10.10.0	C. Maude	66/1
Fell	Diwali Dancer	8.10.0	R. Thornton	100/1
Fell	Do Rightly	9.10.0	P. Holley	100/1
Fell	Fabricator	12.10.0	J. Supple	150/1
Fell	Pashto	11.10.0	J.R. Kavanagh	100/1
Fell	Choisty	8.10.0	R. McGrath	40/1
Fell	Griffins Bar	10.10.0	G. Tormey	200/1
Pulled-Up	Rough Quest	12.11.4	M.A. Fitzgerald	11/1
Pulled-Up	General Crack	9.10.1	Mr J. Tizzard	40/1
Pulled-Up	Go Universal	10.10.0	Mr S. Durack	66/1
Pulled-Up	Into The Red	14.10.0	D. Gallagher	50/1
Pulled-Up	Yeoman Warrior	11.10.1	Richard Guest	100/1
Pulled-Up	Pond House	9.10.0	T. Dascombe	66/1
Pulled-Up	Hillwalk	12.10.0	Mr R. Wakley	150/1
Pulled-Up	Joe White	12.10.0	Mr T. McCarthy	150/1
Pulled-Up	Radical Choice	9.10.0	B. Storey	66/1
Pulled-Up	Winter Belle	10.10.0	Mr C. Bonner	100/1
Pulled-Up	Maple Dancer	12.10.0	G. Shenkin	200/1
Pulled-Up	Decyborg	7.10.0	P. Carberry	200/1
Unseated Rider	Scotton Banks	9.10.7	L. Wyer	33/1
Unseated Rider	Dun Belle	9.10.0	T.P. Treacy	18/1
Unseated Rider	Greenhill Tare Away	10.10.0	S. McNeill	100/1
Unseated Rider	Brave Highlander	10.10.0	P. Hide	25/1
Refused	Him Of Praise	8.10.0	C. Swan	8/1
Refused	Damas	7.10.0	Jamie Evans	200/1

4 April 1998
Going – Heavy
Sponsor – Martell
Winner – £212,569
Time – 10mins 51.5secs
37 Ran
Favourite – Earth Summit

Top Weight – Suny Bay
Winner trained by Nigel Twiston-
Davies at Naunton, Gloucestershire
Winner owned by The Summit
Partnership
Earth Summit, bay gelding by Celtic
Cone – Win Green Hill.

winner, giving Llewellyn a second National win after the most exhausting of performances. Suny Bay was as gallant a runner-up as there had ever been in the National and had run an heroic race under almost impossible circumstances. He was most unlucky not to have been the first since Red Rum to carry 12 stone to victory. Although the time was the slowest since 1883, it was an indication to just how courageous the first two had been when the Scottish National runner-up Samlee came home an age later in third place for Richard Dunwoody, with St Mellion Fairway in fourth. The Irish horse Gimme Five came fifth, with Killeshin, whose jockey Sean Curran had been knocked off when Him Of Praise refused four out, was remounted to take sixth and last. Rough Quest, who had tired badly late on, was pulled-up wisely by Mick Fitzgerald having run an honourable race. Sadly three horses had been killed early in the race, but the ground was not to blame for the tragic losses of Pashto, Do Rightly and Griffins Bar, while many of the jockeys had sensibly pulled-up their horses on the second circuit.

Earth Summit had out-stayed them all and was a most brave hero in unbelievably testing conditions. For connections, the victory was an emotional one given the horse's injury problems in earlier life. Now he had become, to date, the only horse in history to win the Scottish, Welsh and English Grand Nationals. For what the victory meant, one only had to look at the television coverage that fixed upon assistant trainer Peter Scudamore in the closing stages of the race. Scudamore, one of the toughest, battle-hardened and most determined jockeys to have graced the sport, was reduced to uncontrollable tears as the horse known as 'Digger' slogged his way home for a memorable triumph.

1999

BOBBYJO

Twenty-four long years had passed since the last time an Irish victory was celebrated at Aintree in the Grand National. Ridden by Tommy Carberry, the great chestnut L'Escargot in 1975 had been the last to win the race for Ireland. Since then, a great number of horses had tried and failed to bring racing's greatest prize back to the Emerald Isle. Davy Lad, Tied Cottage, Greasepaint, Drumlargan, Son Of War and Life Of A Lord, to name a few, all arrived at Aintree with high hopes of glory but left disappointed, although Greasepaint went very close to winning on two occasions.

Trained, ironically, by Tommy Carberry in County Meath, a huge gamble developed shortly before the race on Bobbyjo, the previous year's Irish Grand National winner. A lovely bay horse with plenty of scope, Bobbyjo was a fine jumper but had failed to win any of his first five chases in the current season in Ireland – all on soft to heavy ground. Only when the ground improved was Bobbyjo able to get his head in front, winning a Hurdle race at Down Royal three weeks before the National with Tommy's son Paul on board. Gambled down from 20/1 to a starting price of 10/1, Bobbyjo proved extremely popular on the day with conditions ideal for the horse at Aintree.

Ever since the publication of the weights, Double Thriller, a big, strong bay, had stood out as a potential blot on the handicap. Owned, like the 1994 fancy Double Silk, by Mr Reg Wilkins, the horse was a former hunter-chaser put into training with Paul Nicholls at the beginning of the season. Displaying rich promise in winning his first two races with ease, the horse was then sent to Cheltenham for the Gold Cup, where he acquitted himself wonderfully, leading for much of the way before finishing fourth behind his brilliant stablemate See More Business. In the weeks leading up to the National, it seemed Double Thriller would start one of the shortest-priced favourites for years, with his price hovering around 4/1. But in one of the craziest day-of-race National markets for years the horse – ridden by Joe Tizzard – drifted out to 7/1, as a flood of money also arrived for the consistent mare Fiddling The Facts, trained by Nicky

Henderson. Fiddling The Facts rarely ran a bad race and had an abundance of stamina. One of the top staying novices of the season before, the mare had been placed in a host of big chases during the season, including the Hennessy, Welsh National and Greenalls Grand National trial at Haydock and, with recent Gold Cup winner Mick Fitzgerald on board, she started 6/1 favourite.

Among the many interesting side notes to the 1999 National included Jenny Pitman saddling her last National runner before retirement in Nahthen Lad and Richard Dunwoody riding in what would be his last National, fittingly aboard a horse named Call It A Day. Dunwoody, twice a winner of the National and placed in five others, had a particularly strong chance on Call It A Day, the horse having won the previous season's Whitbread Gold Cup and also finishing third in an Irish Grand National for trainer David Nicholson. In addition the overall field, though on the small side with thirty-two runners, possessed more quality in depth than the most recent Nationals, with the Scottish National winner Baronet, Welsh National winner Kendal Cavalier (both greys), 1997 Irish National winner Mudahim and 1996 Hennessy winner Coome Hill all in the field. Earth Summit had won the Becher Chase in November and he and the three placed horses from 1998 ran again, while General Wolfe ran in his second National, having returned to fine form since being pin-fired the year before, winning the season's Peter Marsh Chase at Haydock. Outsider Bells Life had winning experience over the big fences, winning the John Hughes Trophy at the Grand National meeting in 1998 and, with former Tripleprint Gold Cup winner Addington Boy and the ultra-consistent seven-year-old Eudipe also proving popular in the betting, a tremendous race was eagerly anticipated.

Beneath clear blue sky, starter Simon Morant had the field away swiftly, with Earth Summit hesitating slightly as the tape rose. Former Stayers' Hurdle winner Cyborgo, one of four in the race for Martin Pipe, was first to show in the centre, together with Blue Charm, Nahthen Lad and the bright chestnut General Wolfe on the inside, the entire leading group taking the fence in majestic style. Towards the outside in mid-division, the first shock arrived as long-time favourite Double Thriller – who had been slightly on edge in the preliminaries – over-jumped and came down in a typical first-fence fall; a collective sigh was let out from the many punters that had backed the horse ante-post.

The dark grey Baronet was next to go, hidden in the middle of the pack when spiralling to the ground at the fourth. Blue Charm and General Wolfe led on to Becher's, with Cyborgo and Brave Highlander showing prominently. The majority sailed the big fence without trouble, but Nahthen Lad was down on his belly, skidding for a number of strides before Andrew Thornton skilfully recovered him. Further back, young Tamarindo flipped over towards the inside and the tailed-off Mudahim, totally disinterested, unseated veteran Brendan Powell.

Running from out of the handicap, Blue Charm had settled into a smooth rhythm in front under Lorcan Wyer, taking the fences down the back in his stride together with General Wolfe, who was travelling down the inside. Outsider Feels

Like Gold had also come through to join the leaders and, together with Nahthen Lad, this group showed the way back onto the racecourse.

A blunder at the fourteenth caused Sean Curran's saddle to slip on former Aintree Foxhunters' winner Cavalero, the outsider forced out of the contest before The Chair, but the bulk of the field had survived one circuit. With surprisingly few fallers, Blue Charm, bouncing off the good ground, led out for the second circuit with his companions on the first circuit – General Wolfe, Feels Like Gold and Nahthen Lad – still very much in contention. Brave Highlander and Samlee were right there too, with Fiddling The Facts, Eudipe and the Irish horse Bobbyjo creeping into the picture steadily, the latter sticking to the inside rail under the distinctive riding style of Paul Carberry. Racing towards the seventeenth, Earth Summit was still well towards the rear of the field together with one of the rank outsiders, Merry People.

As in so many Nationals before, Becher's Brook second time was to have a huge impact on the race. The leading six of Blue Charm, Brave Highlander, General Wolfe, Nahthen Lad, Bobbyjo and Feels Like Gold got over unscathed. In behind, the drama unfolded. Right on the heels of the leaders and running another big race, Fiddling The Facts was caught out by the drop at Becher's, hitting the deck in agonising style. Towards the outside, the unconsidered but rapidly improving Frazer Island took plenty of spruce with him as he dived out in an ugly fall while, even worse, Eudipe came down extremely heavily, tragically breaking his back as he tracked the leading group towards the inside.

Bobbyjo (red) jumps the last open ditch flanked by Feels Like Gold (green) and Nahthen Lad (16).

The veteran Camelot Knight was brought down and Robert Widger was unlucky to be unseated from Choisty, while the fallen horses badly hampered both Earth Summit and Kendal Cavalier, the latter being knocked sideways as Frazer Island happily rose to his feet.

A band of eight challengers had broken away from the remainder, having jumped away from the Canal Turn and Valentines. Crossing the Melling Road for the final time, Blue Charm still led. But it was Brave Highlander in the Aldaniti colours and the Irish raider Bobbyjo, on either side of the leader, that were travelling best as they made their way back onto the racecourse, with Call It A Day bustling into contention. Merry People arrived from out of nowhere on the wide outside and Feels Like Gold, Nahthen Lad and Addington Boy were also in the contending group.

Philip Hide had enjoyed a dream ride on Josh Gifford's Brave Highlander and, approaching two out with the hotly fancied Call It A Day, the jockey sent the tall bay up to dispute the lead with Blue Charm – with the former touching down the narrowest of leaders. In the rush to the second last, Bobbyjo had been caught slightly flat-footed as his fellow Irish challenger Merry People threw down his challenge on the outside, but Merry People was to fall, almost taking Bobbyjo with him, and again the outlook changed by the final fence.

A huge roar erupted as the racecourse commentator announced that Call It A Day had surged through to take the lead at the final fence under Dunwoody, as Brave Highlander and Blue Charm suddenly came under pressure. Having got his horse back on terms, it was Paul Carberry and Bobbyjo that now loomed up menacingly on the outside and, in a flash, they were over the final fence and away up the run-in. Reaching the elbow, Bobbyjo's powerful surge had seen off all but the rallying Blue Charm. But the Irish horse owned the superior finishing speed and, already a proven stayer, unlike Blue Charm, Bobbyjo galloped relentlessly to the line, Carberry punching the air in triumph as the horse won decisively by ten lengths. Blue Charm had taken to Aintree marvellously, settling into an early rhythm and jumping beautifully all the way round, and he fully deserved to win the battle with Call It A Day for second. Back in fourth came Addington Boy, with Feels Like Gold another to have jumped really well in fifth and Brave Highlander – fast developing into an Aintree specialist – sixth, having jumped and travelled like a winner for much of the way, only tiring in the closing stages. Merry People had come from a long way behind on the second circuit to pose a real threat two out, and he was eventually remounted to finish sixteenth of the eighteen that completed.

Bobbyjo had emphatically ended Ireland's long wait for a Grand National success, despite being 14lbs out of the handicap. The horse was a fine jumper blessed with a telling turn of foot, as evident when screaming clear of Blue Charm and Call It A Day from the last. Fearless and confident, Paul Carberry was perhaps the most naturally gifted young rider on the National Hunt scene and, in guiding Bobbyjo to a convincing victory, he confirmed the promise he had

Jockey Paul Carberry and Bobbyjo win the National in 1999, the first time since 1975 that an Irish horse won.

shown over the big fences aboard outsiders Three Brownies, Buckboard Bounce and Decyborg in previous Nationals. As Bobbyjo was led in by owner Mr Robert Burke, glorious scenes of Irish celebration greeted the horse in the winner's enclosure. Tommy and Paul Carberry had become the first father-and-son team to win since Reg and Bruce Hobbs with Battleship in 1938, and only the sixth successful duo of that relationship ever. In addition, Tommy became only the fourth trainer to win the race having also won as a jockey, the others being Algy Anthony, Fulke Walwyn and Fred Winter. With the post-race party just beginning for connections, it remained to be seen if the drought before the next Irish-trained winner of the Grand National would be as long as the one ended in spectacular fashion by Bobbyjo.

1999 GRAND NATIONAL RESULT

FATE	HORSE	AGE/WEIGHT	JOCKEY	ODDS
1st	BOBBYJO	9.10.0	P. CARBERRY	10/1
2nd	BLUE CHARM	9.10.0	L. WYER	25/1
3rd	CALL IT A DAY	9.10.2	R. DUNWOODY	7/1
4th	ADDINGTON BOY	11.10.7	A. MAGUIRE	10/1
5th	Feels Like Gold	11.10.0	B. Harding	50/1
6th	Brave Highlander	11.10.1	P. Hide	50/1
7th	Kendal Cavalier	9.10.0	B. Fenton	28/1
8th	Earth Summit	11.11.0	C. Llewellyn	16/1
9th	St Mellion Fairway	10.10.2	J. Frost	200/1
10th	Samlee	10.10.0	R. Farrant	50/1
11th	Nahthen Lad	10.10.2	A. Thornton	14/1
12th	General Wolfe	10.11.1	N. Williamson	18/1
13th	Suny Bay	10.11.13	G. Bradley	12/1
14th	Back Bar	11.10.0	D. Gallagher	200/1
15th	Strong Chairman	8.10.0	R. Thornton	50/1
16th	Merry People	11.10.0	G. Cotter (remounted)	200/1
17th	Avro Anson	11.10.0	A. Dobbin	40/1
18th	Coome Hill	10.10.11	S. Wynne	25/1
Fell	Eudipe	7.10.10	A.P. McCoy	10/1
Fell	Double Thriller	9.10.8	J. Tizzard	7/1
Fell	Tamarindo	6.10.4	T.J. Murphy	66/1
Fell	Fiddling The Facts	8.10.3	M.A. Fitzgerald	6/1
Fell	Baronet	9.10.2	R. Johnson	12/1
Fell	Frazer Island	10.10.2	Richard Guest	200/1
Pulled-Up	Cyborgo	9.10.11	C. O'Dwyer	50/1
Pulled-Up	Bells Life	10.10.0	G. Tormey	66/1
Pulled-Up	Commercial Artist	13.10.2	T. Jenks	200/1
Pulled-Up	Cavalero	10.10.0	S. Curran	50/1
Brought Down	Camelot Knight	13.10.0	C. Maude	200/1
Unseated Rider	Mudahim	13.10.0	B. Powell	100/1
Unseated Rider	Castle Coin	7.10.0	A.S. Smith	200/1
Unseated Rider	Choisty	9.10.0	R. Widger	200/1

10 April 1999
Going – Good
Sponsor – Martell
Winner – £242,600
Time – 9mins 14.1secs
32 Ran
Favourite – Fiddling The Facts
Top Weight – Suny Bay
Winner trained by Thomas Carberry at Ashbourne, County Meath, Ireland
Winner owned by Mr R. Burke
Bobbyjo, bay gelding by Bustineto – Markup.

2000

PAPILLON

When the weights were framed for the 2000 Grand National by senior jumps handicapper Phil Smith, it was revealed that a staggering total of sixty-six horses from 108 entries were in the handicap proper. This number was more than double that of every Grand National of the 1990s, and promised to make the 2000 race one of the most open for years. The 'Aintree factor' was used, giving a higher mark to horses with form over the big fences, while Smith also vowed to entice the higher-class, Gold Cup-standard horses to the race by giving them a fair chance at the weights. With prize money ever increasing as well, it all meant that the new millennium began with some of the most competitive-looking Nationals ever to be run. Indeed, the 2000 Grand National was the first since 1992 to have a maximum field of forty, with thirty-three in the handicap proper.

After ending Ireland's long wait for a Grand National winner the year before, Bobbyjo was well fancied to become the first since Red Rum to record consecutive victories. As in the year before, Bobbyjo had run into form over hurdles prior to the race and again found his favoured good ground waiting for him at Aintree. Paul Carberry had sufficiently recovered from a recent injury to take the ride, with the horse eventually starting 12/1 having been morning favourite with many bookmakers. The one worry concerning Bobbyjo on this occasion was the fact he had far more weight to carry, going from 14lbs out of the handicap in 1999 to shouldering 11st 6lbs in 2000.

Both Star Traveller and Dark Stranger came to Aintree on the back of good runs at the Cheltenham Festival. Star Traveller had been one of the most consistent handicap chasers of the season, with his third place behind the high-class Marlborough in the William Hill Handicap Chase thrusting him among the favourites for Aintree. Though there were some concerns whether the little bay would be too small for the course, the horse was clearly the prolific Richard Johnson's best ride yet in the National. Dark Stranger had never won beyond three miles and his stamina was unproven, but he had been mightily impressive when winning the Mildmay of Flete at Cheltenham, having been fitted with

blinkers for the first time. Trained by Martin Pipe and ridden by Tony McCoy (who had already won four Jockeys' Championships), it would be Dark Stranger that started 9/1 favourite for the race, following one of the fiercest betting frenzies for many a National.

Having headed the handicap since the publication of the weights, the Peter Beaumont-trained Young Kenny had long been considered an ideal Grand National horse, possessing real stamina. A big, gross bay with plenty of size to carry 12 stone, Young Kenny had risen to fame the season before with a series of brilliant wins in staying chases, destroying a host of good horses when winning the Greenalls Grand National Trial at Haydock, the Midlands National at Uttoxeter and the Scottish National at Ayr. After a slow start to the current season, the horse had rekindled his winning ways most recently in the Singer & Friedlander at Uttoxeter and, despite fears that the ground would be too quick, the horse was well backed with former winner Brendan Powell in the saddle.

Cases could be made for so many in the 2000 National, with the Becher Chase winner Feels Like Gold and former top-class hunter Earthmover attracting plenty of each-way support, while Ireland's Micko's Dream, a front-running chestnut owned by twenty-four Irish prison officers, appealed to many having won the Thyestes Chase. Though injury had ended the career of Lord Gyllene, owner Mr Stan Clarke had another good New Zealand-bred horse in the big bay Listen Timmy, who had been tubed (like the 1992 hero Party Politics), while other famous National-winning colours were represented by Brave Highlander (Aldaniti) and Stormy Passage (West Tip). But it was another Irish horse that

Trainer Martin Pipe and jockey Tony McCoy. The colours are of race favourite Dark Stranger.

was the subject of an almighty gamble, one unprecedented in National history. Trained by Ted Walsh and ridden by his son Ruby, the well-built bay Papillon had been available at 33/1 overnight, when a storm of raceday money – sparked predominantly by newspaper, telephone and television tipsters – sent his odds tumbling dramatically. Consistently and ruthlessly backed in the build up to the race, Papillon eventually started 10/1, and most bookmakers stood to lose heavily if the horse came in. Papillon was something of a character, but was of good size and jumped very well. The horse's form was patchy but, like Bobbyjo the year before, most of his runs had been on soft ground in Ireland, and a recent third over hurdles on much better ground had left Walsh quietly confident of a big run. Papillon had also been second to Bobbyjo in the 1998 Irish National, giving him weight, and, in Ruby Walsh, he had one of the finest up-and-coming jockeys on board.

Despite an overcast afternoon creating a dull backdrop, the bubbly crowd waited with tremendous excitement for the race to unfold. As the bottom weight Celtic Giant turned to join the other thirty-nine, the maximum field was unleashed in a quick start to enthusiastic cheering. Thundering over the lush green turf, the leaders were going at a terrific pace heading for the first, with the Norwegian representative Trinitro charging furiously at the obstacle. Jockey Robert Bellamy was fighting to keep the horse in check as they just held the lead in the centre, with Bobbyjo, Esprit de Cotte, Torduff Express, Papillon, Art Prince and Micko's Dream among the first to meet the fence. Trinitro jumped right through the first, almost hurdling it, and had no chance of staying on his feet, while Micko's Dream was the first of the fancied runners to crash out on the inside. Listen Timmy displayed impressive strength to withstand a collision with the faller and then leapt over him. With Art Prince also coming down, speed had undone three of the leaders while, further back, Royal Predica and the grey Senor El Betrutti also crashed out.

There were plenty of casualties on the run down to Becher's as Sparky Gayle went at the second, while favourite backers soon knew their fate as Dark Stranger left his back legs in the third, unseating McCoy. Earthmover and Choisty were down at the fourth, as Star Traveller came through to lead the field over Becher's, with Esprit De Cotte, Bobbyjo and Torduff Express all in the front rank. Towards the rear the chestnut Red Marauder – whose assistant trainer and jockey Richard Guest had been particularly sweet on – knuckled over having jumped the previous fences poorly.

Even at an early stage in the race it was proving a fantastically thrilling contest. A horrendous blunder by Bobbyjo at the Foinavon fence sent Carberry shooting up the horse's neck and, with little Star Traveller jumping for fun out in front, they raced over the Canal Turn and down the back. In mid-division towards the outside, Young Kenny hit the tenth hard and crashed out of the race in a rare fall for the big horse, while the outsider Druid's Brook clubbed the twelfth, sending Rupert Wakley high into the air in an extravagant unseating.

Papillon (green) jumps the final fence locked together with Mely Moss.

One of four runners for Paul Nicholls, Torduff Express had been travelling with the leaders when falling by the wayside at the thirteenth. Surrounded by loose horses, the leader Star Traveller made a bad mistake a fence later, and one of the riderless ones preceded the same horse dangerously into The Chair before fortunately running out at the last moment.

With an action-packed first circuit behind them, there were still a large number of horses in contention, as the game Star Traveller led onwards, closely attended by Nicky Henderson's runner Esprit De Cotte, The Last Fling, Papillon, Brave Highlander, Addington Boy and the improving Lucky Town for J.P. McManus on the outside. In the colours of Bula, the great Champion Hurdler of the 1970s, young Village King came down on the heels of the leaders at the twentieth as another Irish horse, the Eider Chase winner and Scottish National runner-up of the previous season Hollybank Buck, moved strongly into the leading positions.

The retreating Esprit De Cotte and Stormy Passage tumbled at Becher's second time (badly interfering with Bobbyjo), as Lucky Town, Papillon and Star Traveller led on. Having run so well, Star Traveller got too close to Valentines and hit it very hard, pulling up two fences later. Sadly he had jarred an old injury and never ran again. Papillon's imposing physical strength had pulled him into a share of the lead with Lucky Town and, coming back across the Melling Road for the final time, the two led former Aintree Foxhunters' second Mely Moss – who had cruised into contention from the second Becher's and posed as a real danger to all concerned coming back onto the racecourse. With Brave Highlander,

Addington Boy, Hollybank Buck and the improving Niki Dee – a stablemate of Young Kenny – all still holding chances, a splendid finish lay in store.

The Irish pair Lucky Town and Hollybank Buck had shown well on the second circuit but began to fade by the second last, where Aintree veteran Brave Highlander lost ground with a mistake. With Papillon somewhat impeded by the riderless Choisty approaching the last, Norman Williamson coolly ghosted through on Mely Moss, still to ask the chestnut a question. Jumping the last, Mely Moss and Papillon quickly surged ahead of Niki Dee and Addington Boy and, finding plenty in reserve, it was Papillon that powered past his rival to take a commanding lead heading for the elbow. Mely Moss, trained by Charlie Egerton, had not run for 346 days but, as the leader idled a little in front, the horse came with a renewed challenge to set up a grandstand finish. Against the inside rails, Mely Moss was cutting into Papillon's lead with every stride and looked to be getting up but, sensing his rival at his quarters, Papillon displayed tremendous desire and fighting spirit and, driven hard by Walsh, denied Mely Moss by a length-and-a-quarter. Papillon, like many other 'thinking' individuals before him, had risen to the unique challenge of Aintree. While Mely Moss ran a brave race in defeat, the winner had him held decisively at the line. In third came Niki Dee, while Brave Highlander battled all the way to the line, delighting his trainer Josh Gifford by taking fourth ahead of Addington Boy. Having seen his chance evaporate at the second Becher's, Bobbyjo was guided home safely by Carberry to finish eleventh.

After twenty-four years without a win, Ireland now had two in a row, remarkably with another father-and-son combination. The scenes as Papillon returned to the winners' enclosure even eclipsed those following Bobbyjo's success, with singing and cheering echoing all around Aintree, aided of course by the many that had helped to spark the enormous gamble on the winner. As a jockey, the personable and entertaining Ted Walsh had ridden Castleruddery in the 1975 National, and now his son had won the race on his first ride, showing the skills that would make him one of the very best in the sport for years to come. Papillon's owner, American Mrs Betty Moran, had harboured doubts over running her horse in such a race but, after seeing the course for herself, decided to let Papillon take his chance. With five horses killed on the first two days of the National meeting, it was to everyone's relief that no tragedies occurred in the big race itself and, with Aintree alive once more with jubilant celebrations, Papillon was hailed as the first Grand National hero of the new millennium.

2000 GRAND NATIONAL RESULT

FATE	HORSE	AGE/WEIGHT	JOCKEY	ODDS
1st	PAPILLON	9.10.12	R. WALSH	10/1
2nd	MELY MOSS	9.10.1	N. WILLIAMSON	25/1
3rd	NIKI DEE	10.10.13	R. SUPPLE	25/1
4th	BRAVE HIGHLANDER	12.10.0	P. HIDE	50/1
5th	Addington Boy	12.11.2	A. Maguire	33/1
6th	Call It A Day	10.10.11	B.J. Geraghty	50/1
7th	The Last Fling	10.11.5	S. Durack	14/1
8th	Lucky Town	9.10.5	D.J. Casey	20/1
9th	Djeddah	9.11.8	T. Doumen	16/1
10th	Hollybank Buck	10.10.4	P. Niven	33/1
11th	Bobbyjo	10.11.6	P. Carberry	12/1
12th	Kendal Cavalier	10.10.6	B. Fenton	33/1
13th	Suny Bay	11.11.12	C. Maude	66/1
14th	Feels Like Gold	12.10.7	B. Harding	28/1
15th	Camelot Knight	14.10.0	O. McPhail	150/1
16th	Kingdom Of Shades	10.10.4	T. Jenks	50/1
17th	Celtic Giant	10.10.0	B. Gibson	100/1
Fell	Young Kenny	9.12.0	B. Powell	14/1
Fell	Stormy Passage	10.11.3	A. Thornton	50/1
Fell	Red Marauder	10.11.2	Richard Guest	18/1
Fell	Buck Rogers	11.11.0	K. Whelan	50/1
Fell	Senor El Betrutti	11.10.12	C. Llewellyn	100/1
Fell	Village King	7.10.11	J. Culloty	50/1
Fell	Micko's Dream	8.10.10	J.F. Titley	14/1
Fell	Esprit De Cotte	8.10.8	M.A. Fitzgerald	50/1
Fell	Earthmover	9.10.5	J. Tizzard	14/1
Fell	Royal Predica	6.10.4	G. Tormey	50/1
Fell	Trinitro	9.10.3	R. Bellamy	100/1
Fell	Torduff Express	9.10.3	R. Thornton	50/1
Fell	The Gopher	11.10.3	W. Marston	66/1
Fell	Choisty	10.10.0	R. Widger	50/1
Fell	Flaked Oats	11.10.0	T.J. Murphy	50/1
Fell	Art Prince	10.10.0	D. Gallagher	100/1
Pulled-Up	Listen Timmy	11.11.5	A. Dobbin	50/1
Pulled-Up	Star Traveller	9.10.11	R. Johnson	10/1
Unseated Rider	Escartefigue	8.11.9	J.A. McCarthy	50/1
Unseated Rider	Sparky Gayle	10.10.8	B. Storey	33/1
Unseated Rider	Dark Stranger	9.10.1	A.P. McCoy	9/1
Unseated Rider	Merry People	12.10.0	G. Cotter	40/1
Unseated Rider	Druid's Brook	11.10.0	R. Wakley	66/1

8 April 2000
Going – Good
Sponsor – Martell
Winner – £290,000
Time – 9mins 9.7secs
40 Ran
Favourite – Dark Stranger

Top Weight – Young Kenny
Winner trained by Ted Walsh at Kill,
   County Kildare, Ireland
Winner owned by Mrs J. Maxwell
   Moran
Papillon, bay gelding by Lafontaine
   – Glens Princess.

2001

RED MARAUDER

More than ever before the Aintree Grand National meeting became the focus of the National Hunt season. The disturbing foot-and-mouth crisis that had blitzed the country and reaped havoc on the nation's farming communities had also greatly disrupted the racing calendar. In the march, the cherished Cheltenham Festival had been lost and all eyes turned to Aintree to salvage what had been a bitterly disappointing yet totally unavoidable conclusion to the season.

The 1990s had produced two of the heaviest-ground Grand Nationals ever witnessed when Miinnehoma won from Just So in 1994 and when Earth Summit out-slogged Suny Bay in 1998. But the Grand National of 2001, in all probability, produced the most treacherous ground the race has ever seen. Three days of torrential rain rendered conditions incredibly testing and, by National day, with driving rain present, the course was near unraceable. The Melling Road was covered with puddles of water and the turf so penetrable that horses returned literally painted in mud.

Irish horses had been advised to stay away from England because of foot-and-mouth, and it appeared they would be missing from Aintree. But a last-minute change of heart saw restrictions lifted, giving Papillon a chance to defend the crown he had won so majestically the year before. Papillon and the horse he defeated in 2000, Mely Moss, had dominated the Grand National market for twelve months, and the defending champion again looked a picture in the paddock, trained to the minute by Ted Walsh, while Mely Moss was having his first run of the season. Although both maintained lofty positions in the betting, the extreme conditions encouraged punters to look for horses with both an abundance of stamina and a real liking for heavy going.

The result was three co-favourites in Edmond, Moral Support and Inis Cara. Edmond was something of a difficult character, talented but frustrating, but on his day and in his ideal conditions he was very good. Two years previously he had won the Welsh National by ten lengths on heavy ground and was immediately considered as a Grand National contender. However the horse's owner, Lady

Knutsford, had not been keen for Edmond to run in the 2000 race. Although the horse's form had been patchy of late, the Henry Daly-trained Edmond was expected to relish the conditions, and had been fitted with blinkers in an attempt to rekindle his best form. The Charlie Mann-trained Moral Support was also a confirmed mudlark and the horse (a half-brother to the excellent Irish chaser Doran's Pride) had started the season with four wins before finishing a game second in the Welsh National. The major surprise of the three was the relatively unknown Inis Cara, a horse that had been trained in Ireland until just days before the National, when a dispute between trainer and owners led to the horse being transferred to the Herefordshire yard of Venetia Williams. In truth, Inis Cara's form in Ireland was poor, despite a decent run behind the 2000 Gold Cup winner Looks Like Trouble earlier in the season, and it seemed a most speculative plunge that amazingly saw the horse's odds fall from 66/1 to 10/1 in the space of forty-eight hours.

Of the others, the top weight and class horse was Beau, runaway victor of the Whitbread Gold Cup at the end of the previous season. Trained by Nigel Twiston-Davies, who had won his battle to convince the horse's owner, Mrs Sylvia Tainton, to let him run, Beau presented Carl Llewellyn with a serious chance of winning a third National. Having won in the mud before, albeit never beyond two-and-a-half miles, Blowing Wind was Tony McCoy's pick of an incredible ten Martin Pipe runners, while Smarty had been a top staying novice chaser before injury intervened. The useful chestnut Noble Lord had been second in the Scottish National and was a first Grand National runner for likeable trainer Richard Phillips. Having generally jumped poorly before falling at Becher's in 2000, Red Marauder had been running consistently well during the season, playing his part in some of the good handicaps at Cheltenham and finishing fifth in the Hennessy. When conditions began to turn in his favour a week before the race, permit holder Norman Mason and assistant and jockey Richard Guest decided to let the horse take his chance again at Aintree.

Wasting no time at all, Simon Morant set the field of forty on their way. The field included Merry People, the first horse to get into the race under the new reserve system, where horses withdrawn after the final declaration stage can be replaced – up until Friday morning – by substitutes ranked in the order they appear in the weights. The most notable aspect of the start was just how slowly the runners set off towards the first, knowing full well that this was a race where every ounce of energy would need to be reserved. The eager Edmond led at the first fence from Beau towards the outside – where the ground was considerably better – and, even though the pace was restrained, young Spanish Main unseated Jamie Goldstein towards the rear, while Art Prince fell at the first for the second consecutive year.

The extremely heavy ground made jumping difficult for many horses. Former Royal & Sun Alliance Chase winner Hanakham fell heavily at the second, where Tresor De Mai knuckled over and the veteran Addington Boy was badly baulked,

Beau, pictured in action at Chepstow, was the unlucky horse of the 2001 National.

unseating J.P. McNamara. Three more went at the big ditch, including the blinkered Paddy's Return, who broke Adrian Maguire's 100 per cent completion record in the race, while Hollybank Buck got too close to the ditch and was swept off his feet on the landing side. The gamble on Inis Cara was thwarted when the horse took a most spectacular dive at the fourth and, with Earthmover and The Last Fling among the other casualties, the field had been heavily depleted by Becher's.

With conditions already taking a heavy toll, Beau, Esprit De Cotte, Edmond and Merry People were the leading quartet over Becher's, where the little bay Northern Starlight, winner of the 2000 John Hughes Trophy, made a mistake and unseated Tom Scudamore. Two more of Pipe's runners fell, Exit Swinger and Strong Tel, the latter at the rear of the field when banking the fence and flopping down in a soft exit. A bad blunder saw the end of Merry People a fence later as the field raced to the Canal Turn.

The riderless Paddy's Return had continued on his way at a strong gallop on the wide outside as he joined the bulk of the field approaching the Canal Turn. Suddenly the horse veered violently along the face of the fence, just avoiding the leading group and coming within a whisker of colliding with Red Marauder, but causing carnage for the rest of the field. With no room to jump, horses refused, were brought down, fell or unseated their rider in a pile-up reminiscent of the Easter Hero affair in 1928. Among the ten put out were the fancied Moral Support and Mely Moss as the race provided another one of the amazing, history-defining moments that have made the Grand National a contest like no other.

With chaos in the background, Beau on the inside and Edmond on the outside led on from Blowing Wind. Esprit De Cotte, with Tom Doyle on board as a last-minute replacement for the injured Mick Fitzgerald, went to refuse the eleventh and unseated the jockey, while Red Marauder made a hash of the same fence and received a reminder from Guest, as a decimated field of thirteen were left to hack back over the Melling Road with well over a circuit still to run and plenty more incident lying in store.

Noble Lord was next to go when he crashed at the thirteenth, while Edmond seemed to show a severe dislike for The Chair, part refusing at the monster fence, and spilling over the obstacle in a shocking fall when right in contention. Brave Highlander displayed some nifty footwork to avoid the fallen horse, but both Moondigua and Supreme Charm unseated their riders with Listen Timmy badly hampered and soon pulled up by Tony Dobbin. It had been one of the most action-packed, drama-filled first circuits ever witnessed, and it was almost surreal to see just seven horses preparing to go round again. As well as the stamina-sapping ground, the survivors also had a vast army of loose horses to worry about, but with each of Beau, Smarty, Blowing Wind, Red Marauder, Papillon, Unsinkable Boxer and Brave Highlander seemingly holding an equal chance, the quest continued.

Of the survivors, Beau was travelling best and appeared full of running, but a mistake at the seventeenth was to cost him dear as Llewellyn was left with reins on only one side and barely in control as the horse switched from the better ground on the outside and came right over to the inner. Then the riderless Edmond played his part in proceedings as, cutting from left to right, he shot right across the face of the nineteenth, nearly smacking into Smarty and giving Blowing Wind nowhere to go. In behind, Papillon and Brave Highlander were stopped in their tracks and refused, while the leg-weary Unsinkable Boxer was soon pulled-up. It was cruel luck on Beau when the horse blundered and unseated the helpless Llewellyn at the twentieth, for the horse was still going strongly and, although the jockey desperately tried to catch he to remount, his pursuit was in vain.

Incredibly, the Grand National was now a match between two horses as, preceded by the main villain of the piece, the riderless Paddy's Return, Smarty and Red Marauder approached Becher's second time. Both Timmy Murphy and Guest had sensibly slowed the pace right down, yet they could not legislate for situations such as Paddy's Return again running across the take-off of the Canal Turn. This time, the Ferdy Murphy-trained runner ran directly between the two survivors as they prepared to jump the fence, narrowly missing both of them.

Racing neck and neck, it was Red Marauder on the inside that appeared to be going the best, but a hesitant jump at the last open ditch four out almost ruined his chance, briefly giving Smarty an advantage of some three lengths. Coming back over the Melling Road, Guest had his mount back in control and, swooping round the turn for home, began to draw right away from the gallant

Smarty, who had given his all. Despite another very tired jump at the second last, Red Marauder soldiered on and, jumping the last to a tremendous roar, the exhausted but unbelievably brave horse came home a distance clear of Smarty, with the winning time, unsurprisingly, by far the slowest in modern times. Immediately, an elated Guest hugged the mud-covered and thoroughly shattered chestnut before dismounting the winner. With Red Marauder and Smarty the only two to complete the course without mishap, Blowing Wind and Papillon were remounted and casually finished at their own pace, McCoy taking third, completing the race for the first time.

Red Marauder, whom Guest described as possibly the worst jumper to win the race, was clearly a horse with enormous heart that had refused to give in under extreme circumstances and had won the most astonishing Grand National in recent history. Guest had once famously thrown his jockey's licence at stewards after becoming disillusioned with race decisions that had gone against him, and it was obvious how much winning the Grand National meant to him. Norman Mason was a multi-millionaire businessman with a team of twenty-one horses, many with the name 'Red' in their title after the trainer had discovered on a visit to China that the colour was thought to be lucky by that nation. Although the state of the ground came in for a lot of criticism, it must be remembered that a loose horse caused the majority of casualties and, with all the horses returning safely, the Grand National had once again proved incomparable as both a race and spectacle.

2001 GRAND NATIONAL RESULT

FATE	HORSE	AGE/WEIGHT	JOCKEY	ODDS
1st	RED MARAUDER	11.10.11	RICHARD GUEST	33/1
2nd	SMARTY	8.10.0	T.J. MURPHY	16/1
3rd	BLOWING WIND	8.10.9	A.P. McCOY (remounted)	16/1
4th	PAPILLON	10.11.5	R. WALSH (remounted)	14/1
Fell	Tresor De Mai	7.11.2	R. Greene	66/1
Fell	Hanakham	12.10.11	B.J. Geraghty	100/1
Fell	Strong Tel	11.10.11	D.J. Casey	33/1
Fell	Noble Lord	8.10.5	J.A. McCarthy	25/1
Fell	Exit Swinger	6.10.5	C. Maude	50/1
Fell	Inis Cara	9.10.3	R. Widger	10/1
Fell	Edmond	9.10.1	R. Johnson	10/1
Fell	Hollybank Buck	11.10.0	F.J. Flood	20/1
Fell	Village King	8.10.0	J. Culloty	25/1
Fell	Kaki Crazy	6.10.0	R. Farrant	66/1
Fell	Art Prince	11.10.0	J. Crowley	150/1
Pulled-Up	Unsinkable Boxer	12.10.10	D. Gallagher	66/1
Pulled-Up	Listen Timmy	12.10.3	A. Dobbin	100/1
Pulled-Up	No Retreat	8.10.2	J.M. Maguire	100/1
Pulled-Up	Lance Armstrong	11.10.2	A. Thornton	50/1
Brought Down	General Wolfe	12.11.0	B.J. Crowley	50/1
Brought Down	Moral Support	9.10.9	N. Fehily	10/1
Brought Down	Amberleigh House	9.10.5	W. Marston	150/1
Brought Down	Mely Moss	10.10.5	N. Williamson	14/1
Brought Down	You're Agoodun	9.10.1	R. Wakley	28/1
Unseated Rider	Beau	8.11.10	C. Llewellyn	12/1
Unseated Rider	Earthmover	10.11.2	J. Tizzard	22/1
Unseated Rider	The Last Fling	11.10.12	S. Durack	20/1
Unseated Rider	Addington Boy	13.10.11	J.P. McNamara	33/1
Unseated Rider	Djeddah	10.10.11	T. Doumen	33/1
Unseated Rider	Northern Starlight	10.10.7	Mr T. Scudamore	50/1
Unseated Rider	Moondigua	9.10.0	J.R. Barry	100/1
Unseated Rider	Spanish Main	7.10.0	J. Goldstein	25/1
Unseated Rider	Esprit De Cotte	9.10.0	T. Doyle	33/1
Unseated Rider	Paddy's Return	9.10.0	A. Maguire	16/1
Unseated Rider	Mister One	10.10.0	M. Bradburne	50/1
Unseated Rider	Supreme Charm	9.10.0	R. Thornton	33/1
Unseated Rider	Merry People	13.10.0	G. Cotter	66/1
Refused	Dark Stranger	10.10.3	K.A. Kelly	25/1
Refused	Feels Like Gold	13.10.0	B. Harding	50/1
Refused	Brave Highlander	13.10.0	P. Hide	33/1

7 April 2001
Going – Heavy
Sponsor – Martell
Winner – £310,000
Time – 11mins 0.1secs
40 Ran
Co-Favourites – Moral Support, Inis Cara and Edmond
Top Weight – Beau
Winner trained by Norman Mason at Crook, County Durham
Winner owned by Mr N.B. Mason
Red Marauder, chestnut gelding by Gunner B – Cover Your Money.

Spattered in mud, Smarty (left) and Red Marauder, the only two horses left in contention, clear the last open ditch on the second circuit.

2002

BINDAREE

With thirty-one horses in the handicap proper, the 2002 Grand National continued the recent trend of greater competitiveness and higher overall quality. The brilliant Irish bay Florida Pearl, twice placed in a Cheltenham Gold Cup, was seriously considered for the race by trainer Willie Mullins and, even though the horse – together with highly touted Aintree candidates such as the injured Welsh National winner Supreme Glory, recent Cheltenham Festival winner Frenchman's Creek and the previous two National winners Papillon and Red Marauder – did not ultimately line-up, another very open renewal was promised.

Favourite at 8/1 was the Martin Pipe-trained Blowing Wind. Despite being partnered by Champion Jockey Tony McCoy and hailing from the highest-profile yard in the country, the fact the horse stood at the top of the market was a surprise to many, for Blowing Wind was considered better suited to trips of around two-and-a-half miles, a distance over which he had recently prevailed in the Mildmay of Flete Chase at Cheltenham. However, Blowing Wind had jumped the fences strongly before being stopped in the 2001 race and, even though there was a fair distance to run, the horse had still been travelling well.

If Blowing Wind was a debatable favourite, the possibilities behind him were endless with a quartet of horses – What's Up Boys, Paris Pike, Ad Hoc and Davids Lad – attracting considerable attention. The blinkered grey What's Up Boys was one of the class animals in the field. A winner of the fiercely competitive Coral Cup (handicap Hurdle) at Cheltenham as a six-year-old, the horse had flashed home late to deny the giant Behrajan in the season's Hennessy Cognac Gold Cup, while he had recently finished fifth behind the new chasing phenomenon Best Mate in the Cheltenham Gold Cup. An occasional-lapse jumper but with stamina assured, What's Up Boys presented the excellent pair of trainer Philip Hobbs and jockey Richard Johnson with a fine chance of winning their first National.

Owned by Major Ivan Straker, Paris Pike had looked an ideal Grand National horse when taking the Scottish equivalent two years previously, only for leg trouble to curtail the following season. Taking a while to return to form, the horse

was generally an excellent jumper that loved the top of the ground and was one of four representatives for trainer Ferdy Murphy (Streamstown, Ackzo and Birkdale were the others). He was ridden by the hero of 2001, Richard Guest.

It had taken the classy Ad Hoc time to find his feet as a chaser. The young horse had suffered a number of crushing falls that dampened his confidence. But, when a good second in the Scottish National was followed by a runaway win in the Whitbread Gold Cup to conclude the previous season, the horse had started to look like the genuine article. A beautiful traveller in his races, Ad Hoc had long been considered a Grand National horse by trainer Paul Nicholls (looking for a change of luck after previous disappointments with Deep Bramble and Double Thriller) and had actually been the long-time ante-post favourite for the 2002 race, eventually starting at 10/1.

The principal Irish hope in the National was the dark bay Davids Lad. Like Blowing Wind normally kept to far shorter distances, Davids Lad had proved himself over further ones when winning the Irish National the season before and, like Papillon in 2000, carried with him to Aintree the aura of a horse whose path to the National had been perfectly plotted by wily trainer Tony Martin. In the saddle, Davids Lad had Timmy Murphy, second aboard Smarty in 2001.

Smarty ran again, as did Beau, while the tough little grey Haydock specialist Kingsmark ran for trainer Martin Todhunter with the high-class Gold Cup fourth Marlborough carrying top weight. In the National field for the first time was the bright chestnut Bindaree, a tough stayer by Royal Athlete's sire Roselier, trained, like Beau, by Nigel Twiston-Davies. An eight-year-old, Bindaree had run over the fences the year before in the John Hughes Trophy and had finished third in the

Trainer Nigel Twiston-Davies and his National hero Bindaree.

Bindaree (21) jumps Valentines on the second circuit followed by Davids Lad (red).

season's Welsh National. Since that run at Chepstow, the horse had produced nothing of note, but with Llewellyn opting for the more fancied Beau, Bindaree was ridden by the man of the moment, Best Mate's jockey Jim Culloty.

The sun was bright, the ground lively and, as the anxious runners lined-up on the tape, the tension was as extreme as any National before. Sent on their way, the forty runners packed together as they charged over the Melling Road, with the Irish mare Wicked Crack the first to show in the centre approaching the first, flanked by Celibate and The Last Fling. The rush to the first appeared vicious, and Wicked Crack came crashing down immediately. Behind her, the grey novice Carryonharry got in too close and paid the price with a heavy fall – in the process knocking into and bringing down the former Australian chaser Logician. The first fence had taken its highest toll since 1951, claiming nine horses, including the fancied pair Marlborough and Paris Pike.

The Last Fling and bottom weight Supreme Charm quickly opened up a lead on the run to Becher's, as Samuel Wilderspin and Niki Dee came down at the fourth, followed by the young chestnut Iris Bleu a fence later. With over a quarter of the field already out of the contest, The Last Fling and Supreme Charm thundered over Becher's in fine style. While chasing in behind were Celibate, Mely Moss, Davids Lad and Beau. Alexander Banquet, sixth in the Gold Cup, unseated Barry Geraghty, but the remainder survived and continued down the back.

Owner Trevor Hemmings had long desired a Grand National win, and his recent purchase of Beau gave him perhaps his best chance yet. Approaching the fourteenth, Beau lay just behind another Hemmings horse, The Last Fling (his Goguenard had fallen at the first), with Supreme Charm, Celibate and Davids Lad next. However, having jumped the fence well, Beau stumbled a stride later, giving Llewellyn no chance of staying on board.

Streaming over The Chair and water, the remaining runners received huge encouragement from the crowd and, heading out for circuit two it was still The Last Fling leading from Supreme Charm, Celibate, Mely Moss, Davids Lad, Bindaree and Majed. Then came two horses carrying the dark blue with yellow crossbelts of owner Mr Peter Deal – Royal Predica and Blowing Wind – with both Kingsmark and Ad Hoc (the pair owned by Sir Robert Ogden) gradually creeping into a fascinating race.

The Last Fling was beginning to jump more erratically and, having clouted the twentieth, he was joined in the lead at Becher's second time by the improving Bindaree, with Davids Lad, Blowing Wind and Royal Predica on the wide outside. Taking a strong advantage, Bindaree surged in front jumping the fence, tracked by a host of dangerous-looking challengers, including Blowing Wind and Davids Lad while, in behind, Ad Hoc, Kingsmark and the French horse Djeddah were hunting up the pacesetters, with What's Up Boys beginning a forward move at the Canal Turn. It was there that the tiring chestnut The Last Fling fell alarmingly, tragically breaking his back in a cruel end for a wonderful horse – one that had provided many moments of pure enjoyment for a number of years.

Surrounded by loose horses, Bindaree marched on up front but, by Valentines and having made tremendous progress, the grey What's Up Boys came to dispute proceedings on the wide outside. However, it was at the last open ditch, four out, where the race changed most dramatically. Still tanking along behind the leaders, Davids Lad crashed out in spectacular style. Directly behind him, Ad Hoc ran straight into the faller and was brought down. Given a wonderfully patient ride by Paul Carberry, Ad Hoc had been yet to make his move and looked seriously unlucky, for both he and Davids Lad were sure to have played a part in the finish, while Djeddah too was hampered by loose horses and unseated Thierry Doumen. With four horses left clear crossing the Melling Road, Bindaree was travelling by far the strongest, leading What's Up Boys, Kingsmark and Blowing Wind. Rounding the turn for home, Culloty had not yet moved aboard the chestnut, while Johnson vigorously shook up What's Up Boys to keep the grey in touch with the leader.

Bindaree and What's Up Boys were clear themselves by two out, although now the grey jumped to the front as Bindaree came under pressure for the first time. To make matters worst, the riderless Beau cut across Culloty's mount approaching the second last, causing the horse to lose ground; jumping the final fences, What's Up Boys was away quicker. Attacking the elbow, What's Up Boys looked like becoming only the third ever grey to win the National until Bindaree began a late rally against the inside rails. In receipt of 16lbs and finishing with rare power, with his white face dazzling in the sun, Bindaree was able to wear down the grey horse, getting up to win the National by a length-and-three-quarters. A long way back came Blowing Wind, third again, followed by the brave Kingsmark, who had injured himself after the third last. Sadly, The Last Fling and Manx Magic had lost their lives in what had been a fairly roughhouse edition of the race.

A titanic duel had resulted in Culloty becoming only the sixth jockey to win the Gold Cup and National in the same season and the first since the late John Burke in 1976. Culloty dedicated the win to Jamie Goldstein, who would have ridden Bindaree but for breaking his leg at Ludlow the previous Wednesday. Culloty had in turn been released by Mark Pitman from riding Browjoshy, who had been first reserve and ultimately did not make the cut for the race. It emerged after Bindaree's win that Twiston-Davies had been set to give up his license, so low was his morale following a torrid season. But the victory of Bindaree provided the necessary inspiration to carry on and, from there, the trainer went on to enjoy sustained success, as the Grand National once more had a far-reaching effect on those that it touched.

2002 GRAND NATIONAL RESULT

FATE	HORSE	AGE/WEIGHT	JOCKEY	ODDS
1st	BINDAREE	8.10.4	J. CULLOTY	20/1
2nd	WHAT'S UP BOYS	8.11.6	R. JOHNSON	10/1
3rd	BLOWING WIND	9.10.6	A.P. McCOY	8/1
4th	KINGSMARK	9.11.9	R. WALSH	16/1
5th	Supreme Charm	10.10.0	R. Thornton	28/1
6th	Celibate	11.10.3	N. Fehily	66/1
7th	You're Agoodun	10.10.8	J.R. Kavanagh	50/1
8th	Royal Predica	8.10.8	J.A. McCarthy	80/1
9th	Streamstown	8.10.8	J.P. McNamara	40/1
10th	Birkdale	11.10.2	J.M. Maguire	50/1
11th	Mely Moss	11.10.2	N. Williamson	25/1
Fell	Marlborough	10.11.12	M.A. Fitzgerald	20/1
Fell	Davids Lad	8.11.1	T.J. Murphy	10/1
Fell	Paris Pike	10.10.13	Richard Guest	10/1
Fell	Majed	6.10.11	B. Fenton	66/1
Fell	Inn At The Top	10.10.8	A.S. Smith	40/1
Fell	Manx Magic	9.10.7	G. Supple	100/1
Fell	The Last Fling	12.10.6	R. McGrath	40/1
Fell	Wicked Crack	9.10.5	C. O'Dwyer	33/1
Fell	Super Franky	9.10.5	P.P. O'Brien	66/1
Fell	Gun 'N Roses II	8.10.2	M. Foley	100/1
Fell	Niki Dee	12.10.3	R. Garritty	66/1
Fell	Goguenard	8.10.0	W. Marston	66/1
Fell	Samuel Wilderspin	10.10.0	T. Doyle	14/1
Fell	Iris Bleu	6.10.0	P. Moloney	100/1
Fell	Carryonharry	8.10.0	R. Wakley	66/1
Pulled-Up	Smarty	9.10.1	T. Scudamore	16/1
Pulled-Up	Murt's Man	8.10.2	A. Thornton	66/1
Pulled-Up	Ackzo	9.10.0	D. Gallagher	25/1
Pulled-Up	Inis Cara	10.10.2	B.J. Crowley	66/1
Brought Down	Ad Hoc	8.11.1	P. Carberry	10/1
Brought Down	Struggles Glory	11.10.3	B. Hitchcott	66/1
Brought Down	Logician	11.10.0	M. Bradburne	80/1
Unseated Rider	Alexander Banquet	9.11.11	B.J. Geraghty	22/1
Unseated Rider	Lyreen Wonder	9.11.4	B.M. Cash	40/1
Unseated Rider	Beau	9.11.1	C. Llewellyn	11/1
Unseated Rider	Frantic Tan	10.10.5	T. Jenks	50/1
Unseated Rider	Red Ark	9.10.0	K. Johnson	50/1
Unseated Rider	Spot Thedifference	9.10.0	D.J. Casey	33/1
Unseated Rider	Djeddah	11.10.2	T. Doumen	66/1

6 April 2002
Going – Good
Sponsor – Martell
Winner – £290,000
Time – 9mins 9secs
40 Ran
Favourite – Blowing Wind

Top Weight – Marlborough
Winner trained by Nigel Twiston-Davies
   at Naunton, Gloucestershire
Winner owned by Mr H.R. Mould
Bindaree, chestnut gelding by Roselier
   – Flowing Tide.

2003

MONTY'S PASS

Five years previously in the 1998 Grand National, just seven horses ran from within the handicap proper. It was a credit to both the official race handicapper and the race organisers and sponsors that a grand figure of thirty-six raced from their correct marks in the 2003 race. Unlike many Nationals of the past that contained a large number of 'no-hopers' running from outside the handicap, each National in current times is almost guaranteed a high-class entry and an extremely open contest. True, the fences are less severe now, but the quality of the National has improved drastically to the extent that making the forty-horse cut-off point is a real achievement, such has become the increased desire to feature in the great race

In a fierce betting market, five horses competed for favouritism on the day of the race, with each of Shotgun Willy, Youlneverwalkalone, Iris Bleu, Ad Hoc and Chives holding similarly strong chances. It was Shotgun Willy that eventually emerged from the gambling dogfight as favourite as punters latched on to the fact that Ruby Walsh had picked the big chestnut over stablemate Ad Hoc. Trained by Paul Nicholls, the powerfully built Shotgun Willy had been one of the leading staying novice chasers two years before and had finished runner-up in the previous season's Scottish National. Shotgun Willy was making his first appearance of the season just a month before the National when showing determination and stamina to win a terrific battle with fellow National runners You're Agoodun and Iris Bleu in the Red Square Vodka Gold Cup (formerly the Greenalls Grand National Trial and De Vere Gold Cup). The race highlighted Shotgun Willy's Aintree prospects, although Nicholls admitted he could not split the chestnut and his other main hope, Ad Hoc, the latter having been campaigned all season with a return to Aintree in mind, where he had been so unlucky in the 2002 National.

Having fallen at the fifth in the 2002 race, Iris Bleu had improved both physically and in his jumping as he chartered a meteoric rise up the handicap during the season. A most attractive, big, raking chestnut with a broad white face,

Iris Bleu had come to prominence with a twenty-three-length destruction of a decent field in Sandown's Agfa Diamond Chase in February, a win that saw him allocated in excess of 11 stone for Aintree. Iris Bleu followed the Sandown win with a strong performance in Shotgun Willy's Haydock race and he became a popular selection for the National when Tony McCoy selected him from Martin Pipe's team of seven.

With the anthem of Liverpool Football Club as his name, the Irish horse Youlneverwalkalone was always going to be well supported by the local crowd at Aintree. Yet, as well as being creatively named, the horse – trained by Christy Roche and owned by J.P. McManus – was a class act, just coming into his own as a staying chaser having been a smart hurdler. A bay horse with a decent frame, Youlneverwalkalone had come firmly into the National picture with a win in the William Hill Handicap Chase at the Cheltenham Festival and enjoyed a fair weight for Aintree. A beautiful traveller in his races, the horse was similar in that respect to Ad Hoc, for he liked to come from off the pace, and some wondered if that would go against the horse in the Grand National, where loose horses and stricken fallers are a serious hazard.

December's Welsh Grand National had proved a useful form guide for Aintree. The race was won by little Mini Sensation (who did not run at Aintree), with Andrew Balding's fancied National runner Gunner Welburn third. Splitting the two was the Trevor Hemmings-owned Chives, an injury-riddled chaser only just establishing himself as a performer of class and ability. A tall, dark bay, Chives was a chaser from the traditional mould, powerful and relentless, as

Gunner Welburn (12) and Chives, pictured at Chepstow, ran fine races in the Welsh National to emerge as leading contenders for Aintree.

Monty's Pass is preceded by only the riderless horse The Bunny Boiler at the final fence.

well as being a fine jumper. The horse was trained by Henrietta Knight and had confirmed himself a serious challenger for the National when performing admirably in the recent Gold Cup, leading for a long way before fading late on into seventh behind stablemate Best Mate.

Among the outsiders were a Becher Chase winner in Amberleigh House, a Peter Marsh Chase winner in Red Striker (a full-brother to Red Marauder), a Welsh National winner in Supreme Glory, a Triumph Hurdle winner in Katarino, and an Irish and Midlands National winner in The Bunny Boiler, giving an indication of the overall strength of the 2003 race. Others that were strongly considered were the giant bay Behrajan (fifth in the Gold Cup), Gingembre, a former Scottish National winner and winner through disqualification of the season's Hennessy, the lightly raced dark horse Killusty and the Irish bay Monty's Pass. The lattermost hailed from the small stable of Jimmy Mangan and had run well over the big fences when second in the 2002 Topham Trophy. The good ground was in the horse's favour and, having been given a light campaign aimed specifically at the National, a lot of shrewd late money came for Monty's Pass – a horse rising star Barry Geraghty had stayed loyal to having been offered the ride on Youlneverwalkalone.

Heading to the first fence, Tremallt led clearly from a field that was nicely spaced out, with the next wave including Blowing Wind, Torduff Express, Royal Predica, Montifault, Maximize, The Bunny Boiler and Bramblehill Duke. Bereft of the carnage of the 2002 race, only The Bunny Boiler dropped out, even he jumped the fence well only to peck on landing, unseating race debutant John Cullen. Having got into the race as first reserve when the unlucky Kingsmark was forced out at the eleventh hour with injury, Bramblehill Duke fell explosively at the second, while the normally reliable Wonder Weasel came down at the big ditch.

With Blowing Wind, Torduff Express and Behrajan on the outside and the blazing chestnut Montifault hacking up the inner, Tremallt led gloriously over Becher's, where the only casualty was Fadalko when towards the rear – although the 2002 hero Bindaree was lucky to stay in the race, slipping down to his belly before continuing a long way behind the rest as the field headed for the Foinavon fence and beyond.

It was from the Canal Turn onwards that the race began to deteriorate for many of the leading fancies. Jumping well just behind the leaders, a mistake at the tenth knocked Iris Bleu back somewhat, while both Shotgun Willy and Ad Hoc were well down the field. Chives was already struggling at the back when he barely clambered over the eleventh before pulling-up after the fence. Chives, as he had in the past, had broken a blood vessel and returned with blood streaming from his nostrils. Happily, Chives returned to the racecourse in future seasons. Not so lucky was Youlneverwalkalone, who fractured his off-fore canon bone going to the twelfth. Through fine work by the veterinary surgeons at the Leahurst College in Liverpool the horse was saved, though sadly his racing career was over. It was a great shame, for he was jumping and travelling very well in the National. In mid-division at the time of the injury, Conor O'Dwyer tried to pull the horse up, only for the brave Youlneverwalkalone to jump the fence anyway.

Former Aintree Foxhunter's winner Gunner Welburn had made his way to the front under Barry Fenton and, at The Chair, had Tremallt, Torduff Express, Montifault and Monty's Pass for company. The leader brought gasps from the crowd when hesitating before the fence, but just as it looked like he may end up in the gaping ditch, he put in a leap that just got him over the huge hurdle. Two horses suffered bad injuries further back as Iris Bleu clouted The Chair so hard he was soon pulled-up, missing the following season, but eventually he too raced again, as did Katarino, who had been harshly knocked into when unseating Mick Fitzgerald. In a heart-warming conclusion, Katarino returned to Aintree in 2005 to win the Foxhunters' over the big fences.

With the dreams of many of the leading contenders lying shattered all over Aintree, the same leading bunch began the second circuit with an exciting race building. Tremallt and Torduff Express were matching strides, then came Monty's Pass and Montifault on the inside with Gunner Welburn. Improving on the outside were Ginger McCain's runner Amberleigh House, Behrajan and the Irish chestnut Cregg House, with Royal Predica still there in the centre and the Duchess of Westminster's colours prominent courtesy of the normally lazy Carbury Cross.

A pile-up ensued back in the field at the nineteenth, where Ad Hoc was among the casualties, and Goguenard blundered so badly he unseated Warren Marston before the horse was slammed into by the trailing Robbo. Sadly, Goguenard sustained fatal injuries, as Trevor Hemmings lost another good horse (after The Last Fling's demise in the 2002 race).

With Shotgun Willy well out of contention when pulled-up and Killusty a faller at Becher's second time when making headway, a group of four suddenly pulled clear, headed by Gunner Welburn. Tracking the chestnut were Monty's Pass, Montifault and Amberleigh House, as long-time leaders Tremallt and Torduff Express – a winner over the fences in the 2002 Foxhunters' – began to fade. Jumping down the back, the first three separated from Montifault, and the trio had the race between them crossing the Melling Road for the final time.

With the Bunny Boiler preceding them riderless, Monty's Pass jumped past the tiring Gunner Welburn two out and, clearing the last, the Irish horse came clear of the chestnut and Amberleigh House. Reaching the elbow, Geraghty pushed out the sheepskin noseband-wearing bay and, keeping up a strong gallop, Irish roars willed Monty's Pass home to a very comfortable triumph, passing the post a twelve-length winner. Supreme Glory came from a mile back to run on for second, and had now finished in the frame in an English, Scottish and Welsh National for likeable trainer Pat Murphy. Amberleigh House took third, the gallant Gunner Welburn fourth and Montifault fifth. From a long way out, these had been the dominant horses in the race, as many of the fancied horses performed badly or were injured. Recovering from his awful mistake at the first Becher's, the defending champion Bindaree came home safely in sixth.

Monty's Pass had ultimately powered to victory with surprising ease having jumped impeccably, travelling in the front rank the entire way and relishing the good ground. With his previous effort in the Topham, Monty's Pass was now a confirmed Aintree specialist and became the third Irish winner in four years. The horse landed a huge gamble of just under £1 million for the frontman of the Dee Racing Syndicate that owned him, Mike Futter, and the National success was an astronomical moment in the training career of the little known County Cork-based Mangan, who had first held a license in 1981. The win also confirmed the belief that Geraghty could now be placed in the same elite class as Tony McCoy and Ruby Walsh, for just three weeks after recording an incredible five wins at the Cheltenham Festival, the jockey had added the greatest race of them all to his résumé aboard the highly impressive Monty's Pass.

2003 GRAND NATIONAL RESULT

FATE	HORSE	AGE/WEIGHT	JOCKEY	ODDS
1st	MONTY'S PASS	10.10.7	B.J. GERAGHTY	16/1
2nd	SUPREME GLORY	10.10.2	L. ASPELL	40/1
3rd	AMBERLEIGH HOUSE	11.10.4	G. LEE	33/1
4th	GUNNER WELBURN	11.10.2	B. FENTON	16/1
5th	Montifault	8.10.4	J. Tizzard	33/1
6th	Bindaree	9.10.11	C. Llewellyn	25/1
7th	Carbury Cross	9.10.12	L. Cooper	25/1
8th	Blowing Wind	10.10.9	T. Scudamore	20/1
9th	Tremallt	12.10.2	J.M. Maguire	200/1
10th	Behrajan	8.11.12	R. Johnson	22/1
11th	Djeddah	12.10.1	T. Doumen	66/1
12th	Majed	7.10.5	R. Greene	200/1
13th	Royal Predica	9.10.2	Mr J.E. Moore	33/1
14th	Southern Star	8.10.8	D. Elsworth	66/1
Fell	Maximize	9.10.4	J. Culloty	16/1
Fell	Wonder Weasel	10.10.5	J.P. McNamara	50/1
Fell	Burlu	9.10.0	G. Supple	200/1
Fell	Killusty	9.10.4	A. Dobbin	12/1
Fell	Bramblehill Duke	11.10.0	B.J. Crowley	200/1
Pulled-Up	Gingembre	9.11.9	A. Thornton	14/1
Pulled-Up	Shotgun Willy	9.11.9	R. Walsh	7/1
Pulled-Up	Chives	8.11.5	Richard Guest	10/1
Pulled-Up	Iris Bleu	7.11.3	A.P. McCoy	8/1
Pulled-Up	Ballinclay King	9.10.12	D.N. Russell	50/1
Pulled-Up	Youlneverwalkalone	9.10.11	C. O'Dwyer	8/1
Pulled-Up	Good Shuil	8.10.3	N. Fehily	200/1
Pulled-Up	Red Ark	10.10.0	K. Johnson	100/1
Pulled-Up	Empereur River	11.10.0	Mr P. Pailhes	250/1
Unseated Rider	Fadalko	10.11.7	S. Durack	100/1
Unseated Rider	Ad Hoc	9.11.1	P. Carberry	9/1
Unseated Rider	The Bunny Boiler	9.10.10	J.L. Cullen	50/1
Unseated Rider	You're Agoodun	11.10.9	R. Thornton	50/1
Unseated Rider	Katarino	8.10.8	M.A. Fitzgerald	50/1
Unseated Rider	Red Striker	9.10.8	Mr L. McGrath	50/1
Unseated Rider	Polar Champ	10.10.4	D.J. Howard	200/1
Unseated Rider	Mantles Prince	9.10.3	O. McPhail	200/1
Unseated Rider	Torduff Express	12.10.3	T.J. Murphy	33/1
Unseated Rider	Goguenard	9.10.2	W. Marston	28/1
Unseated Rider	Robbo	9.10.0	A. Dempsey	100/1
Refused	Cregg House	8.10.3	D.J. Casey	50/1

5 April 2003
Going – Good
Sponsor – Martell Cognac
Winner – £348,000
Time – 9mins 21.70secs
40 Ran
Favourite – Shotgun Willy

Top Weight – Behrajan
Winner trained by James Joseph Mangan
   at Mallow, County Cork, Ireland
Winner owned by Dee Racing
   Syndicate
Monty's Pass, bay gelding by
   Montelimar – Friars Pass.

2004

AMBERLEIGH HOUSE

The fact that bookmakers Ladbrokes had seven horses listed as 11/1 co-favourites on the morning of the 2004 Grand National indicated another enormously competitive race. So many horses had been condensed into the handicap and an intriguing contest again loomed large. Even though Davids Lad and newcomers Hedgehunter and Bear On Board eventually missed out on favouritism, four others proudly sat atop the market in a National offering a plethora of possibilities.

The four horses were Bindaree, Clan Royal, Joss Naylor and Jurancon II, the quartet starting 10/1 co-favourites. Having suffered disappointments with the likes of Challenger Du Luc, Eudipe, Dark Stranger and Iris Bleu in recent Nationals, Tony McCoy again partnered a Martin Pipe contender in 2004, this time the seven-year-old Jurancon II. Like those four former National runners as well as twice third Blowing Wind, Jurancon II was French-bred. No horse with that distinction had won the National since Lutteur III in 1909, yet Jurancon II was a stamina-rich bay, progressive and had impressed mightily when winning the Red Square Vodka Gold Cup at Haydock, beating another improving stayer, the Alan King-trained Bear On Board.

The 2002 Grand National winner Bindaree had received treatment in the summer for a back problem and, consequently, the chestnut had returned to his best form. Bindaree had emerged victorious from a thrilling slog in the Welsh National in December – showing form that would prove outstanding in time. On that day, Bindaree outfought Sir Rembrandt, who would subsequently finish a close runner-up to Best Mate in the Gold Cup, future Aintree star Hedgehunter, the Gold Cup runner-up the following season in Take A Stand and also Jurancon II.

As a jockey, Jonjo O'Neill had endured nothing but misery in the Grand National. Now one of the most successful trainers in the land, he was searching for a better fate in his new sphere. O'Neill's first runner in the race, Carbury Cross, had finished seventh in 2003 and his two runners in 2004, though both lightly raced, were very strong fancies. Fast developing into an Aintree specialist,

the gross, hard-pulling bay Clan Royal had won both the Topham Chase and the Becher Chase over the National fences, jumping brilliantly on both occasions. There were questions surrounding Clan Royal's stamina, yet he was heavily supported on the day, while the dark horse for the race was the rarely sighted Joss Naylor, a smaller horse but a superb jumper. Joss Naylor was owned by Mr Darren Mercer, who had been second with Mely Moss, and Joss Naylor had finished second to the fine young chaser Strong Flow in the season's Hennessy Cognac Gold Cup.

A fascinating field included the former excellent staying hurdler Le Coudray as top weight; Artic Jack, a big bay horse trained by Sue Smith that had won the season's Peter Marsh Chase at Haydock; the 2003 hero Monty's Pass, raised 14lbs from the year before; useful hunter-chaser Lord Atterbury and the Hennessy fourth Hedgehunter from Ireland – as well as a host of horses previously placed in the National. Included in this latter group was Amberleigh House, a compact little brown horse similar in size to the most diminutive of National winners such as The Lamb and Battleship, though his frame was packed with power. No horse in the field had as much experience over the National fences as Amberleigh House, for as well as running in two Nationals (finishing third in 2003), the horse had won and been second twice in the Becher Chase and also finished ninth in a Topham Chase, each time jumping the huge fences with efficiency and grace. His trainer Ginger McCain had maintained a love affair with the National, saddling many runners since the great Red Rum's last triumph in 1977, but most of these had been outsiders such as Imperial Black, Dudie, Hotplate and

Davy Russell is unseated from Takagi at The Chair as Bear On Board (yellow) and Smarty surge on. Jumping the fence are Amberleigh House (noseband) and Just In Debt (red).

Back Bar. But in Amberleigh House the trainer was adamant he had a horse capable of winning a National, for which the gelding had been specifically purchased from Ireland to do. With the good ground very much in his favour, Amberleigh House started the race a live each-way chance at 16/1.

In the middle of the track, Alcapone, Bramblehill Duke, Artic Jack, Akarus and Southern Star led a strong charge to the first from stablemates Hedgehunter and Alexander Banquet on the inside. Artic Jack over-jumped the fence and was the first one to go while, back in the field, the blinkered Luzcadou fell, bringing down the French raider Kelami. Very quickly, Hedgehunter and Alcapone took up the leading positions and, both jumping superbly, headed down to Becher's. The quietly fancied Shardam unseated Tom Scudamore at the big ditch and McCoy's poor National record continued a fence later when Jurancon II miscalculated the fourth and came down.

On the wide outside Shardam had continued riderless and, as the field came to Becher's, his white face could be seen knifing towards the centre of the obstacle. As a result, Akarus was badly hampered and fell, in turn causing much grief to those in the vicinity. Bindaree, Skycab and Risk Accessor were all impeded and unseated their riders, Bramblehill Duke and Blowing Wind were both stopped in their tracks and refused, Montreal fell, the trailing grey What's Up Boys was brought down, while away from the carnage, the 2002 Attheraces (Whitbread) Gold Cup winner Bounce Back also came down – and would later fall twice more when riderless. Nine had been eliminated at Becher's. Amberleigh House had suffered bad interference, bravely clearing the fence from a virtual standstill, leaving him well to the rear.

Jumping with mesmerising brilliance, the two leaders attacked the fences down the back, taking Valentines in symmetrical beauty, Hedgehunter in particular fencing magnificently. Next came the two-mile chaser Puntal, clearly relishing the challenge, Lord Atterbury, Gunner Welburn, Monty's Pass and Alexander Banquet. By the tenth, the field were already well strung out, with Bear On Board and Clan Royal travelling nicely in mid-division but Joss Naylor seemingly unnerved by the experience and struggling mightily at the back.

Hedgehunter soared the eleventh and, returning to the racecourse, the Irish horse was tracked by Puntal, Lord Atterbury and Alcapone. A bunch of loose horses, including Kelami and Risk Accessor, threatened to reap havoc at The Chair but, happily, chaos was averted, with the only casualty at the biggest and widest fence on the course being Takagi – the Irish runner clipping the top of the fence with his back legs when starting to move through the field, rocketing Davy Russell from the saddle.

The pace dictated by Hedgehunter had been searching and, come the start of the second circuit, many were in trouble. Puntal and Lord Atterbury gave chase, with a gap to Alcapone, Monty's Pass, the rapidly improving Clan Royal, Gunner Welburn, Alexander Banquet, Bear On Board and Amberleigh House. Alexander Banquet was a faller at the eighteenth, while the tiring Gunner Welburn was

Ginger McCain trained a record-equalling fourth National winner in 2004.

soon pulled-up, together with the bitterly disappointing Joss Naylor. When a mistake by Puntal ended his race at the big ditch, Hedgehunter was joined by Clan Royal and Lord Atterbury, the three approaching Becher's together.

Hedgehunter was bowling along merrily, but it was noticeable just how strongly Clan Royal was travelling, literally pulling jockey Liam Cooper's arms out as the horse tried to force his way to the front. Top weight Le Coudray had slowly crept into the race but, when he fell at Becher's when lying seventh, six horses pulled clear, with the 2004 Grand National lying between the leading trio of Hedgehunter, Clan Royal and Lord Atterbury, as well as the chasing Amberleigh House, Monty's Pass and Bear On Board.

Clan Royal clattered the twenty-sixth but survived and, heading back over the Melling Road, the front three had now broken free of the remainder, with only Amberleigh House running on from behind. It was at the second last where Hedgehunter came under pressure for the first time, Clan Royal surging past him, with Mark Bradburne also sending the chestnut Lord Atterbury past the long-time leader as well as Hedgehunter suddenly got very tired. Passing Hedgehunter, Clan Royal had looked all over the winner, yet he too dramatically emptied approaching the last, his tail swishing violently, the horse was most untidy at the fence.

As the first two set sail for home, Hedgehunter crumbled to the ground in a heartbreaking fall. He had run very freely under David Casey but had jumped like a stag and did not deserve his misfortune – most likely he would have taken fourth place. Although he lay exhausted on the ground for some time, the horse had proved an Aintree natural and, when he finally rose to his feet to unanimous applause, connections immediately turned their attentions to the 2005 Grand National and began plotting alternative tactics.

Meanwhile an enthralling finish was developing. Cooper had dropped his whip and his mount was legless, running up and down on the spot. At one point, Clan Royal veered so wearily to the left it appeared he may take the wrong course, but somehow Cooper steered him round the elbow, almost colliding with Lord Atterbury in the process. Lord Atterbury was even more punch-drunk than Clan Royal, and he could find no more at the elbow. Meanwhile, coming from a long way back under Graham Lee, Amberleigh House was devouring the ground like a starved beast and, at the elbow, was flying on the outside. Fifty yards from the line the three horses were inseparable but, with Clan Royal and Lord Atterbury unable to rally sufficiently, Amberleigh House was able to cut them down, staying on best of all to win in dramatic fashion by three lengths and two. Clan Royal and Lord Atterbury had run magnificent races, but could not match the superior stamina of the winner, while a long way back in fourth came Monty's Pass.

There was much sympathy as well as admiration for the second and third, as well as Hedgehunter, but a gripping renewal of the race had been won by Amberleigh House, at twelve the oldest horse to win since Royal Athlete in 1995. It was a fairytale result, providing Ginger McCain with his fourth National winner, equalling the record set by Fred Rimell. Seventy-three-years old, McCain was proved right in his belief that Amberleigh House could win a National, and the satisfaction was obvious in his beaming red face at the end of the race. The National meant so much to McCain and the trainer was quick to heap praise on rising star Lee, the jockey himself being overcome with emotion at the finish having brought Amberleigh House from a long way back to deliver his challenge.

It was a truly magical conclusion to the 2004 Grand National, offering a mystical, almost surreal feeling in linking the present to the halcyon days of the greatest National horse of all time. Almost three decades had passed since the last of Red Rum's wins, and now his trainer was celebrating another success with the newest Aintree hero Amberleigh House, a horse that, though diminutive in size, had a touch of 'Rummy' about him as he jumped his way into history.

2004 GRAND NATIONAL RESULT

FATE	HORSE	AGE/WEIGHT	JOCKEY	ODDS
1st	AMBERLEIGH HOUSE	12.10.10	G. LEE	16/1
2nd	CLAN ROYAL	9.10.5	L. COOPER	10/1
3rd	LORD ATTERBURY	8.10.1	M. BRADBURNE	40/1
4th	MONTY'S PASS	11.11.10	B.J. GERAGHTY	20/1
5th	Spot Thedifference	11.10.4	R. McGrath	50/1
6th	Smarty	11.10.0	A. Tinkler	100/1
7th	Ardent Scout	12.10.3	W. Marston	50/1
8th	Bear On Board	9.10.1	R. Thornton	14/1
9th	Kingsmark	11.11.7	M.A. Fitzgerald	66/1
10th	The Bunny Boiler	10.10.8	R. Geraghty	33/1
11th	Davids Lad	10.11.4	T.J. Murphy	12/1
Fell	Le Coudray	10.11.12	C. O'Dwyer	28/1
Fell	Alexander Banquet	11.11.8	J.R. Barry	100/1
Fell	Artic Jack	8.11.7	D. Elsworth	20/1
Fell	Hedgehunter	8.10.12	D.J. Casey	11/1
Fell	Jurancon II	7.10.7	A.P. McCoy	10/1
Fell	Akarus	9.10.4	R. Greene	33/1
Fell	Bounce Back	8.10.4	A. Thornton	50/1
Fell	Luzcadou	11.10.0	B. Harding	200/1
Fell	Montreal	7.10.0	J.P. Elliott	200/1
Pulled-Up	Alcapone	10.11.0	N. Fehily	80/1
Pulled-Up	Southern Star	9.10.13	J. Tizzard	25/1
Pulled-Up	Joss Naylor	9.10.11	P. Carberry	10/1
Pulled-Up	Gunner Welburn	12.10.8	A. Dobbin	22/1
Pulled-Up	Royal Atalza	7.10.6	P. Moloney	100/1
Pulled-Up	Exit To Wave	8.10.5	R.P. McNally	50/1
Pulled-Up	Mantles Prince	10.10.1	O. McPhail	250/1
Pulled-Up	Wonder Weasel	11.10.6	J.P. McNamara	200/1
Brought Down	What's Up Boys	10.11.9	R. Johnson	25/1
Brought Down	Kelami	6.10.7	T. Doumen	66/1
Unseated Rider	Risk Accessor	9.11.4	S. Durack	66/1
Unseated Rider	Bindaree	10.11.4	C. Llewellyn	10/1
Unseated Rider	Puntal	8.10.13	D.J. Howard	150/1
Unseated Rider	Shardam	7.10.11	T. Scudamore	18/1
Unseated Rider	Takagi	9.10.11	D.N. Russell	25/1
Unseated Rider	Just In Debt	8.10.5	J. Culloty	33/1
Unseated Rider	Skycab	12.10.1	L. Aspell	200/1
Refused	Blowing Wind	11.10.1	J.A. McCarthy	33/1
Refused	Bramblehill Duke	12.10.0	James Davies	200/1

3 April 2004
Going – Good
Sponsor – Martell Cognac
Winner – £348,000
Time – 9mins 20.30secs
39 Ran
Co-Favourites – Bindaree, Joss Naylor,
  Jurancon II and Clan Royal

Top Weight – Le Coudray
Winner trained by Donald McCain at
  Cholmondeley, Cheshire
Winner owned by Halewood
  International Ltd
Amberleigh House, brown gelding by
  Buckskin – Chancy Gal.

2005

HEDGEHUNTER

They say the best things come to those who wait. Multi-millionaire owner Trevor Hemmings had wanted to win the Grand National since 1971, when his boss Mr Fred Pontin acquired Specify to win the race that year. The National had become an obsession and life goal for Hemmings, yet the sixty-nine-year old had endured cruel luck in the race he had supported so well. His fancied hopes of recent Nationals – Beau, Chives and Artic Jack – had all failed to get round, while The Last Fling and Goguenard had both lost their lives in the race carrying the owner's famous yellow and green-quartered colours. Indeed, only two of his horses had completed the race, Rubika in 1992 and Southern Star in 2003. Making no secret of his burning desire to win, Hemmings was represented in 2005 by the strapping bay Hedgehunter and newcomer Europa. The most heartbreaking sight of the 2004 National had been Hedgehunter falling at the last fence having led the whole way, jumping superbly until that moment. Trainer Willie Mullins realised the horse had run too free then, blazing a trail that left him exhausted in the closing stages, and now, with the brilliant Ruby Walsh on board, knew more restraint was needed to avoid a similar scenario. Mullins reasoned Hedgehunter was now a far stronger horse and, with a light campaign of Hurdle races followed by a chase win at Fairyhouse leading the horse back to Aintree, the horse was extremely popular, eventually starting 7/1 favourite.

The 2005 Grand National appeared full of potential fairytales. From a huge original entry of 152, eighty-five were declared at the five-day stage, with countless decent horses balloted out as the final cut was made, including Kim Bailey's promising Longshanks and former National runner-up Supreme Glory. With Native Emperor, former winner of the National Hunt Chase at the Cheltenham Festival, getting a late call-up as first reserve for the injured outsider Turnium, all forty horses were in the handicap proper, an incredible feat, with even Native Emperor carrying 10st 5lbs. Dominating the build-up was the very realistic prospect of a female jockey riding the winner for the first time. Only two ladies had completed the course in fourteen previous attempts, but never before had any woman held such a chance as Carrie Ford did with Forest Gunner in 2005. At the 2004 Grand

Forest Gunner and Carrie Ford (red cap) get over The Chair in between Ad Hoc (left) and Just In Debt. Take The Stand unseats Leighton Aspell (yellow) while jumping are eventual placed horses Royal Auclair (purple cap) and Simply Gifted (green cap).

National meeting Ford had captured public hearts by winning the Foxhunters' on Forest Gunner just ten weeks after giving birth and, when the horse had been confirmed for the National earlier in the season, she announced she would be coming temporarily out of retirement to partner him again. Trained by Carrie's husband Richard, Forest Gunner was a superb jumper of the National fences, and had set Aintree alight in November when running his rivals ragged in the Grand Sefton Chase, displaying a flare and relish for the fences rarely witnessed. A little chestnut with a big white face, Forest Gunner had some stamina worries, yet a brave, winning performance in Haydock's Red Square Vodka Gold Cup seemed to lessen those fears. When Ginger McCain, who again ran Amberleigh House, stated categorically that 'women do not win Grand Nationals', fuel was added enticingly to the fire, creating a huge sense of anticipation ahead of the big race, for which Ford found many supporters – Forest Gunner starting 8/1 second favourite.

It would be hard to oppose the opinion that the 2005 Grand National had greater strength in depth than any National before, for there were very few no-hopers, with the list of potential winners plentiful. With the handicap as competitive as could be imagined, even those above the dreaded 11 stone mark were strongly and realistically considered. Amberleigh House carried the extreme confidence of McCain, while fellow former winners Bindaree and Monty's Pass ran again, as did Clan Royal and Lord Atterbury. Tony McCoy had switched stables since the 2004 race, joining the Jonjo O'Neill yard, and, in Clan Royal, the jockey partnered a proven Aintree horse that came to the race fresh.

Of the newcomers, serious claims were made for Take The Stand, Strong Resolve, Colnel Rayburn and Joly Bey. Trained in Wales by Peter Bowen, Take The Stand had run the race of his life to finish second to the new Irish superstar Kicking King in the Gold Cup although, having belted a few fences at Cheltenham, there were justifiable concerns over the horse's ability to jump round Aintree. The stamina-packed grey Strong Resolve had finished second in the Welsh National in December and was a fine jumper looking to make Lucinda Russell the first Scottish-based trainer to win the National since John Leadbetter with Rubstic in 1979. The Irish giant Colnel Rayburn was by far the biggest horse in the field, and was a resolute galloper from the up-and-coming County Wexford yard of Paul Nolan. Despite his unusual 'parrot mouth', Colnel Rayburn jumped well and had good form in Ireland, although he was at his best in very soft ground. One of the best-looking horses in the race, the rich chestnut Joly Bey was trained by Nick Gifford, who had taken over for his retired father Josh. Joly Bey had cruised to victory at Sandown in February and had been travelling like the winner of the Topham Trophy, only to crumble four out in that race in 2004. As then, the horse would be ridden by his young amateur rider and owner David Dunsdon.

Sponsored for the first time by John Smiths with a staggering overall value of £700,000, the Grand National got underway, with runners slightly more restrained than usual. Even so, the leaders still attacked the first fence with venom, headed from outside to inner by Strong Resolve, Spot Thedifference, Glenelly Gale, Frenchman's Creek, Lord Atterbury, Double Honour and Colnel Rayburn. The chestnut Lord Atterbury crashed hard at the first, with Frenchman's Creek blundering badly and unseating Jimmy McCarthy. The grey Strong Resolve over-jumped and was down on his nose – looking sure to crumble – yet, miraculously, he stayed on his feet, relinquishing little ground in the process.

The suspect jumper Risk Accessor went at the second, while Ballycassidy unseated Seamus Durack fifty yards after the fence, despite the rider trying desperately to stay aboard. Going down to Becher's, the Irish runner Glenelly Gale had carved a sizeable lead over Double Honour, Monty's Pass, Colnel Rayburn, Strong Resolve and the outsider Astonville, with Carrie Ford and Forest Gunner travelling smoothly on the tails of the leaders.

Following the Canal Turn and Valentines, Hedgehunter – restrained on the inside by Walsh – made a slight mistake at the tenth, where the cheek piece-wearing Merchant's Friend came down, while Clan Royal, again eager to pull himself to the front, moved up to track Glenelly Gale, with Double Honour on the inside. The Jonjo O'Neill stable had endured a torrid season due to a crippling virus. Many of his recent runners had disappointed woefully as they slowly returned to action and, with Clan Royal not sighted since the previous December, many wondered if the 2004 National runner-up would flop as well. But here was a horse that clearly loved the unique make-up of the National course. Running keenly,

Clan Royal was soon striding along in his familiar low head-carrying, low-jumping style, and was disputing the lead retuning to the racecourse.

Fearing the horse had gone lame, Brian Crowley pulled Astonville up approaching the thirteenth, though thankfully the horse was fine. Receiving the usual inspiring roar from the crowd, the field streamed over the mighty Chair. Take The Stand's jumping had stood up well on the first circuit and the horse had steadily moved through the field but, clipping the giant fence, he gave Leighton Aspell no chance of staying in the saddle and his race was over. Normally one of the cleanest of jumpers, Strong Resolve dragged his back legs through the water, losing momentum.

With thirty-two surviving a circuit, a tremendous race was developing as Clan Royal led on from Glenelly Gale and Double Honour, with a tightly packed band of challengers close up. They were headed by Colnel Rayburn and included Hedgehunter, Monty's Pass, the French horse Innox, Just In Debt, Forest Gunner, Ad Hoc, Heros Collonges, Simply Gifted, Fondmort, the Gold Cup fourth Royal Auclair and the rapidly improving Joly Bey, travelling widest of all.

Clan Royal was tanking along in front in the company of the riderless pair Merchant's Friend and Take The Stand, but it was approaching Becher's where Tony McCoy's Grand National luck turned rotten once more. Forced slightly wide by Take The Stand, McCoy cut inside trying to avoid the loose horses. Merchant's Friend cut right along the face of the fence, followed by Take The Stand. Denied a clean take-off, Clan Royal instinctively followed the loose ones and, in bitterly unlucky fashion, the horse was carried out. It was a long way out, but so purposely was Clan Royal

Hedgehunter is in control by the final fence.

going that he might well have been involved in the finish. That possibility was of no solace to McCoy, the disbelieving jockey apparently burdened with the most soul-destroying of Grand National curses. In retrospect, it was fortunate Clan Royal had been so far ahead, as countless others would have been hampered. As it was, those on the inside were snatched up slightly as the loose horses tore in front of them. Most affected was Colnel Rayburn, forced to jump Becher's from a standstill, losing ground and momentum. Ad Hoc fell in mid-division, as suddenly Hedgehunter was left in front on the inside from Innox in the centre and Joly Bey on the outside.

However, many horses were travelling confidently as they jumped down the back with Just In Debt, Heros Collonges, Royal Auclair and Simply Gifted hunting up the leading three, with Forest Gunner also still in contention. But none were going better than Hedgehunter, eased masterfully into contention by Walsh and jumping every bit as brilliantly as he had done the year before. As the leading group were joined by the Martin Pipe duo It Takes Time and rank outsider Polar Red, eleven horses crossed the Melling Road for the final time with every chance. As the challengers thundered into position behind him, Hedgehunter was allowed to quicken slightly, stealing a couple of lengths jumping the second last.

Jumping the final fence in style with those chasing him under real pressure, Hedgehunter cruised onwards, yet to be asked a question by Walsh. As the crowd rose to their feet, the gifted horseman finally let Hedgehunter go at the elbow, and the horse responded by sprinting away decisively, storming home to win by an emphatic fourteen lengths – one of the finest winners of recent times. Hedgehunter had carried 11st 1lb to victory, the first since Corbiere won in 1983 to shoulder in excess of 11 stone. With an even greater weight, Royal Auclair bravely followed him home, confirming his class, while the unconsidered Simply Gifted provided O'Neill with a slice of compensation by running into third, ahead of It Takes Time in fourth. Given a splendid ride by Carrie Ford, Forest Gunner came home in fifth, the jockey equalling the best ever finish of a female rider in the race, though Ford's effort was surely superior to Rosemary Henderson's in 1994 given the competitiveness of the finish and Forest Gunner's proximity to the winner. Indeed, Forest Gunner had been one of many in contention at the third last, yet none could live with Hedgehunter, whose triumph was totally convincing and deserving, and whose success was a second in the National for his sire Montelimar (Monty's Pass).

A fourth Irish winner in seven years, Hedgehunter's victory was heart-warming for all involved, not least for Hemmings for fulfilling his ambition following many years of misfortune and Mullins for adding a Grand National to his impressive résumé. Ruby Walsh had given the horse the most beautiful ride, never panicking despite being left in front following the exit of Clan Royal. For many, the jockey was now the best in the business. Walsh had also won the Welsh and Irish Nationals during the season and after Aintree came agonisingly close to adding the Scottish version as well. But most of all it was wonderful for Hedgehunter for, twelve months after running his heart out only to fall at the last, the horse had returned to Aintree to add his name to the most famous roll of honour.

2005 GRAND NATIONAL RESULT

FATE	HORSE	AGE/WEIGHT	JOCKEY	ODDS
1st	HEDGEHUNTER	9.11.1	R. WALSH	7/1
2nd	ROYAL AUCLAIR	8.11.10	CHRISTIAN WILLIAMS	40/1
3rd	SIMPLY GIFTED	10.10.6	B. HARDING	66/1
4th	IT TAKES TIME	11.10.11	T.J. MURPHY	18/1
5th	Forest Gunner	11.10.7	Carrie Ford	8/1
6th	Nil Desperandum	8.10.11	J. Culloty	16/1
7th	Innox	9.10.6	R. Thornton	16/1
8th	Heros Collonges	10.10.11	J.P. McNamara	66/1
9th	Just In Debt	9.10.7	A. Dobbin	33/1
10th	Amberleigh House	13.11.3	G. Lee	16/1
11th	Bindaree	11.11.3	C. Llewellyn	33/1
12th	Iznogoud	9.10.9	T. Scudamore	125/1
13th	Polar Red	8.10.8	T. J. Malone	100/1
14th	Joly Bey	8.10.10	Mr D.H. Dunsdon	16/1
15th	L'Aventure	6.10.5	R.P. McNally	66/1
16th	Monty's Pass	12.11.6	B.J. Geraghty	33/1
17th	Strong Resolve	9.10.6	P. Buchanan	9/1
18th	Spot Thedifference	12.10.7	R.M. Power	25/1
19th	Arctic Copper	11.10.6	D.N. Russell	200/1
20th	Europa	9.10.6	J.M. Maguire	150/1
21st	Shamawan	10.10.6	J.R. Barry	200/1
Fell	Foly Pleasant	11.11.0	A. Thornton	50/1
Fell	Ad Hoc	11.10.12	J. Tizzard	33/1
Fell	Lord Atterbury	9.10.6	M. Bradburne	25/1
Fell	Merchants Friend	10.10.6	N. Fehily	80/1
Pulled-Up	Le Coudray	11.11.12	C. O'Dwyer	33/1
Pulled-Up	Fondmort	9.11.6	M.A. Fitzgerald	50/1
Pulled-Up	Astonville	11.10.13	B.J. Crowley	100/1
Pulled-Up	Glenelly Gale	11.10.11	Mr T. Greenall	150/1
Pulled-Up	Jakari	8.10.10	R. Johnson	33/1
Pulled-Up	Colnel Rayburn	9.10.7	P. Carberry	20/1
Unseated Rider	Take The Stand	9.11.5	L. Aspell	16/1
Unseated Rider	Ballycassidy	9.11.5	S. Durack	66/1
Unseated Rider	Risk Accessor	10.11.4	A.P. Crowe	100/1
Unseated Rider	Frenchman's Creek	11.10.9	J.A. McCarthy	50/1
Unseated Rider	Double Honour	7.10.8	P.J. Brennan	25/1
Unseated Rider	Marcus Du Berlais	8.10.5	B.M. Cash	25/1
Unseated Rider	Native Emperor	9.10.5	D. Elsworth	100/1
Refused	Ballybough Rasher	10.11.4	A. Dempsey	100/1
Carried Out	Clan Royal	10.10.11	A.P. McCoy	9/1

9 April 2005
Going – Good to Soft (Good in places)
Sponsor – John Smith's
Winner – £406,000
Time – 9mins 20.80secs
40 Ran
Favourite – Hedgehunter

Top Weight – Le Coudray
Winner trained by Willie Mullins at
Bagenalstown, County Carlow, Ireland
Winner owned by Mr Trevor Hemmings
Hedgehunter, bay gelding by Montelimar
– Aberedw.

Other titles published by Tempus

If you are interested in purchasing other books published by Tempus, or in case you have difficulty finding any Tempus books in your local bookshop, you can also place orders directly through our website www.tempus-publishing.com

FESTIVAL GOLD FORTY YEARS OF CHELTENHAM RACING
STEWART PETERS

Set in the beautiful surroundings of the Cotswold Hills, the Cheltenham Festival creates an atmosphere which is a unique blend of colour, romance and excitement. The festival is host to the Gold Cup one of racing's greatest events. This volume looks at forty year's history of this famous festival and is superbly illustrated throughout with photographs from Bernard Parkin, the official Cheltenham course photographer.

0 7524 2817 9

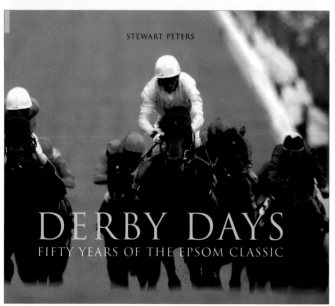

DERBY DAYS FIFTY YEARS OF THE EPSOM CLASSIC
STEWART PETERS

Since it was first run in 1780, the Epsom Derby has become one of the great events in the sporting calendar. The most prestigious and important flat race event of the year, it attracts crowds in excess of 50,000 every year from all walks of life. This book covers the runners and riders of the last fifty years, with a dramatic retelling of all the major action and many excellent photographs.

0 7524 3202 8